TOP 10
OF EVERYTHING
2004

TOP 10

OF EVERYTHING
2004
RUSSELL ASH

DK Publishing

Contents

LONDON, NEW YORK, MUNICH, MELBOURNE, DELHI

Senior Editor Nicki Lampon
Senior Art Editor Kevin Ryan
DTP Designer Rajen Shah
Production Controller Heather Hughes

Managing Editor Adèle Hayward
Managing Art Editor
Karen Self
Category Publisher Stephanie Jackson

Produced for Dorling Kindersley by
The Bridgewater Book Company,
The Old Candlemakers, West Street,
Lewes, East Sussex BN7 2NZ

Editors Hazel Songhurst,
Stephanie Horner
Designers Lisa McCormick,
Richard Constable

Author's Project Manager Aylla Macphail

Published in Great Britain in 2003 by
Dorling Kindersley Limited, 80 Strand,
London WC2R 0RL

2 4 6 8 10 9 7 5 3 1

A Cataloging in Publication record is available from
the Library of Congress.

0-7894-9639-9 (hc)
0-7894-9659-3 (pb)

Reproduction by Colourscan, Singapore
Printed and bound by GGP Media GmbH, Germany
See our complete catalogue at
www.dk.com

Contents

Introduction

ACCORDING TO HISTORIAN Edward Creasy, there were Fifteen Decisive Battles of the World. The planet Uranus has 15 moons, while in *Treasure Island* there are "15 Men on a Dead Man's Chest." Now, with the publication of this book, there have been 15 editions of *The Top 10 of Everything*. It's all too easy to slip into this list-geared mode, since we are constantly assailed with lists: from the 100 Greatest Film Stars and the FBI's 10 Most Wanted to the bestselling DVDs and the most-visited Internet sites, lists have become a part of our world view.

A SENSE OF PERSPECTIVE

One function of *The Top 10 of Everything* is to distil down a wealth of data by drawing together a diversity of quantitative superlatives. They are not anyone's "10 bests" (which are qualitative judgements), but there are some "10 worsts" in the case of accidents and disasters, since, sadly, these can be gauged by numbers of victims. The only "bests" are bestsellers, because sales can be measured. There are the results of major polls and also some "firsts" and "latests," which recognize pioneers, most recent achievers, and award winners.

SOURCE MATERIAL

My data sources include "official" and government departments, from the United Nations and sports governing bodies to commercial organizations and research groups, every one of whom has granted me privileged access to their databases. Among the most rewarding sources of all are the private individuals who are specialists in everything from poisonous creatures to the world's tallest buildings, and who have been generous enough to share with me the results of their researches.

AS TIME GOES BY...

Entry-levels for Top 10 lists have changed, often dramatically, over the 15 annual publications of *The Top 10 of Everything*: the richest American of 15 years ago had a mere $6.7 billion, while Bill Gates is today more than six times wealthier. We have ever-bigger cruise liners, spiralling transfer fees for sporting superstars, and increasing levels of worldwide box office income—the criterion on which the film lists are mostly based—which means that *Star Wars*, the highest-earning film in 1990, is now ranked tenth.

A COMEDY OF ERRORS

I endeavour to ensure that the information in *The Top 10 of Everything* is as up to date and as accurate as possible, but arguments continue to rage over the precise lengths of rivers, how many copies of the Bible have ever been sold, how fast a bee flies, and so on, and just as other sources disagree with each other, some may disagree with me. But then at least I don't claim—as certain respected reference books have—that Mt. Pico in the Azores is 67,713 ft (20,639 m) high (more than twice the height of Everest), that Iceland has 1,754 tractors per 2.5 acres (hence a total of 180 billion tractors), or that Manila has a population of 21 people per square foot...

KEEP IN CONTACT

Do please send me your comments and any corrections or ideas for new lists by writing to me c/o the publishers or by e-mailing me direct at ash@pavilion.co.uk

Other recent Dorling Kindersley books by Russell Ash:
The Factastic Book of 1,001 Lists
The Factastic Book of Comparisons
Great Wonders of the World
The Top 10 of Sport (with Ian Morrison)
The Top 10 of Film

SPECIAL FEATURES

• Over 700 lists on everything under—and beyond—the Sun

• Completely updated with many innovative lists, from pop star film debuts and films from song titles, to the strongest men and the most valuable comics

• "First Fact" features throughout on such diverse subjects as the first in-flight wedding and the first million-selling soundtrack album to the first computer games and the first 200 mph car

• Further Information—a valuable guide to the Top 10 websites to explore for each of the principal themes in *The Top 10 of Everything*

THE UNIVERSE
& THE EARTH

Heavenly Bodies

COMETS COMING CLOSEST TO THE EARTH

	COMET	DATE*	(AU)#	DISTANCE (MILES)	(KM)
1	Comet of 1491	Feb. 20, 1491	0.0094	873,784	1,406,220
2	Lexell	July 1, 1770	0.0151	1,403,633	2,258,928
3	Tempel-Tuttle	Oct. 26, 1366	0.0229	2,128,688	3,425,791
4	IRAS-Araki-Alcock	May 11, 1983	0.0313	2,909,516	4,682,413
5	Halley	Apr. 10, 837	0.0334	3,104,724	4,996,569
6	Biela	Dec. 9, 1805	0.0366	3,402,182	5,475,282
7	Grischow	Feb. 8, 1743	0.0390	3,625,276	5,834,317
8	Pons-Winnecke	June 26, 1927	0.0394	3,662,458	5,894,156
9	Comet of 1014	Feb. 24, 1014	0.0407	3,783,301	6,088,633
10	La Hire	Apr. 20, 1702	0.0437	4,062,168	6,537,427

* Of closest approach to the Earth

\# Astronomical Units: 1 AU = mean distance from the Earth to the Sun (92,955,793 miles/149,597,870 km)

LARGEST METEORITES EVER FOUND

	LOCATION	ESTIMATED WEIGHT (TONS)
1	Hoba West, Grootfontein, Namibia	more than 66.0
2	Ahnighito ("The Tent"), Cape York, West Greenland	63.1
3	Campo del Cielo, Argentina	45.6
4	Canyon Diablo*, Arizona	33.0
5	Sikhote-Alin, Russia	29.7
6	Chupaderos, Mexico	26.6
7	Bacuberito, Mexico	24.2
8	Armanty, Western Mongolia	22.0
9	Mundrabilla#, Western Australia	18.7
10	Mbosi, Tanzania	17.6

* Formed meteor crater; fragmented; total in public collections is around 12.6 tons

\# In two parts

ASTEROID DISCOVERED!

FIRST FACT

ON NEW YEAR'S DAY, 1801, at the observatory at Palermo, Sicily, Giuseppe Piazzi (1746–1826), a monk, astronomer, and professor of mathematics, was working on what was later published as a catalog of 7,646 stars when he observed an object in the constellation of Taurus. Having recorded its location, he noted over the next six weeks that it had moved, thus demonstrating the existence of asteroids—rocks orbiting between Mars and Jupiter. Named Ceres, the asteroid has been examined by the Hubble Space Telescope, and NASA's *Dawn* mission, scheduled launch in 2006, will make a close study of Ceres in 2014.

LARGEST ASTEROIDS

	ASTEROID	YEAR DISCOVERED	DIAMETER (MILES)	(KM)
1	Ceres	1801	582	936
2	Pallas	1802	377	607
3	Vesta	1807	322	519
4	Hygeia	1849	279	450
5	Euphrosyne	1854	229	370
6	Interamnia	1910	217	349
7	Davida	1903	200	322
8	Cybele	1861	192	308
9	Europa	1858	179	288
10	Patientia	1899	171	275

NASA's NEO (Near Earth Object) program monitors close approaches of asteroids and other space objects to the Earth. "Near" in this context means within 28 million miles (45 million km) of Earth's orbit.

LARGEST PLANETARY MOONS

	MOON	PLANET	DIAMETER (MILES)	(KM)
1	Ganymede	Jupiter	3,274	5,269
2	Titan	Saturn	3,200	5,150
3	Callisto	Jupiter	2,986	4,806
4	Io	Jupiter	2,262	3,642
5	Moon	Earth	2,159	3,475
6	Europa	Jupiter	1,945	3,130
7	Triton	Neptune	1,680	2,704
8	Titania	Uranus	980	1,578
9	Rhea	Saturn	949	1,528
10	Oberon	Uranus	946	1,522

▶ **Galileo and Ganymede**
The cratered surface of Ganymede, seventh-largest of Jupiter's moons and larger than the planet Mercury. Ganymede was discovered by Italian astronomer Galileo on January 7, 1610, and investigated by NASA's aptly named *Galileo* probe, which reached it in 1996.

TOP 10 | GALAXIES CLOSEST TO THE EARTH

	GALAXY	DISTANCE (LIGHT-YEARS)
1	Large Cloud of Magellan	169,000
2	Small Cloud of Magellan	190,000
3	Ursa Minor dwarf	250,000
4	Draco dwarf	260,000
5	Sculptor dwarf	280,000
6	Fornax dwarf	420,000
7 =	Leo I dwarf	750,000
=	Leo II dwarf	750,000
9	Barnard's Galaxy	1,700,000
10	Andromeda Spiral	2,200,000

These and other galaxies are members of the so-called "Local Group," although with vast distances such as these, "local" is clearly a relative term.

▶ **By Jupiter!**
The Solar System's largest planet is more massive than all the other eight planets combined. The prominent Great Red Spot, seen here on the right, turns counterclockwise and is easily large enough to swallow Earth.

TOP 10 | LARGEST BODIES IN THE SOLAR SYSTEM

	BODY	MAXIMUM DIAMETER (MILES)	(KM)
1	Sun	865,036	1,392,140
2	Jupiter	88,846	142,984
3	Saturn	74,898	120,536
4	Uranus	31,763	51,118
5	Neptune	30,778	49,532
6	Earth	7,926	12,756
7	Venus	7,520	12,103
8	Mars	4,222	6,794
9	Ganymede	3,274	5,269
10	Titan	3,200	5,150

Most of the planets are visible to the naked eye and have been the object of systematic study since ancient times. The planets that are too small to be seen unaided are Uranus, discovered on March 13, 1781, by British astronomer William Herschel; Neptune, found by German astronomer Johann Galle, who announced his discovery on September 23, 1846; and, outside the Top 10, Pluto, located by US astronomer Clyde Tombaugh on March 13, 1930.

TOP 10 | STARS CLOSEST TO THE EARTH*

	STAR	(LIGHT-YEARS)	DISTANCE (MILES [MILLIONS])	(KM [MILLIONS])
1	Proxima Centauri	4.22	24,792,500	39,923,310
2	Alpha Centauri	4.35	25,556,250	41,153,175
3	Barnard's Star	5.98	35,132,500	56,573,790
4	Wolf 359	7.75	45,531,250	73,318,875
5	Lalande 21185	8.22	48,292,500	77,765,310
6	Luyten 726-8	8.43	49,526,250	79,752,015
7	Sirius	8.65	50,818,750	81,833,325
8	Ross 154	9.45	55,518,750	89,401,725
9	Ross 248	10.40	61,100,000	98,389,200
10	Epsilon Eridani	10.80	63,450,000	102,173,400

Excluding the Sun

A spaceship traveling at 25,000 mph (40,237 km/h)—which is faster than any human has yet traveled in space—would take more than 113,200 years to reach the Earth's closest stellar neighbor, Proxima Centauri.

Exploring the Universe

TOP 10 LONGEST SPACE MISSIONS*

	COSMONAUT#	MISSION DATES	DURATION DAYS:HRS:MINS
1	Valeri V. Polyakov	Jan. 8, 1994–Mar. 22, 1995	437:17:59
2	Sergei V. Avdeyev	Aug. 13, 1998–Aug. 28, 1999	379:14:52
3 =	Musa K. Manarov	Dec. 21, 1987–Dec. 21, 1988	365:22:39
=	Vladimir G. Titov	Dec. 21, 1987–Dec. 21, 1988	365:22:39
5	Yuri V. Romanenko	Feb. 5–Dec. 5, 1987	326:11:38
6	Sergei K. Krikalyov	May 18, 1991–Mar. 25, 1992	311:20:01
7	Valeri V. Polyakov	Aug. 31, 1988–Apr. 27, 1989	240:22:35
8 =	Oleg Y. Atkov	Feb. 8–Oct. 2, 1984	236:22:50
=	Leonid D. Kizim	Feb. 8–Oct. 2, 1984	236:22:50
=	Anatoli Y. Solovyov	Feb. 8–Oct. 2, 1984	236:22:50

* To January 1, 2003

All Soviet/Russian

Space-medicine specialist Valeri Vladimirovich Polyakov (born April 27, 1942) spent his 52nd birthday in space during his record-breaking mission aboard the Mir space station. One of the purposes of his mission was to study the effects on the human body of long-duration spaceflight.

TOP 10 LARGEST REFLECTING TELESCOPES

	TELESCOPE	LOCATION	APERTURE (FT)	(M)
1 =	Keck I Telescope*	Mauna Kea, Hawaii	32.8	0.0
=	Keck II Telescope*	Mauna Kea, Hawaii	32.8	0.0
3	Hobby-Eberly Telescope	Mount Fowlkes, Texas	30.9	9.2
4	Subaru Telescope	Mauna Kea, Hawaii	27.2	8.3
5 =	Antu Telescope	Cerro Paranal, Chile	26.9	8.2
=	Kueyen Telescope	Cerro Paranal, Chile	26.9	8.2
=	Melipal Telescope	Cerro Paranal, Chile	26.9	8.2
=	Yepun Telescope	Cerro Paranal, Chile	26.9	8.2
9 =	Gemini North Telescope*	Mauna Kea, Hawaii	26.5	8.1
=	Gemini South Telescope*	Cerro Pachon, Chile	26.5	8.1

* Twins

Antu, Kueyen, Melipal, and Yepun are soon to be combined to form the appropriately named Very Large Telescope, which will take first place in this list with an aperture of 53.8 ft (16.4 m). The Keck telescopes work in tandem to produce the largest reflecting surface. They are to be combined with several smaller scopes to form the 47.9-ft (14.6-m) Keck Interferometer.

◀ Callisto's Craters
First observed by Galileo, Callisto, the second-largest of Jupiter's satellites, has the most heavily cratered surface of any body in the Solar System: Valhalla, the crater seen here on the right-hand side of Callisto, is 373 miles (600 km) in diameter.

THE 10 FIRST PLANETARY MOONS TO BE DISCOVERED

	MOON	PLANET	DISCOVERER	YEAR
1	Moon	Earth	—	Ancient
2	Io	Jupiter	Galileo Galilei (Italian)	1610
3	Europa	Jupiter	Galileo Galilei	1610
4	Ganymede	Jupiter	Galileo Galilei	1610
5	Callisto	Jupiter	Galileo Galilei	1610
6	Titan	Saturn	Christian Huygens (Dutch)	1655
7	Iapetus	Saturn	Giovanni Cassini (Italian/French)	1671
8	Rhea	Saturn	Giovanni Cassini	1672
9	Tethys	Saturn	Giovanni Cassini	1684
10	Dione	Saturn	Giovanni Cassini	1684

While Earth's Moon has been observed since ancient times, it was not until the development of the telescope that Galileo was able to discover (on January 7, 1610) the first moons of another planet.

TOP 10 | COUNTRIES WITH MOST SPACEFLIGHT EXPERIENCE*

	COUNTRY	ASTRONAUTS	(DAYS)	DURATION OF MISSION (HRS)	(MINS)	(SECS)
1	USSR/Russia#	96	15,806	13	16	36
2	US	271	8,509	08	48	22
3	France	9	384	23	38	00
4	Kazakhstan	2	349	14	59	03
5	Germany	10	309	17	08	56
6	Canada	8	122	13	30	58
7	Japan	5	88	06	00	40
8	Italy	4	76	06	34	09
9	Switzerland	1	42	12	05	32
10	South Africa	1	24	22	28	22

* To January 1, 2003

\# Russia became a independent state on December 25, 1991

The USSR, and now Russia, has clocked up its considerable lead on the rest of the world (with 61 percent of the total time spent by humans in space) largely through the long-duration stays of its cosmonauts on board the Mir space station. The US has had almost three times as many astronauts in space—principally aboard the Space Shuttle—but its missions have been of shorter duration. Up to January 1, 2003, the USSR/Russia and the US had hosted representatives of 28 further countries. Of these, Mexico's space experience is the shortest: a single six-day mission.

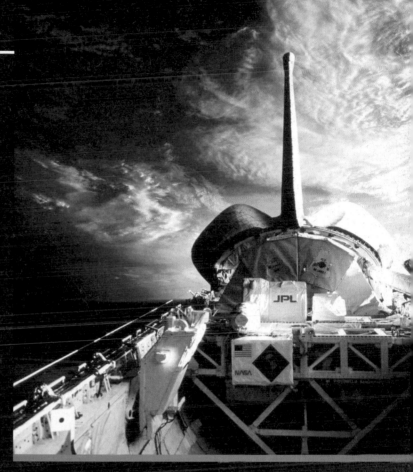

▲ **Space Shuttle**
The Space Shuttle's cargo bay is 60 ft (18.3 m) long and 15 ft (4.6 m) in diameter. The bay has a Remote Manipulator System arm to maneuver and deploy the Shuttle's cargo, and also contains the docking systems that are used during missions to the Spacelab.

THE 10 | FIRST UNMANNED MOON LANDINGS

	CRAFT	COUNTRY	DATE (LAUNCH/IMPACT)
1	Lunik 2	USSR	Sept. 12/14, 1959
2	Ranger 4*	US	Apr. 23/26, 1962
3	Ranger 6	US	Jan. 30/Feb. 2, 1964
4	Ranger 7	US	July 28/31, 1964
5	Ranger 8	US	Feb. 17/20, 1965
6	Ranger 9	US	Mar. 21/24, 1965
7	Luna 5*	USSR	May 9/12, 1965
8	Luna 7*	USSR	Oct. 4/8, 1965
9	Luna 8*	USSR	Dec. 3/7, 1965
10	Luna 9	USSR	Jan. 31/Feb. 3, 1966

* Crash-landing

TOP 10 | LONGEST SPACE SHUTTLE FLIGHTS*

	SPACE SHUTTLE	FLIGHT DATES	(DAYS)	DURATION OF MISSION (HRS)	(MINS)	(SECS)
1	STS-80 Columbia	Nov. 19–Dec. 7, 1996	17	08	53	18
2	STS-78 Columbia	June 20–July 7, 1996	16	21	48	30
3	STS-67 Endeavour	Mar. 2–18, 1995	16	15	09	46
4	STS-73 Columbia	Oct. 20–Nov. 5, 1995	15	21	53	16
5	STS-90 Columbia	Apr. 17–May 3, 1998	15	21	15	58
6	STS-75 Columbia	Feb. 22–Mar. 9, 1996	15	17	41	25
7	STS-94 Columbia	July 1–17, 1997	15	16	46	01
8	STS-87 Atlantis	Sept. 25–Oct. 6, 1997	15	16	35	01
9	STS-65 Columbia	July 8–23, 1994	14	17	55	00
10	STS-58 Columbia	Oct. 18–Nov. 1, 1993	14	00	12	32

* To January 1, 2003

Water World

TOP 10 LARGEST OCEANS AND SEAS

OCEAN/SEA	APPROXIMATE AREA* (SQ MILES)	(SQ KM)
1 Pacific Ocean	64,186,600	166,242,500
2 Atlantic Ocean	33,420,160	86,557,800
3 Indian Ocean	28,350,640	73,427,800
4 Arctic Ocean	5,105,740	13,223,800
5 South China Sea	1,148,499	2,974,600
6 Caribbean Sea	971,400	2,515,900
7 Mediterranean Sea	969,120	2,510,000
8 Bering Sea	873,020	2,261,100
9 Sea of Okhotsk	589,800	1,527,570
10 Gulf of Mexico	582,100	1,507,600

Excluding tributary seas

The Coral, Weddell, and Tasman Seas would be eligible for this list, but most authorities consider them part of the Pacific Ocean. The Bering Sea is more commonly identified as an independent sea, rather than part of the Pacific.

TOP 10 LONGEST RIVERS

RIVER	LOCATION	LENGTH (MILES)	(KM)
1 Nile	Burundi/Dem. Rep. of Congo/Egypt/Eritrea/ Ethiopia/Kenya/Rwanda/Sudan/Tanzania/Uganda	4,158	6,695
2 Amazon	Peru/Brazil	4,007	6,448
3 Chang Jiang (Yangtze)	China	3,964	6,378
4 Huang He (Yellow)	China	3,395	5,464
5 Amur	China/Russia	2,744	4,415
6 Lena	Russia	2,734	4,400
7 Congo	Angola/Dem. Rep. of Congo	2,718	4,373
8 Irtysh	China/Kazakhstan/Mongolia/Russia	2,640	4,248
9 Mackenzie	Canada	2,635	4,241
10 Mekong	Tibet/China/Myanmar/Laos/ Cambodia/Vietnam	2,600	4,183

TOP 10 DEEPEST DEEP-SEA TRENCHES

	TRENCH*	DEEPEST POINT (FT)	(M)
1	Marianas	35,837	10,924
2	Tonga#	35,430	10,800
3	Philippine	34,436	10,497
4	Kermadec#	32,960	10,047
5	Bonin	32,786	9,994
6	New Britain	32,609	9,940
7	Kuril	31,985	9,750
8	Izu	31,805	9,695
9	Puerto Rico	28,229	8,605
10	Yap	27,973	8,527

* With the exception of the Puerto Rico (Atlantic), all the trenches are in the Pacific

\# Some authorities consider these parts of the same feature

TOP 10 HIGHEST WATERFALLS

	WATERFALL	RIVER	LOCATION	TOTAL DROP (FT)	(M)
1	Angel	Carrao	Venezuela	3,212*	979
2	Tugela	Tugela	South Africa	3,107	947
3	Utigård	Jostedal Glacier	Nesdale, Norway	2,625	800
4	Mongefossen	Monge	Mongebekk, Norway	2,540	774
5	Yosemite	Yosemite Creek	California	2,425	739
6	Østre Mardøla Foss	Mardals	Eikisdal, Norway	2,152	656
7	Tyssestrengane	Tysso	Hardanger, Norway	2,120	646
8	Cuquenán	Arabopo	Venezuela	2,000	610
9	Sutherland	Arthur	South Island, New Zealand	1,904	580
10	Kjellfossen	Naero	Gudvangen, Norway	1,841	561

* Longest single drop 2,648 ft (807 m)

TOP 10 COUNTRIES WITH THE LARGEST AREAS OF CORAL REEF

	COUNTRY	REEF AREA (SQ MILES)	PERCENTAGE OF WORLD TOTAL
1	Indonesia	19,699	17.95
2	Australia	18,903	17.22
3	Philippines	9,676	8.81
4	France (overseas territories)	5,514	5.02
5	Papua New Guinea	5,344	4.87
6	Fiji	3,869	3.52
7	Maldives	3,444	3.14
8	Saudi Arabia	2,571	2.34
9	Marshall Islands	2,539	2.15
10	India	2,305	2.04
	World total (including those not in Top 10)	109,768	100.00

Source: World Atlas of Coral Reefs

◀ **Beneath the waves**
Coral reefs have taken millions of years to form and, as habitats for a huge variety of sea life, are subject to stringent controls.

TOP 10 DEEPEST LAKES

	LAKE	LOCATION	GREATEST DEPTH (FT)	(M)
1	Baikal	Russia	5,371	1,637
2	Tanganyika	Burundi/ Tanzania/ Dem. Rep. of Congo/ Zambia	4,825	1,471
3	Caspian Sea	Azerbaijan/ Iran/Kazakhstan/ Russia/Turkmenistan	3,363	1,025
4	Malawi	Malawi/ Mozambique/ Tanzania	2,316	706
5	Issyk-kul	Kyrgyzstan	2,257	688
6	Great Slave	Canada	2,015	614
7	Crater	Oregon	1,932	589
8	Toba	Sumatra, Indonesia	1,736	529
9	Hornindals	Norway	1,686	514
10 =	Sarez	Tajikistan	1,657	505
=	Tahoe	California/ Nevada	1,657	505

Lake Baikal contains some 20 percent of the world's unfrozen fresh water, a volume of 5,518 cubic miles (23,000 km³).

Island Treasure

TOP 10 LARGEST ISLANDS

	ISLAND	AREA* (SQ MILES)	(SQ KM)
1	**Greenland** (Kalaatdlit Nunaat)	840,003.9	2,175,600.0
2	**New Guinea**	303,381.0	785,753.0
3	**Borneo** (Indonesia/Malaysia/Brunei)	288,869.3	748,168.1
4	**Madagascar** (Malagasy Republic)	226,917.3	587,713.1
5	**Baffin Island,** Canada	194,573.9	503,944.0
6	**Sumatra,** Indonesia	171,068.7	443,065.8
7	**Great Britain**	88,786.9	229,957.0
8	**Honshu,** Japan	87,182.0	225,800.3
9	**Victoria Island,** Canada	85,154.2	220,548.2
10	**Ellesmere Island,** Canada	71,029.1	183,964.6

* Mainlands, including areas of inland water, but excluding offshore islands

Australia is regarded as a continental landmass rather than an island; otherwise it would rank first, at 2,941,517 sq miles (7,618,493 sq km), or 35 times the size of Great Britain. The largest US island is Hawaii, which measures 4,037 sq miles (10,456 sq km), and the largest off mainland US is Kodiak, Alaska, at 3,672 sq miles (9,510 sq km).

TOP 10 LARGEST ISLAND COUNTRIES

	COUNTRY	AREA (SQ MILES)	(SQ KM)
1	**Indonesia**	705,192	1,826,440
2	**Madagascar**	224,534	581,540
3	**Papua New Guinea**	174,406	451,709
4	**Japan**	152,411	394,744
5	**Malaysia**	126,853	328,549
6	**Philippines**	115,124	298,171
7	**New Zealand**	103,734	268,671
8	**Cuba**	42,803	110,860
9	**Iceland**	38,707	100,251
10	**Sri Lanka**	24,996	64,740

Source: *US Census Bureau, International Data Base*

All of the countries on this list are completely self-contained island countries. Because Ireland and Northern Ireland share an island, the UK and Ireland are both excluded from this list. Had it been included, the UK would take 8th place with an area of 93,278 sq miles (241,590 sq km).

TOP 10 MOST IMPORTANT ISLANDS FOR CONSERVATION

	ISLAND/LOCATION	ENDEMIC SPECIES	THREATENED SPECIES	CONSERVATION IMPORTANCE INDEX
1	**New Caledonia,** Southwest Pacific	2,688	172	115
2	**Mauritius,** Indian Ocean	316	223	85
3	**Malta,** Mediterranean Sea	32	230	63
4	**Lord Howe Island,** Australia	130	79	58
5	**St. Helena,** South Atlantic	62	54	50
6	**Rapa Iti,** Southwest Pacific	225	51	49
7	**Madeira,** Atlantic Ocean	230	136	48
8	**Henderson,** Pitcairn, South Pacific	21	2	47
9	**Viti Levu,** Fiji, Southwest Pacific	9	4	44
10 =	**Jamaica,** Caribbean Sea	1,020	13	42
=	**Vanua Levu,** Fiji Southwest Pacific	2	3	42

Source: *United Nations System-Wide Earthwatch*

The United Nations' Conservation Importance Index ranks islands according to terrestrial and marine conservation importance, endemic and threatened species, vulnerability, and features such as seabird rookeries and sea turtle nesting areas.

TOP 10 SMALLEST ISLAND COUNTRIES

	COUNTRY/LOCATION	AREA (SQ MILES)	(SQ KM)
1	**Nauru,** Pacific Ocean	8	21
2	**Tuvalu,** Pacific Ocean	10	26
3	**Marshall Islands,** Pacific Ocean	70	181
4	**Maldives,** Indian Ocean	116	300
5	**Malta,** Mediterranean Sea	124	321
6 =	**Grenada,** Caribbean Sea	131	339
=	**St. Vincent and the Grenadines,** Caribbean Sea	131	339
8	**St. Kitts and Nevis,** Caribbean Sea	139	360
9	**Barbados,** Caribbean Sea	166	430
10	**Antigua and Barbuda,** Caribbean Sea	170	440

Source: *US Census Bureau, International Data Base*

▶ Easter Island

Guarded by over 600 giant statues, or "moais," of mysterious origin, Easter Island was discovered by Jacob Roggeveen on Easter Day, 1722. It lies more than 2,000 miles (3,200 km) from the nearest population centers in Tahiti and Chile, making it the world's most isolated inhabited island.

MOST ISOLATED INHABITED ISLANDS

	ISLAND/LOCATION	ISOLATION INDEX
1	**Easter Island,** South Pacific	149
2	**Rapa Iti**, Southwest Pacific	130
3	**Kiritimati,** Line Islands, Central Pacific	129
4	**Jarvis Island,** Central Pacific	128
5 =	**Kosrae,** Micronesia, Pacific	126
=	**Malden,** Line Islands, Central Pacific	126
=	**Starbuck,** Line Islands, Central Pacific	126
=	**Vostok,** Line Islands, Central Pacific	126
9 =	**Bouvet Island,** South Atlantic	125
=	**Gough Island,** South Atlantic	125
=	**Palmyra Island,** Central Pacific	125

Source: *United Nations*

The United Nation's isolation index is calculated by adding together the square roots of the distances to the nearest island, group of islands, and continent.

LARGEST VOLCANIC ISLANDS

	ISLAND/LOCATION	TYPE	AREA (SQ MILES)	AREA (SQ KM)
1	**Sumatra,** Indonesia	Active volcanic	171,068.7	443,065.8
2	**Honshu,** Japan	Volcanic	87,182.0	225,800.3
3	**Java,** Indonesia	Volcanic	53,588.5	138,793.6
4	**North Island,** New Zealand	Volcanic	43,082.4	111,582.8
5	**Luzon,** Philippines	Active volcanic	42,457.7	109,964.9
6	**Iceland**	Active volcanic	39,315.2	101,826.0
7	**Mindanao,** Philippines	Active volcanic	37,656.5	97,530.0
8	**Hokkaido,** Japan	Active volcanic	30,394.7	78,719.4
9	**New Britain,** Papua New Guinea	Volcanic	13,569.4	35,144.6
10	**Halmahera,** Indonesia	Active volcanic	6,965.1	18,039.6

Source: *United Nations*

High & Mighty

TOP 10 HIGHEST MOUNTAINS

	MOUNTAIN/LOCATION	FIRST ASCENT	TEAM LEADER(S)' NATIONALITY	HEIGHT* (FT)	(M)
1	Everest, Nepal/China	May 29, 1953	British/New Zealander	29,035	8,850
2	K2 (Chogori), Pakistan/China	July 31, 1954	Italian	28,238	8,607
3	Kangchenjunga, Nepal/India	May 25,1955	British	28,208	8,598
4	Lhotse, Nepal/China	May 18, 1956	Swiss	27,923	8,511
5	Makalu I, Nepal/China	May 15, 1955	French	27,824	8,481
6	Lhotse Shar II, Nepal/China	May 12, 1970	Austrian	27,504	8,383
7	Dhaulagiri I, Nepal	May 13, 1960	Swiss/Austrian	26,810	8,172
8	Manaslu I (Kutang I), Nepal	May 9, 1956	Japanese	26,760	8,156
9	Cho Oyu, Nepal	Oct. 19, 1954	Austrian	26,750	8,153
10	Nanga Parbat (Diamir), Kashmir	July 3, 1953	German/Austrian	26,660	8,126

Height of principal peak; lower peaks of the same mountain are excluded

The current "official" height of Everest was announced in November 1999 following analysis of data beamed from sensors on Everest's summit to GPS (Global Positioning System) satellites. This superseded the previous "official" measurement of 29,028 ft (8,848 m), recorded on April 20, 1993.

TOP 10 HIGHEST ACTIVE VOLCANOES

	VOLCANO/LOCATION	LATEST ACTIVITY	HEIGHT (FT)	(M)
1	Cerro Pular, Chile	1990	20,449	6,233
2	San Pedro, Chile	1960	20,161	6,145
3	Antofallar, Argentina	1911	20,013	6,100
4	Aracar, Argentina	1993	19,954	6,082
5	Guallatiri, Chile	1985	19,918	6,071
6	Tupungatito, Chile	1986	19,685	6,000
7	Tacora, Chile	1937	19,619	5,980
8	Sabancaya, Peru	2000	19,577	5,967
9	Cotopaxi, Ecuador	1942	19,393	5,911
10	Putana, Chile	1972	19,324	5,890

This list includes only volcanoes that were active at some time during the 20th century. Activity cannot always be confirmed beyond a doubt, due to the remoteness of the volcanoes, which can often make it difficult to ascertain precisely which volcano has erupted. The tallest currently active volcano in Europe is Mt. Etna, Sicily, at 10,855 ft (3,311 m), which was responsible for numerous deaths in earlier times.

TOP 10 HIGHEST MOUNTAINS IN NORTH AMERICA

	MOUNTAIN	COUNTRY	HEIGHT* (FT)	(M)
1	McKinley	US (Alaska)	20,320	6,194
2	Logan	Canada	19,545	5,959
3	Citlaltépetl (Orizaba)	Mexico	18,409	5,611
4	St. Elias	US (Alaska)/Canada	18,008	5,489
5	Popocatépetl	Mexico	17,887	5,452
6	Foraker	US (Alaska)	17,400	5,304
7	Ixtaccihuatl	Mexico	17,343	5,286
8	Lucania	Canada	17,147	5,226
9	King	Canada	16,971	5,173
10	Steele	Canada	16,644	5,073

Height of principal peak; lower peaks of the same mountain are excluded

▶ **Peak performance**
The Andes, the world's longest mountain range, stretches the length of South America, from Lago de Maracaibo in the north to Tierra del Fuego in the south.

TOP 10 HIGHEST MOUNTAINS IN EUROPE

	MOUNTAIN/COUNTRY	HEIGHT* (FT)	(M)
1	**Mont Blanc,** France/Italy	15,771	4,807
2	**Monte Rosa,** Switzerland	15,203	4,634
3	**Zumsteinspitze,** Italy/Switzerland	14,970	4,564
4	**Signalkuppe,** Italy/Switzerland	14,941	4,555
5	**Dom,** Switzerland	14,911	4,545
6	**Liskamm,** Italy/Switzerland	14,853	4,527
7	**Weisshorn,** Switzerland	14,780	4,505
8	**Täschorn,** Switzerland	14,733	4,491
9	**Matterhorn,** Italy/Switzerland	14,688	4,477
10	**Mont Maudit,** France/Italy	14,649	4,466

* Height of principal peak, lower peaks of the same mountain are excluded

THE 10 FIRST MOUNTAINEERS TO CLIMB EVEREST

	MOUNTAINEER/NATIONALITY	DATE
1	**Edmund Hillary,** New Zealander	May 29, 1953
2	**Tenzing Norgay,** Nepalese	May 29, 1953
3	**Jürg Marmet,** Swiss	May 23, 1956
4	**Ernst Schmied,** Swiss	May 23, 1956
5	**Hans-Rudolf von Gunten,** Swiss	May 24, 1956
6	**Adolf Reist,** Swiss	May 24, 1956
7	**Wang Fu-chou,** Chinese	May 25, 1960
8	**Chu Ying-hua,** Chinese	May 25, 1960
9	**Konbu,** Tibetan	May 25, 1960
10 =	**Nawang Gombu,** Indian	May 1, 1963
=	**James Whittaker,** American	May 1, 1963

Hillary and Tenzing's conquest of Everest followed at least 16 unsuccessful expeditions from 1921 to 1952. Whether George Leigh Mallory and Andrew Irvine, the British climbers who died on the 1924 expedition, reached the summit is still controversial. Mallory's body was discovered in 1999 at an elevation of 27,000 ft (8,230 m). Nawang Gombu and James Whittaker are 10th equal as neither wished to deny the other the privilege of being first, so they ascended the last steps to the summit side-by-side.

TOP 10 LONGEST MOUNTAIN RANGES

	RANGE/LOCATION	LENGTH (MILES)	(KM)
1	**Andes,** South America	4,500	7,242
2	**Rocky Mountains,** North America	3,750	6,035
3	**Himalayas/Karakoram/Hindu Kush,** Asia	2,400	3,862
4	**Great Dividing Range,** Australia	2,250	3,621
5	**Trans-Antarctic Mountains,** Antarctica	2,200	3,541
6	**Brazilian East Coast Range,** Brazil	1,900	3,058
7	**Sumatran/Javan Range,** Sumatra, Java	1,800	2,897
8	**Tien Shan,** China	1,400	2,253
9	**Eastern Ghats,** India	1,300	2,092
10 =	**Altai,** Asia	1,250	2,012
=	**Central New Guinean Range,** Papua New Guinea	1,250	2,012
=	**Urals,** Russia	1,250	2,012

Face of the Earth

LONGEST CAVES

	CAVE/LOCATION	TOTAL KNOWN LENGTH (MILES)	(KM)
1	**Mammoth Cave System,** Kentucky	346	557
2	**Optimisticheskaya,** Ukraine	131	212
3	**Jewel Cave,** South Dakota	128	206
4	**Hölloch,** Switzerland	114	184
5	**Lechuguilla Cave,** New Mexico	109	176
6	**Wind Cave,** South Dakota	106	171
7	**Fisher Ridge System,** Kentucky	105	169
8	**Siebenhengstehohle,** Switzerland	90	145
9	**Ozernaya,** Ukraine	73	117
10	**Gua Air Jernih,** Malaysia	68	109

Source: *Tony Waltham, BCRA*

▼ An immense and ancient land

The Sahara's boundaries are the Atlantic Ocean to the west, the Atlas Mountains and the Mediterranean Sea to the north, the Red Sea and Egypt to the east, and the Sudan and the Niger River to the south. Over 8,000 years ago the Sahara was a fertile area where millet and other crops were cultivated. As conditions gradually became drier, however, and the desert began to form, the farmers abandoned their land.

DEEPEST DEPRESSIONS

	DEPRESSION/LOCATION	MAXIMUM DEPTH BELOW SEA LEVEL (FT)	(M)
1	**Dead Sea,** Israel/Jordan	1,312	400
2	**Lake Assal,** Djibouti	511	156
3	**Turfan Depression,** China	505	154
4	**Qattâra Depression,** Egypt	436	133
5	**Mangyshlak Peninsula,** Kazakhstan	433	132
6	**Danakil Depression,** Ethiopia	383	117
7	**Death Valley,** US	282	86
8	**Salton Sink,** US	235	72
9	**Zapadny Chink Ustyurta,** Kazakhstan	230	70
10	**Prikaspiyskaya Nizmennost',** Kazakhstan/Russia	220	67

The shore of the Dead Sea is the lowest exposed ground below sea level, but the bed of the Sea actually reaches 2,388 ft (728 m) below sea level, and that of Lake Baikal, Russia, attains 4,872 ft (1,485 m) below sea level. Much of Antarctica is below sea level—some as low as 8,326 ft (2,538 m)—but the land there is covered by an ice cap that averages 6,890 ft (2,100 m) in depth. Lake Assal is Africa's lowest point and reputedly the world's saltiest body of water, 10 times as salty as the average for seawater, and saltier even than the notorious Dead Sea, which causes intense irritation to the eyes of swimmers, who are advised instead to take advantage of their unusual buoyancy and simply float. The Top 10 includes the lowest elevations in the continents of Asia, Africa, Europe, and North America; the lowest point in South America is the Valdes Peninsula, Argentina, at 131 ft (40 m) below sea level, and in Australia, Lake Eyre, 52 ft (16 m) below sea level.

TOP 10 LAND MASSES WITH THE LOWEST ELEVATIONS

	LAND MASS/LOCATION/COUNTRY	HIGHEST POINT (FT)	(M)
1	**Kingman Reef,** North Pacific Ocean (US)	3.2	1
2	**Palmyra Atoll,** North Pacific Ocean (US)	6.5	2
3 =	**Bassas da India,** Mozambique Channel, Southern Africa (French)	7.8	2.4
=	**Wingili Island in the Addu Atoll,** Maldives	7.8	2.4
5 =	**Ashmore and Cartier Islands,** Indian Ocean (Australian)	9.8	3
=	**Howland Island,** North Pacific Ocean (US)	9.8	3
7	**Spratly Islands,** South China Sea (claimed by China, Taiwan, Vietnam, Malaysia, and Philippines)	13.1	4
8 =	**Cocos (Keeling) Islands,** Indian Ocean (Australia)	16.4	5
=	**Johnston Atoll,** North Pacific Ocean (US)	16.4	5
=	**Tokelau,** South Pacific Ocean (New Zealand)	16.4	5
=	**Tuvalu,** South Pacific Ocean	16.4	5

Source: *CIA, The World Factbook 2001*

These 10 locations are definitely off the agenda if you are planning a climbing vacation, none of them possessing a single elevation taller than a small house. Beyond these exceptionally low-lying places, several countries, including Gambia and the Marshall Islands, lack a rise greater than 33 ft (10 m). Compared with these, even the Netherlands' 1,050-ft (321-m) Vaalserberg hill makes the country's appellation as one of the "Low Countries" seem almost unfair.

TOP 10 LARGEST DESERTS

	DESERT/LOCATION	APPROX. AREA (SQ MILES)	(SQ KM)
1	**Sahara,** Northern Africa	3,500,000	9,100,000
2	**Australian,** Australia*	1,300,000	3,400,000
3	**Arabian Peninsula,** Southwest Asia#	1,000,000	2,600,000
4	**Turkestan,** Central Asia†	750,000	1,900,000
5 =	**Gobi,** Central Asia	500,000	1,300,000
=	**North American Desert,** US/Mexico§	500,000	1,300,000
7	**Patagonia,** Southern Argentina	260,000	670,000
8	**Thar,** Northwest India/Pakistan	230,000	600,000
9	**Kalahari,** Southwestern Africa	220,000	570,000
10	**Takla Makan,** Northwestern China	185,000	480,000

* *Includes Gibson, Great Sandy, Great Victoria, and Simpson*

Includes an-Nafud and Rub ul-Khali

† *Includes Kara-Kum and Kyzylkum*

§ *Includes Great Basin, Mojave, Sonorah, and Chihuahuan*

This Top 10 presents the approximate areas and ranking of the world's great deserts, which are often broken down into smaller desert regions—the Australian Desert into the Gibson, Great Sandy, Great Victoria, and Simpson, for example. The world total is more than double that of the Top 10 at some 13,616,000 sq miles (35,264,000 sq km), or about one-quarter of the world's land area. However, deserts may range from the extremely arid and typical barren sandy desert (about 4 percent of the total land surface of the globe), through arid (15 percent) to semiarid (almost 15 percent), and most exhibit features that encompass all these degrees of aridity, with one zone merging almost imperceptibly into the next.

MOST COMMON ELEMENTS IN THE EARTH'S CRUST

ELEMENT	PARTS PER MILLION*
1 Oxygen	460,000
2 Silicon	270,000
3 Aluminum	82,000
4 Iron	63,000
5 Calcium	50,000
6 Magnesium	29,000
7 Sodium	23,000
8 Potassium	15,000
9 Titanium	6,600
10 Hydrogen	1,500

* mg per kg

This is based on the average percentages of the elements in igneous rock. Of every million atoms, some 200,000 are silicon, 63,000 aluminum, and 31,000 hydrogen—although in the Universe as a whole, hydrogen is by far the most common element, comprising some 930,000 out of every million atoms.

HEAVIEST ELEMENTS

ELEMENT	DISCOVERER/ COUNTRY	YEAR DISCOVERED	DENSITY*
1 Osmium	Smithson Tennant, UK	1804	22.59
2 Iridium	Smithson Tennant, UK	1804	22.56
3 Platinum	Julius Caesar Scaliger, Italy/France[#]; Charles Wood, UK[†]	1557 1741	21.45
4 Rhenium	Walter K. Noddack et al., Germany	1925	21.01
5 Neptunium	Edwin Mattison McMillan/ Philip H. Abelson, US	1940	20.47
6 Plutonium	Glenn Theodore Seaborg et al., US	1940	20.26
7 Gold		Prehistoric	19.29
8 Tungsten	Juan José and Fausto de Elhuijar, Spain	1783	19.26
9 Uranium	Martin Heinrich Klaproth, Germany	1789	19.05
10 Tantalum	Anders Gustav Ekeberg, Sweden	1802	16.67

* Grams per cubic centimeter at 20° C

[#] Earliest reference to

[†] Discovered

The two heaviest elements, the metals osmium and iridium, were discovered at the same time by the British chemist Smithson Tennant (1761–1815), who was also the first to prove that diamonds are made of carbon. A cubic foot (0.028317 m³) of osmium weighs 1,410 lb (640 kg).

MOST COMMON ELEMENTS ON THE MOON

ELEMENT	PERCENTAGE
1 Oxygen	40.0
2 Silicon	19.2
3 Iron	14.3
4 Calcium	8.0
5 Titanium	5.9
6 Aluminum	5.6
7 Magnesium	4.5
8 Sodium	0.33
9 Potassium	0.14
10 Chromium	0.002

This Top 10 is based on the analysis of the 45.8 lb (20.77 kg) of rock samples brought back to Earth by the crew of the 1969 Apollo 11 lunar mission. One of the minerals they discovered was named Armalcolite in honor of the three astronauts—Armstrong, Aldrin, and Collins.

HYDROGEN DISCOVERED!

THE EXISTENCE OF HYDROGEN, the lightest and most abundant element in the Universe, was first demonstrated in 1766 by British scientist Henry Cavendish (1731– 1810). He called it "inflammable air," but because it produces water when it burns in oxygen, it was given a name that means "water-forming." Soon after Cavendish's discovery, techniques for extracting hydrogen were developed, which led to one of its earliest practical uses by enabling the first hydrogen balloon flight, by Jacques Charles and Nicholas-Louis Robert, to take place in France on December 1, 1783. Following their debut two-hour flight from Paris to Nesle, Charles took off alone, thus becoming the world's first solo flier.

FIRST FACT

MOST COMMON ELEMENTS IN THE SUN

ELEMENT	PARTS PER MILLION*
1 Hydrogen	750,000
2 Helium	230,000
3 Oxygen	9,000
4 Carbon	3,000
5 = Iron	1,000
= Neon	1,000
= Nitrogen	1,000
8 Silicon	900
9 Magnesium	700
10 Sulfur	400

* mg per kg

More than 70 elements have been detected in the Sun, the most common of which correspond closely to those found in the Universe as a whole, but with some variations in their ratios, including a greater proportion of the principal element, hydrogen.

TOP 10 MOST COMMON ELEMENTS IN THE UNIVERSE

	ELEMENT	PARTS PER MILLION*
1	Hydrogen	750,000
2	Helium	230,000
3	Oxygen	10,000
4	Carbon	5,000
5	Neon	1,300
6	Iron	1,100
7	Nitrogen	1,000
8	Silicon	700
9	Magnesium	600
10	Sulfur	500

mg per kg

Hydrogen is the simplest atom—a single proton circled by a single electron. The atoms of hydrogen in the Universe outnumber those of all the other elements combined.

TOP 10 PRINCIPAL COMPONENTS OF AIR

	COMPONENT	PERCENTAGE BY VOLUME
1	Nitrogen	78.110
2	Oxygen	20.953
3	Argon	0.934
4	Carbon dioxide	0.01–0.10
5	Neon	0.001818
6	Helium	0.000524
7	Methane	0.0002
8	Krypton	0.000114
9 =	Hydrogen	0.00005
=	Nitrous oxide	0.00005

► **Gas light**
A cloud of electrons whirls around an atom of helium, the lightest and most abundant element after hydrogen. Helium was discovered in the Sun's spectrum during an eclipse in 1868, and isolated on Earth in 1895.

Weather Extremes

HOTTEST PLACES—EXTREMES

	LOCATION	HIGHEST TEMPERATURE (°F)	(°C)
1	**Al'Azīzīyah,** Libya	136.4	58.0
2	**Greenland Ranch,** Death Valley, California	134.0	56.7
3 =	**Ghudamis,** Libya	131.0	55.0
=	**Kebili,** Tunisia	131.0	55.0
5	**Tombouctou,** Mali	130.1	54.5
6	**Araouane,** Mali	130.0	54.4
7	**Tirat Tavi,** Israel	129.0	53.9
8	**Ahwāz,** Iran	128.3	53.5
9	**Agha Jārī,** Iran	128.0	53.3
10	**Wadi Halfa,** Sudan	127.0	52.8

Maximum of two places per country listed

Source: *Philip Eden*

The hottest temperature on Earth was that recorded by meteorologists from the National Geographic Society at Al'Azīzīyah, 40 km (25 miles) south of Tripoli, Libya, on 13 September 1922.

COLDEST PLACES—EXTREMES

	LOCATION	LOWEST TEMPERATURE (°F)	(°C)
1	**Vostok*,** Antarctica	-138.6	-89.2
2	**Plateau Station*,** Antarctica	-129.2	-84.0
3	**Oymyakon,** Russia	-96.0	-71.1
4	**Verkhoyansk,** Russia	-90.0	-67.7
5	**Northice*,** Greenland	-87.0	-66.0
6	**Eismitte*,** Greenland	-85.0	-64.9
7	**Snag,** Yukon, Canada	-81.4	-63.0
8	**Prospect Creek,** Alaska	-79.8	-62.1
9	**Fort Selkirk,** Yukon, Canada	-74.0	-58.9
10	**Rogers Pass,** Montana	-69.7	-56.5

Maximum of two places per country listed

* *Present or former scientific research base*

Source: *Philip Eden*

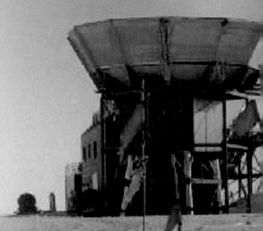

▼ **Freezing point**
The Martin A. Pomerantz Observatory at the Amundsen-Scott base at the South Pole. The American scientific research facility is located in almost the coldest place on Earth.

PLACES WITH THE MOST CONTRASTING SEASONS*

	LOCATION	WINTER (°F)	(°C)	SUMMER (°F)	(°C)	DIFFERENCE (°F)	(°C)
1	**Verkhoyansk,** Russia	-58.5	-50.3	56.5	13.6	115.0	63.9
2	**Yakutsk,** Russia	-49.0	-45.0	63.5	17.5	112.5	62.5
3	**Manzhouli,** China	-15.0	-26.1	69.0	20.6	84.0	46.7
4	**Fort Yukon,** Alaska	-20.2	-29.0	61.4	16.3	81.6	45.3
5	**Fort Good Hope,** Northwestern Territory, Canada	-21.8	-29.9	59.5	15.3	81.3	45.2
6	**Brochet,** Manitoba, Canada	-20.5	-29.2	59.7	15.4	80.2	44.6
7	**Tunka,** Mongolia	-16.0	-26.7	61.0	16.1	77.0	42.8
8	**Fairbanks,** Alaska	-11.2	-24.0	60.1	15.6	71.3	39.6
9	**Semipalatinsk,** Kazakhstan	0.5	-17.7	69.0	20.6	68.5	38.3
10	**Jorgen Bronlund Fjørd,** Greenland	-23.6	-30.9	43.5	6.4	67.1	37.3

Maximum of two places per country listed

* *Biggest differences between mean monthly temperatures in summer and winter*

Source: *Philip Eden*

Whether based on the differences in its mean winter and summer temperatures, or on its extremes, having recorded a winter temperature as low as -90° F (-68° C) and summer temperatures as high as 98° F (37° C), Verkhoyansk, a river port in northeast Siberia, has the most extreme climate on the planet.

TOP 10 PLACES WITH THE LEAST CONTRASTING SEASONS*

LOCATION	COOLEST (°F)	COOLEST (°C)	WARMEST (°F)	WARMEST (°C)	DIFFERENCE (°F)	DIFFERENCE (°C)
1 = **Lorengau**, New Guinea	80.0	26.7	81.0	27.2	1.0	0.5
= **Malacca**, Malaysia	80.0	26.7	81.0	27.2	1.0	0.5
= **Malden Island**, Kiribati	82.0	27.8	83.0	28.3	1.0	0.5
= **Ocean Island**, Kiribati	82.0	27.8	83.0	28.3	1.0	0.5
5 = **Kavieng**, New Guinea	81.0	27.2	82.0	27.8	1.0	0.6
= **Quito**, Ecuador	58.0	14.4	59.0	15.0	1.0	0.6
7 = **Andagoya**, Colombia	81.0	27.2	82.4	28.0	1.4	0.8
= **Labuhan**, Indonesia	81.0	27.2	82.4	28.0	1.4	0.8
= **Mwanza**, Tanzania	72.7	22.6	74.1	23.4	1.4	0.8
10 **Belém**, Brazil	79.0	26.1	80.5	26.9	1.5	0.8

Maximum of two places per country listed

* *Smallest differences between mean monthly temperature of warmest and coolest months*

Source: *Philip Eden*

TOP 10 WETTEST PLACES—AVERAGE

LOCATION	AVERAGE ANNUAL RAINFALL* (IN)	AVERAGE ANNUAL RAINFALL* (MM)
1 **Cherrapunji**, India	498.0	12,649
2 **Mawsynram**, India	467.4	11,872
3 **Waialeale**, Hawaii	451.0	11,455
4 **Debundscha**, Cameroon	404.6	10,277
5 **Quibdó**, Colombia	353.9	8,989
6 **Bellenden Ker Range**, Australia	340.0	8,636
7 **Andagoya**, Colombia	281.0	7,137
8 **Henderson Lake**, British Columbia, Canada	256.0	6,502
9 **Kikori**, Papua New Guinea	232.9	5,916
10 **Tavoy**, Myanmar	214.6	5,451

Maximum of two places per country listed

* *Annual rainfall total, averaged over a long period of years*

Source: *Philip Eden*

TOP 10 COLDEST PLACES—AVERAGE

LOCATION	AVERAGE TEMPERATURE* (°F)	AVERAGE TEMPERATURE* (°C)
1 **Plateau#**, Antarctica	-70.0	-56.7
2 **Amundsen-Scott#**, Antarctica	-56.2	-49.0
3 **Northice#**, Greenland	-22.0	-30.0
4 **Eismitte#**, Greenland	-20.5	-29.2
5 **Resolute**, NWT, Canada	-11.6	-24.2
6 **Eureka**, NWT, Canada	-3.5	-19.7
7 **Ostrov Bol'shoy**, Lyakhovskiy, Russia	5.5	-14.7
8 **Barrow Point**, Alaska	9.8	-12.3
9 **Barter Island**, Alaska	10.2	-12.1
10 **Ostrov Vrangela**, Russia	11.0	-11.7

Maximum of two places per country listed

* *Lowest long-term temperature averaged throughout the year*

Present or former scientific research base

Source: *Philip Eden*

TOP 10 HOTTEST PLACES—AVERAGE

LOCATION*	AVERAGE TEMPERATURE* (°F)	AVERAGE TEMPERATURE* (°C)
1 **Dallol**, Ethiopia	94.3	34.6
2 **Assab**, Eritrea	86.8	30.4
3 **Néma**, Mauritania	86.5	30.3
4 **Berbera**, Somalia	86.2	30.1
5 **Hombori**, Mali	86.1	30.1
6 **Perm Island**, South Yemen	86.0	30.0
7 **Djibouti**, Djibouti	85.8	29.9
8 **Atbara**, Sudan	85.7	29.8
9 = **Bender Qaasim**, Somalia	85.5	29.7
= **Kamarãn Island**, North Yemen	85.5	29.7

Maximum of two places per country listed

* *Highest long-term temperature averaged throughout the year*

Source: *Philip Eden*

Natural Disasters

THE 10 WORST EARTHQUAKES

	LOCATION	DATE	ESTIMATED NO. KILLED
1	**Near East/Mediterranean**	May 20, 1202	1,100,000
2	**Shenshi,** China	Feb. 2, 1556	820,000
3	**Calcutta,** India	Oct. 11, 1737	300,000
4	**Antioch,** Syria	May 20, 526	250,000
5	**Tang-shan,** China	July 28, 1976	242,419
6	**Nan-Shan,** China	May 22, 1927	200,000
7	**Yeddo,** Japan	Dec. 30, 1703	190,000
8	**Kansu,** China	Dec. 16, 1920	180,000
9	**Messina,** Italy	Dec. 28, 1908	160,000
10	**Tokyo/Yokohama,** Japan	Sept. 1, 1923	142,807

There are discrepancies between the "official" death tolls in many earthquakes and the estimates of other authorities: a figure of 750,000 is sometimes quoted for the 1976 Tang-shan earthquake, for example, and totals ranging from 58,000 to 250,000 for the quake that devastated Messina in 1908. In more recent times, the Armenian earthquake of December 7, 1988, killed more than 55,000 (28,854 officially), and that in Iran on June 21, 1990, killed over 55,000 (50,000 officially).

THE 10 WORST TSUNAMIS

	LOCATIONS AFFECTED	DATE	ESTIMATED NO. KILLED
1	**Krakatoa,** Sumatra, Java*	Aug. 27, 1883	36,380
2	**Sanriku,** Japan	June 15, 1896	28,000
3	**Agadir,** Morocco#	Feb. 29, 1960	12,000
4	**Lisbon,** Portugal	Nov. 1, 1755	10,000
5	**Papua New Guinea**	July 18, 1998	8,000
6	**Chile/Pacific islands/Japan**	May 22, 1960	5,700
7	**Philippines**	Aug. 17, 1976	5,000
8	**Hyuga to Izu,** Japan	Oct. 28, 1707	4,900
9	**Sanriku,** Japan	Mar. 3, 1933	3,000
10	**Japan#**	July 9, 1854	2,400

* Combined effect of volcanic eruption and tsunamis

 # Combined effect of earthquake and tsunamis

Tsunamis (from the Japanese *tsu*, port and *nami*, wave) are waves caused by undersea disturbances such as earthquakes or volcanic eruptions. They are often mistakenly called tidal waves, which are another phenomenon. Tsunamis can cross entire oceans, devastating islands and coastal regions in their paths.

THE 10 WORST VOLCANIC ERUPTIONS

	LOCATION	DATE	ESTIMATED NO. KILLED
1	**Tambora,** Indonesia	Apr. 5–12, 1815	92,000

The eruption of Tambora on the island of Sumbawa killed about 10,000 islanders immediately, with a further 82,000 dying subsequently from disease and famine resulting from crops being destroyed. An estimated 1,840,000 tons (1,700,000 metric tons) of ash were hurled into the atmosphere. This blocked out the sunlight and affected the weather over the globe during the following year. An effect of this was to produce brilliantly colored sunsets, depicted strikingly in paintings from the period, especially those of J.M.W. Turner.

	LOCATION	DATE	ESTIMATED NO. KILLED
2	**Unsen,** Japan	Apr. 1, 1793	53,000

During a period of intense volcanic activity in the area, the island of Unsen, or Unzen, completely disappeared, killing all its inhabitants.

	LOCATION	DATE	ESTIMATED NO. KILLED
3	**Mont Pelée,** Martinique	May 8, 1902	40,000

After lying dormant for centuries, Mont Pelée began to erupt in April 1902. Assured that there was no danger, the 30,000 residents of the main city, St. Pierre, stayed in their homes and were there when, at 7:30 a.m. on May 8, the volcano burst apart and showered the port with molten lava, ash, and gas, destroying virtually all life and property.

	LOCATION	DATE	ESTIMATED NO. KILLED
4	**Krakatoa,** Sumatra/Java	Aug. 26–27, 1883	36,380

The uninhabited island of Krakatoa exploded after a series of eruptions over the course of several days, and was audible up to 3,000 miles (4,800 km) away. Some sources put the fatalities as high as 200,000, most of them killed by subsequent tsunamis that reached 100 ft (30 m) high. The events were portrayed in the 1969 film *Krakatoa, East of Java*, but purists should note that Krakatoa is actually *west* of Java.

	LOCATION	DATE	ESTIMATED NO. KILLED
5	**Nevado del Ruiz,** Colombia	Nov. 13, 1985	22,940

The Andean volcano gave signs of erupting, but the decision to evacuate came too late. The steam, rocks, and ash ejected from Nevado del Ruiz melted its ice cap, resulting in a mudslide that completely engulfed the town of Armero.

	LOCATION	DATE	ESTIMATED NO. KILLED
6	**Mt. Etna,** Sicily	Mar. 11, 1669	over 20,000

Europe's largest volcano at 10,760 ft (3,280 m) has erupted frequently, but killed most people in 1669 when lava engulfed Catania, killing at least 20,000.

	LOCATION	DATE	ESTIMATED NO. KILLED
7	**Laki,** Iceland	Jan.–June 1783	20,000

Events on the Laki volcanic ridge in 1783 culminated on June 11 with the largest ever recorded lava flow, up to 50 miles (80 km) long and 100 ft (30 m) deep. Many villages were engulfed and those who managed to escape were killed by poisonous gases released from the lava.

	LOCATION	DATE	ESTIMATED NO. KILLED
8	**Vesuvius,** Italy	Aug. 24, AD 79	16–20,000

When the previously dormant Vesuvius erupted, Herculaneum was engulfed by a mud flow while Pompeii was buried under a vast layer of pumice and volcanic ash—which preserved it in a near-perfect state that was revealed by archaeological excavations that began in 1738 and continue to this day.

	LOCATION	DATE	ESTIMATED NO. KILLED
9	**Vesuvius,** Italy	Dec. 16–17, 1631	up to 18,000

The next major cataclysm after that of AD 79 was almost as disastrous when lava and mud flows poured into surrounding towns, including Naples.

	LOCATION	DATE	ESTIMATED NO. KILLED
10	**Mt. Etna,** Sicily	1169	over 15,000

Large numbers died sheltering in Catania cathedral, and more were killed when a tsunami caused by the eruption hit the port of Messina.

THE 10 WORST AVALANCHES AND LANDSLIDES*

	LOCATION	INCIDENT	DATE	ESTIMATED NO. KILLED
1	**Alps,** Italy	Avalanche	Oct. 218 BC	18,000
2	**Yungay,** Peru	Landslide	May 31, 1970	17,500
3	**Italian Alps**	Avalanche	Dec. 13, 1916	10,000
4	**Huarás,** Peru	Avalanche	Dec. 13, 1941	5,000
5	**Nevada Huascaran,** Peru	Avalanche	Jan. 10, 1962	3,500
6	**Chiavenna,** Italy	Landslide	Sept. 4, 1618	2,427
7	**Plurs,** Switzerland	Avalanche	Sept. 4, 1618	1,496
8	**Goldau Valley,** Switzerland	Landslide	Sept. 2, 1806	800
9	**Medellin,** Colombia	Landslide	Sept. 27, 1987	683
10	**Chungar,** Peru	Avalanche	Mar. 19, 1971	600

* Excluding those where most deaths resulted from flooding, earthquakes, volcanoes etc., associated with landslides

▼ Landslide tragedy
The Villa Tina area of Medellin, Colombia, was engulfed in a mudslide in 1987. Although 183 bodies were recovered, a further 500 inhabitants disappeared completely and 200 were injured, leaving just 117 survivors.

THE 10 WORST FLOODS

	LOCATION	DATE	ESTIMATED NO. KILLED
1	**Huang He River,** China	Aug. 1931	3,700,000
2	**Huang He River,** China	Spring 1887	1,500,000
3	**Netherlands**	Nov. 1, 1530	400,000
4	**Kaifong,** China	1642	300,000
5	**Henan,** China	Sept.–Nov. 1939	over 200,000
6	**Bengal,** India	1876	200,000
7	**Yangtze River,** China	Aug.–Sept. 1931	140,000
8	**Netherlands**	1646	110,000
9	**North Vietnam**	Aug. 30, 1971	over 100,000
10 =	**Friesland,** Netherlands	1228	100,000
=	**Dort,** Netherlands	Apr. 16, 1421	100,000
=	**Canton,** China	June 12, 1915	100,000
=	**Yangtze River,** China	Sept. 1911	100,000

Records of floods caused by China's Huang He, or Yellow River, date back to 2297 BC. Since then, it has flooded at least 1,500 times, resulting in millions of deaths and giving it the nickname "China's Sorrow." According to some accounts, the flood of 1887 may have resulted in as many as 6 million deaths.

LIFE ON EARTH

Land Animals

HEAVIEST PRIMATES

	PRIMATE	LENGTH* (IN)	LENGTH* (CM)	WEIGHT (LB)	WEIGHT (KG)
1	Gorilla	79	200	485	220
2	Man	70	177	170	77
3	Orangutan	54	137	165	75
4	Chimpanzee	36	92	110	50
5 =	Baboon	39	100	99	45
=	Mandrill	37	95	99	45
7	Gelada baboon	30	75	55	25
8	Proboscis monkey	30	76	53	24
9	Hanuman langur	42	107	44	20
10	Siamung gibbon	35	90	29	13

* Excluding tail

The largest primates (including humans) and all the apes derive from the Old World (Africa, Asia and Europe). Only one member of a New World species of monkey (the Guatemalan howler, at 36 in/91 cm, 20 lb/9 kg) is a close contender for the Top 10. The difference between the prosimians (primitive primates), great apes, lesser apes, and monkeys has more to do with shape than size, though the great apes mostly fill out the table.

TEST-TUBE GORILLA!

ROSIE, A LOWLAND GORILLA living at the Cincinnati Zoo, Ohio, produced her seventh baby, a female named Timu ("team" in Swahili), on October 9, 1995. Timu was the first gorilla ever born by *in vitro* fertilization, using the same technique that produced the first human test-tube baby, Louise Brown, in 1978. An egg from Rosie had been fertilized by sperm from Mosuba, a male gorilla at Henry Doorly Zoo in Omaha, Nebraska, as part of a program to ensure the survival of this threatened species.

FIRST FACT

◄ **Great ape**
Gorillas are the heaviest primates. The largest on record was N'gagi, a male living at the San Diego Zoo, California from 1931 to 1944, whose peak weight was 683 lb (310 kg).

TOP 10 | SNAKES WITH THE DEADLIEST BITES

	SNAKE	EST. LETHAL DOSE FOR HUMANS (MG)	AVE. VENOM PER BITE (MG)	POTENTIAL HUMANS KILLED PER BITE
1	**Coastal taipan** (*Oxyuranus scutellatus*)	1	120	120
2	**Common krait** (*Bungarus caeruleus*)	0.5	42	84
3	**Philippine cobra** (*Naja naja philippinensis*)	2	120	60
4 =	**King cobra** (*Ophiophagus hannah*)	20	1,000	50
=	**Russell's viper** (*Daboia russelli*)	3	150	50
6	**Black mamba** (*Dendroaspis polyepis*)	3	135	45
7	**Yellow-jawed tommygoff** (*Bothrops asper*)	25	1,000	40
8 =	**Multibanded krait** (*Bungarus multicinctus*)	0.8	28	35
=	**Tiger snake** (*Notechis scutatus*)	1	35	35
10	**Jararacussu** (*Bothrops jararacussu*)	25	800	32

This list represents the results of a comprehensive survey of the various factors that determine the relative danger posed by poisonous snakes. These include the strength of the venom (and hence the estimated lethal dose for an adult), and the amount injected per bite; most snakes inject about 15 percent of their venom per bite. Some snakes are rare and seldom come into contact with humans, while the likelihood of death as a result of snake bite varies according to the availability of antivenom and medical treatment. The common krait has the highest fatality rate of any snake on record: in one study, of 32 victims admitted to hospitals in India after bites, only two survived. Bites by Russell's vipers have been known to cause death within 15 minutes.

TOP 10 | FASTEST MAMMALS

	MAMMAL	MAXIMUM RECORDED SPEED (MPH)	(KM/H)
1	**Cheetah**	65	105
2	**Pronghorn antelope**	55	89
3 =	**Mongolian gazelle**	50	80
=	**Springbok**	50	80
5 =	**Grant's gazelle**	47	76
=	**Thomson's gazelle**	47	76
7	**Brown hare**	45	72
8	**Horse**	43	69
9 =	**Greyhound**	42	68
=	**Red deer**	42	68

Although several animals on the list are capable of higher speeds, these figures are based on controlled measurements of average speeds over 0.25 miles (0.4 km). Charging lions can achieve 50 mph (80 km/h) over very short distances, while various members of the antelope family, wildebeests, elks, dogs, coyotes, foxes, hyenas, zebras, and Mongolian wild asses have all been credited with unsustained spurts of 40 mph (64 km/h) or more. Compare these figures with the top speed of the three-toed sloth, which is 0.12 mph (0.2 km/h).

TOP 10 | HEAVIEST CARNIVORES

	CARNIVORE	LENGTH (FT)	(IN)	(M)	WEIGHT (LB)	(KG)
1	**Southern elephant seal**	21	4	6.5	7,716	3,500
2	**Walrus**	12	6	3.8	2,646	1,200
3	**Steller sea lion**	9	8	3.0	2,425	1,100
4	**Grizzly bear**	9	8	3.0	1,720	780
5	**Polar bear**	8	6	2.6	1,323	600
6	**Tiger**	9	2	2.8	661	300
7	**Lion**	6	3	1.9	551	250
8	**American black bear**	6	0	1.8	500	227
9	**Giant panda**	5	0	1.5	353	160
10	**Spectacled bear**	6	0	1.8	309	140

Only three marine carnivores have been included, to make room for the terrestrial heavyweights. The polar bear is probably the largest land carnivore if shoulder height (when the animal is on all fours) is taken into account; it tops an awesome 5.3 ft (1.6 m) compared with the 4 ft (1.2 m) of its nearest rival, the grizzly.

TOP 10 | HEAVIEST TERRESTRIAL MAMMALS

	MAMMAL	LENGTH (FT)	(M)	WEIGHT (LB)	(KG)
1	**African elephant**	24	7.3	14,432	7,000
2	**White rhinoceros**	14	4.2	7,937	3,600
3	**Hippopotamus**	13	4.0	5,512	2,500
4	**Giraffe**	19	5.8	3,527	1,600
5	**American bison**	13	3.9	2,205	1,000
6	**Arabian camel** (dromedary)	12	3.5	1,521	690
7	**Polar bear**	8	2.6	1,323	600
8	**Moose**	10	3.0	1,213	550
9	**Siberian tiger**	11	3.3	661	300
10	**Gorilla**	7	2.0	485	220

The list excludes domesticated cattle and horses. It also avoids comparing close kin such as the African and Indian elephants, highlighting instead the sumo stars within distinctive large mammal groups such as the bears, deer, big cats, primates, and bovines (oxlike mammals).

Flying Animals

HEAVIEST FLIGHTED BIRDS

BIRD*	WINGSPAN		WEIGHT		
	(IN)	(CM)	(LB)	(OZ)	(KG)
1 Mute swan	93	238	49	6	22.50
2 Kori bustard	106	270	41	8	19.00
3 = Andean condor	126	320	33	1	15.00
= Great white pelican	141	360	33	1	15.00
5 Black vulture (Old World)	116	295	27	5	12.50
6 Sarus crane	110	280	26	9	12.24
7 Himalayan griffon (vulture)	122	310	26	5	12.00
8 Wandering albatross	137	350	24	9	11.30
9 Steller's sea eagle	104	265	19	8	9.00
10 Marabou stork	113	287	19	6	8.90

* By species

Source: *Chris Mead*

Wing size does not necessarily correspond to weight in flighted birds: the huge wingspan of the marabou stork, for example, is greater than that of species twice its weight. When laden with a meal of carrion, however, the voracious marabou can double its weight and needs all the lift it can get to take off. It often fails totally and has to put up with flightlessness until digestion takes its course.

FASTEST BIRDS

BIRD	SPEED	
	(MPH)	(KM/H)
1 Common eider	47	76
2 Bewick's swan	44	72
3 = Barnacle goose	42	68
= Common crane	42	68
5 Mallard	40	65
6 = Red-throated diver	38	61
= Wood pigeon	38	61
8 Oyster catcher	36	58
9 = Pheasant	33	54
= White-fronted goose	33	54

Source: *Chris Mead*

Recent research reveals that, contrary to popular belief, swifts are not fast fliers, but very efficient with long thin wings like gliders and low wing-loading. Fast fliers generally have high wing-loading and fast wing beats. The fastest swimming birds are penguins that can achieve speeds of 21 mph (35 km/h). The fastest running bird is the ostrich which can reach a speed of 44 mph (72 km/h), and maintain it for 20 minutes – ostrich racing with human jockeys or drawing chariots is pursued in South Africa and other countries.

TOP 10 SMALLEST BATS

BAT/HABITAT	LENGTH (IN)	(CM)	WEIGHT (OZ)	(G)
1 Kitti's hognosed bat (*Craseonycteris thonglongyai*), Thailand	1.10	2.9	0.07	2.0
2 Proboscis bat (*Rhynchonycteris naso*), Central and South America	1.50	3.8	0.09	2.5
3 = Banana bat (*Pipistrellus nanus*), Africa	1.50	3.8	0.11	3.0
= Smoky bat (*Furipterus horrens*), Central and South America	1.50	3.8	0.11	3.0
5 = Little yellow bat (*Rhogeessa mira*), Central America	1.57	4.0	0.12	3.5
= Lesser bamboo bat (*Tylonycteris puchypus*), Southeast Asia	1.57	4.0	0.12	3.5
7 Disc-winged bat (*Thyroptera tricolor*), Central and South America	1.42	3.6	0.14	4.0
8 = Lesser horseshoe bat (*Rhinolophus hipposideros*), Europe and Western Asia	1.46	3.7	0.18	5.0
= California myotis (*Myotis californienses*), North America	1.69	4.3	0.18	5.0
10 Northern blossom bat (*Macroglossus minimus*), Southeast Asia to Australia	2.52	6.4	0.53	15.0

The minute Kitti's hognosed bat, the world's smallest mammal, is found only in a group of caves in Thailand. It is named after Kitti Thonglongya, who discovered it in 1973.

TOP 10 LONGEST BIRD MIGRATIONS

BIRD	APPROXIMATE DISTANCE (MILES)	(KM)
1 Pectoral sandpiper	11,806	19,000*
2 Wheatear	11,184	18,000
3 Slender-billed shearwater	10,874	17,500*
4 Ruff	10,314	16,600
5 Willow warbler	10,128	16,300
6 Arctic tern	10,066	16,200
7 Arctic skua	9,693	15,600
8 Swainson's hawk	9,445	15,200
9 Knot	9,320	15,000
10 Swallow	9,258	14,900

* *Thought to be only half of the path taken during a whole year*

Source: *Chris Mead*

This list is of the likely extremes for a normal migrant, not one that has gotten lost and wandered into new territory. All migrant birds fly far longer than is indicated by the direct route. Many species fly all year, except when they come to land to breed or, in the case of seabirds, to rest on the sea. Such species include the albatross, petrel, tern, and some types of swift and house martin. The annual distance covered by these birds may range from 93,200 miles (150,000 km) to almost 186,115 miles (300,000 km).

TOP 10 HEAVIEST OWLS

OWL	WINGSPAN (IN)	(CM)	WEIGHT (LB)	(OZ)	(KG)
1 Eurasian eagle-owl	29	75	9	4	4.20
2 Verraux's eagle-owl	26	65	6	14	3.11
3 Snowy owl	28	70	6	8	2.95
4 Great horned owl	24	60	5	8	2.50
5 Pel's fishing-owl	25	63	5	2	2.32
6 Pharaoh eagle-owl	20	50	5	1	2.30
7 Cape eagle-owl	23	58	3	15	1.80
8 Great grey owl	27	69	3	12	1.70
9 Powerful owl	24	60	3	5	1.50
10 Ural owl	24	62	2	14	1.30

* *Some owls closely related to these species may be of similar size; most measurements are from female owls as they are usually larger*

Source: *Chris Mead*

◀ **Big wings**
The Andean condor has one of the greatest total wing areas of any bird. The celebrated British mountaineer Edward Whymper encountered one in Ecuador in 1892 with wings that measured 10 ft 6 in (3.2 m) from tip to tip.

Marine Animals

THE 10 COUNTRIES WITH THE MOST-THREATENED FISH SPECIES

COUNTRY/MOST THREATENED SPECIES*	TOTAL NO. OF THREATENED FISH
1 US	131
Alabama sturgeon#, cu-cui#, Charalito chihuahua, White River spinedace#, Moapa dace#, Cahaba shiner#, Cape Fear shiner#, Leon Spring pupfish#, Pecos pupfish,# California black sea bass, Alabama cavefish#, shortnose cisco, Apache trout	
2 Mexico	88
Perrito de potosi# (extinct in the wild), Cachorrito de charco palmal# (extinct in the wild), black-blotch pupfish# (extinct in the wild), butterfly splitfin# (extinct in the wild), golden skiffia# (extinct in the wild), charal de Alchichica#, *Cyprinella alvarezdelvillari*# (no common name), sardinita bocagrande#, sardinita quijarrona#, charalito saltillo#, charalito chihuahua, sardinita de tepelmene#, cachorrito de Mezquital#, cachorrito cabezon#, cachorrito de dorsal larga,# cachorrito de charco azul#, Cuatrocienegas killifish#, blackspot allotoca#, Mexclapique#, Turners hocklandkärpfling#, balsas hocklandkärpfling#, guayacon bocon#, broad-spotted molly#, molly del Teapa#, Monterrey platyfish#, black sea bass, totoaba#, Boccacio rockfish	
3 Indonesia	67
Sentani rainbowfish#, duck-bill poso minnow#, elongate poso minnow#, *Betta miniopinna*# (no common name), *Betta spilotogena*# (no common name), poso bungu#, *Encheloclarias kelioides*# (no common name)	
4 Australia	44
Red-finned blue-eye#, spotted handfish#, swan galaxias#, barred galaxias#, Clarence galaxias#, pedder galaxias#, Elizabeth Springs goby#, Edgbaston goby#, Mary River cod#	
5 China	33
Dabry's sturgeon#, Chinese paddlefish#	

COUNTRY/MOST THREATENED SPECIES*	TOTAL NO. OF THREATENED FISH
6 South Africa	30
Twee River redfin#, border barb#, Clanwilliam sandfish#, Berg redfin#, Barnard's rock-catfish#, Incomati suckermouth#, river pipefish#	
7 Philippines	28
Cephalakoompsus pachycheilus# (no common name), manumbok#, bagangan#, bitungu#, pait#, baolan#, disa#, katapa-tapa#, *Puntius herrei*# (no common name), katolo#, kandar#, manalak#, tras#, palata#, dwarf pygmy goby#	
8 = Cameroon	27
Dikume#, konye#, myaka#, pungu#, fissi#, blackbelly tilapia#, keppi#, kululu#, nsess#, mongo#, pindu#, *Clarias maclareni*# (no common name)	
= Uganda	27
Allochromis welcommei# (no common name), *Astatotilapia latifasciata*# (no common name), *Haplochromis annectidens*# (no common name), *Harpagochromis worthingtoni*# (no common name), *Lipochromis "backflash cryptodon"*# (no common name), *Paralabidochromis beadlei*# (no common name), *Xystichromis "Kyoga flameback"*# (no common name)	
10 Turkey	22
Baltic/European sturgeon, *Aphanius splendens*# (no common name), *Aphanius sureyanus*# (no common name), *Aphanius transgrediens*# (no common name), flathead trout#	

* Listed as Critically Endangered on the IUCN Red List 2000, except where otherwise indicated

 # Found in no other countries

Source: *2000 IUCN Red List of Threatened Species/UNEP-WCMC Animals of the World Database*

TOP 10 HEAVIEST MARINE MAMMALS

	MAMMAL	LENGTH (FT)	(M)	WEIGHT (TONS)
1	Blue whale	110.0	33.5	151.0
2	Bowhead whale (Greenland right)	65.0	20.0	95.0
3	Northern right whale (black right)	60.0	18.6	85.6
4	Fin whale (common rorqual)	82.0	25.0	69.9
5	Sperm whale	59.0	18.0	48.2
6	Gray whale	46.0	14.0	38.5
7	Humpback whale	49.2	15.0	38.1
8	Sei whale	60.0	18.5	32.4
9	Bryde's whale	47.9	14.6	22.0
10	Baird's whale	18.0	5.5	13.3

Source: *Lucy T. Verma*

Probably the largest animal that ever lived, the blue whale dwarfs even the other whales listed here, all but one of which far outweigh the biggest land animal, the elephant. The elephant seal, with a weight of 3.9 tons, is the largest marine mammal that is not a whale.

TOP 10 HEAVIEST SHARKS

	SHARK	MAXIMUM WEIGHT (LB)	(KG)
1	Whale shark	67,240	30,500
2	Basking shark	20,410	9,258
3	Great white shark	7,731	3,507
4	Greenland shark	2,224	1,009
5	Tiger shark	2,043	927
6	Great hammerhead shark	1,889	857
7	Six-gill shark	1,327	602
8	Gray nurse shark	1,243	564
9	Mako shark	1,221	554
10	Thresher shark	1,097	498

Source: *Lucy T. Verma*

Such is the notoriety of sharks that many accounts of their size are exaggerated, and this list should be taken as an approximate ranking based on best available evidence. The rare whale shark is also the largest fish, measuring up to 41 ft 6 in (12.65 m). First discovered in 1828, it is a plankton-eater and consequently not a threat to swimmers.

TOP 10 HEAVIEST TURTLES

	TURTLE	MAXIMUM WEIGHT (LB)	(KG)
1	Pacific leatherback turtle*	1,552	704 4
2	Atlantic leatherback turtle*	1,018	463.0
3	Green sea turtle	783	355.3
4	Loggerhead turtle	568	257.8
5	Alligator snapping turtle#	220	100.0
6	Flatback (sea) turtle	171	78.2
7	Hawksbill (sea) turtle	138	62.7
8	Kemps Ridley turtle	133	60.5
9	Olive Ridley turtle	110	49.9
10	Common snapping turtle#	85	38.5

* One species, differing in size according to where they live

Freshwater species

Source: *Lucy T. Verma*

The largest leatherback turtle ever recorded is a male found beached at Harlech, Wales, in 1988, measuring 9 ft 5½ in (2.9 m) and weighing 2,120 lb (961 kg). It is now displayed in the National Museum of Wales, Cardiff.

◀ **Threatened turtle**
Having been hunted as food and for their shells, many of the world's largest turtles are endangered and under threat of extinction.

A Bug's Life

TOP 10 MOST COMMON INSECTS*

SPECIES (SCIENTIFIC NAME)	APPROXIMATE NO. OF KNOWN SPECIES
1 **Beetles** (*Coleoptera*)	400,000
2 **Butterflies and moths** (*Lepidoptera*)	165,000
3 **Ants, bees, and wasps** (*Hymenoptera*)	140,000
4 **True flies** (*Diptera*)	120,000
5 **Bugs** (*Hemiptera*)	90,000
6 **Crickets, grasshoppers, and locusts** (*Orthoptera*)	20,000
7 **Caddisflies** (*Trichoptera*)	10,000
8 **Lice** (*Phthiraptera/Psocoptera*)	7,000
9 **Dragonflies and damselflies** (*Odonata*)	5,500
10 **Lacewings** (*Neuroptera*)	4,700

* By number of known species

This list includes only species that have been discovered and named; it is surmised that many thousands of species still await discovery. It takes no account of the absolute numbers of each species, which are truly colossal. There are at least one million insects for each of the Earth's 6.3 billion humans; all together, the insects would weigh at least 12 times as much as the human race and at least three times as much as the combined weight of all other living animals. There are at least five quadrillion individuals, among the most common of which are ants, flies, beetles, and the little-known springtails, which inhabit moist topsoil all over the world. The latter alone probably outweigh the entire human race.

▶ **Leaf beetle**
Almost one-third of all known animal species are beetles, with more than 25,000 species of leaf beetles among the 400,000 recorded.

TOP 10 LARGEST MOLLUSKS*

SPECIES (SCIENTIFIC NAME)	CLASS	LENGTH (IN)	(MM)
1 **Giant squid** (*Architeuthis* species)	Cephalopod	660	16,764#
2 **Giant clam** (*Tridacna gigas*)	Marine bivalve	51	1,300
3 **Australian trumpet** (*Syrus aruanus*)	Marine snail	30	770
4 *Hexabranchus sanguineus*	Sea slug	20	520
5 *Carinaria cristata*	Heteropod	19	500
6 **Steller's Coat of Mail shell** (*Cryptochiton stelleri*)	Chiton	18	470
7 **Freshwater mussel** (*Cristaria plicata*)	Freshwater bivalve	11	300
8 **Giant African snail** (*Achatina achatina*)	Land snail	7	200
9 **Tusk shell** (*Dentalium vernedi*)	Scaphopod	5	138
10 **Apple snail** (*Pila werneri*)	Freshwater snail	4	125

* Largest species within each class

\# Estimated; actual length unknown

There are over 60,000 species of mollusks, including octopuses, snails, slugs, and shellfish, of which these are the largest—although tales of the largest, the giant squid, attacking and sinking ships are in the realm of sailors' tall tales. The giant clam is noted for its longevity, with lifespans of up to 150 years being claimed by some experts.

TOP 10 LARGEST BUTTERFLIES

BUTTERFLY (SCIENTIFIC NAME)	WINGSPAN (IN)	(MM)
1 **Queen Alexandra's birdwing** (*Ornithoptera alexandrae*)	11.0	280
2 **African giant swallowtail** (*Papilio antimachus*)	9.1	230
3 **Goliath birdwing** (*Ornithoptera goliath*)	8.3	210
4 = **Buru opalescent birdwing** (*Troides prattorum*)	7.9	200
= *Trogonoptera trojana*	7.9	200
= *Troides hypolitus*	7.9	200
7 = **Chimaera birdwing** (*Ornithoptera chimaera*)	7.5	190
= *Ornithoptera lydius*	7.5	190
= *Troides magellanus*	7.5	190
= *Troides miranda*	7.5	190

The rare Queen Alexandra's birdwing is found only in Papua New Guinea. Females, which are usually larger than males, weigh up to ⁹⁄₁₀ oz (25 g).

TOP 10 FASTEST INSECT FLIERS

	SPECIES (SCIENTIFIC NAME)	SPEED (MPH)	SPEED (KM/H)
1	**Hawkmoth** (*Sphingidaei*)	33.3	53.6
2 =	**West Indian butterfly** (*Nymphalidae prepona*)	30.0	48.0
=	**Deer botfly** (*Cephenemyia pratti*)	30.0	48.0
4	**Deer botfly** (*Chrysops*)	25.0	40.0
5	**West Indian butterfly** (*Hesperiidae* species)	18.6	30.0
6	**Dragonfly** (*Anax parthenope*)	17.8	28.6
7	**Hornet** (*Vespa crabro*)	13.3	21.4
8	**Bumblebee** (*Bombus lapidarius*)	11.1	17.9
9	**Horsefly** (*Tabanus bovinus*)	8.9	14.3
10	**Honey bee** (*Apis mellifera*)	7.2	11.6

▶ **Hive of activity**
With its wings beating at an amazing rate of 11,000 times a minute, the honey bee can fly extremely fast.

TOP 10 DEADLIEST SPIDERS

	SPIDER (SCIENTIFIC NAME)	LOCATION
1	**Banana spider** (*Phonenutria nigriventer*)	Central and South America
2	**Sydney funnel web** (*Atrax robustus*)	Australia
3	**Wolf spider** (*Lycosa raptoria/erythrognatha*)	Central and South America
4	**Black widow** (*Latrodectus* species)	Widespread
5	**Violin spider/Recluse spider**	Widespread
6	**Sac spider**	Southern Europe
7	**Tarantula** (*Eurypelma rubropilosum*)	Neotropics
8	**Tarantula** (*Acanthoscurria atrox*)	Neotropics
9	**Tarantula** (*Lasiodora klugi*)	Neotropics
10	**Tarantula** (*Pamphobeteus* species)	Neotropics

This list ranks spiders according to their "lethal potential"—their venom yield divided by their venom potency. The banana spider, for example, yields 6 mg of venom, with 1 mg the estimated lethal dose in man. However, few spiders are capable of killing humans—there were just 14 recorded deaths caused by black widows in the US in the entire 19th century—since their venom yield is relatively low compared with that of the most dangerous snakes; the tarantula, for example, produces 1.5 mg of venom, but its lethal dose for an adult human is 12 mg. Anecdotal evidence suggests that the Thailand and Sumatran black birdeaters may be equally dangerous, but insufficient data are available.

TOP 10 MOST COMMON ANIMAL PHOBIAS

	ANIMAL	MEDICAL TERM
1	Spiders	Arachnophobia or arachnephobia
2	Bees and wasps	Bees: Apiphobia, apiophobia, or melissophobia; wasps: spheksophobia
3	Reptiles	Batrachophobia
4	Snakes	Ophidiophobia, ophiophobia, ophiciophobia, herpetophobia, or snakephobia
5	Mice	Musophobia or muriphobia
6	Dogs	Cynophobia or kynophobia
7	Birds	Ornithophobia
8	Frogs	Batrachophobia
9 =	Ants	Myrmecophobia
=	Horses	Hippophobia or equinophobia
=	Rats	No medical term

Not all phobias are completely irrational. Creatures that may bite or sting, or carry disease, such as rabid dogs or cats, are very wisely avoided.

▼ **Death rattle**
The fear of snakes is among the most common of all phobias—although with species such as this rattlesnake, there are good reasons.

THE 10 COUNTRIES THAT CATCH THE MOST WHALES

	COUNTRY	CATCH (2000) SPERM AND PILOT WHALES	BLUE AND FIN WHALES	TOTAL
1	Japan	16,937	552	17,489
2	Brazil	861	–	861
3	Norway	–	487	487
4	Argentina	445	–	445
5	France	213	–	213
6	US	172	35	207
7	Russia	22	180	202
8	South Korea	95	79	174
9	Greenland	–	162	162
10	UK	46	3	49

Source: *Food and Agriculture Organization of the United Nations*

Whaling has been banned in the majority of these countries; most of the whales listed in this Top 10 have been caught accidentally in fishing nets.

THE 10 LATEST GENESIS AWARDS FOR BEST FEATURE FILM

YEAR	FILM
2003	Spirit: Stallion of the Cimarron
2002	Doctor Dolittle 2
2001	Chicken Run
2000	Instinct
1999	Mighty Joe Young
1998	Shiloh
1997	Fly Away Home
1996	Babe
1995	Black Beauty
1994	Free Willy

Source: *The Ark Trust*

Since 1986 the Ark Trust, Inc., a US animal rights and welfare charity, has been presenting the Genesis Awards, including one for the best animal feature film that raises such issues.

THE 10 COUNTRIES WITH THE MOST IVORY SEIZURES

	COUNTRY	SEIZURES (1989–99)
1	US	1,435
2	Namibia	409
3	France	375
4	UK	367
5	Germany	261
6	Belgium	237
7	Tanzania	210
8	South Africa	155
9	Malawi	132
10	Zambia	104
	World	4,361

Source: *The Elephant Trade Information System (ETIS)*

The records indicate that nearly 130 tons of ivory have been seized across the world in the period 1989–99, representing some 28,319 tusks and pieces of raw ivory, 204,215 semi-worked ivory blocks, and 187,950 ivory products.

TOP 10 FILMS STARRING ANIMALS

	FILM	YEAR	ANIMAL
1	Jaws	1975	Shark
2	101 Dalmatians	1996	Dogs
3	Doctor Dolittle	1998	Various
4	Babe	1995	Pig
5	Jaws 2	1978	Shark
6	Cats & Dogs	2001	Cats/dogs
7	The Horse Whisperer	1998	Horses
8	102 Dalmatians	2000	Dogs
9	Doctor Dolittle 2	2001	Various
10	Deep Blue Sea	1999	Sharks

This list is of movies where real animals are central, rather than secondary, characters. It excludes dinosaurs, fantasy creatures such as dragons, and humans disguised as animals (hence eliminating *Planet of the Apes*) as well as animated films and the eponymous stars of animated/live-action combinations such as *Who Framed Roger Rabbit*, *Stuart Little*, and *Scooby-Doo*. With new technology, the line between real, animatronic, and computer generated animals is becoming increasingly blurred.

Jaws of death
Star of *Jaws*, the great white shark is responsible for more human attacks (254) and fatalities (67) than any other species in attacks recorded between 1580 and 2001.

THE 10 PLACES WHERE MOST PEOPLE ARE ATTACKED BY SHARKS

COUNTRY/STATE	FATAL ATTACKS	LAST FATAL ATTACK	TOTAL ATTACKS*
1 US (continental)	69	2001	855
2 Australia	152	2000	323
3 South Africa	43	1999	225
4 Hawaii	19	1992	99
5 Brazil	20	1998	78
6 Papua New Guinea	31	2000	65
7 New Zealand	9	1968	53
8 The Bahamas	1	1968	42
9 Mexico	21	1997	39
10 Fiji Islands	10	2000	25

* Including non-fatal

Source: *International Shark Attack File/American Elasmobranch Society/Florida Museum of Natural History*

The International Shark Attack File monitors worldwide incidents, a total of more than 2,000 of which have been recorded since the 16th century. The 1990s had the highest attack total (536) of any decade, while 76 unprovoked attacks were recorded in 2001 alone. This upward trend is believed to reflect the increase in the numbers of people engaging in scuba diving and other aquatic activities.

THE 10 ANIMALS USED IN THE MOST EXPERIMENTATION IN THE US

ANIMAL	NO. USED (2001)
1 Rabbits	267,351
2 Guinea pigs	256,193
3 Other animals	242,251
4 Hamsters	167,231
5 Other farm animals	75,169
6 Dogs	70,082
7 Pigs	60,253
8 Primates	49,382
9 Sheep	26,236
10 Cats	22,755
Total	1,236,903

* Includes animals used in research, experiments, testing, and teaching

Source: *US Department of Agriculture*, Animal Welfare Report, Fiscal Year 2001

Rats, mice, and all non-mammals are excluded from the above list because they are not covered by any protective laws and there is no legal requirement for data to be collected. These unreported species are thought to make up 85–95 percent of animals used in experimentation in the US, so it is possible that the total number of animals used in experiments could exceed 20 million.

Pet Power

TOP 10 PETS IN THE US

PET	EST. NO.*
1 Dogs	40,000,000
2 Cats	34,700,000
3 Freshwater fish	12,200,000
4 Small animal pets#	5,500,000
5 Reptiles	4,000,000
6 Cockatiels	2,600,000
7 Parakeets	2,100,000
8 Saltwater fish	700,000
9 Finches	600,000
10 Parrots	500,000

Number of households owning, rather than individual specimens

Includes rabbits and small rodents—ferrets, hamsters, guinea pigs, and gerbils

Source: *American Pet Products Manufacturers Association*

TOP 10 PET DOG POPULATIONS

COUNTRY	EST. PET DOG POPULATION (2002)
1 US	61,080,000
2 Brazil	30,051,000
3 China	22,908,000
4 Japan	9,650,000
5 Russia	9,600,000
6 South Africa	9,100,000
7 France	8,150,000
8 Italy	7,600,000
9 Poland	7,520,000
10 Thailand	6,900,000

Source: *Euromonitor*

The estimate for the US dog population represents a ratio of more than one dog for every two of the 104,705,000 households in the country, but since multiple ownership is common, there are more dog-free homes than those with a canine inhabitant.

TOP 10 PET BIRD POPULATIONS

COUNTRY	EST. PET BIRD POPULATION (2002)
1 China	71,474,000
2 Japan	21,300,000
3 US	18,740,000
4 Brazil	17,254,000
5 Indonesia	14,842,000
6 Italy	13,000,000
7 Turkey	9,200,000
8 Spain	7,734,000
9 Australia	7,100,000
10 France	6,500,000

Source: *Euromonitor*

TOP 10 PET FISH POPULATIONS

COUNTRY	EST. PET FISH POPULATION (2002)
1 US	168,990,000
2 China	121,852,000
3 Germany	50,000,000
4 Japan	34,100,000
5 Italy	30,000,000
6 France	28,000,000
7 UK	23,900,000
8 Russia	20,600,000
9 Australia	12,900,000
10 Sweden	9,480,000

Source: *Euromonitor*

◀ **Tanks a lot**
Fish are kept as domestic pets, rather than for food, all over the world. China's particular fondness for them is a long-standing tradition.

THE 10 LATEST WINNERS OF "BEST IN SHOW" AT THE WESTMINSTER KENNEL CLUB DOG SHOW

YEAR	BREED	CHAMPION
2003	Kerry blue terrier	Torums Scarf Michael
2002	Miniature poodle	Surrey Spice Girl
2001	Bichon frise	Special Times Just Right
2000	English springer spaniel	Salilyn 'n Erin's Shameless
1999	Papillon	Loteki Supernatural Being
1998	Norwich terrier	Fairewood Frolic
1997	Standard schnauzer	Parsifal Di Casa Netzer
1996	Clumber spaniel	Clussexx Country Sunrise
1995	Scottish terrier	Gaelforce Post Script
1994	Norwich terrier	Chidley Willum The Conqueror

Source: *Westminster Kennel Club*

▲ **Cool for cats**
Ownership of pedigree cats, such as this Siamese, contributes to the substantial feline population of many Western countries. In developing parts of the world, cats continue their traditional role as domestic mouse-catchers.

TOP 10 PET CAT POPULATIONS

	COUNTRY	EST. PET CAT POPULATION (2002)
1	US	76,430,000
2	China	53,100,000
3	Russia	12,700,000
4	Brazil	12,466,000
5	France	9,600,000
6	Italy	9,400,000
7	UK	7,700,000
8	Ukraine	7,350,000
9	Japan	7,300,000
10	Germany	7,000,000

Source: *Euromonitor*

TOP 10 PET SMALL MAMMAL POPULATIONS

	COUNTRY	EST. PET SMALL MAMMAL POPULATION (2002)
1	US	20,930,000
2	Germany	6,400,000
3	Russia	4,700,000
4	UK	4,200,000
5	Japan	3,000,000
6	France	2,400,000
7	Italy	2,100,000
8	China	1,748,000
9	Canada	1,153,000
10	Spain	1,112,000

Source: *Euromonitor*

TOP 10 REASONS FOR PET CAT RELINQUISHMENT IN THE US

	REASON	PERCENTAGE
1	Too many animals in household	11
2 =	Allergies in family	8
=	Moving	8
4 =	Cost of pet maintenance	6
=	Landlord not allowing pet	6
=	No homes available for littermates	6
7	House soiling	5
8	Owner having personal problems	4
9 =	Inadequate facilities	2
=	Incompatibility with other pets	2

Source: *National Council on Pet Population Study and Policy (NCPPSP)*

Trees & Forests

TOP 10 COUNTRIES WITH THE LARGEST AREAS OF FOREST

	COUNTRY	AREA (2000) (SQ MILES)	(SQ KM)
1	Russia	3,287,243	8,513,920
2	Brazil	2,100,359	5,439,905
3	Canada	944,294	2,445,710
4	US	872,564	2,259,930
5	China	631,200	1,634,800
6	Australia	596,678	1,545,390
7	Dem. Rep. of Congo	522,037	1,352,070
8	Indonesia	405,353	1,049,860
9	Angola	269,329	697,560
10	Peru	251,796	652,150
	World	14,888,715	38,561,590

Source: *Food and Agriculture Organization of the United Nations*, State of the World's Forests, 2001

The world's forests occupy some 29 percent of the total land area of the planet. Just under half of Russia is forested—a total area that is almost the size of the whole of Brazil.

TOP 10 COUNTRIES WITH THE LARGEST AREAS OF TROPICAL FOREST

	COUNTRY	AREA (SQ MILES)	(SQ KM)
1	Brazil	1,163,222	3,012,730
2	Dem. Rep. of Congo	521,512	1,350,710
3	Indonesia	343,029	887,440
4	Peru	292,032	756,360
5	Bolivia	265,012	686,380
6	Venezuela	214,730	556,150
7	Colombia	205,352	531,860
8	Mexico	176,700	457,650
9	India	171,622	444,500
10	Angola	145,035	375,640
	World	5,434,964	14,076,490

▼ Tropical forest
The world's tropical forests are among Earth's most important resources, and are home to more than half the planet's plant and animal species. The vast forests of Brazil occupy an area greater than the whole of India.

TOP 10 BIGGEST TREES IN THE US*

	SPECIES	LOCATION	POINTS
1	General Sherman giant sequoia	Sequoia National Park, California	1,312
2	Coast redwood	Jedidiah Smith State Park, California	1,291
3	Western redcedar	Olympic National Park, Washington	931
4	Sitka spruce	Olympic National Park, Washington	922
5	Coast Douglas fir	Olympic National Forest, Washington	804
6	Bluegum eucalyptus	Petrolia, California	759
7	Common baldcypress	Cat Island, Louisiana	748
8	California laurel	Grass Valley, California	684
9	Sugar pine	Dorrington, Califonia	681
10	Port-orford-cedar	Siskiyou National Forest, Oregon	680

*By species (i.e., the biggest known example of each of the 10 biggest species)

Source: National Register of Big Trees, *American Forestry Association*

The American Forestry Association operates a National Register of Big Trees which is constantly updated as new "champion trees" are nominated. Their method of measurement, which gives this Top 10 by species, is based not solely on height, but also takes account of the thickness of the trunk and spread of the upper branches and leaves, or crown.

▲ Deforesting countries
In the 1990s the net loss of the world's forest (the difference between deforestation and increase by new planting) declined from 15,302,887 sq miles (39,634,290 sq km) to 14,940,051 sq miles (38,694,550 sq km), an average of 362,836 sq miles (939,740 sq km) a year.

TOP 10 COUNTRIES WITH THE HIGHEST DEFORESTATION RATE

	COUNTRY	ANNUAL FOREST COVER LOSS (1990–2000) (SQ MILES)	(SQ KM)
1	Brazil	8,915	23,090
2	Indonesia	5,065	13,120
3	Sudan	3,702	9,590
4	Zambia	3,286	8,510
5	Mexico	2,436	6,310
6	Dem. Rep. of Congo	2,054	5,320
7	Myanmar	1,996	5,170
8	Nigeria	1,537	3,980
9	Zimbabwe	1,235	3,200
10	Argentina	1,100	2,850

Source: *Food and Agriculture Organization of the United Nations*, State of the World's Forests, 2001

During the 1990s, deforestation—the permanent loss of forest when trees are felled to enable the land to be used for other purposes—resulted in the decline of Brazil's rain forests from 2,189,192 sq miles (5,669,980 sq km) to 2,100,029 sq miles (5,439,050 sq km).

TOP 10 MOST FORESTED COUNTRIES

	COUNTRY	PERCENTAGE FOREST COVER (2000)
1	French Guiana	90.0
2	Solomon Islands	87.8
3	Suriname	86.4
4	Gabon	81.5
5	Guyana	78.5
6	Brunei	76.6
7	Palau	76.1
8	Finland	72.0
9	North Korea	68.1
10	Sweden	66.8
	US	24.7

Source: *Food and Agriculture Organization of the United Nations*

These countries have the greatest area of forest as a percentage of their total land area. Deforestation has caused the world average to fall from about 32 percent in 1972 to its present 29 percent.

TOP 10 TIMBER-PRODUCING COUNTRIES

	COUNTRY	ROUNDWOOD PRODUCTION (2001) (CU FT)	(CU M)
1	US	16,989,640,250	481,092,992
2	China	10,151,909,030	287,470,024
3	Brazil	8,349,172,609	236,422,218
4	Canada	6,239,819,672	176,692,000
5	Russia	5,731,570,941	162,300,000
6	Indonesia	4,134,273,302	117,069,572
7	Ethiopia	3,223,648,197	91,283,543
8	Dem. Rep. of Congo	2,465,235,465	69,807,688
9	Nigeria	2,440,792,910	69,115,552
10	Sweden	2,292,627,376	64,920,000
	World	108,075,688,600	3,060,362,410

Source: *Food and Agriculture Organization of the United Nations*

Enough roundwood is produced annually to build more than 3,000 buildings with the volume of the Empire State Building, all constructed in solid wood!

Crops & Livestock

CEREAL CROPS

	CROP	PRODUCTION (2001) (TONS)
1	Corn	677,061,124
2	Rice (paddy)	656,170,874
3	Wheat	650,222,915
4	Barley	157,704,863
5	Sorghum	64,741,231
6	Millet	31,856,932
7	Oats	29,707,508
8	Rye	25,665,580
9	Triticale (wheat/rye hybrid)	11,479,909
10	Buckwheat	2,840,707

Source: *Food and Agriculture Organization of the United Nations*

◀ Top of the crops
Terraced rice cultivation in Indonesia, a leading producer of one of the world's most important crops. Worldwide, more than 579,000 sq miles (1.5 million sq km) are devoted to rice growing.

RICE-PRODUCING COUNTRIES

	COUNTRY	PRODUCTION* (2001) (TONS)
1	China	197,648,870
2	India	150,554,893
3	Indonesia	55,221,431
4	Bangladesh	42,439,019
5	Vietnam	35,241,031
6	Thailand	29,711,797
7	Myanmar	22,707,631
8	Philippines	14,280,344
9	Japan	12,478,174
10	Brazil	11,238,513
	World	656,170,874
	US	10,652,260

* Paddy

Source: *Food and Agriculture Organization of the United Nations*

VEGETABLE CROPS

	CROP*	PRODUCTION (2001) (TONS)
1	Sugar cane	1,403,652,112
2	Potatoes	340,952,401
3	Sugar beet	252,889,825
4	Soybeans	194,564,886
5	Sweet potatoes	149,305,474
6	Tomatoes	115,819,432
7	Cabbages	65,331,138
8	Onions (dry)	54,470,856
9	Yams	42,515,462
10	Cucumbers	38,600,276

* Excluding cereals

Source: *Food and Agriculture Organization of the United Nations*

The two leading crops exemplify the two-way traffic history of vegetable cultivation: sugar cane originated in India but was taken to the Caribbean, while the potato, indigenous to the Americas, was transported to Europe, where it became a staple crop.

TRACTOR COUNTRIES

		AGRICULTURAL TRACTORS IN USE (2000)	
	COUNTRY	TOTAL	PER 1,000 INHABITANTS
1	Slovenia	114,188	57.44
2	Ireland	167,000	43.91
3	Austria	330,000	40.84
4	Yugoslavia	397,391	37.66
5	Finland	194,000	37.51
6	Estonia	50,624	36.34
7	Poland	1,306,700	33.85
8	Iceland	9,019	32.33
9	Italy	1,750,000	30.42
10	Norway	133,000	29.76
	World	26,409,666	4.36
	US	4,800,000	16.95

Source: *Food and Agriculture Organization of the United Nations*

TOP 10 CATTLE COUNTRIES

COUNTRY	CATTLE (2001)
1 India	219,642,000
2 Brazil	176,000,000
3 China	106,175,000
4 US	96,700,000
5 Argentina	50,369,000
6 Sudan	38,325,000
7 Ethiopia	34,500,000
8 Mexico	30,600,000
9 Australia	28,768,000
10 Colombia	27,000,000
World	1,360,475,620

Source: *Food and Agriculture Organization of the United Nations*

In addition to its symbolic and religious significance, the dairy cow has long been a crucial component of India's economy. The country's cattle population has more than quadrupled in the past century.

TOP 10 TYPES OF LIVESTOCK

ANIMAL	WORLD STOCKS (2001)
1 Chickens	15,420,137,000
2 Cattle	1,360,475,620
3 Sheep	1,044,045,120
4 Ducks	947,525,000
5 Pigs	939,318,631
6 Rabbits	497,082,000
7 Geese	245,731,000
8 Turkeys	242,802,000
9 Buffalo	166,418,998
10 Goats	146,514,641

Source: *Food and Agriculture Organization of the United Nations*

In sheer numbers, chickens clearly rule the roost, with more than two chickens for every human on the planet. As well as providing meat, they produce some 880 billion eggs per annum, 337 billion of them in China alone—enough to make an omelet larger than Denmark!

▶ **Getting the goat**
There are more than 60 countries in the world with one million or more goats. Worldwide, goats produce over 13 million tons of milk a year, while more than 300 million are slaughtered annually to provide meat and goatskin.

Fruit & Nuts

TOP 10 | FRUIT-PRODUCING COUNTRIES

	COUNTRY	PRODUCTION* (2001) (TONS)
1	China	83,523,210
2	India	59,018,097
3	Brazil	38,634,147
4	US	36,574,299
5	Italy	22,205,269
6	Spain	18,130,196
7	Mexico	17,274,956
8	Iran	14,299,956
9	Philippines	13,514,278
10	France	13,411,870
	World	568,980,548

* Excluding melons

Source: *Food and Agriculture Organization of the United Nations*

TOP 10 | ALMOND-PRODUCING COUNTRIES

	COUNTRY	PRODUCTION (2001) (TONS)
1	US	457,457
2	Spain	312,278
3	Italy	137,075
4	Iran	118,037
5	Morocco	99,418
6	Greece	67,153
7	Syria	60,131
8	Turkey	51,033
9	Pakistan	40,384
10	Lebanon	40,097
	World	1,616,460

Source: *Food and Agriculture Organization of the United Nations*

TOP 10 | FRUIT CROPS

	CROP	PRODUCTION (2001) (TONS)
1	Watermelons	95,191,761
2	Bananas	83,218,842
3	Oranges	76,023,478
4	Grapes	74,421,533
5	Apples	71,293,185
6	Coconuts	61,431,315
7	Plantains	35,030,943
8	Mangoes	31,162,574
9	Cantaloupes and other melons	23,299,323
10	Tangerines, etc.	22,081,791

Source: *Food and Agriculture Organization of the United Nations*

About 70 percent of watermelons, the world's top fruit crop, are grown in China, where they have been cultivated since the 10th century.

TOP 10 | WALNUT-PRODUCING COUNTRIES

	COUNTRY	PRODUCTION (2001) (TONS)
1	US	336,203
2	China	306,623
3	Iran	204,172
4	Turkey	140,950
5	Ukraine	66,987
6	Romania	41,241
7	India	37,667
8	France	35,451
9	Yugoslavia	28,675
10	Greece	26,642

Source: *Food and Agriculture Organization of the United Nations*

◀ **In a nutshell**
Walnuts were exported to the US from England and introduced into California in 1867, starting a state industry that today produces 99 percent of the US total and a major proportion of the world's supply.

TOP 10 | NUT CROPS

	CROP	PRODUCTION (2001) (TONS)
1	Groundnuts (in shell)	43,893,839
2	Cashew nuts	1,949,697
3	Almonds	1,616,460
4	Walnuts	1,514,317
5	Chestnuts	1,166,431
6	Hazelnuts	959,535
7	Karite nuts (sheanuts)	786,770
8	Areca nuts (betel)	783,934
9	Tung nuts	678,494
10	Pistachios	357,769

Source: *Food and Agriculture Organization of the United Nations*

Groundnuts, or peanuts, are native to Peru and Brazil, from where they spread to Asia and Africa. The modern peanut industry owes its origins to African-American agriculturalist George Washington Carver (1864–1943), who pioneered improved methods of cultivation, devising no fewer than 325 products based on peanuts, ranging from shampoo to shoe polish.

TOP 10 | GRAPE-PRODUCING COUNTRIES

	COUNTRY	PRODUCTION (2001) (TONS)
1	Italy	10,921,710
2	France	8,847,746
3	US	7,222,927
4	Spain	6,210,694
5	China	4,574,838
6	Turkey	3,949,045
7	Iran	3,058,014
8	Argentina	2,986,206
9	Chile	1,907,692
10	Australia	1,884,605
	World	74,421,533

Source: *Food and Agriculture Organization of the United Nations*

TOP 10 | DATE-PRODUCING COUNTRIES

	COUNTRY	PRODUCTION (2001) (TONS)
1	Egypt	1,352,724
2	Iran	1,063,185
3	United Arab Emirates	920,553
4	Saudi Arabia	893,091
5	Iraq	789,808
6	Pakistan	767,566
7	Algeria	449,583
8	Oman	301,899
9	Sudan	215,071
10	Libya	160,999
	World	7,452,058
	US	19,289

Source: *Food and Agriculture Organization of the United Nations*

▶ **It's a date**
There are some 90 million date palms in the world, 64 million of them in Arab countries. Only female trees produce fruit—as much as 150 lb (68 kg) a year each.

THE HUMAN WORLD

Human Body & Health

TOP 10 HEALTHIEST COUNTRIES

	COUNTRY	HEALTHY LIFE EXPECTANCY AT BIRTH*
1	Japan	73.6
2	Switzerland	72.8
3	San Marino	72.2
4	Sweden	71.8
5	Australia	71.6
6 =	France	71.3
=	Monaco	71.3
8	Iceland	71.2
9 =	Austria	71.0
=	Italy	71.0
	US	67.6

* Average number of years expected to be spent in good health

Source: World Health Organization, World Health Report 2002

▶ **Long life**
Diet and other factors have enabled Japanese healthy life expectancy to top the world league table.

THE 10 LEAST HEALTHY COUNTRIES

	COUNTRY	HEALTHY LIFE EXPECTANCY AT BIRTH*
1	Sierra Leone	26.5
2	Malawi	29.8
3	Zambia	30.9
4	Botswana	32.9
5	Niger	33.2
6 =	Afghanistan	33.4
=	Lesotho	33.4
8	Burundi	33.7
9	Rwanda	33.8
10	Swaziland	33.9

* Average number of years expected to be spent in good health

Source: World Health Organization, World Health Report 2002

THE 10 MOST COMMON HEALTH DISORDERS

DISORDERS AFFECTING MALES	% TOTAL*		DISORDERS AFFECTING FEMALES	% TOTAL*
Depression	9.7	1	Depression	14.0
Alcohol-use disorders	5.5	2	Iron-deficiency disorders	4.9
Hearing loss, adult onset	5.1	3	Hearing loss, adult onset	4.2
Iron-deficiency anemia	4.1	4	Osteoarthritis	3.5
Chronic obstructive pulmonary disease	3.8	5	Chronic obstructive pulmonary disease	2.9
Injuries resulting from falls	3.3	6	Schizophrenia	2.7
Schizophrenia	3.0	7	Manic depression	2.4
Injuries resulting from road traffic accidents	2.7	8	Injuries resulting from falls	2.3
Manic depression	2.6	9	Alzheimer's/other dementias	2.2
Osteoarthritis	2.5	10	Obstructed labor	2.1

* Total includes other disorders not listed above

Source: World Health Organization, World Health Report 2001

TOP 10 LONGEST BONES IN THE HUMAN BODY

	BONE	AVERAGE LENGTH (IN)	(CM)
1	**Femur** (thighbone—upper leg)	19⅞	50.50
2	**Tibia** (shinbone—inner lower leg)	16¹⁵⁄₁₆	43.03
3	**Fibula** (outer lower leg)	15¹⁵⁄₁₆	40.50
4	**Humerus** (upper arm)	14⁵⁄₁₆	36.46
5	**Ulna** (inner lower arm)	11⅛	28.20
6	**Radius** (outer lower arm)	10⁵⁄₁₆	26.42
7	**7th rib**	9⁷⁄₁₆	24.00
8	**8th rib**	9¹⁄₁₆	23.00
9	**Innominate bone** (hipbone—half pelvis)	7½	18.50
10	**Sternum** (breastbone)	6¹¹⁄₁₆	17.00

These are average dimensions of the bones of an adult male measured from their extremities (ribs are curved, and the pelvis measurement is taken diagonally). The same bones in the female skeleton are usually 6 to 13 percent smaller, with the exception of the sternum, which is virtually identical.

THE 10 MOST COMMON ALLERGENS

FOOD		ENVIRONMENTAL
Nuts	1	House dust mite (*Dermatophagoldes pteronyssinus*)
Shellfish/seafood	2	Grass pollens
Milk	3	Tree pollens
Wheat	4	Cats
Eggs	5	Dogs
Fresh fruit (apples, oranges, strawberries, etc.)	6	Horses
Fresh vegetables (potatoes, cucumber, etc.)	7	Molds (*Aspergillus, fumigatus, Alternaria cladosporium*, etc.)
Cheese	8	Birch pollen
Yeast	9	Weed pollen
Soya protein	10	Wasp/bee venom

An allergy has been defined as "an unpleasant reaction to foreign matter, specific to that substance, which is altered from the normal response and peculiar to the individual concerned."

TOP 10 LARGEST HUMAN ORGANS

	ORGAN	AVERAGE WEIGHT (OZ)	(G)
1	**Skin**	384.0	10,886
2	**Liver**	55.0	1,560
3	**Brain**		
	male	49.7	1,408
	female	44.6	1,263
4	**Lungs**		
	right	20.5	580
	left	18.0	510
	total	38.5	1,090
5	**Heart**		
	male	11.1	315
	female	9.3	265
6	**Kidneys**		
	right	4.9	140
	left	5.3	150
	total	10.2	290
7	**Spleen**	6.0	170
8	**Pancreas**	3.5	98
9	**Thyroid**	1.2	35
10	**Prostate** (male only)	0.7	20

THE 10 MOST COMMON PHOBIAS

	OBJECT OF PHOBIA	MEDICAL TERM
1	**Spiders**	Arachnephobia or arachnophobia
2	**People and social situations**	Anthropophobia or sociophobia
3	**Flying**	Aerophobia or aviatophobia
4	**Open spaces**	Agoraphobia, cenophobia, or kenophobia
5	**Confined spaces**	Claustrophobia, cleisiophobia, cleithrophobia, or clithrophobia
6 =	**Heights**	Acrophobia, altophobia, hypsophobia, or hypsiphobia
=	**Vomiting**	Emetophobia or emitophobia
8	**Cancer**	Carcinomaphobia, carcinophobia, carcinomatophobia, cancerphobia, or cancerophobia
9	**Thunderstorms**	Brontophobia or keraunophobia; related phobias are those associated with lightning (astraphobia), cyclones (anemophobia), and hurricanes and tornadoes (lilapsophobia)
10 =	**Death**	Necrophobia or thanatophobia
=	**Heart disease**	Cardiophobia

A phobia is a morbid fear that is out of all proportion to the object of the fear. Many people would admit to being uncomfortable about these principal phobias, as well as others, but most do not become obsessive about them and allow such fears to rule their lives. True phobias often arise from some incident in childhood when a person has been afraid of some object and has developed an irrational fear that persists into adulthood. Perhaps surprisingly, the Top 10 does not remain static as "new" phobias become more common; although outside the Top 10, "technophobia," the fear of modern technology such as computers, is increasingly reported. Today phobias can be cured by taking special desensitization courses—for example to conquer one's fear of flying.

Medicine & Health Care

TOP 10 COUNTRIES WITH THE MOST HOSPITALS

	COUNTRY	BEDS PER 10,000 (1990–99)	HOSPITALS (1998)
1	China	17	69,105
2	India	8	15,067
3	Vietnam	17	12,500
4	Nigeria	2	11,588*
5	Russia	121	11,200
6	Japan	164	9,413#
7	Egypt	21	7,411
8	South Korea	55	6,446#
9	Brazil	31	6,410#
10	US	36	6,097

* 1993 data

1997 data

▼ Babes in arms

Despite its single-child policy, China's hospitals still have to deal with a proportion of the country's 20 million births a year.

TOP 10 COUNTRIES THAT SPEND THE MOST ON HEALTH CARE

	COUNTRY	HEALTH SPENDING PER CAPITA (1995–99) ($)
1	US	4,271
2	Switzerland	3,857
3	Norway	3,182
4	Denmark	2,785
5	Germany	2,697
6	France	2,288
7	Japan	2,243
8	Netherlands	2,173
9	Sweden	2,145
10	Belgium	2,137

Source: *World Bank*, World Development Indicators 2002

An annual average of $12 per capita is estimated to provide minimal health services, but many poor countries fall short of this figure. Ethiopia, for example, spends only $4 per capita on health care.

TOP 10 DRUGS PRESCRIBED IN THE US

	DRUG/THERAPEUTIC CLASSIFICATION	DRUG PRESCRIPTIONS (2000)
1	**Claritin**, antihistamines	17,145,000
2	**Lipitor**, hyperlipidemia	16,267,000
3	**Synthroid**, thyroid agents	15,999,000
4	**Premarin**, estrogens/progestins	14,775,000
5	**Amoxicillin**, penicillins	13,068,000
6	**Tylenol**, nonnarcotic analgesics	12,789,000
7	**Lasix**, diuretics	12,577,000
8	**Celebrex**, nonsteroidal anti-inflammatory drugs (NSAIDs)	12,161,000
9	**Glucophage**, blood glucose regulators	11,468,000
10	**Albuterol sulfate**, calcium channel blockers	10,862,000
	Total of all prescriptions (including those not in Top 10)	1,263,503,000

Source: *National Center for Health Statistics*

THE 10 COUNTRIES THAT SPEND THE MOST ON PRIVATE HEALTH CARE

	COUNTRY	PRIVATE HEALTH SPENDING AS PERCENTAGE OF GDP* (1995–99)
1	Lebanon	9.7
2	United Arab Emirates	7.6
3	Uruguay	7.3
4	US	7.1
5	Cambodia	6.3
6	Argentina	6.1
7	Kenya	5.5
8	Honduras	4.7
9	El Salvador	4.6
10	Sierra Leone	4.4

* Gross domestic product

Source: World Bank, World Development Indicators 2002

Expenditure on private health care is high both in countries where inhabitants are sufficiently wealthy to choose this option and in some where the lack of state medicine makes it a necessity.

TOP 10 COUNTRIES THAT SPEND THE MOST ON PUBLIC HEALTH CARE

	COUNTRY	PUBLIC HEALTH SPENDING AS PERCENTAGE OF GDP* (1995–99)
1	Croatia	9.5
2	Nicaragua	8.5
3	Bosnia and Herzegovina	8.0
4	Germany	7.9
5	Switzerland	7.6
6	France	7.3
7	Norway	7.0
8	Denmark	6.9
9	Slovenia	6.7
10 =	Canada	6.6
=	Czech Republic	6.6
=	Sweden	6.6
	US	5.7

* Gross domestic product

Source: World Bank, World Development Indicators 2002

TOP 10 MOST COMMON REASONS FOR TIME SPENT IN SHORT-STAY HOSPITALS IN THE US

	PRINCIPAL REASON	STAYS (2000)
1	Diseases of the circulatory system	6,294,000
2	Diseases of the respiratory system	3,444,000
3	Diseases of the digestive system	3,143,000
4	Injury and poisoning	2,466,000
5	Mental disorders	2,147,000
6	Diseases of the genitourinary system	1,743,000
7	Diseases of the musculo-skeletal system and connective tissue	1,530,000
8	Endocrine, nutritional, and metabolic disease and immunity disorders	1,455,000
9	Cancer	1,156,000
10	Infectious and parasitic diseases	787,000
	Total stays (including those not in Top 10)	31,706,000

Source: National Center for Health Statistics

THE 10 COUNTRIES WITH THE MOST PATIENTS PER DOCTOR

	COUNTRY	PATIENTS PER DOCTOR*
1	Malawi	49,118
2	Liberia	43,434
3	Mozambique	36,320
4	Eritrea	33,240
5	Chad	30,260
6	Ethiopia	30,195
7	Gambia	28,791
8	Central African Republic	28,600
9	Niger	28,560
10	Burkina Faso	27,158
	US	370

* In those countries/latest year for which data available

TOP 10 COUNTRIES WITH THE FEWEST PATIENTS PER DOCTOR

	COUNTRY	PATIENTS PER DOCTOR*
1	Italy	169
2	Monaco	170
3	Cuba	188
4 =	Belarus	227
=	Georgia	227
6	Russia	238
7	Greece	243
8	Lithuania	250
9	Israel	256
10	Belgium	263
	US	370

* In latest year for which data available

THE 10 MOST COMMON HOSPITAL ER CASES

	REASON FOR VISIT	VISITS (2000)
1	Stomach and abdominal pain, cramps, and spasms	6,759,000
2	Chest pain and related symptoms	5,798,000
3	Fever	4,383,000
4	Headache, pain in head	2,962,000
5	Shortness of breath	2,701,000
6	Back symptoms	2,595,000
7	Cough	2,592,000
8	Pain, unspecific	2,335,000
9	Laceration and cuts, upper body	2,322,000
10	Throat symptoms	2,043,000
	Total visits (including those not in Top 10)	108,017,000

Source: National Ambulatory Medical Care Survey/ Center for Disease Control/National Center for Health Statistics

Birth & Lifespan

TOP 10 COUNTRIES WITH THE HIGHEST BIRTH RATE

	COUNTRY	EST. BIRTH RATE (LIVE BIRTHS PER 1,000 POPULATION IN 2004)
1	Niger	48.8
2	Mali	47.5
3	Chad	46.7
4	Uganda	46.6
5	Somalia	46.0
6	Angola	45.4
7	Liberia	45.0
8 =	Dem. Rep. of Congo	44.7
=	Marshall Islands	44.7
10	Ethiopia	43.7

Source: *US Census Bureau, International Data Base*

The countries with the highest birth rates are often among the poorest in the world. In these places, people often have large families so that their children can contribute to the family income.

TOP 10 COUNTRIES WITH THE LOWEST BIRTH RATE

	COUNTRY	EST. BIRTH RATE (LIVE BIRTHS PER 1,000 POPULATION IN 2004)
1	Bulgaria	8.0
2	Italy	8.6
3	Germany	8.7
4 =	Czech Republic	8.9
=	Latvia	8.9
6 =	Hungary	9.2
=	Slovenia	9.2
8 =	Andorra	9.3
=	Austria	9.3
=	Spain	9.3
	US	*14.1*

Source: *US Census Bureau, International Data Base*

◄ **Baby boom**
Mali and most of the other countries with high birth rates have rural economies that depend on large families to provide the required labor force.

TOP 10 COUNTRIES WITH THE HIGHEST LIFE EXPECTANCY

	COUNTRY	LIFE EXPECTANCY AT BIRTH (2004)
1	Andorra	83.5
2	San Marino	81.5
3	Japan	81.1
4	Singapore	80.5
5	Australia	80.2
6 =	Sweden	80.1
=	Switzerland	80.1
8 =	Canada	79.9
=	Iceland	79.9
10 =	Italy	79.4
=	Liechtenstein	79.4
=	Monaco	79.4
	US	77.5

Source: *US Census Bureau, International Data Base*

Life expectancy represents the average life span of a newborn child. A century ago the world average life expectancy was about 30 years; today it is more than double that, but to achieve this average there are countries with a much higher expectancy, as well as those that fall below it.

THE 10 COUNTRIES WITH THE HIGHEST INFANT MORTALITY

	COUNTRY	EST. DEATH RATE PER 1,000 LIVE BIRTHS (2004)
1	Angola	187.5
2	Afghanistan	140.2
3	Sierra Leone	140.0
4	Mozambique	137.2
5	Liberia	125.7
6	Guinea	123.1
7	Niger	119.5
8	Somalia	118.5
9	Malawi	117.6
10	Mali	115.9
	US	6.5

Source: *US Census Bureau, International Data Base*

With the exception of Afghanistan, which has experienced its own unique range of social and medical problems, all the countries in the Top 10 are in sub-Saharan Africa.

◀ **Lease on life**
Japan was the first country to attain an average lifespan of over 80 years more than double that of many less-developed countries.

THE 10 COUNTRIES WITH THE LOWEST LIFE EXPECTANCY

	COUNTRY	LIFE EXPECTANCY AT BIRTH (2004)
1	Botswana	32.3
2	Mozambique	33.7
3	Swaziland	34.2
4	Zimbabwe	35.3
5	Malawi	35.6
6	Namibia	36.1
7	Zambia	37.4
8	Rwanda	38.0
9	Central African Republic	43.1
10	Ethiopia	43.3

Source: *US Census Bureau, International Data Base*

TOP 10 COUNTRIES WITH THE MOST BIRTHS

	COUNTRY	EST. BIRTHS (2004)
1	India	24,579,788
2	China	19,506,042
3	Nigeria	5,220,326
4	Indonesia	5,057,950
5	Pakistan	4,423,638
6	US	4,025,868
7	Bangladesh	3,379,322
8	Ethiopia	3,111,374
9	Brazil	3,094,876
10	Dem. Rep. of Congo	2,614,438
	World	131,471,559

Source: *US Census Bureau, International Data Base*

TOP 10 COUNTRIES WITH THE LOWEST INFANT MORTALITY

	COUNTRY	EST. DEATH RATE PER 1,000 LIVE BIRTHS (2004)
1	Sweden	3.40
2	Iceland	3.48
3	Singapore	3.55
4	Finland	3.70
5	Japan	3.77
6	Norway	3.83
7	Andorra	4.05
8	Netherlands	4.21
9	Austria	4.28
10	Switzerland	4.30

Source: *US Census Bureau, International Data Base*

Marriage & Divorce

THE 10 COUNTRIES WITH THE HIGHEST DIVORCE RATES

	COUNTRY	DIVORCE RATE PER 1,000*
1	Maldives	10.97
2	Belarus	4.65
3	US	4.19
4	Panama	3.82
5	Russia	3.66
6	Estonia	3.65
7	Puerto Rico	3.61
8	Ukraine	3.59
9	Costa Rica	3.58
10	Cuba	3.54

In those countries/latest year for which data available

Source: *United Nations*

TOP 10 COUNTRIES WITH THE LOWEST DIVORCE RATES

	COUNTRY	DIVORCE RATE PER 1,000*
1	Libya	0.24
2	Georgia	0.36
3	Mongolia	0.38
4	= Armenia	0.42
	= Chile	0.42
6	Italy	0.47
7	Mexico	0.48
8	El Salvador	0.49
9	= Macedonia	0.51
	= Turkey	0.51

In those countries/latest year for which data available

Source: *United Nations*

THE 10 FIRST WEDDING ANNIVERSARY GIFTS

	GIFT
1	Paper
2	Cotton (or calico)
3	Leather
4	Linen (or silk)
5	Wood
6	Iron (or candy)
7	Wool (or copper)
8	Bronze (or small electrical appliances)
9	Willow (or pottery)
10	Tin (or aluminum)

The custom of celebrating different wedding anniversaries by presenting specific types of gift has a long tradition, but has been much modified over the years, the association of electrical appliances with the 8th anniversary testifying to the intrusion of modern commercialism into the practice.

TOP 10 COUNTRIES WITH THE HIGHEST PROPORTION OF TEENAGE BRIDES

	COUNTRY	PERCENTAGE OF 15–19-YEAR-OLD GIRLS WHO HAVE EVER BEEN MARRIED*
1	Dem. Rep. of Congo	74.2
2	Congo	55.0
3	Afghanistan	53.7
4	Bangladesh	51.3
5	Uganda	49.8
6	Mali	49.7
7	Guinea	49.0
8	Chad	48.6
9	Mozambique	47.1
10	Senegal	43.8
	US	3.9

In latest year for which data available

Source: *United Nations*

TOP 10 COUNTRIES WITH THE HIGHEST PROPORTION OF TEENAGE HUSBANDS

	COUNTRY	PERCENTAGE OF 15–19-YEAR-OLD BOYS WHO HAVE EVER BEEN MARRIED*
1	Iraq	14.9
2	Nepal	13.5
3	Congo	11.8
4	Uganda	11.4
5	Central African Republic	8.1
6	India	9.5
7	Afghanistan	9.2
8	Guinea	8.2
9	Guatemala	7.8
10	Colombia	7.7
	US	1.3

In latest year for which data available

Source: *United Nations*

IN-FLIGHT WEDDINGS!

FIRST FACT

HOLDING WEDDINGS IN UNUSUAL locations is not a strictly modern phenomenon: the first marriage to take place in the air was in a balloon a mile above Cincinnati, Ohio, on October 19, 1874. A publicity stunt for showman Phineas T. Barnum's Great Roman Hippodrome circus, the balloonist was daredevil Washington Harrison Donaldson, the first person to ride a bicycle on a tightrope. Before 50,000 spectators, Donaldson piloted a huge gas balloon named *P. T. Barnum*, which also carried the bride, Mary Elizabeth Walsh (a horseback rider in Barnum's circus), the groom, Charles M. Colton, and, to conduct the airborne ceremony, minister Rev. Howard B. Jeffries.

COUNTRIES WITH THE HIGHEST MARRIAGE RATES

	COUNTRY	MARRIAGES PER 1,000 PER ANNUM*
1	Antigua and Barbuda	21.0
2	Maldives	20.1
3	Barbados	13.5
4	Liechtenstein	12.8
5	Cyprus	12.1
6 =	Seychelles	11.5
=	South Africa	11.5
8	Jamaica	10.3
9 =	Ethiopia	10.2
=	Iran	10.2
	US	8.3

* In those countries/latest year for which data available

Source: *United Nations*

COUNTRIES WITH THE MOST MARRIAGES

	COUNTRY	MARRIAGES PER ANNUM*
1	US	2,244,000
2	Bangladesh	1,181,000
3	Russia	911,162
4	Japan	784,595
5	Brazil	734,045
6	Mexico	704,456
7	Ethiopia	630,290
8	Iran	511,277
9	Egypt	493,787
10	Turkey	485,112

* In those countries/latest year for which data available

Source: *United Nations*

This list, based on United Nations statistics, regrettably excludes certain large countries such as India, Indonesia, and Pakistan, which fail to provide accurate data.

▼ **Viva Las Vegas**
More than 110,000 people tie the knot in Las Vegas each year, including celebrities such as Frank Sinatra and Mia Farrow (1966), Elvis Presley and Priscilla Beaulieu (1967), and Bruce Willis and Demi Moore (1987).

Death & Disease

THE 10 MOST COMMON CAUSES OF DEATH BY NONCOMMUNICABLE DISORDERS

CAUSE	APPROXIMATE DEATHS (2001)
1 Ischemic heart disease	7,181,000
2 Cancers	7,115,000
3 Cerebrovascular disease	5,454,000
4 Chronic obstructive pulmonary disease	2,672,000
5 Perinatal conditions	2,504,000
6 Road traffic accidents	1,194,000
7 Neuropsychiatric disorders	1,023,000
8 Diabetes mellitus	895,000
9 Hypertensive heart disease	874,000
10 Self-inflicted injury	849,000

Source: *World Health Organization*, World Health Report 2002

WHO estimates identify 33,077,000 deaths in 2001 resulting from noncommunicable conditions. These exclude a further 5,103,000 caused by injuries such as road traffic accidents, fires, and drowning.

THE 10 WORST GLOBAL DISEASES*

DISEASE	PERCENTAGE OF TOTAL BURDEN OF DISEASE#†
1 Neuropsychiatric disorders	13.0
2 Cardiovascular diseases	9.8
3 Lower respiratory infections	6.2
4 HIV/AIDS	6.0
5 Cancers	5.2
6 = Diarrheal diseases	4.3
= Respiratory diseases (noncommunicable)	4.3
8 Digestive diseases	3.4
9 Childhood diseases	3.3
10 Malaria	2.9

* *Those diseases that cause the highest total levels of disability worldwide*

Measured in Disability-Adjusted Life Years (DALYs): a measure of the difference between a population's health and a normative goal of living in full health

† *Total percentage includes injuries at 12.2%, maternal conditions at 2.1%, nutritional deficiencies at 2.2%, perinatal conditions at 6.7%*

Source: *World Health Organization*, World Health Report 2002

THE 10 MOST COMMON CAUSES OF DEATH BY INFECTIOUS AND PARASITIC DISEASES

CAUSE	APPROXIMATE DEATHS (2001)
1 Lower respiratory infections	3,871,000
2 HIV/AIDS	2,866,000
3 Diarrhea (including dysentery)	2,001,000
4 Tuberculosis	1,644,000
5 Malaria	1,124,000
6 Measles	745,000
7 Whooping cough (pertussis)	285,000
8 Neonatal tetanus	282,000
9 Meningitis	173,000
10 Syphilis	167,000

Source: *World Health Organization*, World Health Report 2002

Infectious and parasitic diseases—those listed here and many outside the 10 principal causes—were responsible for 10,937,000 deaths worldwide in 2001. Extending the parameters to encompass all communicable diseases, maternal and perinatal conditions, and nutritional deficiencies increases the total to 18,374,000.

THE 10 COUNTRIES WITH THE HIGHEST DEATH RATE

COUNTRY	EST. DEATH RATE PER 1,000 (2004)
1 Botswana	33.6
2 Mozambique	30.9
3 Angola	25.9
4 Lesotho	24.8
5 Zambia	24.4
6 Zimbabwe	23.3
7 Swaziland	23.1
8 Malawi	23.0
9 Rwanda	21.9
10 Niger	21.5

Source: *US Census Bureau, International Data Base*

All 10 of the countries with the highest death rates are in Africa, with all but Niger and Rwanda located between 10° and 30° south latitude.

THE 10 WORST EPIDEMICS

EPIDEMIC	LOCATION	DATES	EST. DEATHS
1 Black Death	Europe/Asia	1347–51	75,000,000
2 AIDS	Worldwide	1981–	21,800,000
3 Influenza	Worldwide	1918–20	21,640,000
4 Bubonic plague	India	1896–1948	12,000,000
5 Typhus	Eastern Europe	1914–15	3,000,000
6 = "Plague of Justinian"	Europe/Asia	541–90	millions*
= Cholera	Worldwide	1846–60	millions*
= Cholera	Europe	1826–37	millions*
= Cholera	Worldwide	1893–94	millions*
10 Smallpox	Mexico	1530–45	>1,000,000

* *No precise figures available*

Pandemics—epidemics spread over widespread geographical areas—have affected human populations since ancient times. The Black Death—bubonic plague—was the worst of all time, annihilating entire communities and decimating countries. After spreading throughout Asia, it reached Constantinople in 1347 and then spread to Europe, where it killed half the population of many cities, recurring at intervals in later centuries.

THE 10 MOST SUICIDAL COUNTRIES

	COUNTRY	SUICIDES PER 100,000 POPULATION*
1	Lithuania	42.0
2	Russia	35.3
3	Belarus	33.5
4	Estonia	33.2
5	Hungary	33.1
6	Latvia	31.4
7	Slovenia	29.7
8	Ukraine	28.8
9	Kazakhstan	26.8
10	Finland	23.8
	US	11.3

* In those countries/latest year for which data available

Source: United Nations

It is perhaps surprising that the highest suicide rates are not generally recorded in the poorest countries in the world. Suicide rates in many African countries are very low, maybe because of the strong extended family networks, as well as the cultural and religious taboos attached to suicide. It is also difficult to obtain reliable figures for such countries.

THE 10 COUNTRIES WITH THE HIGHEST DEATH RATE FROM LUNG CANCER

	COUNTRY	DEATH RATE PER 100,000 FEMALE	MALE*
1	Hungary	36.02	123.92
2	Belgium	18.69	119.73
3	Croatia	18.61	105.65
4	Italy	18.60	98.08
5	Greece	15.42	92.69
6	Netherlands	24.70	90.72
7	Luxembourg	19.61	86.66
8	Poland	17.84	86.55
9	Estonia	17.09	85.17
10	UK	44.19	84.58
	World	9.74	26.58

* Ranked by incidence in male population

Source: International Agency for Research on Cancer, Globocan 2000

Denmark has the highest incidence of deaths from lung cancer among women, with an average of 50.4 women in every 100,000 dying from the disease.

THE 10 COUNTRIES WITH THE HIGHEST DEATH RATE FROM HEART DISEASE

	COUNTRY	DEATH RATE PER 100,000
1	Ukraine	896.0
2	Bulgaria	891.2
3	Russia	746.6
4	Latvia	745.7
5	Belarus	741.3
6	Romania	736.8
7	Hungary	728.4
8	Estonia	715.6
9	Georgia	603.7
10	Croatia	594.5
	US	349.3

* In those countries/latest year for which data available

Source: United Nations

▼ Buried alive!
The specter of premature burial heightened the terror as the Black Death swept across Europe and Asia.

What's in a Name?

TOP 10 | FEMALE FIRST NAMES IN THE US

NAME	% OF ALL FIRST NAMES
1 Mary	2.629
2 Patricia	1.073
3 Linda	1.035
4 Barbara	0.980
5 Elizabeth	0.937
6 Jennifer	0.932
7 Maria	0.828
8 Susan	0.794
9 Margaret	0.768
10 Dorothy	0.727

Source: *US Census Bureau*

The Top 10 female names according to an analysis of the 1990 US Census account for 10.703 percent of all names. It should be noted that this list represents names of people of all age groups enumerated, and not the current popularity of first names. When name data from the Census 2000 are made available, it will reveal the extent to which these traditional names have become diluted by the more fashionable and volatile names of the modern era.

TOP 10 | MALE FIRST NAMES IN THE US

NAME	% OF ALL FIRST NAMES
1 James	3.318
2 John	3.271
3 Robert	3.143
4 Michael	2.629
5 William	2.451
6 David	2.363
7 Richard	1.703
8 Charles	1.523
9 Joseph	1.404
10 Thomas	1.380

Source: *US Census Bureau*

The Top 10 male names account for 23.185 percent of all names, pointing to their relative lack of diversity compared with those of females. As with its female counterpart, this list represents names of people of all age groups enumerated, and hence differs from the names given to babies, which reflect contemporary fashion.

TOP 10 | FIRST NAMES IN THE US, 2001

GIRLS		BOYS
Emily	1	Jacob
Hannah	2	Michael
Madison	3	Joshua
Samantha	4	Matthew
Ashley	5	Andrew
Sarah	6	Joseph
Elizabeth	7	Nicholas
Kayla	8	Anthony
Alexis	9	Tyler
Abigail	10	Daniel

The Top 10 is based on a one percent sample of Social Security applications for the period January to August 2001. In 1999 Michael, which had been the most popular boys name in the US since 1962 (when it ousted David), was replaced by Jacob; in 2000 David returned to its preeminent position before exchanging places with Jacob yet again in 2001.

GIRLS' AND BOYS' NAMES IN THE US 50 YEARS AGO*

GIRLS		BOYS
Mary	1	Robert
Deborah	2	Michael
Linda	3	John
Debra	4	James
Patricia	5	David
Susan	6	William
Barbara	7	Richard
Maria	8	Thomas
Karen	9	Mark
Nancy	10	Gary

* Based on a sample of 25,384 male and 23,846 female birth registrations in 1954

 **US PATRONYMS**

	NAME/ORIGIN	% OF ALL US NAMES
1	Johnson ("son of John")	0.810
2	Williams ("son of William")	0.699
3	Jones ("son of John")	0.621
4	Davis ("son of Davie/David")	0.480
5	Wilson ("son of Will")	0.339
6 =	Anderson ("son of Andrew")	0.311
=	Thomas ("son of Thomas")	0.311
8	Jackson ("son of Jack")	0.310
9	Harris ("son of Harry")	0.275
10	Martin ("son of Martin")	0.273

Patronyms are names recalling a father or other ancestor. Up to one-third of all US surnames may be patronymic in origin. Several US Presidents have borne such names, including Andrew Johnson, Lyndon Johnson, Woodrow Wilson, Andrew Jackson, William Henry, Benjamin Harrison, Thomas Jefferson, and James Madison.

▼ Jacob and Emily?
The fraught business of choosing names for their children results in many parents opting for those in the list of the most popular.

SURNAMES IN THE US

	NAME	% OF ALL SURNAMES
1	Smith	1.006
2	Johnson	0.810
3	Williams	0.699
4 =	Brown	0.621
=	Jones	0.621
6	Davis	0.480
7	Miller	0.424
8	Wilson	0.339
9	Moore	0.312
10 =	Anderson	0.311
=	Taylor	0.311
=	Thomas	0.311

The Top 10 (or, in view of those in equal 10th place, 12) US surnames together make up over six percent of the entire US population—in other words, one American in every 16 bears one of these names. Extending the list, some 28 different names comprise 10 percent of the entire population, 115 names 20 percent, 315 names 30 percent, 733 names 40 percent, 1,712 names 50 percent, and 3,820 names 60 percent. Beyond this, large numbers of less common—and in some instances, unique—names make up the remainder.

Pomp & Power

FIRST FEMALE PRIME MINISTERS AND PRESIDENTS

	PRIME MINISTER OR PRESIDENT	COUNTRY	FIRST PERIOD IN OFFICE
1	**Sirimavo Bandaranaike** (PM)	Sri Lanka	July 1960–Mar. 1965
2	**Indira Gandhi** (PM)	India	Jan. 1966–Mar. 1977
3	**Golda Meir** (PM)	Israel	Mar. 1969–June 1974
4	**Maria Estela Perón** (President)	Argentina	July 1974–Mar. 1976
5	**Elisabeth Domitien** (PM)	Central African Republic	Jan. 1975–Apr. 1976
6	**Margaret Thatcher** (PM)	UK	May 1979–Nov. 1990
7	**Maria Lurdes Pintasilgo** (PM)	Portugal	Aug. 1979–Jan. 1980
8	**Mary Eugenia Charles** (PM)	Dominica	July 1980–June 1995
9	**Vigdís Finnbogadóttir** (President)	Iceland	Aug. 1980–Aug. 1996
10	**Gro Harlem Brundtland** (PM)	Norway	Feb.–Oct. 1981

Sirimavo Bandaranaike (1916–2000) became the world's first female prime minister on July 21, 1960, when the Sri Lanka Freedom Party, founded by her assassinated husband Solomon Bandaranaike, won the general election. She held the position on three occasions, and her daughter Chandrika Kumaratunga also became prime minister and later president.

TOP 10 PARLIAMENTS WITH THE HIGHEST PERCENTAGE OF WOMEN MEMBERS*

	PARLIAMENT/ELECTION	WOMEN MEMBERS	TOTAL MEMBERS	PERCENTAGE WOMEN
1	**Sweden,** 2002	158	349	45.3
2	**Denmark,** 2001	68	179	38.0
3	**Netherlands,** 2003	55	150	36.7
4	**Finland,** 1999	73	200	36.5
5	**Norway,** 2001	60	165	36.4
6	**Costa Rica,** 2002	20	57	35.1
7	**Iceland,** 1999	22	63	34.9
8	**Austria,** 2002	62	183	33.9
9	**Germany,** 2002	194	603	32.2
10	**Argentina,** 2001	79	257	30.7
	US, 2002	*62*	*435*	*14.3*

* As of March 1, 2003

Source: *Inter-Parliamentary Union*

This list is based on the most recent election results for all democracies, and based on the lower chamber where the parliament comprises two chambers. Forty-one countries now have at least 20 percent female members of parliament.

TOP 10 LONGEST-REIGNING MONARCHS

	MONARCH	COUNTRY	REIGN	AGE AT ACCESSION	REIGN YEARS
1	**King Louis XIV**	France	1643–1715	5	72
2	**King John II**	Liechtenstein	1858–1929	18	71
3	**Emperor Franz-Josef**	Austria-Hungary	1848–1916	18	67
4	**Queen Victoria**	Great Britain	1837–1901	18	63
5	**Emperor Hirohito**	Japan	1926–89	25	62
6	**Emperor K'ang Hsi**	China	1661–1722	8	61
7	**King Sobhuza II***	Swaziland	Dec. 22, 1921–Aug. 21, 1982	22	60
8	**Emperor Ch'ien Lung**	China	Oct. 18, 1735–Feb. 9, 1796	25	60
9	**King Christian IV**	Denmark	Apr. 4, 1588–Feb. 21, 1648	11	59
10	**King George III**	Great Britain	Oct. 26, 1760–Jan. 29, 1820	22	59

* Paramount chief until 1967, when Great Britain recognized him as king with the granting of internal self-government

TOP 10 LONGEST-REIGNING LIVING MONARCHS*

	MONARCH	COUNTRY	DATE OF BIRTH	ACCESSION
1	**Bhumibol Adulyadej**	Thailand	Dec. 5, 1927	June 9, 1946
2	**Prince Rainier III**	Monaco	May 31, 1923	May 9, 1949
3	**Elizabeth II**	UK	Apr. 21, 1926	Feb. 6, 1952
4	**Malietoa Tanumafili II**	Samoa	Jan. 4, 1913	Jan. 1, 1962[#]
5	**Taufa'ahau Tupou IV**	Tonga	July 4, 1918	Dec. 16, 1965[†]
6	**Haji Hassanal Bolkiah**	Brunei	July 15, 1946	Oct. 5, 1967
7	**Sayyid Qaboos ibn Saidal-Said**	Oman	Nov. 18, 1942	July 23, 1970
8	**Margrethe II**	Denmark	Apr. 16, 1940	Jan. 14, 1972
9	**Jigme Singye Wangchuk**	Bhutan	Nov. 11, 1955	July 24, 1972
10	**Carl XVI Gustaf**	Sweden	Apr. 30, 1946	Sept. 19, 1973

* Including hereditary rulers of principalities, dukedoms, etc.

[#] Sole ruler since April 15, 1963

[†] Full sovereignty from June 5, 1970, when British protectorate ended

There are 28 countries that have emperors, kings, queens, princes, dukes, sultans, or other hereditary rulers as their heads of state. This list formerly included Birendra Bir Bikram Shah Dev, King of Nepal since January 31, 1972. On June 1, 2001, he was shot dead by his own son, Crown Prince Dipendra, who then committed suicide.

TOP 10 LONGEST-SERVING PRESIDENTS TODAY

	PRESIDENT	COUNTRY	TOOK OFFICE
1	General Gnassingbé Eyadéma	Togo	Apr. 14, 1967
2	El Hadj Omar Bongo	Gabon	Dec. 2, 1967
3	Colonel Mu'ammar Gadhafi	Libya	Sept. 1, 1969*
4	Zayid ibn Sultan al-Nuhayyan	United Arab Emirates	Dec. 2, 1971
5	Fidel Castro	Cuba	Nov. 2, 1976
6	France-Albert René	Seychelles	June 5, 1977
7	Ali Abdullah Saleh	Yemen	July 17, 1978
8	Maumoon Abdul Gayoom	Maldives	Nov. 11, 1978
9	Teodoro Obiang Nguema Mbasogo	Equatorial Guinea	Aug. 3, 1979
10	José Eduardo Dos Santos	Angola	Sept. 21, 1979

* Since a reorganization in 1979, Colonel Gadhafi has held no formal position, but continues to rule under the ceremonial title of "Leader of the Revolution"

All the presidents in this list have been in power for over 20 years, and some in excess of 30 years. Fidel Castro was prime minister of Cuba from February 1959. Since he was also chief of the army, and there was no opposition party, he effectively ruled as dictator from then, but he was not technically president until the Cuban constitution was revised in 1976. Among those no longer in office, Abu Sulayman Hafiz al-Assad, President of Syria, died on June 10, 2000, after serving as leader of his country since February 22, 1971.

THE 10 FIRST COUNTRIES TO GIVE WOMEN THE VOTE

	COUNTRY	YEAR
1	New Zealand	1893
2	Australia (South Australia 1894; Western Australia 1898; Australia united in 1901)	1902
3	Finland (then a Grand Duchy under the Russian Crown)	1906
4	Norway (restricted franchise; all women over 25 in 1913)	1907
5	Denmark and Iceland (a Danish dependency until 1918)	1915
6 =	Netherlands	1917
=	USSR	1917
8 =	Austria	1918
=	Canada	1918
=	Germany	1918
=	Great Britain and Ireland (Ireland part of the United Kingdom until 1921; women over 30 only—lowered to 21 in 1928)	1918
=	Poland	1918

Although not a country, the Isle of Man was the first place to give women the vote, in 1880. Until 1920 the only other European countries to enfranchise women were Sweden in 1919 and Czechoslovakia in 1920. Certain US states gave women the vote at earlier dates (Wyoming in 1869, Colorado in 1894, Utah in 1895, and Idaho in 1896), but it was not granted nationally until 1920. A number of countries, such as France and Italy, did not give women the vote until 1945. In certain countries, such as Saudi Arabia, women are not allowed to vote at all—but neither are men.

◀ **Head of state**
Leader of the Revolution and Supreme Commander of the Armed Forces, Colonel Mu'ammar Gadhafi has been the controversial leader of Libya since the overthrow of the monarchy in 1969.

Crime & Punishment

THE 10 COUNTRIES WITH THE MOST EXECUTIONS

	COUNTRY	EXECUTIONS (1998)
1	China	1,067
2	Dem. Rep. of Congo	100
3	US	68
4	Iran	66
5	Egypt	48
6	Belarus	33
7	Taiwan	32
8	Saudi Arabia	29
9	Singapore	28
10 =	Rwanda	24
=	Sierra Leone	24

Source: *Amnesty International*

At least 80 countries in the world retain the death penalty, with China consistently the leading practitioner of this ultimate sanction.

► Hot seat

The electric chair has been introduced in few countries outside the US, where it has been used since 1890. It remains the official execution method in 10 of the 38 states that retain the death penalty.

THE 10 COUNTRIES WITH THE HIGHEST REPORTED BURGLARY RATES

	COUNTRY	RATE*
1	Netherlands	3,100.40
2	Australia	2,280.82
3	New Zealand	2,153.66
4	Scotland	2,118.73
5	Antigua and Barbuda	2,071.99
6	Denmark	1,868.06
7	England and Wales	1,832.69
8	St. Kitts and Nevis	1,790.00
9	Estonia	1,699.95
10	Finland	1,690.52

* Reported crime per 100,000 population, in latest year for which data available

Source: *Interpol*

TOP 10 COUNTRIES WITH THE LOWEST REPORTED CRIME RATES

	COUNTRY	RATE*
1	Burkina Faso	9.30
2	Mali	10.03
3	Syria	42.26
4	Cambodia	47.97
5	Yemen	63.22
6	Myanmar	64.54
7	Angola	71.52
8	Cameroon	78.17
9	Vietnam	83.56
10	Bangladesh	89.66

* Reported crime per 100,000 population, in latest year for which data available

Source: *Interpol*

There are just 12 countries in the world with reported crime rates of fewer than 100 per 100,000 inhabitants; the other two are Mauritania (95.40) and Niger (99.09). It should be noted that these figures are based on reported crimes. For propaganda purposes, many countries do not publish accurate figures, while in certain countries crime is so common and law enforcement so inefficient or corrupt that countless incidents are unreported.

THE 10 COUNTRIES WITH THE HIGHEST PRISON POPULATION RATES

	COUNTRY	TOTAL PRISON POPULATION*	PRISONERS PER 100,000
1	US	1,962,220	686
2	Russia	919,330	638
3	Belarus	56,000	554
4	Kazakhstan	84,000	522
5	Turkmenistan	22,000	489
6	Belize	1,097	459
7	Suriname	1,933	437
8	Dominica	298	420
9	Bahamas	1,280	416
10	Maldives	1,098	414

* Includes pre-trial detainees; most figures relate to dates between 1999–2002

Source: *UK Home Office*, World Prison Population List (4th ed.)

The US incarceration rate has increased dramatically in recent years. The total first exceeded 100,000 in 1927 and 200,000 in 1958, since when it has escalated rapidly, far outstripping the rate of population increase.

THE 10 MOST COMMON OFFENSES FOR WHICH PEOPLE ARE IMPRISONED IN THE US

	OFFENSE	PRISONERS*	PERCENTAGE OF PRISON POPULATION
1	Drug offenses	77,791	55.1
2	Firearms, explosives, and arson	13,581	9.6
3	Immigration offenses	12,905	9.1
4	Robbery	8,740	6.2
5	Property offenses	7,335	5.2
6	Extortion, fraud, and bribery	6,844	4.8
7	Disorderly conduct	6,561	4.6
8	Homicide, aggravated assault, and kidnapping	2,685	1.9
9	White collar offenses	1,054	0.8
10	Sex offenses	1,013	0.7

* As of May 30, 2002

Source: *US Department of Justice, Federal Bureau of Prisons*

THE 10 COUNTRIES WITH THE HIGHEST REPORTED CRIME RATES

	COUNTRY	RATE*
1	Iceland	14,726.95
2	Sweden	13,455.08
3	New Zealand	12,586.64
4	Grenada	10,177.89
5	Norway	10,086.72
6	England and Wales	9,823.28
7	Denmark	9,460.38
8	Finland	8,697.37
9	Scotland	8,428.73
10	Canada	4,123.97

* Reported crime per 100,000 population, in latest year for which data available

Source: *Interpol*

THE 10 COUNTRIES WITH THE HIGHEST REPORTED CAR THEFT RATES

	COUNTRY	RATE*
1	Switzerland	962.80
2	New Zealand	818.01
3	England and Wales	752.93
4	Sweden	738.47
5	Australia	726.19
6	Denmark	604.18
7	Scotland	555.33
8	Italy	537.00
9	Canada	521.20
10	Norway	518.25
	US	414.17

* Reported car thefts per 100,000 population, in latest year for which data available

Source: *Interpol*

FIRST SPEEDING TICKET!

FIRST FACT

THE WORLD'S FIRST AUTOMOBILE speeding ticket was issued in the UK on January 28, 1896 to Walter Arnold. He was charged with driving at 8 mph in an area of Paddock Wood, Kent, that had a limit of 2 mph, hurtling past the house of a policeman, who gave chase on his bicycle. Arnold was fined one shilling (25 cents). In the US on May 20, 1899, Jacob German became the first driver arrested for speeding when he was caught driving an electric taxicab at a "breakneck speed" of 12 mph on New York's Lexington Avenue— for which he was jailed.

Murder by Numbers

TOP 10 COUNTRIES WITH THE LOWEST MURDER RATES

	COUNTRY	REPORTED MURDERS PER 100,000 POPULATION (2000*)
1	Iceland	0.00
2	Senegal	0.33
3 =	Burkina Faso	0.38
=	Cameroon	0.38
5 =	Finland	0.71
=	Gambia	0.71
=	Mali	0.71
=	Saudi Arabia	0.71
9	Mauritania	0.76
10	Oman	0.91

Or latest year for which data are available

Source: *Interpol*

The murder rate in Iceland has been so exceptionally low for many years that it is often excluded altogether from comparative international statistics.

THE 10 COUNTRIES WITH THE HIGHEST MURDER RATES

	COUNTRY	REPORTED MURDERS PER 100,000 POPULATION (2000*)
1	Honduras	154.02
2	South Africa	121.91
3	Swaziland	93.32
4	Colombia	69.98
5	Lesotho	50.41
6	Rwanda	45.08
7	Jamaica	37.21
8	El Salvador	36.88
9	Venezuela	33.20
10	Bolivia	31.98

Or latest year for which data are available

Source: *Interpol*

These figures should be viewed with caution: not all countries record or define crimes identically or use the same statistical methods in reporting rates.

TOP 10 RELATIONSHIPS OF HOMICIDE VICTIMS TO PRINCIPAL SUSPECTS IN THE US

	RELATIONSHIP	VICTIMS (2001)
1	Acquaintance	2,979
2	Stranger	1,803
3	Wife	600
4	Girlfriend	434
5	Friend	342
6	Son	253
7	Daughter	218
8	Boyfriend	153
9	Husband	142
10	Father	110

Source: FBI Uniform Crime Reports

Over 21 percent of the 13,752 murders committed in the US in 2001 were committed by acquaintances, and another 13 percent by strangers.

THE 10 WORST GUN MASSACRES*

	PERPETRATOR/LOCATION/DATE/CIRCUMSTANCES	KILLED
1	**Woo Bum Kong** Sang-Namdo, South Korea, Apr. 28, 1982. Off-duty policeman Woo Bum Kong, 27, killed 57 and injured 38 during a drunken rampage with rifles and hand grenades before blowing himself up with a grenade.	57
2	**Martin Bryant** Port Arthur, Tasmania, Australia, Apr. 28, 1996. Bryant, a 28-year-old Hobart resident, began killing with a high-powered rifle and was eventually captured when he fled in flames from a guesthouse in which he had held three hostages.	35
3	**Baruch Goldstein** Hebron, occupied West Bank, Israel, Feb. 25, 1994. Goldstein, a 42-year-old US immigrant doctor, massacred Palestinians at prayer at the Tomb of the Patriarchs before being beaten to death by the crowd.	29
4	**Campo Elias Delgado** Bogota, Colombia, Dec. 4, 1986. Delgado, a Vietnamese war veteran, stabbed two and shot a further 26 people before being killed by police.	28
5 =	**George Jo Hennard** Killeen, Texas, Oct. 16, 1991. Hennard drove his truck through a café window and killed 22 with semiautomatic guns before shooting himself.	22
=	**James Oliver Huberty** San Ysidro, California, July 18, 1984. Huberty, aged 41, opened fire in a McDonald's restaurant before being shot dead by a SWAT marksman.	22
7 =	**Thomas Hamilton** Dunblane, Stirling, UK, Mar. 13, 1996. Hamilton, 43, shot 16 children and a teacher in Dunblane Primary School before killing himself in the UK's worst ever shooting incident.	17
=	**Robert Steinhäuser** Erfurt, Germany, Apr. 26, 2002. Former student Steinhäuser returned to Johann Gutenberg secondary school and killed 14 teachers, two students, and a police officer with a handgun before shooting himself.	17
9 =	**Michael Ryan** Hungerford, Berkshire, UK, Aug. 19, 1987. Ryan, 26, shot 14 dead and wounded 16 others (two of whom died later) before shooting himself.	16
=	**Ronald Gene Simmons** Russellville, Arkansas, Dec. 28, 1987. Simmons killed 16, including 14 members of his own family, by shooting or strangling. After being caught, he was sentenced to death on Feb. 10, 1989.	16
=	**Charles Joseph Whitman** Austin, Texas, July 31–Aug. 1, 1966. Twenty-five-year-old ex-Marine marksman Whitman killed his mother and wife and the following day went to the University of Texas at Austin, where he took the elevator to the 27th floor of the campus tower and ascended to the observation deck. From here he shot 14 and wounded 34 before being shot dead by police officers Romero Martinez and Houston McCoy.	16

By individuals, excluding terrorist and military actions; totals exclude perpetrator

THE 10 MOST PROLIFIC SERIAL KILLERS*

MURDERER/COUNTRY/CRIMES	VICTIMS
1 Behram (India)	931

Behram (or Buhram) was the leader of the Thugee cult in India, which it is believed was responsible for the deaths of up to two million people. At his trial, Behram was found guilty of 931 murders between 1790 and 1830, mostly by ritual strangulation with the cult's traditional cloth known as a "ruhmal."

2 Countess Erszébet Báthory (Hungary)	up to 650

In the period up to 1610 in Hungary, Báthory (1560–1614), known as "Countess Dracula," was alleged to have murdered between 300 and 650 girls (her personal list of 610 victims was described at her trial) in the belief that drinking their blood would prevent her from aging. She was eventually arrested in 1611; tried and found guilty, she died on August 21, 1614, walled up in her own castle in Csejthe.

3 Pedro Alonso López (Colombia)	300

Captured in 1980, López, nicknamed the "Monster of the Andes," led police to 53 graves, but probably murdered at least 300 in Colombia, Ecuador, and Peru. He was sentenced to life imprisonment.

4 Dr. Harold Shipman (UK)	215

In January 2000, Manchester doctor Shipman was found guilty of the murder of 15 women patients; the official inquiry into his crimes put the figure at 215, with 45 possible further cases, but some authorities believe that the total could be as high as 400.

5 Henry Lee Lucas (US)	200

Lucas (1936–2001) admitted in 1983 to 360 murders, many with his partner-in-crime Ottis Toole. He died while on Death Row in Huntsville Prison, Texas.

MURDERER/COUNTRY/CRIMES	VICTIMS
6 Gilles de Rais (France)	up to 200

A wealthy aristocrat, Gilles de Laval, Baron de Rais (1404–40), was accused of having kidnapped between 60 and 200 children, and killed them as sacrifices during black magic rituals. After being tried, tortured, and found guilty, he was strangled and his body burned in Nantes on October 25, 1440.

7 Hu Wanlin (China)	196

Posing as a doctor specializing in Chinese medicine, Hu Wanlin was given a 15-year sentence on October 1, 2000, for three deaths, but he is thought to have been responsible for 20 in Taiyuan, 146 in Shanxi, and 30 in Shangqui.

8 Luis Alfredo Garavito (Colombia)	189

Garavito confessed in 1999 to a spate of murders. On May 28, 2000, he was sentenced to a total of 835 years imprisonment.

9 Hermann Webster Mudgett (US)	up to 150

Mudgett (1860–96) was believed to have lured over 150 women to his Chicago "castle" of soundproofed cells equipped for torture, murder, and the disposal of bodies. Arrested and found guilty of the murder of an ex-partner, he confessed to 27 killings, but 200 victims' remains were thought to have been found. Mudgett was hanged in Moyamensing Prison on May 7, 1896.

10 Dr. Jack Kevorkian (US)	130

In 1999, Kevorkian, who admitted to assisting in 130 suicides since 1990, was convicted of second-degree murder. His appeal against his 10- to 25-year prison sentence was rejected on November 21, 2001.

* Includes only individual murderers; excludes murders by bandits, terrorist groups, political and military atrocities, and gangland slayings

▶ **Hand gun**
In 2001, firearms were used in 8,719 murders in the US, with handguns accounting for some 6,790 of them.

War & Peace

THE 10 BATTLES WITH THE MOST CASUALTIES

	BATTLE/WAR/DATES	CASUALTIES*
1	**Stalingrad,** World War II, 1942–43	2,000,000
2	**Somme River I,** World War I, 1916	1,073,900
3	**Po Valley,** World War II, 1945	740,000
4	**Moscow,** World War II, 1941–42	700,000
5	**Verdun,** World War I, 1916	595,000
6	**Gallipoli,** World War I, 1915	500,000
7	**Artois-Loos,** World War I, 1915	428,000
8	**Berezina,** War of 1812	400,000
9	**38th Parallel,** Korean War, 1951	320,000
10	**Somme River II,** World War I, 1918	300,000

* Estimated total of military and civilian dead, wounded, and missing

Source: *Alexis Tregenza*

Total numbers of casualties in the Battle of Stalingrad are at best estimates, but it was undoubtedly one of the longest battles—and almost certainly the bloodiest—of all time. Fought between German (with Hungarian, Romanian, and Italian troops also under German command) and Soviet forces, it continued from August 19, 1942, to February 2, 1943, with huge losses on both sides.

THE 10 20TH-CENTURY WARS WITH THE MOST MILITARY FATALITIES

	WAR	DATES	EST. MILITARY FATALITIES
1	**World War II**	1939–45	15,843,000
2	**World War I**	1914–18	8,545,800
3	**Korean War**	1950–53	1,893,100
4	**Sino-Japanese War**	1937–41	1,200,000
5	**Biafra–Nigeria Civil War**	1967–70	1,000,000
6	**Spanish Civil War**	1936–39	611,000
7	**Vietnam War**	1961–75	546,000
8	**French Vietnam War**	1945–54	300,000
9 =	**India–Pakistan War**	1947	200,000
=	**USSR invasion of Afghanistan**	1979–89	200,000
=	**Iran–Iraq War**	1980–88	200,000

The statistics of warfare has always been an imperfect science. Not only are battle deaths seldom recorded accurately, but figures are often deliberately inflated by both sides in a conflict. These figures therefore represent military historians' "best guesses"—and fail to take into account the enormous toll of deaths among civilian populations during the many wars that beset the 20th century.

THE 10 COUNTRIES SUFFERING THE GREATEST CIVILIAN LOSSES IN WORLD WAR II

	COUNTRY	EST. CIVILIAN FATALITIES
1	**China**	8,000,000
2	**USSR**	6,500,000
3	**Poland**	5,300,000
4	**Germany**	2,350,000
5	**Yugoslavia**	1,500,000
6	**France**	470,000
7	**Greece**	415,000
8	**Japan**	393,400
9	**Romania**	340,000
10	**Hungary**	300,000

Civilian deaths in World War II—many resulting from famine and internal purges, such as those in China and the USSR—were colossal, but they were less well documented than those among fighting forces. An estimate of 60,600 civilian deaths resulting from bomb and rocket attacks on the UK represents less than one-quarter of the total military deaths. Although the figures are the best available from authoritative sources, and present a broad picture of the scale of civilian losses, the precise numbers will never be known.

THE 10 LATEST YEARS OF THE NOBEL PEACE PRIZE

PRIZE YEAR	WINNER(S)	COUNTRY
2002	Jimmy Carter	US
2001	Kofi Annan/United Nations	Ghana/International body
2000	Kim Dae Jung	South Korea
1999	Médecins Sans Frontières	Belgium
1998	John Hume/David Trimble	UK
1997	International Campaign to Ban Landmines/Jody Williams	International body/US
1996	Carlos Filipe Ximenes Belo/José Ramos-Horta	East Timor
1995	Joseph Rotblat	UK
1994	Yasser Arafat/Shimon Peres/Itzhak Rabin	Palestine/Israel
1993	Nelson Rolihlahla Mandela/Frederik Willem de Klerk	South Africa

Former US president Jimmy Carter was awarded the Nobel Peace Prize in 2002 "for his decades of untiring effort to find peaceful solutions to international conflicts, to advance democracy and human rights, and to promote economic and social development."

THE 10 COUNTRIES SUFFERING THE GREATEST MILITARY LOSSES IN WORLD WAR II

	COUNTRY	EST. MILITARY FATALITIES
1	USSR	13,600,000*
2	Germany	3,300,000
3	China	1,324,516
4	Japan	1,140,429
5	British Empire#	357,116
6	Romania	350,000
7	Poland	320,000
8	Yugoslavia	305,000
9	US	292,131
10	Italy	279,800
	Total	21,268,992

* Total, of which 7,800,000 are battlefield deaths

Including Australia, Canada, India, New Zealand, etc.; UK figure 264,000

The massive losses among the 30 million Soviet troops who bore arms include 7 million battlefield deaths, 2 million from wounds or disease received in battle, and 3 million prisoners who died in captivity.

THE 10 LONGEST WARS

	WAR	COMBATANTS	DATES	YEARS
1	Hundred Years' War	France and England	1337–1453	116
2	Greco-Persian Wars	Greece and Persia	499–448 BC	51
3 =	Wars of the Roses	Lancaster and York	1455–85	30
=	Thirty Years' War	Catholics and Protestants	1618–48	30
5	Second Peloponnesian War	Peloponnesian League (Sparta, Corinth, etc.) and Delian League (Athens, etc.)	432–404 BC	28
6 =	First Punic War	Rome and Carthage	264–241 BC	23
=	Napoleonic Wars	France and other European countries	1792–1815	23
8	Second Great Northern War	Russia and Sweden and Baltic states	1700–21	21
9	Vietnam War	South Vietnam (with US support) and North Vietnam	1957–75	18
10	Second Punic War	Rome and Carthage	219–202 BC	17

Source: Alexis Tregenza

It may be argued that the total period of the Crusades (fought by Christians and Muslims) constitutes one long single conflict spanning a total of 195 years from 1096 to 1291, rather than a series of nine short ones, in which case it ranks as the longest war ever. Similarly, if all the Punic Wars between 264 and 146 BC are taken as one, they would rank second at 118 years. The War of the Spanish Succession (1701–14) is the only other major conflict to have lasted more than 10 years, with the War of the Austrian Succession (1740–48), the American Revolution (1775–83), and the Chinese–Japanese War (1937–45) each lasting eight years.

▼ Siege of Stalingrad
The German army besieged Stalingrad, USSR, in 1942. The ensuing battle lasted almost six months and was the bloodiest in history.

Modern Military

NUCLEAR SUBMARINE

ALTHOUGH SUBMARINES HAD BEEN used militarily for almost 100 years, it was not until January 21, 1954, that the first nuclear-powered vessel was launched, at Groton, Connecticut. It was named *Nautilus* after the submarine in Jules Verne's novel *20,000 Leagues Under the Sea*, and on August 3, 1958, it became the first submarine ever to cross beneath the North Pole, with 116 men on board. By 1979, after 25 years in service and having traveled a record of almost 500,000 miles (804,672 km), *Nautilus* was decommissioned and towed to Groton where it joined the Submarine Force Museum. Designated a National Historic Landmark, it is also Connecticut's official State Ship.

FIRST FACT

▲ **Sub power**

The US submarine fleet, the world's largest, is principally composed of Los Angeles Class nuclear-powered hunter-killers, named after the first, USS *Los Angeles*, which was commissioned in 1976.

TOP 10 COUNTRIES WITH THE MOST SUBMARINES

	COUNTRY	SUBMARINES
1	US	73
2	China	69
3	Russia (and associated states)	56
4	North Korea	26
5	South Korea	19
6	= India	16
	= Japan	16
	= UK	16
9	Germany	14
10	Turkey	13

TOP 10 COUNTRIES WITH THE MOST COMBAT AIRCRAFT*

	COUNTRY	COMBAT AIRCRAFT
1	US	3,939
2	China	2,900
3	Russia	2,636
4	India	738
5	North Korea	621
6	Egypt	580
7	South Korea	555
8	Ukraine	543
9	Taiwan	482
10	France	473

* Air force only, excluding long-range strike/attack aircraft

TOP 10 COUNTRIES WITH THE LARGEST ARMIES

	COUNTRY	ARMY PERSONNEL
1	China	1,600,000
2	India	1,100,000
3	North Korea	950,000
4	South Korea	560,000
5	Pakistan	550,000
6	US	477,800
7	Vietnam	412,000
8	Turkey	402,000
9	Iraq	375,000
10	Russia	321,000

Slight reductions in numbers have been made over the past few years, but recent heightenings in international tension since the September 11, 2001, terrorist attacks and ongoing disputes have put further reductions "on hold."

TOP 10 COUNTRIES WITH THE LARGEST NAVIES

	COUNTRY	NAVY PERSONNEL*
1	US	366,100
2	China	250,000
3	Russia	171,500
4	Taiwan	62,000
5	South Korea	60,000
6 =	India	53,000
=	Turkey	53,000
8	North Korea	46,000
9	France	45,600
10	UK	43,530

Including naval air forces and marines

Along with other factors, the increasing reliance on technology rather than manpower in modern naval warfare led to reductions in numbers during the 1990s, but all the major powers remain capable of putting substantial forces to sea.

TOP 10 COUNTRIES WITH THE LARGEST DEFENSE BUDGETS

	COUNTRY	BUDGET ($)
1	US	291,100,000,000
2	Russia	44,000,000,000
3	Japan	40,400,000,000
4	UK	34,000,000,000
5	Saudi Arabia	27,200,000,000
6	France	25,300,000,000
7	Germany	21,000,000,000
8	China	17,000,000,000
9	India	15,600,000,000
10	Italy	15,500,000,000

The so-called "peace dividend"—the savings made as a consequence of the end of the Cold War between the West and the former Soviet Union—means that both the numbers of personnel and the defense budgets of many countries have been cut. That of the US has gone down from its 1989 peak of $303.6 billion.

TOP 10 COUNTRIES WITH THE HIGHEST MILITARY/ CIVILIAN RATIO

	COUNTRY	RATIO (2002)*
1	North Korea	441
2	Israel	258
3	United Arab Emirates	253
4	Qatar	202
5	Syria	195
6	Iraq	190
7	Bahrain	176
8	Taiwan	167
9	Oman	162
10	Jordan	146
	US	49

Military personnel per 10,000 population

▶ **People's army**
China's armed forces make up the world's largest military machine. At 18, male citizens are officially drafted into service for two years, but in practice conscription is selective.

World Religions

TOP 10 RELIGIOUS BELIEFS

	RELIGION	FOLLOWERS (2002)
1	Christianity	2,050,616,000
2	Islam	1,239,029,000
3	Hinduism	836,543,000
4	Non-religion	780,557,000
5	Buddhism	367,538,000
6	Ethnic religion	234,341,000
7	Atheism	150,804,000
8	New religion	104,280,000
9	Sikhism	24,124,000
10	Judaism	14,670,000

Source: *David B. Barrett & Todd M. Johnson,*
International Bulletin of Missionary Research,
January 2002

TOP 10 CHRISTIAN TRADITIONS IN THE MOST COUNTRIES

	CHRISTIAN TRADITION	COUNTRIES
1	Roman Catholic	235
2	Protestant	231
3	Independent	230
4	Jehovah's Witnesses	212
5	Adventist	199
6	Baptist	163
7	Anglican	162
8	New Apostolic	149
9	Reformed, Presbyterian	141
10	Orthodox	133

Source: *David B. Barrett & Todd M. Johnson,* World
Christian Trends, *William Carey Library, 2001*

◀ **Buddhist statue in China**
Despite its suppression during the
Cultural Revolution, Buddhism has
survived in China, where it now has
more than 100 million followers.

TOP 10 LARGEST BUDDHIST POPULATIONS

	COUNTRY	BUDDHIST POPULATION (2000)
1	China	105,829,000
2	Japan	69,931,000
3	Thailand	52,383,000
4	Vietnam	39,534,000
5	Myanmar	33,145,000
6	Sri Lanka	12,879,000
7	Cambodia	9,462,000
8	India	7,249,000
9	South Korea	7,174,000
10	Taiwan	4,686,000
	World	*359,981,757*

Source: *David B. Barrett & Todd M. Johnson,* World Christian Trends, *William Carey Library, 2001*

Buddhism originated in India in the 6th century BC. Its espousal of peace and tolerant coexistence ensured its appeal and encouraged its spread throughout Asia and beyond.

TOP 10 LARGEST HINDU POPULATIONS

	COUNTRY	HINDU POPULATION (2000)
1	India	755,135,000
2	Nepal	18,354,000
3	Bangladesh	15,995,000
4	Indonesia	7,259,000
5	Sri Lanka	2,124,000
6	Pakistan	1,868,000
7	Malaysia	1,630,000
8	US	1,032,000
9	South Africa	959,000
10	Myanmar	893,000

Source: *David B. Barrett & Todd M. Johnson,* World Christian Trends, *William Carey Library, 2001*

Claimed as the world's oldest organized religion, Hinduism is also the third largest after Christianity and Islam, with an estimated total world population of at least 900 million.

TOP 10 RELIGIONS IN THE US

	RELIGION	EST. NO. OF FOLLOWERS (2001)
1	Christianity	159,030,000
2	Judaism	1,104,000
3 =	Buddhism	1,082,000
=	Islam	1,082,000
5	Hinduism	766,000
6	Unitarian/Universalism	629,000
7	Paganism	140,000
8	Wiccan	134,000
9	Spiritualist	116,000
10	Native American	103,000

Source: *American Religious Identity Survey (ARIS) 2001*

Estimates of how many followers a religion has can vary hugely. This list is ranked by weighted estimates of followers, based on self-declared religious identity. The figures are based on the results of a random digit-dialed telephone survey of 50,281 US households during the period February–June 2001.

TOP 10 LARGEST MUSLIM POPULATIONS

	COUNTRY	MUSLIM POPULATION (2000)
1	Pakistan	150,365,000
2	India	122,570,000
3	Indonesia	116,105,000*
4	Bangladesh	110,849,000
5	Turkey	64,714,000
6	Iran	64,707,000
7	Egypt	57,780,000
8	Nigeria	49,000,000
9	Algeria	30,442,000
10	Morocco	27,736,000

* An additional 46 million people are considered Muslims by the Indonesian government but are more properly categorized as New Religionists (Islamisized syncretistic religions)

Source: *David B. Barrett & Todd M. Johnson,* World Christian Trends, *William Carey Library, 2001*

TOP 10 RELIGIOUS BRANCHES

	BRANCH/RELIGION	FOLLOWERS (2000)
1	**Roman Catholic,** Christianity	1,057,328,093
2	**Sunni,** Islam	1,002,542,801
3	**Vaishnavite,** Hinduism	549,583,323
4	**Protestant,** Christianity	342,001,605
5	**Sufi,** Islam	237,400,000
6	**Shaivite,** Hinduism	216,260,000
7	**Animist,** ethno-religion	216,160,890
8	**Orthodox,** Christianity	215,128,717
9	**Mahayana,** Buddhism	202,232,757
10	**Shia,** Islam	170,100,000

Source: *David B. Barrett & Todd M. Johnson,* World Christian Trends, *William Carey Library, 2001*

The world's religions are far from homogenous: within each major religion there are often numerous branches often conflicting—sometimes fiercely—with others. This list represents the 10 largest branches that share a common historical heritage and a proportion of doctrines or practices.

TOP 10 RELIGIOUS TRADITIONS WITH THE MOST MARTYRS

	RELIGIOUS TRADITION	MARTYRS
1	**Russian Orthodox**	21,626,000
2	**Assyrian or Nestoran** (East Syrian, Messihaye)	12,379,000
3	**Latin-rite Catholic**	11,024,000
4	**Ukrainian Orthodox**	3,500,000
5	**Armenian Orthodox** (Gregorian)	1,215,000
6	**Coptic Orthodox**	1,068,000
7	**Pentecostal** (Protestant, Classical Pentecostal)	1,021,000
8 =	**Messianic Jewish**	1,000,000
=	**Quasi-Christians**	1,000,000
10	**Lutheran**	987,000

Source: *David B. Barrett & Todd M. Johnson,* World Christian Trends, *William Carey Library, 2001*

According to some authorities, some 70 million Christians have been martyred for their faith during the past 2,000 years, while other major religions also claim figures running into the millions.

TOWN & COUNTRY

Countries of the World

TOP 10 COUNTRIES WITH THE MOST NEIGHBORS*

	COUNTRY/NEIGHBORS	NO. OF NEIGHBORS
1	**China** Afghanistan, Bhutan, India, Kazakhstan, Kyrgyzstan, Laos, Macau, Mongolia, Myanmar, Nepal, North Korea, Pakistan, Russia, Tajikistan, Vietnam	15
2	**Russia** Azerbaijan, Belarus, China, Estonia, Finland, Georgia, Kazakhstan, Latvia, Lithuania, Mongolia, North Korea, Norway, Poland, Ukraine	14
3	**Brazil** Argentina, Bolivia, Colombia, French Guiana, Guyana, Paraguay, Peru, Suriname, Uruguay, Venezuela	10
4 =	**Dem. Rep. of Congo** Angola, Burundi, Central African Republic, Congo, Rwanda, Sudan, Tanzania, Uganda, Zambia	9
=	**Germany** Austria, Belgium, Czech Republic, Denmark, France, Luxembourg, Netherlands, Poland, Switzerland	9
=	**Sudan** Central African Republic, Chad, Dem. Rep. of Congo, Egypt, Eritrea, Ethiopia, Kenya, Libya, Uganda	9
7 =	**Austria** Czech Republic, Germany, Hungary, Italy, Liechtenstein, Slovakia, Slovenia, Switzerland	8
=	**France** Andorra, Belgium, Germany, Italy, Luxembourg, Monaco, Spain, Switzerland	8
=	**Turkey** Armenia, Azerbaijan, Bulgaria, Georgia, Greece, Iran, Iraq, Syria	8
10 =	**Mali** Algeria, Burkina Faso, Cote d'Ivoire, Guinea, Mauritania, Niger, Senegal	7
=	**Niger** Algeria, Benin, Burkina Faso, Chad, Libya, Mali, Nigeria	7
=	**Saudi Arabia** Iraq, Jordan, Kuwait, Oman, Qatar, United Arab Emirates, Yemen	7
=	**Tanzania** Burundi, Kenya, Malawi, Mozambique, Rwanda, Uganda, Zambia	7
=	**Ukraine** Belarus, Hungary, Moldova, Poland, Romania, Russia, Slovakia	7
=	**Zambia** Angola, Dem. Rep. of Congo, Malawi, Mozambique, Namibia, Tanzania, Zimbabwe	7

It should be noted that some countries have more than one discontinuous border with the same country; this has been counted only once.

▼ **Canadian coastline**
The coast of mainland Canada comprises 35,889 miles (57,759 km) of its total coastline length, the balance being the total coastline lengths of its 52,455 offshore islands.

TOP 10 COUNTRIES WITH THE LONGEST COASTLINES

	COUNTRY	TOTAL COASTLINE LENGTH (MILES)	(KM)
1	**Canada**	151,485	243,791
2	**Indonesia**	33,999	54,716
3	**Russia**	23,396	37,653
4	**Philippines**	22,559	36,289
5	**Japan**	18,486	29,751
6	**Australia**	16,007	25,760
7	**Norway**	13,624	21,925
8	**US**	12,380	19,924
9	**New Zealand**	9,404	15,134
10	**China**	9,010	14,500
	World	*221,208*	*356,000*

Including all of its islands, the coastline of Canada is more than six times as long as the distance around the Earth at the equator, which is 24,902 miles (40,076 km).

TOP 10 LARGEST LANDLOCKED COUNTRIES

	COUNTRY/NEIGHBORS	AREA (SQ MILES)	(SQ KM)
1	Kazakhstan, China, Kyrgyzstan, Russia, Turkmenistan, Uzbekistan	1,049,156	2,717,300
2	Mongolia, China, Russia	604,250	1,565,000
3	Niger, Algeria, Benin, Burkina Faso, Chad, Libya, Mali, Nigeria	489,075	1,266,699
4	Chad, Cameroon, Central African Republic, Libya, Niger, Nigeria, Sudan	486,180	1,259,201
5	Mali, Algeria, Burkina Faso, Côte d'Ivoire, Guinea, Mauritania, Niger, Senegal	471,044	1,219,999
6	Ethiopia, Djibouti, Eritrea, Kenya, Somalia, Sudan	432,312	1,119,683
7	Bolivia, Argentina, Brazil, Chile, Paraguay, Peru	418,685	1,084,389
8	Zambia, Angola, Dem. Rep. of Congo, Malawi, Mozambique, Namibia, Tanzania, Zimbabwe	285,993	740,719
9	Afghanistan, China, Iran, Pakistan, Tajikistan, Turkmenistan, Uzbekistan	250,001	647,500
10	Central African Republic, Cameroon, Chad, Congo, Dem. Rep. of Congo, Sudan	240,534	622,980

Source: *US Census Bureau, International Data Base*

TOP 10 SMALLEST LANDLOCKED COUNTRIES

	COUNTRY/NEIGHBORS	AREA (SQ MILES)	(SQ KM)
1	Vatican City, Italy	0.2	0.44
2	San Marino, Italy	23	60
3	Liechtenstein, Austria, Switzerland	62	161
4	Andorra, Spain, France	174	451
5	Luxembourg, Germany, Belgium, France	998	2,585
6	Swaziland, South Africa, Mozambique	6,641	17,200
7	Rwanda, Burundi, Dem. Rep. of Congo, Uganda, Tanzania	9,633	24,949
8	Burundi, Rwanda, Tanzania, Dem. Rep. of Congo	9,903	25,649
9	Macedonia, Yugoslavia, Bulgaria, Greece, Albania	9,928	25,713
10	Armenia, Azerbaijan, Georgia, Iran, Turkey	11,506	29,800

Source: *US Census Bureau, International Data Base*

Liechtenstein is one of only two doubly landlocked countries in the world. These are countries that are surrounded by other countries that are also landlocked; the other is Uzbekistan, whose neighbours are Afghanistan, Kazakhstan, Kyrgyzstan, Tajikistan, and Turkmenistan.

TOP 10 LARGEST COUNTRIES

	COUNTRY	PERCENTAGE OF WORLD TOTAL	AREA (SQ MILES)	(SQ KM)
1	Russia	13.0	6,592,850	17,075,400
2	China	7.1	3,600,948	9,326,411
3	Canada	7.0	3,560,237	9,220,970
4	US	6.9	3,539,245	9,166,601
5	Brazil	6.4	3,265,077	8,456,511
6	Australia	5.8	2,941,300	7,617,931
7	India	2.2	1,148,148	2,973,190
8	Argentina	2.1	1,056,642	2,736,690
9	Kazakhstan	2.1	1,049,155	2,717,300
10	Algeria	1.8	919,595	2,381,741
	World	*100.0*	*50,580,568*	*131,003,055*

Source: *US Census Bureau, International Data Base*

TOP 10 SMALLEST COUNTRIES

	COUNTRY	AREA (SQ MILES)	(SQ KM)
1	Vatican City	0.2	0.44
2	Monaco	0.7	2
3	Nauru	8	21
4	Tuvalu	10	26
5	San Marino	23	60
6	Liechtenstein	62	161
7	Marshall Islands	70	181
8	Maldives	115	300
9	Malta	124	321
10	Grenada	131	339

Source: *US Census Bureau, International Data Base*

The "country" status of the Vatican is questionable, since its government and other features are intricately linked with those of Italy.

Country Populations

TOP 10 | COUNTRIES WITH THE OLDEST POPULATIONS

	COUNTRY	PERCENTAGE OVER 65 (2004 EST.)
1	Monaco	22.4
2	Italy	19.3
3	Japan	18.8
4	Greece	18.6
5	Germany	17.9
6 =	Spain	17.5
=	Sweden	17.5
8	Belgium	17.4
9	Bulgaria	17.1
10	San Marino	16.7
	World	*7.2*
	US	*12.6*

Source: *US Census Bureau International Data Base*

Nine of the 10 countries with the oldest populations are in Europe, implying that this region has lower death rates and a higher life expectancy than the rest of the world. On average, one in every 6.6 people in Europe is over the age of 65 (15.7 percent).

TOP 10 | MOST POPULATED COUNTRIES

	COUNTRY	POPULATION (2004 EST.)
1	China	1,305,625,273
2	India	1,077,116,060
3	US	285,522,555
4	Indonesia	239,259,710
5	Brazil	178,998,012
6	Pakistan	153,705,278
7	Russia	144,112,353
8	Bangladesh	137,650,588
9	Nigeria	136,514,807
10	Japan	127,295,333

Source: *US Census Bureau, International Data Base*

▶ **Dense Tokyo**
Japan is one of the world's most highly populated island countries, and only just fails to rank among the most densely populated.

COUNTRIES WITH THE YOUNGEST POPULATIONS

	COUNTRY	PERCENTAGE UNDER 15 (2004 EST.)
1	Uganda	50.5
2	Marshall Islands	48.7
3	Dem. Rep. of Congo	48.1
4	Chad	47.8
5	São Tomé and Príncipe	47.7
6	Niger	47.6
7	Ethiopia	47.3
8 =	Burkina Faso	47.0
=	Mali	47.0
10	Benin	46.8
	World	28.4
	US	20.7

Source: *US Census Bureau, International Data Base*

Countries with high proportions of their population under the age of 15 are usually characterized by high birth rates and high death rates.

LEAST POPULATED COUNTRIES

	COUNTRY	POPULATION (2004 EST.)
1	Tuvalu	11,468
2	Nauru	12,809
3	Palau	20,016
4	San Marino	28,503
5	Monaco	32,270
6	Liechtenstein	33,436
7	St. Kitts and Nevis	38,836
8	Antigua and Barbuda	68,320
9	Dominica	69,278
10	Andorra	69,865

Source: *US Census Bureau, International Data Base*

These are all independent countries, but there are numerous dependencies with even smaller populations, including the Falkland Islands (2,121) and the Pitcairn Islands, which were settled in 1790 by mutineers from the ship *Bounty*, and which have a population of 54. Another well-known small "country" is the Vatican City, with a population of 738. While it is an independent country, for some purposes and some statistics, it is counted as part of Italy.

MOST POPULATED ISLAND COUNTRIES

	COUNTRY	POPULATION (2004 EST.)
1	Indonesia	239,259,710
2	Japan	127,295,333
3	Philippines	87,891,082
4	Malaysia	23,522,482
5	Taiwan	22,898,115
6	Sri Lanka	19,905,165
7	Madagascar	17,501,871
8	Cuba	11,301,850
9	Dominican Republic	9,005,285
10	Haiti	7,269,957

Source: *US Census Bureau, International Data Base*

There are 17 island countries in the world with populations of more than one million, of which these are the Top 10. Australia is regarded as a continental landmass, rather than an island, but if it were included, its 19,546,792 population would put it in sixth place. The UK (59,778,002) is also excluded, as it is not a self-contained island state.

MOST DENSELY POPULATED COUNTRIES

	COUNTRY	AREA (SQ MILES)	POPULATION (2004 EST.)	POPULATION PER SQ MILE
1	Monaco	0.75	37,270	49,693.3
2	Singapore	241	4,767,974	19,784.1
3	Malta	124	403,342	3,254.8
4	Maldives	116	339,330	2,925.3
5	Bahrain	239	677,886	2,836.3
6	Bangladesh	51,703	137,650,588	2,662.3
7	Taiwan	12,455	22,898,115	1,838.4
8	Mauritius	714	1,220,481	1,709.4
9	Barbados	166	279,157	1,681.7
10	Nauru	8	12,809	1,601.1
	World	50,580,279	6,386,027,015	126.3
	US	3,535,177	285,522,555	80.8

Source: *US Census Bureau, International Data Base*

LEAST DENSELY POPULATED COUNTRIES

	COUNTRY	AREA (SQ MILES)	POPULATION (2004 EST.)	POPULATION PER SQ MILE
1	Mongolia	604,246	2,775,768	4.6
2	Namibia	317,872	1,857,619	5.8
3	Australia	2,941,283	19,913,144	6.8
4 =	Botswana	226,011	1,587,782	7.0
=	Suriname	62,343	440,862	7.0
6	Iceland	38,706	282,151	7.3
7	Mauritania	397,837	2,998,563	7.5
8	Libya	679,358	5,631,585	8.3
9	Canada	3,560,216	32,507,874	9.1
10	Guyana	76,003	703,680	9.3

Source: *US Census Bureau, International Data Base*

In addition to these sparsely populated countries, there are several territories where one could be really alone—the Western Sahara with 0.30 people per square mile, and Greenland with 0.01 people, or almost 15 sq miles per person.

World Cities

MOST URBANIZED COUNTRIES

COUNTRY	POPULATION LIVING IN URBAN AREAS (2001) TOTAL	PERCENTAGE
1 = Hong Kong	6,961,000	100.0
= Monaco	34,000	100.0
= Nauru	13,000	100.0
= Singapore	4,108,000	100.0
= The Vatican	1,000	100.0
6 Belgium	5,444,000	97.4
7 Kuwait	1,894,000	96.1
8 Qatar	534,000	92.9
9 Iceland	261,000	92.7
10 Bahrain	603,000	92.5
World	2,923,182,000	47.7
US	221,408,000	77.4

Source: *United Nations Population Division*, World Urbanization Prospects: The 2001 Revision

LARGEST CITIES IN THE US

CITY/STATE	POPULATION (2002*)
1 **New York** (including Newark and Paterson, New Jersey), New York	21,650,000
2 **Los Angeles** (including Riverside and Anaheim), California	16,900,000
3 **Chicago**, Illinois	9,400,000
4 **Washington** (including Baltimore, Maryland), D.C.	7,850,000
5 **San Francisco** (including Oakland and San Jose), California	7,300,000
6 **Philadelphia**, Pennsylvania	6,300,000
7 **Boston**, Massachusetts	5,950,000
8 **Detroit** (including Windsor, Canada), Michigan	5,850,000
9 **Dallas** (including Fort Worth), Texas	5,600,000
10 **Houston**, Texas	4,950,000

* Of urban agglomeration

Source: *Th. Brinkhoff:* The Principal Agglomerations of the World, *http://www.citypopulation.de,* November 12, 2002

COUNTRIES WITH THE MOST PEOPLE LIVING IN LARGE CITIES

COUNTRY	% POPULATION IN CITIES OF OVER 1 MILLION* (2002)
1 Hong Kong	100
2 Singapore	89
3 Dominican Republic	61
4 Kuwait	60
5 Portugal	57
6 Australia	56
7 = Lebanon	47
= South Korea	47
9 = Argentina	41
= Congo	41
= Germany	41
US	38

* In those countries for which data available

Source: *World Bank*, World Development Indicators, 2002

COUNTRIES WITH THE LARGEST URBAN POPULATIONS

COUNTRY	EST. TOTAL URBAN POPULATION (2005)
1 China	535,958,000
2 India	312,887,000
3 US	232,080,000
4 Brazil	151,925,000
5 Indonesia	104,048,000
6 Russia	102,731,000
7 Japan	101,831,000
8 Mexico	80,073,000
9 Germany	72,405,000
10 Nigeria	62,623,000
World	3,176,892,000

* In those countries for which data available

Source: *United Nations Population Division*, World Urbanization Prospects: The 2001 Revision

▶ **City and nation**
Singapore City and the nation of Singapore are synonymous, as a result of which Singapore is considered a totally urbanized country.

TOP 10 | LARGEST CITIES 100 YEARS AGO

	CITY/COUNTRY	POPULATION*
1	**London,** UK	6,581,000
2	**New York,** New York	3,437,000
3	**Paris,** France	2,714,000
4	**Berlin,** Germany	1,889,000
5	**Chicago,** Illinois	1,699,000
6	**Vienna,** Austria	1,675,000
7	**Wuhan,** China	1,500,000
8	**Tokyo,** Japan	1,440,000
9	**Philadelphia,** Pennsylvania	1,294,000
10	**St. Petersburg,** Russia	1,265,000

* Including adjacent suburban areas

TOP 10 | LARGEST CITIES

	CITY/COUNTRY	EST. POPULATION (2002)
1	**Tokyo,** Japan	35,100,000
2	**New York,** US	21,650,000
3	**Seoul,** South Korea	21,330,000
4	**Mexico City,** Mexico	20,950,000
5	**São Paulo,** Brazil	19,900,000
6	**Mumbai** (Bombay), India	18,400,000
7	**Osaka,** Japan	18,050,000
8	**Delhi,** India	17,500,000
9	**Los Angeles,** US	16,900,000
10	**Jakarta,** Indonesia	16,050,000

Source: *Th. Brinkhoff:* The Principal Agglomerations of the World, *http://www.citypopulation.de, November 12, 2002*

TOP 10 | FASTEST-GROWING CITIES*

	CITY/COUNTRY	AVERAGE ANNUAL POPULATION GROWTH RATE (PERCENT) (2000–05)
1	**Ansan,** South Korea	9.15
2	**Toluca,** Mexico	6.15
3	**Sana`a,** Yemen	5.83
4	**Niamey,** Niger	5.70
5	**Songnam,** South Korea	5.47
6	**P'ohang,** South Korea	5.43
7	**Rajshahi,** Bangladesh	5.29
8	**Kabul,** Afghanistan	5.10
9 =	**Antananarivo,** Madagascar	5.05
=	**Campo Grande,** Brazil	5.05

* Of urban agglomerations with 750,000 inhabitants or more

Source: *United Nations Population Division,* World Urbanization Report: The 2001 Revision

Place Names

COUNTRIES WITH THE LONGEST OFFICIAL NAMES

	OFFICIAL NAME*	COMMON ENGLISH NAME	LETTERS
1	al-Jamāhīrīyah al-'Arabīyah al-Lībīyah ash-Sha bīyah al-Ishtirākīyah	Libya	59
2	al-Jumhūrīyah al-Jazā'irīyah ad-Dīmuqrātīyah ash-Sha' bīyah	Algeria	51
3	United Kingdom of Great Britain and Northern Ireland	United Kingdom	45
4 =	Srī Lankā Prajātāntrika Samājavādī Janarajaya	Sri Lanka	41
=	Jumhurīyat al-Qumur al-Ittihādīyah al-Islāmīyah	The Comoros	41
6	República Democrática de São Tomé e Príncipe São Tomé	Príncipe	38
7	al-Jūmhurīyah al-Islāmīyah al-Mūrītānīyah	Mauritania	36
8 =	al-Mamlakah al-Urdunnīyah al-Hāshimīyah	Jordan	34
=	Sathalanalat Paxathipatai Paxaxôn Lao	Laos	34
10	Federation of Saint Christopher and Nevis	St. Kitts and Nevis	33

* Some official names have been transliterated from languages that do not use the Roman alphabet; their length may vary according to the method used

There is clearly no connection between the length of names and the longevity of the nation-states that bear them, for since this list was first published in 1991, three countries have ceased to exist: Socijalisticka Federativna Republika Jugoslavija (Yugoslavia, 45 letters), Soyuz Sovetskikh Sotsialisticheskikh Respublik (USSR, 43) and Ceskoslovenská Socialistická Republika (Czechoslovakia, 36). Uruguay's official name of La República Oriental del Uruguay is sometimes given in full as the 38-letter La República de la Banda Oriental del Uruguay, which would place it in 6th position.

▶ **The long and the short of it**
A bustling market in Libya. The country's short and commonly used name appeared in Egyptian hieroglyphics 4,000 years ago and is a fraction of the length of its modern official name, adopted on March 8, 1977, which means "The Great Socialist People's Libyan Arab Jamahiriya."

LONGEST PLACE NAMES*

	NAME	LETTERS
1	Krung thep mahanakhon bovorn ratanakosin mahintharayutthaya mahadilok pop noparatratchathani burirom udomratchanivetmahasathan amornpiman avatarnsathit sakkathattiyavisnukarmprasit	167

When the poetic name of Bangkok, capital of Thailand, is used, it is usually abbreviated to "Krung Thep" (city of angels).

2	Taumatawhakatangihangakoauauotamateaturipukakapiki-maungahoronukupokaiwhenuakitanatahu	85

This is the longer version (the other has a mere 83 letters) of the Maori name of a hill in New Zealand. It translates as "The place where Tamatea, the man with the big knees, who slid, climbed and swallowed mountains, known as land-eater, played on the flute to his loved one."

3	Gorsafawddachaidraigddanheddogleddollônpenrhyn-areurdraethceredigion	67

A name contrived by the Fairbourne Steam Railway, Gwynedd, North Wales, for publicity purposes and in order to outdo its rival, No. 4. It means "The Mawddach station and its dragon teeth at the Northern Penrhyn Road on the golden beach of Cardigan Bay."

4	Llanfairpwllgwyngyllgogerychwyrndrobwllllantysiliogogogoch	58

This is the place in Gwynedd famed especially for the length of its railway tickets. It means "St. Mary's Church in the hollow of the white hazel near the rapid whirlpool of the church of St. Tysilio near the Red Cave." Its official name, however, comprises only the first 20 letters, and the full name appears to have been invented as a hoax in the 19th century by a local tailor.

5	El Pueblo de Nuestra Señora la Reina de los Ángeles de la Porciúncula	57

The site of a Franciscan mission and the full Spanish name for the city of Los Angeles; it means "The town of Our Lady the Queen of the Angels of the Little Portion."

6	Chargoggagoggmanchaugagoggchaubunagungamaug	43

The longest US place name, a lake near Webster, Massachusetts. Its Indian name, loosely translated, means "You fish on your side, I'll fish on mine, and no one fishes in the middle." It is said to be pronounced "Char-gogg-a-gogg (pause) man-chaugg-a-gog (pause) chau-bun-a-gung-a-maug." It is, however, an invented extension of its real name (Chabunagungamaug, or "boundary fishing place"), devised in the 1920s by Larry Daly, the editor of the *Webster Times*.

7 =	Lower North Branch Little Southwest Miramichi	40

Canada's longest place name—a short river in New Brunswick.

=	Villa Real de la Santa Fé de San Francisco de Asis	40

The full Spanish name of Santa Fe, New Mexico, translates as "Royal city of the holy faith of St. Francis of Assisi."

9	Te Whakatakanga-o-te-ngarehu-o-te-ahi-a-Tamatea	38

The Maori name of Hammer Springs, New Zealand; like the second name in this list, it refers to a legend of Tamatea, explaining how the springs were warmed by "the falling of the cinders of the fire of Tamatea."

10	Meallan Liath Coire Mhic Dhubhghaill	32

The longest multiple name in Scotland, a place near Aultanrynie, Highland, alternatively spelled Meallan Liath Coire Mhic Dhughaill (30 letters).

* Including single-word, hyphenated, and multiple names

LARGEST COUNTRIES* NAMED AFTER REAL PEOPLE

	COUNTRY	NAMED AFTER	AREA (SQ MILES)	(SQ KM)
1	United States of America	Amerigo Vespucci (Italy; 1451–1512)	3,539,245	9,166,601
2	Saudi Arabia	Abdul Aziz ibn-Saud (Nejd; 1882–1953)	830,000	2,149,690
3	Bolivia	Simón Bolívar (Venezuela; 1783–1830)	418,685	1,084,389
4	Colombia	Christopher Columbus (Italy; 1451–1506)	401,044	1,038,699
5	Philippines	Philip II (Spain; 1527–98)	115,124	298,171
6	Falkland Islands	Lucius Cary, 2nd Viscount Falkland (UK; c. 1610–43)	4,700	12,173
7	Northern Mariana	Maria Theresa (Austria; 1717–80)	184	477
8	Wallis & Futuna	Samuel Wallis (UK; 1728–95)	105	274
9	Cook Islands	Capt. James Cook (UK; 1728–79)	93	241
10	Marshall Islands	Capt. John Marshall (UK; 1748–after 1818)	70	181

* Including dependencies

Many countries were named after mythical characters, or saints of dubious historical authenticity—often because they were discovered on the saint's day—but these are all named after real people. It is questionable whether China is named after the Emperor Chin, but if so, it would rank first.

MOST COMMON PLACE NAMES IN THE US

	PLACE NAME	OCCURRENCES
1	Fairview	287
2	Midway	252
3	Riverside	180
4	Oak Grove	179
5	Five Points	155
6	Oakland	149
7	Greenwood	145
8 =	Bethel	141
=	Franklin	141
10	Pleasant Hill	140

Source: *US Geological Survey*

Great Buildings

TALLEST TELECOMMUNICATIONS TOWERS

	TOWER/LOCATION	YEAR COMPLETED	HEIGHT (FT)	(M)
1	**CN Tower,** Toronto, Canada	1975	1,821	555
2	**Ostankino Tower*,** Moscow, Russia	1967	1,762	537
3	**Oriental Pearl Broadcasting Tower,** Shanghai, China	1995	1,535	468
4	**Borj-e Milad Telecommunications Tower,** Tehran, Iran	2003#	1,426	435
5	**Menara Telecom Tower,** Kuala Lumpur, Malaysia	1996	1,381	421
6	**Tianjin TV and Radio Tower,** Tianjin, China	1991	1,362	415
7	**Central Radio and TV Tower,** Beijing, China	1994	1,328	405
8	**TV Tower,** Tashkent, Uzbekistan	1983	1,230	375
9	**Liberation Tower,** Kuwait City, Kuwait	1998	1,220	372
10	**Alma-Ata Tower,** Kazakhstan	1983	1,215	370

* Severely damaged by fire, August 2000

Under construction; scheduled completion date

CANADA'S FIRST WORLD RECORD TOWER

WHILE EVER-TALLER HABITABLE BUILDINGS have seized the record in recent years, the CN Tower, Toronto, Canada, has retained its place as Canada's and the world's tallest freestanding structure for almost 30 years. Built by 1,537 construction workers between February 5, 1973, and April 2, 1975, the finished tower weighs 130,000 tons (117,910 metric tons). It features a glass floor at a height of 1,122 ft (342 m), across which brave visitors can walk while looking straight down.

TALLEST HOTELS

	HOTEL*/LOCATION/YEAR COMPLETED	STOREYS	HEIGHT# (FT)	(M)
1	**Jin Mao Tower,** Shanghai, China, 1998 *Grand Hyatt Hotel occupies floors 53–87*	88	1,214	370
2	**Shimao International Plaza,** Shanghai, China, 2004† *48 floors of hotel occupancy proposed*	60	1,093	333
3	**Baiyoke Tower 2,** Bangkok, Thailand, 1997 *Baiyoke Sky Hotel occupies floors 22–74*	89	1,013	309
4	**Burj Al Arab,** Dubai, United Arab Emirates, 1999	60	885	270
5	**Emirates Tower 2,** Dubai, United Arab Emirates, 1999	50	858	262
6	**Thai Wah Tower II,** Bangkok, Thailand, 1996 *Westin Banyan Tree Hotel occupies floors 33–60*	60	853	260
7	**Grand Duta Hyatt,** Kuala Lumpur, Malaysia, 2004†	60	798	243
8	**Four Seasons Hotel and Tower,** Miami, Florida, USA, 2002, *Hotel occupies lower floors*	54	788	241
9	**JR Central Towers,** Nagoya, Japan, 1999	53	787	240
10	**Grand Gateway,** Shanghai, China (twin towers), 2002	52	765	233

* Including mixed occupancy (hotel + residential/office) buildings

Excluding spires

† Under construction; scheduled completion date

◀ **High life**
The striking, sail-like Burj Al Arab hotel, Dubai, is the world's tallest all-hotel building. The structure stands on a man-made island and contains a record-breaking 590-ft (180-m) atrium.

TOP 10 TALLEST HABITABLE BUILDINGS

BUILDING/LOCATION	YEAR COMPLETED	STORIES	HEIGHT* (FT)	(M)
1 **Union Square,** Hong Kong, China	2008#	101	1,575	480
2 **Petronas Towers,** Kuala Lumpur, Malaysia	1996	96	1,482	452
3 **Taipei Financial Center,** Taipei, China	2003#	101	1,470	448
4 **Sears Tower,** Chicago, IL	1974	110	1,454	443
5 **Two International Financial Center,** Hong Kong, China	2003#	88	1,350	412
6 **Jin Mao Building,** Shanghai, China	1997	93	1,255	382
7 **Empire State Building,** New York, NY	1931	102	1,250	381
8 **Tuntex & Chien-Tai Tower,** Kao-hsiung, Taiwan	1997	85	1,142	348
9 **AON Building,** Chicago, IL	1973	80	1,136	346
10 **John Hancock Center,** Chicago, IL	1969	100	1,127	343

* Excluding spires

 # Under construction; scheduled completion date

TOP 10 TALLEST CATHEDRALS AND CHURCHES

CATHEDRAL OR CHURCH/LOCATION	YEAR COMPLETED	HEIGHT (FT)	(M)
1 **Chicago Methodist Temple*,** Chicago, IL	1924	568	173
2 **Sagrada Familia,** Barcelona, Spain	2020#	558	170
3 **Santuario de los Santos Mártires de Cristo Rey y Santa María de Guadalupe,** Tlaquepaque, Mexico	2004#	551	168
4 **Ulm Cathedral,** Ulm, Germany	1890	528	161
5 **Notre Dame de la Paix,** Yamoussoukro, Côte d'Ivoire	1989	519	158
6 **Cologne Cathedral,** Cologne, Germany	1880	513	156
7 **Rouen Cathedral,** Rouen, France	1876	485	148
8 **St. Nicholas,** Hamburg, Germany	1847	475	145
9 **Notre Dame,** Strasbourg, France	1439	465	142
10 **Queen of Peace Shrine and Basilica,** Lichen, Poland	—#	459	140

* Sited on top of a 25-story, 328-ft (100-m) building

 # Under construction; scheduled completion date (where announced)

▶ **Tall temple**
The Chicago Methodist Temple was completed in 1924 at a cost of $3 million. It was the tallest building in the city until the Chicago Board of Trade was completed in 1930, but it remains the world's tallest church.

Under & Over

TOP 10 | LONGEST CABLE-STAYED BRIDGES

	BRIDGE/LOCATION	YEAR COMPLETED	LENGTH OF MAIN SPAN (FT)	(M)
1	**Tatara,** Onomichi-Imabari, Japan	1999	2,920	890
2	**Pont de Normandie,** Le Havre, France	1994	2,808	856
3	**Second Nanjing,** Nanjing, China	2001	2,060	628
4	**Third Yangtze,** Wuhan, China	2000	2,000	618
5	**Qinghzhou Minjiang,** Fozhou, China	1996	1,985	605
6	**Yang Pu,** Shanghai, China	1993	1,975	602
7	= **Meiko-chuo,** Nagoya, Japan	1997	1,936	590
	= **Xu Pu,** Shanghai, China	1997	1,936	590
9	**Patras,** Greece	—*	1,837	560
10	**Skarnsundet,** Trondheim Fjord, Norway	1991	1,739	530

* Under construction

The first true cable-stayed bridge, a design in which large steel uprights transmit the load to the deck via steel cables, was built at Strömsund, Sweden, in 1956. After this, the technology was used extensively in Germany before being adopted in Asia, where seven of the world's Top 10 are now located.

TOP 10 | LONGEST SUSPENSION BRIDGES

	BRIDGE/LOCATION	YEAR COMPLETED	LENGTH OF MAIN SPAN (FT)	(M)
1	**Akashi-Kaikyo,** Kobe-Naruto, Japan	1998	6,532	1,991
2	**Izmit Bay,** Turkey	—*	5,472	1,668
3	**Great Belt,** Denmark	1997	5,328	1,624
4	**Humber Estuary,** UK	1980	4,626	1,410
5	**Jiangyin,** China	1998	4,544	1,385
6	**Tsing Ma,** Hong Kong, China	1997	4,518	1,377
7	**Verrazano Narrows,** New York, NY	1964	4,260	1,298
8	**Golden Gate,** San Francisco, CA	1937	4,200	1,280
9	**Höga Kusten** (High Coast), Veda, Sweden	1997	3,970	1,210
10	**Mackinac Straits,** Michigan	1957	3,800	1,158

* Under construction

The Messina Strait Bridge between Sicily and Calabria, Italy, received the go-ahead in June 2002, with work to begin in 2004–05; it will take 5–6 years and cost 4.6 billion ($4.9 billion). It will have by far the longest center span of any bridge at 10,827 ft (3,300 m), although at 12,828 ft (3,910 m) Japan's Akashi-Kaikyo bridge, completed in 1998, and with a main span of 1,990 m (6,529 ft), is the world's longest overall.

TOP 10 | LONGEST STEEL-ARCH BRIDGES

	BRIDGE/LOCATION	YEAR COMPLETED	LONGEST SPAN (FT)	(M)
1	**New River Gorge,** Fayetteville, West Virginia	1977	1,700	518
2	**Kill van Kull,** Bayonne, New Jersey/ Staten Island, New York	1931	1,652	504
3	**Sydney Harbor,** Australia	1932	1,650	503
4	**Wanxian,** Yangtse River, China	1997	1,378	420
5	**Fremont,** Portland, Oregon	1973	1,257	383
6	**Port Mann,** Vancouver, Canada	1964	1,200	366
7	**Thatcher Ferry,** Panama Canal	1962	1,128	344
8	**Laviolette,** Quebec, Canada	1967	1,100	335
9	**Zdákov,** Lake Orlik, Czech Republic	1967	1,083	330
10	**Runcorn-Widnes,** UK	1961	1,082	330

▶ **Longest bridge so far**
The longest, tallest, and most expensive bridge in the world, Japan's Akashi-Kaikyo measures 12,828 ft (3,910 m) overall. It was built to withstand winds of up to 180 mph (290 km/h) and earthquakes of up to 8.5 on the Richter Scale.

TOP 10 LONGEST UNDERWATER TUNNELS

	TUNNEL/LOCATION	YEAR COMPLETED	LENGTH (FT)	LENGTH (M)
1	Seikan, Japan	1988	176,673	53,850
2	Channel Tunnel, France/England	1994	165,518	50,450
3	Dai-Shimizu, Japan	1982	72,904	22,221
4	Shin-Kanmon, Japan	1975	61,286	18,680
5	Tokyo Bay Aqualine Expressway*, Japan	1997	31,440	9,583
6	Great Belt Fixed Link (Eastern Tunnel), Denmark	1997	26,325	8,024
7	Bømlafjord*, Norway	2000	25,988	7,921
8	Oslofjord*, Norway	2000	23,819	7,260
9	Severn, UK	1886	22,992	7,008
10	Magerøysund*, Norway	1999	22,556	6,875

* Road; others rail

The need to connect the Japanese islands of Honshu, Kyushu, and Hokkaido has resulted in a recent wave of undersea tunnel building, with the Seikan the most ambitious project of all. Connecting Honshu and Hokkaido, 14.4 miles (23.3 km) of the tunnel is 328 ft (100 m) below the seabed, bored through strata that presented such enormous engineering problems that it took 24 years to complete.

TOP 10 LONGEST RAIL TUNNELS

	TUNNEL/LOCATION	YEAR COMPLETED	LENGTH (MILES)	LENGTH (KM)
1	Seikan, Japan	1988	33.46	53.85
2	Channel Tunnel, France/England	1994	31.35	50.45
3	Moscow Metro (Medvedkovo/Belyaevo section), Russia	1979	19.07	30.70
4	London Underground (East Finchley/ Morden, Northern Line), UK	1939	17.30	27.84
5	Hakkoda, Japan	—*	16.44	26.46
6	Iwate, Japan	—*	16.04	25.81
7	Iiyama, Japan	—*	13.98	22.50
8	Dai-Shimizu, Japan	1982	13.81	22.22
9	Simplon II, Italy/Switzerland	1922	12.31	19.82
10	Simplon I, Italy/Switzerland	1906	12.30	19.80

* Under construction

The world's longest rail tunnel, the Gotthard AlpTransit, Switzerland, is scheduled for completion in 2010, and will measure 35.46 miles (57.07 km). Further rail tunnels over 12.43 miles (20 km) in length are in the planning stages in Austria, France, Italy, Spain, and Switzerland.

TOP 10 LONGEST ROAD TUNNELS

	TUNNEL/LOCATION	YEAR COMPLETED	LENGTH (FT)	LENGTH (M)
1	Laerdal, Norway	2000	80,413	24,510
2	Zhongnanshan, China	2007*	59,186	18,040
3	St. Gotthard, Switzerland	1980	55,505	16,918
4	Arlberg, Austria	1978	45,850	13,972
5	Pinglin Highway, Taiwan	2003*	42,323	12,900
6	Fréjus, France/Italy	1980	42,306	12,895
7	Mont-Blanc, France/Italy	1965	38,094	11,611
8	Gudvangen, Norway	1991	37,493	11,428
9	Folgefonn, Norway	2001	36,417	11,100
10	Kan-Etsu II (southbound), Japan	1990	36,122	11,010

* Under construction; scheduled completion date

Nos. 1, 3, 4, and 7 have all held the record as "world's longest road tunnel." Previous record-holders include the 19,206-ft (5,854-m) Grand San Bernardo (Italy–Switzerland; 1964), the 16,841-ft (5,133-m) Alfonso XIII or Viella (Spain; 1948), the 10,620-ft (3,237-m) Queensway (Mersey) Tunnel (connecting Liverpool and Birkenhead, UK; 1934), and the 10,453-ft (3,186-m) Col de Tende (France–Italy; 1882), originally built as a rail tunnel and converted in 1928.

CULTURE & LEARNING

Mind Your Language

TOP 10 — MOST WIDELY SPOKEN LANGUAGES

	LANGUAGE	APPROX. NO. OF SPEAKERS
1	Chinese (Mandarin)	874,000,000
2	Hindustani*	426,000,000
3	Spanish	358,000,000
4	English	341,000,000
5	Bengali	207,000,000
6	Arabic#	206,000,000
7	Portuguese	176,000,000
8	Russian	167,000,000
9	Japanese	125,000,000
10	German (standard)	100,000,000

Hindi and Urdu are essentially the same language, Hindustani; as the official language of Pakistan it is written in modified Arabic script and called Urdu; as the official language of India it is written in the Devanagari script and called Hindi

Includes 16 variants of the Arabic language

TOP 10 — LANGUAGES OFFICIALLY SPOKEN IN THE MOST COUNTRIES

	LANGUAGE	COUNTRIES
1	English	57
2	French	33
3	Arabic	23
4	Spanish	21
5	Portuguese	7
6 =	Dutch	5
=	German	5
8 =	Chinese (Mandarin)	3
=	Danish	3
=	Italian	3
=	Malay	3

There are many countries in the world with more than one official language—both English and French are recognized officially in Canada, for example. English is used in numerous countries as the lingua franca, the common language that enables people who speak mutually unintelligible languages to communicate with each other.

TOP 10 — COUNTRIES WITH THE MOST ENGLISH-LANGUAGE SPEAKERS

	LANGUAGE	APPROX. NO. OF SPEAKERS*
1	US	237,320,000
2	UK	58,090,000
3	Canada	18,218,000
4	Australia	15,561,000
5	Ireland	3,720,000
6	South Africa	3,700,000
7	New Zealand	3,338,000
8	Jamaica#	2,460,000
9	Trinidad and Tobago#†	1,245,000
10	Guyana#	764,000

People for whom English is their mother tongue

Includes English Creole

† *Trinidad English*

The Top 10 represents the countries with the greatest numbers of inhabitants who speak English as their mother tongue, rather than those who understand or speak it as a second language.

TOP 10 COUNTRIES WITH THE MOST FRENCH-LANGUAGE SPEAKERS

	COUNTRY	APPROX. NO. OF SPEAKERS*
1	France	55,100,000
2	Canada	7,158,000
3	Haiti#	6,868,000
4	Belgium†	3,350,000
5	US§	2,250,000
6	Switzerland	1,380,000
7	Mauritius§	878,000
8	Réunion#	660,000
9	Guadeloupe§	407,000
10	Martinique§	372,000

* People for whom French is their mother tongue

French Creole

† Walloon French

§ French/French Creole

TOP 10 COUNTRIES WITH THE MOST SPANISH-LANGUAGE SPEAKERS

	COUNTRY	APPROX. NO. OF SPEAKERS*
1	Mexico	91,080,000
2	Colombia	41,880,000
3	Argentina	35,860,000
4	Spain#	29,860,000
5	Venezuela	23,310,000
6	US	20,720,000
7	Peru	20,470,000
8	Chile	13,640,000
9	Ecuador	11,760,000
10	Dominican Republic	8,270,000

* People for whom Spanish is their mother tongue

Castilian Spanish

TOP 10 ONLINE LANGUAGES

	LANGUAGE	INTERNET ACCESS*
1	English	280,000,000
2	Chinese	170,000,000
3	Japanese	90,000,000
4	Spanish	68,000,000
5	German	62,000,000
6	Korean	43,000,000
7	French	41,000,000
8	Italian	35,000,000
9	Portuguese	32,000,000
10	Russian	23,000,000
	World total	940,000,000

* Online population estimate for 2004

Source: Global Reach

THE FIRST DICTIONARY

FIRST FACT

In London in 1604, Robert Cawdrey's *A Table Alphabeticall, containing the true writing and understanding of hard usuall English wordes*, considered the first ever English dictionary, was published. Cawdrey assembled a collection that originally contained 2,543 words, expanded to over 3,200 in later editions. The definitions are simple one-line entries, using 17th-century spelling, so "medicine" is defined as "remedie, or cure" and "corps" as "deade bodie." A single copy of this pioneering book survives.

◀ **Chinese whispers**
Mandarin, the official Chinese dialect based on the pronunciation used in Beijing, is spoken by more than two-thirds of the population, making it the world's most used language.

TOP 10 COUNTRIES WITH THE MOST GERMAN-LANGUAGE SPEAKERS

	COUNTRY	APPROX. NO. OF SPEAKERS*
1	Germany	75,060,000
2	Austria	7,444,000
3	Switzerland	4,570,000
4	US	1,850,000
5	Brazil	910,000
6	Poland	500,000
7	Canada	486,000
8	Kazakhstan	460,000
9	Russia	350,000
10	Italy	310,000

* People for whom German is their mother tongue

German is the national language of Germany and Austria, and is one of four official languages in Switzerland. As a result of the diaspora, whereby more than seven million people emigrated from Germany to the US and settled in many other parts of the world, German is spoken by expatriate groups in countries as far flung as Paraguay and Namibia.

TOP 10 COUNTRIES WITH THE MOST ARABIC-LANGUAGE SPEAKERS

	COUNTRY	APPROX. NO. OF SPEAKERS*
1	Egypt	65,080,000
2	Algeria	26,280,000
3	Saudi Arabia	20,920,000
4	Morocco	18,730,000
5	Iraq	17,490,000
6	Yemen	17,400,000
7	Sudan	17,320,000
8	Syria	14,680,000
9	Tunisia#	6,710,000
10	Libya	4,910,000

* People for whom Arabic is their mother tongue

Another 2,520,000 people speak Arabic-French and 300,000 speak Arabic-English

Islamic invasions carried Arabic throughout the Middle East and North Africa, while certain Arabic words, such as alcohol, giraffe, and magazine, reached Europe, where they were adopted into English.

Libraries of the World

LARGEST LIBRARIES

	LIBRARY	LOCATION	FOUNDED	BOOKS
1	Library of Congress	Washington DC, US	1800	24,616,867
2	National Library of China	Beijing, China	1909	22,000,00
3	Library of the Russian Academy of Science	St. Petersburg, Russia	1714	20,000,000
4	Deutsche Bibliothek*	Frankfurt, Germany	1990	16,593,000
5	National Library of Canada	Ottawa, Canada	1953	16,000,000
6	British Library#	London, UK	1753	15,000,000
7	Harvard University Library	Cambridge, Massachusetts, US	1638	14,437,361
8	Institute for Scientific Information on the Social Sciences of the Russian Academy of Science	Moscow, Russia	1969	13,500,000
9	Vernadsky Central Scientific Library of the National Academy of Sciences	Kiev, Ukraine	1919	13,000,000
10	Bibliothèque National de France	Paris, France	1400	11,000,000

Formed in 1990 through the unification of the Deutsche Bibliothek, Frankfurt (founded 1947) and the Deutsche Bucherei, Leipzig

 # Founded as part of the British Museum, 1753; became an independent body in 1973

FIRST PUBLIC LIBRARIES IN THE US

	LIBRARY/LOCATION	FOUNDED
1	**Peterboro Public Library,** Peterboro, NH	1833
2	**New Orleans Public Library,** New Orleans, LA	1843
3	**Boston Public Library,** Boston, MA	1852
4	**Public Library of Cincinnati and Hamilton County,** Cincinnati, OH	1853
5	**Springfield City Library,** Springfield, MA	1857
6	**Worcester Public Library,** Worcester, MA	1859
7	**Multnomah County Library,** Portland, OR	1864
8 =	**Detroit Public Library,** Detroit, MI	1865
=	**St. Louis Public Library,** St. Louis, MO	1865
10	**Atlanta-Fulton Public Library,** Atlanta, GA	1867

Source: *Public Library Association*

Shelf life
The founding of the National Library of Austria dates from 1368, when Archduke Albrecht III established it in the Imperial Castle, Vienna.

LARGEST UNIVERSITY LIBRARIES IN THE US

	LIBRARY	VOLUMES HELD
1	Harvard University Library	14,437,361
2	Yale University Library	10,492,812
3	University of Illinois-Urbana Library	9,469,620
4	University of California-Berkeley Library	9,107,757
5	University of Texas-Austin Library	7,935,540
6	University of California-Los Angeles Library	7,517,303
7	University of Michigan-Ann Arbor Library	7,348,360
8	Stanford University Library	7,286,437
9	Columbia University-Main Division Library	7,266,499
10	Cornell University	6,609,332

Source: *American Library Association*

FIRST PRESIDENTIAL LIBRARIES

	LIBRARY	FOUNDED
1	Franklin D. Roosevelt Library	July 4, 1940
2	Harry S. Truman Library	July 6, 1957
3	Herbert Hoover Library	Aug. 10, 1962
4	Lyndon Baines Johnson Library	May 22, 1971
5	Dwight D. Eisenhower Library	May 1, 1972
6	John Fitzgerald Kennedy Library	Oct. 20, 1979
7	Gerald R. Ford Library	Apr. 27, 1981
8	Jimmy Carter Library	Oct. 1, 1986
9	Ronald Reagan Library	Nov. 4, 1991
10	George Bush Library	Nov. 6, 1997

The founding of the George Bush Library in 1997 brought the total number of presidential libraries to 10.

▶ **Reading room**
The New York Public Library is one of the world's largest public libraries. In addition to its holdings of books, it houses over 30 million cataloged items.

OLDEST NATIONAL LIBRARIES

	LIBRARY/LOCATION	FOUNDED
1	**Narodní Knihovne Ceské Republiky** National Library of the Czech Republic, Prague, Czech Republic	1366
2	**Österreichische Nationalbibliothek** National Library of Austria, Vienna, Austria	1368
3	**Biblioteca Nazionale Marciana,** Venice, Italy	1468
4	**Bibliothèque Nationale de France** National Library of France, Paris, France	1480
5	**National Library of Malta,** Valetta, Malta	1555
6	**Bayericsche Staatsbibliothek,** Munich, Germany	1558
7	**Bibliothèque Royale Albert 1er** National Library of Belgium, Brussels, Belgium	1559
8	**Nacionalna i Sveucilisna Knjiznica** Zagreb National and University Library, Zagreb, Croatia	1606
9	**Helsingin Yliopiston Kirjasto** National Library of Finland, Helsinki, Finland	1640
10	**Kongeligie Bibliotek** National Library of Denmark, Copenhagen, Denmark	1653

LARGEST PUBLIC LIBRARIES

	LIBRARY/BRANCHES	LOCATION	FOUNDED	BOOKS
1	**Chicago Public Library** (79)	Chicago, IL	1872	10,994,943
2	**New York Public Library** (The Branch Libraries) (85)	New York, NY	1895*	10,608,570[#]
3	**Queens Borough Public Library** (62)	Jamaica, New York, NY	1896	10,357,159
4	**Public Library of Cincinnati and Hamilton County** (41)	Cincinnati, OH	1853	9,952,009
5	**County of Los Angeles Public Library** (85)	Los Angeles, CA	1872	8,235,100
6	**Shanghai Public Library**	Shanghai, China	1952[†]	8,200,000
7	**Boston Public Library** (25)	Boston, MA	1852	7,736,451
8	**Brooklyn Public Library** (58)	Brooklyn, New York, NY	1896	7,189,998
9	**Free Library of Philadelphia** (52)	Philadelphia, PA	1891	6,225,098
10	**Los Angeles Public Library** (67)	Los Angeles, CA	1872	6,023,257

* Astor Library founded 1848; consolidated with Lenox Library and Tilden Trust to form New York Public Library, 1895

[#] Lending library and reference library holdings available for loan

[†] Opened to the public 1996

Schooling & Further Education

TOP 10 COUNTRIES SPENDING THE MOST ON EDUCATION

	COUNTRY	PUBLIC EXPENDITURE AS PERCENTAGE OF GNP* (1999/2000)
1	Zimbabwe	11.05
2	Papua New Guinea	10.00
3	Botswana	9.32
4	Saudi Arabia	9.27
5	Denmark	8.04
6	St. Lucia	8.01
7	Lesotho	7.93
8 =	Namibia	7.89#
=	Seychelles	7.89
10	Sweden	7.86
	US	5.04

* Gross National Product; in those countries for which data are available

1998/1999 data

Source: UNESCO

If the Marshall Islands were a country, it would top this list, with the 1998/1999 public expenditure on education at 15.39 percent of this US territory's gross national income.

TOP 10 COUNTRIES WITH THE FEWEST PRIMARY SCHOOL PUPILS PER TEACHER

	COUNTRY	PUPIL/TEACHER RATIO IN PRIMARY SCHOOLS (1999/2000)
1	San Marino	5.36
2	Libya	8.44*
3	Denmark	10.12
4	Hungary	10.71
5	Iceland	10.93
6	Italy	10.96
7	Cuba	11.50
8	Sweden	11.84
9	Saudi Arabia	11.99
10	Brunei	13.10

* 1998/1999

Source: UNESCO

▼ A class of their own
Relatively small elementary school class sizes in such countries as Hungary contrast with those in some African countries, which may be up to five times as large.

THE 10 COUNTRIES WITH THE LOWEST PERCENTAGE OF CHILDREN IN ELEMENTARY SCHOOL

	COUNTRY	% CHILDREN ENROLLED IN ELEMENTARY SCHOOL (1999/2000)*		
		GIRLS	BOYS	TOTAL
1	Niger	20.58	21.82	21.19
2	Angola	29.22	25.42	27.32
3	Djibouti	34.85	26.29	30.59
4	Ethiopia	34.46	27.74	31.11
5	Dem. Rep. of Congo	33.44	31.82	32.63#
6	Burkina Faso	34.63	28.31	34.63
7	Eritrea	43.28	37.39	40.34
8	Mali	50.71	35.89	43.32#
9	Burundi	49.35	39.57	44.46
10	Sudan	48.60	40.75	44.74
	US	94.67	94.60	94.64

* In those countries for which data are available

1998/1999

Source: UNESCO

TOP 10 COUNTRIES WITH THE HIGHEST PERCENTAGE OF HIGH SCHOOL GRADS IN FURTHER EDUCATION

	COUNTRY	% HIGH SCHOOL GRADS IN FURTHER EDUCATION (1999/2000)*		
		FEMALE	MALE	TOTAL
1	Finland	83.79	91.89	76.01
2	South Korea	51.97	90.28	71.69
3	US	81.45	62.17	71.62
4	Norway	81.59	55.74	68.40
5	Sweden	79.05	54.17	66.32
6	New Zealand	80.25	53.04	66.31
7	Russia	72.99	57.38	65.10
8	Australia	69.80	56.51	63.00
9	Canada	68.82	51.57	59.99
10	Spain	62.32	53.01	57.56

* Total enrollment in further education taken as a percentage of the five-year age-group following on from high school graduation age; in those countries for which data is available

Source: UNESCO

TOP 10 BACHELOR'S DEGREES IN THE US (MALE)

	DEGREE	NO. CONFERRED ON MEN (1999–2000)
1	Business administration and management	48,747
2	Engineering	46,525
3	Communications	21,289
4	Biology, general	18,239
5	Computer and information sciences, general	16,261
6	Psychology, general	16,193
7	Teacher education, academic and vocational programs	15,557
8	Finance, general and banking and financial support services	15,537
9	History	14,866
10	Political science and government	14,544
	All subjects	530,367

Source: National Center for Educational Statistics

TOP 10 BACHELOR'S DEGREES IN THE US (FEMALE)

	DEGREE	NO. CONFERRED ON WOMEN (1999–2000)
1	Psychology	52,552
2	General teacher education	52,331
3	Business administration and management	48,402
4	Nursing	35,622
5	Communications	34,471
6	Biology, general	26,743
7	English language and literature	25,940
8	Accounting	21,262
9	Teacher education academic and vocational programs	18,229
10	Sociology	17,969
	All subjects	707,508

Source: National Center for Educational Statistics

By the Book

TOP 10 BESTSELLING PENGUIN CLASSICS

	TITLE/AUTHOR	WRITTEN/FIRST PUBLISHED*
1	**Emma,** Jane Austen	1816
2	**Pride and Prejudice,** Jane Austen	1813
3	**Wuthering Heights,** Emily Brontë	1847
4	**Jane Eyre,** Charlotte Brontë	1847
5	**The Canterbury Tales,** Geoffrey Chaucer	1387
6	**Great Expectations,** Charles Dickens	1862
7	**The Odyssey,** Homer	*c.* 8th cent. BC
8	**The Prince,** Niccolò Machiavelli	1513
9	**The Republic,** Plato	*c.* 368 BC
10	**Frankenstein,** Mary Shelley	1818

* In book form (some 19th-century novels were originally issued in weekly parts before appearing as books)

The Penguin Classics series was started in 1946 by classicist E. V. Rieu (1887–1972), whose own translation of Homer's *Odyssey*, undertaken during World War II and the first title published, remains in the Top 10, having sold almost three million copies. The series now comprises some 850 titles, with about 60 additions annually.

PENGUIN CLASSICS

JANE AUSTEN
Emma

TOP 10 US HARDBACK NONFICTION BESTSELLERS, 2002

	TITLE/AUTHOR	SALES
1	**Self Matters,** Phillip C. McGraw	1,350,000
2	**A Life God Rewards,** Bruce Wilkinson with David Kopp	1,186,000
3	**Let's Roll!,** Lisa Beamer with Ken Abraham	958,208
4	**Guinness World Records 2003**	919,953
5	**Who Moved My Cheese?,** Spencer Johnson	850,000
6	**Leadership,** Rudolph W. Giuliani	801,470
7	**Prayer of Jabez for Women,** Darlene Wilkinson	704,626
8	**Bush at War,** Bob Woodward	690,000
9	**Portrait of a Killer,** Patricia Cornwell	683,340
10	**Body for Life,** Bill Phillips	676,464

Source: Publishers Weekly

The US nonfiction bestsellers list has been dominated for years by self-help books, led in 2002 by "Dr. Phil" McGraw's *Self Matters*, whose subtitle, "Creating Your Life from the Inside Out," and that of Johnson's *Who Moved My Cheese?* ("An Amazing Way to Deal With Change in Your Work and Your Life") summarize the aspirations of such titles. Personal accounts of the events of and in the wake of 9/11 in Beamer's *Let's Roll!* and Giuliani's *Leadership* also proved immensely popular during the year.

◀ Pride of place
Almost 200 years after they were written, Jane Austen's *Emma,* followed by her *Pride and Prejudice,* top the Penguin Classics bestseller list.

TOP 10 HARDBACK FICTION TITLES IN THE US, 2002

	TITLE/AUTHOR	SALES
1	**The Summons,** John Grisham	2,625,000
2	**Red Rabbit,** Tom Clancy	1,970,932
3	**Remnant,** Jerry B. Jenkins and Tim LaHaye	1,880,549
4	**The Lovely Bones,** Alice Seybold	1,841,825
5	**Prey,** Michael Crichton	1,496,807
6	**Skipping Christmas,** John Grisham	1,225,000
7	**The Shelters of Stone,** Jean M. Auel	1,223,105
8	**Four Blind Mice,** James Patterson	1,060,470
9	**Everything's Eventual,** Stephen King	925,000
10	**The Nanny Diaries,** Emma McLaughlin and Nicola Kraus	852,021

Source: Publishers Weekly

Grisham, Clancy, Crichton, and King have dominated the US fiction bestsellers lists for many years, while movies derived from their novels, including Grisham's *The Firm* (1993), Clancy's *Clear and Present Danger* (1994), Crichton's *Jurassic Park* (1993), and King's *The Green Mile* (1999), are among the biggest box-office hits of the past 10 years.

TOP 10 MASS-MARKET PAPERBACK BESTSELLERS, 2002

	TITLE/AUTHOR	SALES
1	The Summons, John Grisham	3,965,000
2	The Lord of the Rings: The Two Towers, J. R. R. Tolkien	2,828,087
3	Face the Fire, Nora Roberts	2,700,269
4	The Villa, Nora Roberts	2,204,755
5	Midnight Bayou, Nora Roberts	2,034,602
6	On the Street Where You Live, Mary Higgins Clark	1,796,342
7	The Lord of the Rings: The Fellowship of the Ring, J. R. R. Tolkien	1,718,720
8	The Hobbit, J. R. R. Tolkien	1,710,430
9	The Kiss, Danielle Steel	1,610,000
10	Isle of Dogs, Patricia Cornwell	1,601,026

Source: Publishers Weekly

As the link between books and films has been increasingly exemplified in recent years, 2002 saw a surge in interest in the works of J. R. R. Tolkien resulting from the release and worldwide success of the movies of *The Lord of the Rings: The Fellowship of the Ring* and *The Lord of the Rings: The Two Towers*. They, and J. K. Rowling's *Harry Potter* phenomenon, have also created a new enthusiasm for books featuring magic and wizardry, which Nora Roberts has skillfully woven into her Three Sisters Island trilogy, of which *Face the Fire* was the concluding part. A permanent resident of the fiction bestseller list since 1981, with every book going to No. 1, and with 390 consecutive weeks in the *New York Times* bestseller list, Danielle Steel is in a class apart, with a total of more than 350 million copies of her books in print. Patricia Cornwell's *Isle of Dogs* was a surprising, albeit successful, departure in that it was a comic novel that did not feature her popular Chief Medical Examiner character Kay Scarpetta.

▲ **Summons at the summit**
John Grisham's *The Summons* topped both the hardback and paperback bestseller lists in 2002, with cumulative sales of over 6.5 million.

TOP 10 BESTSELLING BOOKS OF ALL TIME

	BOOK/AUTHOR/FIRST PUBLISHED	APPROX. SALES
1	The Bible, c. 1451–55	more than 6,000,000,000
2	Quotations from the Works of Mao Tse-tung, 1966	900,000,000
3	The Lord of the Rings, J. R. R. Tolkien, 1954–55	over 100,000,000
4	American Spelling Book, Noah Webster, 1783	up to 100,000,000
5	The Guinness Book of Records (now *Guinness World Records*), 1955	more than 92,000,000*
6	World Almanac, 1868	73,500,000*
7	The McGuffey Readers, William Holmes McGuffey, 1836	60,000,000
8	The Common Sense Book of Baby and Child Care, Benjamin Spock, 1946	more than 50,000,000
9	A Message to Garcia, Elbert Hubbard, 1899	up to 40,000,000
10 =	In His Steps: What Would Jesus Do?, Rev. Charles Monroe Sheldon, 1896	more than 30,000,000
=	Valley of the Dolls, Jacqueline Susann, 1966	more than 30,000,000

* Aggregate sales of annual publication

TOP 10 CHILDREN'S HARDBACK TITLES IN THE US, 2002

	TITLE/AUTHOR	SALES
1	The Carnivorous Carnival, Lemony Snicket and Brett Helquist (illustrator) (A Series of Unfortunate Events #9)	726,543
2	The Bad Beginning, Lemony Snicket and Brett Helquist (illustrator) (A Series of Unfortunate Events #1)	681,019
3	Harry Potter and the Goblet of Fire, J. K. Rowling	654,000
4	Goodnight, Margaret Wise Brown and Clement Hurd (illustrator) (board book)	639,694
5	If You Take a Mouse to School, Laura Numeroff and Felicia Bond (illustrator)	526,008
6	The Reptile Room, Lemony Snicket and Brett Helquist (illustrator) (A Series of Unfortunate Events #2)	504,964
7	Green Eggs and Ham, Dr. Seuss	497,772
8	Oh, The Places You'll Go!, Dr. Seuss	426,424
9	Five Little Monkeys Jumping on the Bed, Eileen Christelow (board book)	412,000
10	The Wide Window, Lemony Snicket and Brett Helquist (illustrator) (A Series of Unfortunate Events #3)	409,909

Source: Publishers Weekly

Literary Classics

THE 10 LATEST BOOKER PRIZE WINNERS

YEAR	AUTHOR	TITLE
2002	Yann Martel	Life of Pi
2001	Peter Carey	True History of the Kelly Gang
2000	Margaret Atwood	The Blind Assassin
1999	J. M. Coetzee	Disgrace
1998	Ian McEwan	Amsterdam
1997	Arundhati Roy	The God of Small Things
1996	Graham Swift	Last Orders
1995	Pat Barker	The Ghost Road
1994	James Kelman	How Late It Was, How Late
1993	Roddy Doyle	Paddy Clarke Ha Ha Ha

Two authors, South African J. M. Coetzee and Australian Peter Carey, have won the Booker prize twice: Coetzee in 1999 with *Disgrace* and in 1983 with *Life and Times of Michael K*; Carey with *Oscar and Lucinda* in 1988 and *True History of the Kelly Gang* in 2001.

THE 10 LATEST WINNERS OF THE NOBEL PRIZE FOR LITERATURE

YEAR	AUTHOR	COUNTRY
2002	Imre Kertész	Hungary
2001	V. S. Naipaul	UK
2000	Gao Xingjian	China
1999	Günter Grass	Germany
1998	José Saramago	Portugal
1997	Dario Fo	Italy
1996	Wislawa Szymborska	Poland
1995	Seamus Heaney	Ireland
1994	Kenzaburo Oe	Japan
1993	Toni Morrison	US

The Nobel Prize for Literature has been awarded since 1901, when it was won by the French poet Sully Prudhomme.

THE 10 LATEST WINNERS OF THE NATIONAL BOOK AWARD FOR FICTION

YEAR	AUTHOR	TITLE
2002	Julia Glass	Three Junes
2001	Jonathan Franzen	The Corrections
2000	Susan Sontag	In America
1999	Ha Jin	Waiting
1998	Alice McDermott	Charming Billy
1997	Charles Frazier	Cold Mountain
1996	Andrea Barrett	Ship Fever and Other Stories
1995	Philip Roth	Sabbath's Theater
1994	William Gaddis	A Frolic of His Own
1993	E. Annie Proulx	The Shipping News

This Award, now under the aegis of the National Book Foundation, has been presented since 1950.

◄ **Life story**
Canadian writer Yann Martel celebrates winning the prestigious Booker Prize for his surreal novel *Life of Pi*.

THE 10 LATEST WINNERS OF THE PULITZER PRIZE FOR FICTION

YEAR	AUTHOR	TITLE
2003	Jeffrey Eugenides	Middlesex
2002	Richard Russo	Empire Falls
2001	Michael Chabon	The Amazing Adventures of Kavalier & Clay
2000	Jhumpa Lhiri	Interpreter of Maladies
1999	Michael Cunningham	The Hours
1998	Philip Roth	American Pastoral
1997	Steven Millhauser	Martin Dressler: The Tale of an American Dreamer
1996	Richard Ford	Independence Day
1995	Carol Shields	The Stone Diaries
1994	E. Annie Proulx	The Shipping News

The Pulitzer Prize for Fiction has been awarded since 1915, with past recipients including Margaret Mitchell for *Gone with the Wind* (1937) and John Steinbeck for *The Grapes of Wrath* (1940).

TOP 10 MOST ANTHOLOGIZED ENGLISH POEMS

	POEM/POET	APPEARANCES
1	**The Tyger,** William Blake (British; 1757–1827)	170
2	**How Do I Love Thee? (Sonnet 42),** Elizabeth Barrett Browning (British; 1806–61)	136
3	**London,** William Blake (British; 1757–1827)	122
4	**With how sad steps, O Moon, thou climb'st the skies (Sonnet 31),** Philip Sidney (British; 1554–86)	98
5	**She dwelt among the untrodden ways ("Lucy"),** William Wordsworth (British; 1770–1850)	97
6	**Kubla Khan,** Samuel Taylor Coleridge (British; 1772–1834)	95
7	**La Belle Dame sans Merci,** John Keats (British; 1795–1821)	92
8	**To His Coy Mistress,** Andrew Marvell (British; 1621–78)	87
9	**Stopping by Woods on a Snowy Evening,** Robert Frost (American; 1874–1963)	85
10	**Love ("Love bade me welcome but my soul drew back"),** George Herbert (British; 1593–1633)	84

"Appearances" refers to the number of anthologies in which the poem is found, out of a total of more than 400 listed in *The Columbia Granger's Index to Poetry in Anthologies* (12th edition, Columbia University Press, 2002), a guide to poems that can be found in anthologies, which has been published since 1904.

THE 10 LATEST WINNERS OF THE PULITZER PRIZE FOR POETRY

YEAR	POET	POETRY
2003	**Paul Muldoon**	Moy Sand and Gravel
2002	**Carl Dennis**	Practical Goods
2001	**Stephen Dunn**	Different Hours
2000	**C. K. Williams**	Repair
1999	**Mark Strand**	Blizzard of One
1998	**Charles Wright**	Black Zodiac
1997	**Lisel Mueller**	Alive Together: New and Selected Poems
1996	**Jorie Graham**	The Dream of the Unified Field
1995	**Philip Levine**	The Simple Truth
1994	**Yusef Komunyakaa**	Neon Vernacular: New and Selected Poems

Although a poetry prize funded by the Poetry Society was presented alongside the Pulitzers in 1918 and 1919, the first Pulitzer Prize for Poetry dates from 1922, when it was won by Edward Arlington Robinson for his *Collected Poems*. Notable winners have included Robert Frost (on four occasions), W. H. Auden, and Sylvia Plath, whose award was posthumous.

TOP 10 MOST POPULAR POEMS IN THE WORLD

	POEM	POET
1	**Do Not Go Gentle into that Good Night**	Dylan Thomas
2	**The Tyger**	William Blake
3	**The Raven**	Edgar Allan Poe
4	**Stopping by Woods on a Snowy Evening**	Robert Frost
5	**Jabberwocky**	Lewis Carroll
6	**How Do I Love Thee? Let Me Count the Ways**	Elizabeth Barrett Browning
7	**There's a Certain Slant of Light**	Emily Dickinson
8	**Shall I Compare Thee to a Summer's Day**	William Shakespeare
9	**Because I Could Not Stop for Death**	Emily Dickinson
10	**Mending Wall**	Robert Frost

Source: *The Poetry Poll*

These are the Top 10 poems voted for in an international poll to discover the most popular poetry in the world. The poll, in which some 50,000 people participated, was conducted on the Internet over the six-year period 1992–98. Dylan Thomas's winning poem was written in 1951 in a verse style known as a villanelle, which has only two rhymes throughout.

TOP 10 BESTSELLING POETRY BOOKS IN THE US*

	BOOK/AUTHOR OR EDITOR/DATE	EST. SALES
1	**The Prophet,** Kahlil Gibran (1923)	6,000,000
2	**101 Famous Poems,** R. J. Cook (ed.) (1916)	up to 6,000,000
3	**The Pocket Book of Verse,** M. E. Speare (ed.) (1940)	2,719,600
4	**Listen to the Warm,** Rod McKuen (1967)	2,025,000
5	**Stanyan Street and Other Sorrows,** Rod McKuen (1967)	1,500,000
6	**Pocket Book of Ogden Nash,** Ogden Nash (1955)	1,121,000
7	**Anthology of Robert Frost's Poems,** Robert Frost (ed. Louis Untermeyer) (1949)	1,054,910
8	**Immortal Poems of the English Language,** Oscar Williams (ed.) (1952)	1,054,500
9	**A Heap O' Livin',** Edgar Guest (1916)	1,000,000
10	**John Brown's Body,** Stephen Vincent Bénet (1928)	755,630

* Based on a survey of bestsellers in the US during the period 1895–1975

Poetry books rarely sell in large numbers, so these multimillion sellers, as revealed by an extensive survey of sales in the US over an 80-year period, are exceptional.

Newspapers & Magazines

TOP 10 ENGLISH-LANGUAGE DAILY NEWSPAPERS

	NEWSPAPER	COUNTRY	AVERAGE DAILY CIRCULATION
1	The Sun	UK	3,472,841
2	The Daily Mail	UK	2,476,625
3	The Mirror	UK	2,187,960
4	USA Today	US	2,610,255
5	Times of India	India	1,879,000
6	Wall Street Journal	US	1,800,607
7	New York Times	US	1,109,000
8	The Daily Telegraph	UK	1,020,889
9	Daily Express	UK	957,574
10	Los Angeles Times	US	944,000

Source: *World Association of Newspapers/ Audit Bureau of Circulations*

The Sun was founded on September 15, 1964, as the successor to the *Daily Herald*. By 1978, it had achieved the highest circulation of any English-language newspaper.

TOP 10 COUNTRIES WITH THE HIGHEST NEWSPAPER CIRCULATIONS

	COUNTRY	AVERAGE DAILY CIRCULATION
1	China	117,815,000
2	Japan	71,694,000
3	US	55,578,000
4	India	29,482,000
5	Germany	23,838,000
6	UK	17,899,000
7	France	8,597,000
8	Russia	7,850,000
9	Brazil	7,670,000
10	Italy	6,100,000

Source: *World Association of Newspapers*

China's huge population is served by several of the highest-circulation newspapers in the world, among them *Sichuan Ribao*, which sells some eight million copies daily, making it the biggest-selling outside Japan.

TOP 10 SUBSCRIPTION MAGAZINES IN THE US

	MAGAZINE/ ISSUES PER YEAR	AVERAGE SUBSCRIPTION CIRCULATION*
1	NRTA/AARP Bulletin (10)	21,712,410
2	Modern Maturity# (36)	17,538,189
3	Reader's Digest (12)	11,527,098
4	TV Guide (52)	8,103,380
5	Better Homes and Gardens (12)	7,268,408
6	National Geographic Magazine (12)	6,630,182
7	Time (54)	3,948,602
8	My Generation# (36)	3,843,250
9	Ladies' Home Journal (12)	3,746,271
10	Good Housekeeping (12)	3,707,740

* January–July 2002

\# Now combined in AARP The Magazine

Source: *Audit Bureau of Circulations/Magazine Publishers of America*

THE FIRST ENGLISH NEWSPAPER

ALTHOUGH THERE HAD BEEN short-lived predecessors, the first real daily newspaper in the English language was the *London Gazette*, originally published on November 15, 1665, in Oxford, England, as the *Oxford Gazette*, while the royal court resided there during an outbreak of the plague. It moved to London with the court and changed its name, in its second year recording the momentous events of the Great Fire of London, and is still published today.

FIRST FACT

TOP 10 NEWSSTAND MAGAZINES IN THE US

	MAGAZINE/ ISSUES PER YEAR	AVERAGE SINGLE COPY CIRCULATION*
1	Cosmopolitan (12)	2,043,873
2	Family Circle (17)	1,607,143
3	National Enquirer (52)	1,575,731
4	National Enquirer (52)	1,467,702
5	Woman's Day (17)	1,419,322
6	People (52)	1,392,465
7	First For Women (17)	1,304,063
8	Star (52)	1,194,676
9	Glamour (12)	1,007,224
10	Good Housekeeping (12)	1,001,224

* January–July 2002

Source: *Audit Bureau of Circulations/Magazine Publishers of America*

TOP 10 WOMEN'S MAGAZINES IN THE US

	MAGAZINE/ ISSUES PER YEAR	AVERAGE CIRCULATION*
1	Better Homes and Gardens (12)	7,602,575
2	Good Housekeeping (12)	4,708,964
3	Family Circle (17)	4,671,052
4	Woman's Day (17)	4,167,052
5	Ladies' Home Journal (12)	4,101,280
6	Rosie (12)	3,503,993
7	Cosmopolitan (12)	2,963,351
8	Glamour (12)	2,509,566
9	Redbook (12)	2,380,410
10	Martha Stewart Living (12)	2,275,599

* January–July 2002

Source: *Audit Bureau of Circulations/Magazine Publishers of America*

▲ Newspapers
Despite the proliferation of new media, from TV to the internet, traditional papers retain their international appeal as an accessible source of information and entertainment.

TOP 10 NEWSPAPERS IN THE US

	NEWSPAPER/FREQUENCY	AVERAGE CIRCULATION*
1	**USA Today** (daily edition)	2,610,225
2	**Wall Street Journal** (daily edition)	1,800,607
3	**New York Times** (Sunday edition)	1,671,865
4	**Los Angeles Times** (Sunday edition)	1,376,932
5	**Washington Post** (Sunday edition)	1,048,122
6	**Chicago Tribune** (Sunday edition)	1,012,240
7	**New York Daily News** (Sunday edition)	801,292
8	**Denver Post/Rocky Mountain News** (Sunday edition)	789,137
9	**The Dallas Morning News** (Sunday edition)	784,905
10	**Philadelphia Inquirer** (Sunday edition)	747,969

Through September 30, 2002

Source: *Audit Bureau of Circulations*

TOP 10 OLDEST NEWSPAPERS IN THE US

	NEWSPAPER	YEAR ESTABLISHED
1	**The Hartford Courant,** Hartford, Connecticut	1764
2 =	**Poughkeepsie Journal,** Poughkeepsie, New York	1785
=	**The Augusta Chronicle**, Augusta, Georgia	1785
=	**Register Star,** Hudson, New York	1785
5 =	**Pittsburgh Post Gazette,** Pittsburgh, Pennsylvania	1786
=	**Daily Hampshire Gazette,** Northampton, Massachusetts	1786
7	**The Berkshire Eagle,** Pittsfield, Massachusetts	1789
8	**Norwich Bulletin,** Norwich, Connecticut	1791
9	**The Recorder,** Greenfield, Massachusetts	1792
10	**Intelligencer Journal,** Lancaster, Pennsylvania	1794

Source: *Editor & Publisher Year Book*

Art on Show

TOP 10 **BEST-ATTENDED EXHIBITIONS AT THE METROPOLITAN MUSEUM OF ART, NEW YORK**

	EXHIBITION	YEARS	TOTAL ATTENDANCE
1	The Treasures of Tutankhamun	1978–79	1,226,467
2	Mona Lisa	1963	1,007,521
3	The Vatican Collection: The Papacy and Art	1983	896,743
4	Glory of Russian Costume	1976–77	835,862
5	Origins of Impressionism	1994–95	794,108
6	Romantic and Glamorous Hollywood	1974–75	788,665
7	The Horses of San Marco	1980	742,221
8	Man and the Horse	1984–85	726,523
9	Masterpiece of Fifty Centuries	1979–81	690,471
10	Seurat	1991–92	642,408

Source: *Metropolitan Museum of Art*

TOP 10 **BEST-ATTENDED EXHIBITIONS AT THE NATIONAL GALLERY, WASHINGTON, D.C.**

	EXHIBITION	YEARS	TOTAL ATTENDANCE
1	Rodin Rediscovered	1981–82	1,053,223
2	Treasure Houses of Britain	1985–86	990,474
3	The Treasures of Tutankhamun	1976–77	835,924
4	Archaeological Finds of the People's Republic of China	1974–75	684,238
5	Ansel Adams: Classic Images	1985–86	651,652
6	The Splendor of Dresden	1978	620,089
7	The Art of Paul Gauguin	1988	596,058
8	Circa 1492: Art in the Age of Exploration	1991–92	568,192
9	Andrew Wyeth: The Helga Pictures	1987	558,433
10	Post Impressionism: Cross Currents in European & American Painting	1980	557,533

Source: *National Gallery*

Although the *Rodin Rediscovered* show holds the Gallery's record, the show was open for 307 days, while the *Treasure Houses of Britain* came a close second, despite being open for just 153 days.

◀ **Behind the mask**
Held in the 1970s, the
Treasures of Tutankhamun
exhibition retains its
record as the biggest
crowd-pulling art show
of all time in both
New York and London.

TOP 10 BEST-ATTENDED ART EXHIBITIONS, 2002

	EXHIBITION/VENUE/CITY	DATES	ATTENDANCE TOTAL	DAILY
1	**Van Gogh and Gauguin,** Van Gogh Museum, Amsterdam	Feb. 9–June 2	739,117	6,719
2	**Van Gogh and Gauguin,** Art Institute of Chicago, Chicago	Sept. 22, 2001–Jan. 13, 2002	690,951	6,281
3	**Masterpieces from the Prado Museum,** National Museum of Western Art, Tokyo	Mar. 5–June 16	516,711	5,616
4	**Matisse/Picasso,** Tate Modern, London	May 11–Aug. 18	467,166	4,671
5	**Surrealist Revolution,** Centre Georges Pompidou, Paris	Mar. 6–June 24	450,000*	4,500
6	**The Artists of the Pharaohs,** Musée du Louvre, Paris	Apr. 19–Aug. 5	450,000*	4,285
7	**The Secret Gallery and the Nude,** Museo del Prado, Madrid	June 28–Sept. 29	289,239	4,074
8	**Andy Warhol,** Tate Modern, London	Feb. 7–Apr. 1	218,801	4,052
9	**Treasures of Ancient Egypt,** National Gallery of Art, Washington, D.C.	June 30–Oct. 14	430,772	4,026
10	**Gerhard Richter,** Museum of Modern Art, New York	Feb. 14–May 21	333,695	4,020

* Approximate totals provided by museums

Source: The Art Newspaper

TOP 10 BEST-ATTENDED ART EXHIBITIONS IN NEW YORK, 2002

	EXHIBITION/VENUE	ATTENDANCE TOTAL	DAILY
1	**Gerhard Richter,** Museum of Modern Art	333,695	4,020
2	**Gauguin in New York Collections,** Metropolitan Museum	421,239	3,865
3	**Alberto Giacometti,** Museum of Modern Art	267,412	3,518
4	**Norman Rockwell,** Guggenheim Museum	355,895	3,326
5	**Thomas Eakins,** Metropolitan Museum	261,399	3,309
6	**Surrealism: Desire Unbound,** Metropolitan Museum	269,593	3,248
7	**Jeff Koons,** Guggenheim Museum	134,081	2,853
8	**Brazil: Body and Soul,** Guggenheim Museum	561,232	2,849
9	**Paintings from the Ordrupgaard College,** Metropolitan Museum	200,860	2,752
10	**Orazio and Artemesia Gentileschi,** Metropolitan Museum	201,307	2,649

Source: The Art Newspaper

While the Museum of Modern Arts' 40-year retrospective of the work of German artist Gerhard Richter attracted the greatest daily average during its 96-day run, the Guggenheim Museum's *Brazil: Body and Soul* gained the highest total figure during its 222 days.

Art at Auction

TOP 10 | MOST EXPENSIVE PAINTINGS

PAINTING/ARTIST/SALE	PRICE ($)
1 **Portrait du Dr. Gachet,** Vincent van Gogh (Dutch; 1853–90), Christie's, New York, May 15, 1990. *Both this painting and the one in No. 2 position were bought by Ryoei Saito, chairman of the Japanese company Daishowa Paper Manufacturing.*	75,000,000
2 **Au Moulin de la Galette,** Pierre-Auguste Renoir (French; 1841–1919), Sotheby's, New York, May 17, 1990	71,000,000
3 **Massacre of the Innocents,** Sir Peter Paul Rubens (Flemish; 1577–1640), Sotheby's, London, July 10, 2002	68,400,000 (£45,000,000)
4 **Portrait de l'Artiste Sans Barbe,** Vincent van Gogh, Christie's, New York, Nov. 19, 1998	65,000,000
5 **Rideau, Cruchon et Compôtier,** Paul Cézanne (French; 1839–1906), Sotheby's, New York, May 10, 1999	55,000,000
6 **Les Noces de Pierrette, 1905,** Pablo Picasso (Spanish, 1881–1973), Binoche et Godeau, Paris, Nov. 30, 1989. *This painting was sold by Swedish financier Fredrik Roos and bought by Tomonori Tsurumaki, a Japanese property developer, bidding from Tokyo by telephone.*	51,671,920 (F.Fr 315,000,000)

PAINTING/ARTIST/SALE	PRICE ($)
7 **Femme aux Bras Croises,** Pablo Picasso, Christie's Rockefeller, New York, Nov. 8, 2000	50,000,000
8 **Irises,** Vincent van Gogh, Sotheby's, New York, Nov. 11, 1987. *After much speculation, the painting's mystery purchaser was eventually confirmed as Australian businessman Alan Bond. However, because he was unable to pay for it in full, its former status as the world's most expensive work of art has been disputed. Painted in 1938, the work was part of the collection of the cellist and conductor Daniel Saidenberg and his wife Eleanore.*	49,000,000
9 **Femme Assise Dans un Jardin,** Pablo Picasso, Sotheby's, New York, Nov. 10, 1999	45,000,000
10 **Le Rêve,** Pablo Picasso, Christie's, New York, Nov. 10, 1997. *Victor and Sally Ganz had paid $7,000 for this painting in 1941.*	44,000,000

TOP 10 | MOST EXPENSIVE WORKS OF ART BY LIVING ARTISTS

WORK/ARTIST/SALE	PRICE ($)
1 **False Start,** Jasper Johns (American; 1930–), Sotheby's, New York, Nov. 10, 1988	15,500,000
2 **Two Flags,** Jasper Johns, Sotheby's, New York, Nov. 8, 1989	11,000,000
3 = **Henry Moore Bound to Fail, Back View,** Bruce Nauman (American; 1941–), Christie's Rockefeller, New York, May 17, 2001	9,000,000
= **0 Through 9,** Jasper Johns, Christie's Rockefeller, New York, Nov. 13, 2002	9,000,000
5 **Corpse and Mirror,** Jasper Johns, Christie's, New York, Nov. 10, 1997	7,600,000
6 **White Numbers,** Jasper Johns, Christie's, New York, Nov. 10, 1997	7,200,000
7 **Two Flags,** Jasper Johns, Christie's Rockefeller, New York, May 13, 1999	6,500,000
8 **White Flag,** Jasper Johns, Christie's, New York, Nov. 9, 1988	6,400,000
9 **Large Interior, WII,** Lucian Freud (British/German; 1922–), Sotheby's, New York, May 14, 1998	5,300,000
10 = **Michael Jackson and Bubbles,** Jeff Koons (American; 1955–), Sotheby's, New York, May 15, 2001	5,100,000
= **Untitled,** Cy Twombly (American; 1929–), Sotheby's, New York, Nov. 12, 2002	5,100,000

TOP 10 | MOST EXPENSIVE PIECES OF SCULPTURE

SCULPTURE/ARTIST/SALE	PRICE ($)
1 **Danaïde,** Constantin Brancusi (Romanian; 1876–1956), Christie's Rockefeller, New York, May 7, 2002	16,500,000
2 **Grande Femme Debout I,** Alberto Giacometti (Swiss; 1901–66), Christie's Rockefeller, New York, Nov. 8, 2000	13,000,000
3 **La Serpentine Femme à la Stele—l'Araignée,** Henri Matisse (French; 1869–1954), Sotheby's, New York, May 10, 2000	12,750,000
4 **Grande Tête de Diego,** Alberto Giacometti, Sotheby's, New York, May 8, 2002	12,500,000
5 **La Forêt,** Alberto Giacometti, Christie's Rockefeller, New York, May 7, 2002	12,000,000
6 **Figure Decorative,** Henri Matisse, Sotheby's, New York, May 10, 2001	11,500,000
7 **Petite Danseuse de Quatorze Ans,** Edgar Degas, Sotheby's, New York, Nov. 11, 1999	11,250,000
8 **Petite Danseuse de Quatorze Ans,** Edgar Degas, Sotheby's, New York, Nov. 12, 1996	10,800,000
9 **Petite Danseuse de Quatorze Ans,** Edgar Degas (French; 1834–1917), Sotheby's, London, June 27, 2000	10,570,000 (£7,000,000)
10 **The Dancing Faun,** Adriaen de Vries (Dutch; c.1550–1626), Sotheby's, London, Dec. 7, 1989	9,796,000 (£6,200,000)

TOP 10 MOST EXPENSIVE GOUACHE/PASTEL WORKS

WORK/ARTIST/SALE	PRICE ($)
1 Acrobate et Jeune Arlequin, Pablo Picasso (Spanish; 1881–1973), Christie's, London, Nov. 28, 1988	35,530,000 (£19,000,000)
2 Danseuses au Repos, Edgar Degas (French; 1834–1917), Sotheby's, London, June 28, 1999	25,280,000 (£16,000,000)
3 Miss Cassatt au Musée du Louvre, Edgar Degas, Sotheby's, New York, May 8, 2002	15,000,000
4 Famille de l'Arlequin, Pablo Picasso, Christie's, New York, Nov. 14, 1989	14,000,000
5 La Moisson en Provence, Vincent van Gogh (Dutch; 1853–90), Sotheby's, London, June 24, 1997	13,280,001 (£8,000,000)

WORK/ARTIST/SALE	PRICE ($)
6 Danseuse Assise aux Bas Roses, Henri de Toulouse-Lautrec (French; 1864–1901), Christie's, New York, May 12, 1997	13,200,000
7 La Vis, Henri Matisse (French; 1869–1954), Sotheby's, New York, Nov. 3, 1993	12,500,000
8 Portrait de Mme. K, Joan Miró (Spanish; 1893–1983), Christie's Rockefeller, New York, Nov. 6, 2001	11,500,000
9 Garçon à la Collerette, Pablo Picasso, Christie's, New York, Nov. 7, 1995	11,000,000
10 Danseuses, Edgar Degas, Sotheby's, New York, May 13, 1997	10,000,000

While the world's most costly paintings are oils, a number of drawings, sketches, and studies in gouache (a type of watercolor) and pastel (a kind of crayon) have also attained substantial sums at auction. Both media were widely employed by the Impressionists and ideally suited to their fleeting style.

Prima ballerina
Degas's pastel and gouache study of dancers at rest is the most expensive work in this medium by an Impressionist artist.

Collectibles

TOP 10 | MOST EXPENSIVE MUSICAL INSTRUMENTS

INSTRUMENT*/SALE	PRICE ($)
1 **John Lennon's Steinway Model Z upright piano, teak veneered, complete with cigarette burns, played by Lennon at Woodstock, 1969,** Fleetwood-Owen online auction, Hard Rock Café, London and New York, Oct. 17, 2000	2,150,000
2 **"Kreutzer" violin by Antonio Stradivari,** Christie's, London, Apr. 1, 1998	1,582,847 (£946,000)
3 **"Cholmondeley" violincello by Antonio Stradivari,** Sotheby's, London, June 22, 1998	1,141,122 (£682,000)
4 **"Brownie," one of Eric Clapton's favorite electric guitars,** Christie's, New York, June 24, 1999	497,500
5 **Steinway grand piano, decorated by Lawrence Alma-Tadema and Edward Poynter for Henry Marquand, 1884–87,** Sotheby Parke Bernet, New York, Mar. 26, 1980	390,000
6 **Single-manual harpsichord by Joseph Joannes Couchet, Antwerp, 1679,** Sotheby's, London, Nov. 21, 2001	378,004 (£267,500)
7 **Acoustic guitar owned by David Bowie, Paul McCartney, and George Michael,** Christie's, London, May 18, 1994	339,856 (£220,000)
8 **Double bass by Domenico Montagnana,** Sotheby's, London, Mar. 16, 1999	250,339 (£155,500)
9 **Verne Powell's platinum flute,** Christie's, New York, Oct. 18, 1986	187,000
10 **Viola by Giovanni Paolo Maggini,** Christie's, London, Nov. 20, 1984	161,121 (£129,000)

* *Most expensive example only given for each category of instrument*

TOP 10 | MOST EXPENSIVE ITEMS OF POP MEMORABILIA

ITEM*/SALE	PRICE ($)#
1 **John Lennon's 1965 Rolls-Royce Phantom V touring limousine, finished in psychedelic paintwork,** Sotheby's, New York, June 29, 1985	2,299,000
2 **Bernie Taupin's handwritten lyrics for the rewritten** *Candle in the Wind,* **played by Elton John at the funeral of Diana, Princess of Wales,** Christie's, Los Angeles, Feb. 11, 1998 (bought by Diana's brother, Earl Spencer)	400,000
3 **Paul McCartney's handwritten lyrics for** *Getting Better,* 1967, Sotheby's, London, Sept. 14, 1995	249,380 (£161,000)
4 **John Lennon's 1970 Mercedes-Benz 600 Pullman four-door limousine,** Christie's, London, Apr. 27, 1989	232,169 (£137,500)
5 **John Lennon's 1965 Ferrari 330 GT 2+2 two door coupé, right-hand drive,** Fleetwood-Owen online auction, Hard Rock Café, London and New York, Oct. 17, 2000	188,304
6 **Mal Evan's notebook, compiled 1967–68, which includes a draft by Paul McCartney of the lyrics for** *Hey Jude,* Sotheby's, London, Sept. 15, 1998	187,110 (£111,500)
7 **Elvis Presley's 1963 Rolls–Royce Phantom V touring limousine,** Sotheby's, London, Aug. 28, 1986	163,240 (£110,000)
8 **Page of lyrics in John Lennon's hand for** *I Am The Walrus,* **1967, in black ink,** Christie's, London, Sept. 30, 1999	129,500 (£78,500)
9 **Reel-to-reel tape recording of 16-year-old John Lennon singing with the Quarrymen at a church fair in Liverpool on July 6, 1957,** Sotheby's, London, Sept. 15, 1994	122,774 (£78,500)
10 **Recording of John Lennon with his step-daughter Kyoko Cox,** Christie's, London, Apr. 30, 2002	109,747 (£75,200)

* *Excluding musical instruments*

\# *Including 10 percent buyer's premium, where appropriate*

Pioneered by Sotheby's in London, pop memorabilia has become big business—especially if it involves personal association with megastars such as the Beatles. Even such items as the Liverpool birthplace of Ringo Starr, the barber shop mentioned in the Beatles' song "Penny Lane," and a door from John Lennon's house have been offered for sale as artifacts from the archaeology of the Beatles.

◄ **Classic Clapton**
Eric Clapton performing with "Brownie," the 1956 sunburst Fender Stratocaster guitar he used to record the whole of the *Layla* album, sold in aid of a drug rehabilitation charity.

TOP 10 MOST EXPENSIVE ITEMS OF FILM MEMORABILIA

	ITEM*/SALE	PRICE ($)
1	David O. Selznick's Oscar for *Gone with the Wind* (1939), Sotheby's, New York, June 12, 1999 (bought by Michael Jackson)	1,542,500
2	Judy Garland's ruby slippers from *The Wizard of Oz* (1939), Christie's, New York, May 26, 2000	666,000
3	Clark Gable's Oscar for *It Happened One Night* (1934), Christie's, Los Angeles, Dec. 15, 1996	607,500
4	Bette Davis's Oscar for *Jezebel* (1938), Christie's, New York, July 19, 2001 (bought by Steven Spielberg)	578,000
5	Vivien Leigh's Oscar for *Gone with the Wind*, Sotheby's, New York, Dec. 15, 1993	562,500
6	Statue of the Maltese Falcon from *The Maltese Falcon* (1941), Christie's Rockefeller, New York, Dec. 5, 1994	398,500
7	James Bond's Aston Martin DB5 from *Goldfinger* (1964), Sotheby's, New York, June 28, 1986	275,000
8 =	Clark Gable's personal script for *Gone with the Wind*, Christie's, Los Angeles, Dec. 15, 1996	244,500
=	Herman J. Mankiewicz's Oscar for co-writing *Citizen Kane* (1941), Christie's, New York, Nov. 18, 1999	231,000
10	"Rosebud" sled from *Citizen Kane*, Christie's, Los Angeles, Dec. 15, 1996	233,500

* Excluding posters and animation cels

TOP 10 MOST VALUABLE AMERICAN COMICS

	COMIC	VALUE ($)*
1	*Action Comics* No. 1, published in June 1938, the first issue of *Action Comics* marked the original appearance of Superman.	350,000
2	*Detective Comics* No. 27, issued in May 1939, it is prized as the first comic book to feature Batman.	300,000
3	*Marvel Comics* No. 1, The Human Torch and other heroes were first introduced in the issue dated Oct 1939.	250,000
4	*Superman* No. 1, the first comic book devoted to Superman, reprinting the original *Action Comics* story, was published in summer 1939.	210,000
5	*All American Comics* No. 16, The Green Lantern made his debut in the July 1940 issue.	115,000
6 =	*Batman* No. 1, published in spring 1940, this was the first comic book devoted to Batman.	100,000
=	*Captain America Comics* No. 1, published in Mar 1941, this was the original comic book in which Captain America appeared.	
8 =	*Flash Comics* No. 1, dated Jan 1940, featuring The Flash, it is rare as it was issued in only small numbers for promotional purposes, and unique as issue #2 was retitled *Whiz Comics*.	85,000
=	*Whiz Comics* No. 1, published in Feb 1940 – and confusingly numbered "2" – it was the first comic book to feature Captain Marvel.	77,000
10	*More Fun Comics* No. 52, The Spectre made his debut in the issue dated Feb 1940.	72,000

* For example; in "Near Mint" condition

Source: The Overstreet Comic Book Price Guide, No. 32, 2002. ©2002 Gemstone Publishing, Inc. All rights reserved.

Glittering prize
First presented in 1929, the gold-plated Oscar statuette is coveted not only by its recipients but also by collectors of film memorabilia.
©A.M.P.A.S.®

MUSIC & MUSICIANS

Songs & Songwriters

TOP 10 SONGWRITERS IN THE US CHARTS

	SONGWRITER(S)	CHART HITS
1	Brian Holland, Lamont Dozier, and Eddie Holland	128
2	John Lennon and Paul McCartney	118
3	Kenny Gamble and Leon Huff	105
4	Burt Bacharach and Hal David	103
5	Gerry Goffin and Carole King	93
6	Curtis Mayfield	85
7	Jerry Leiber and Mike Stoller	80
8	Diane Warren	76
9	Barry Mann and Cynthia Weil	75
10	Mick Jagger and Keith Richard	63

Source: *Music Information Database*

▼ **Wonder land**
Stevie Wonder is the most recent recipient of the Songwriters Hall of Fame Lifetime Achievement Award, named in honor of legendary songwriter Sammy Cahn (1913–93).

THE 10 LATEST GRAMMY SONGS OF THE YEAR

YEAR	SONG	SONGWRITER(S)
2002	Don't Know Why	Jesse Harris
2001	Fallin'	Alicia Keys
2000	Beautiful Day	U2
1999	Smooth	Itaal Shur and Rob Thomas
1998	My Heart Will Go On	James Horner and Will Jennings
1997	Sunny Came Home	Shawn Colvin
1996	Change the World	Gordon Kennedy, Wayne Kirkpatrick, and Tommy Sims
1995	Kiss From a Rose	Seal
1994	Streets of Philadelphia	Bruce Springsteen
1993	A Whole New World	Alan Menken and Tim Rice

The National Academy of Recording Arts & Sciences was founded in 1957. Awards have been presented annually since 1959, for recordings of the preceding year. In the category "Song of the Year," the award is made to the songwriter rather than the performer. The first winner was *Nel Blu Dipinto di Blu*, written by Domenico Modugno. Subsequent winners represent many songs that are now regarded as classics, as well as some of the biggest-selling singles of all time, among them *Moon River* by Henry Mancini and Johnny Mercer, from the film *Breakfast at Tiffany's* (1961) and *We Are The World* by Michael Jackson and Lionel Richie (1985).

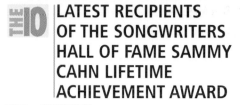

THE 10 LATEST RECIPIENTS OF THE SONGWRITERS HALL OF FAME SAMMY CAHN LIFETIME ACHIEVEMENT AWARD

YEAR	RECIPIENT(S)
2002	Stevie Wonder
2001	Gloria and Emilio Estefan
2000	Neil Diamond
1999	Kenny Rogers
1998	Berry Gordy
1997	Vic Damone
1996	Frankie Laine
1995	Steve Lawrence and Eydie Gorme
1994	Lena Horne
1993	Ray Charles

Source: *National Academy of Popular Music*

The National Academy of Popular Music's most prestigious award is named for Sammy Cahn, who served for 20 years as the Academy's President.

TOP 10 ROCK SONGS OF ALL TIME*

	SONG	ARTIST OR GROUP
1	(I Can't Get No) Satisfaction	The Rolling Stones
2	Respect	Aretha Franklin
3	Stairway to Heaven	Led Zeppelin
4	Like a Rolling Stone	Bob Dylan
5	Born to Run	Bruce Springsteen
6	Hotel California	The Eagles
7	Light My Fire	The Doors
8	Good Vibrations	The Beach Boys
9	Hey Jude	The Beatles
10	Imagine	John Lennon

* Determined by a panel of 700 voters assembled by the music network VH1

The Top 10 from an all-time top 100 list is dominated by songs dating from the 1960s. Within it are no fewer than nine Beatles songs (in addition to John Lennon's *Imagine*), as well as five by the Rolling Stones, four by Elvis Presley, and three each by the Beach Boys, Bob Dylan, Marvin Gaye, and Led Zeppelin. A number of notable artists are perhaps surprisingly represented by a single song, including Chuck Berry's *Johnny B Goode*, David Bowie's *Space Oddity*, the Doors' *Light My Fire*, the Eagles' *Hotel California*, Jimi Hendrix's *Purple Haze*, Little Richard's *Good Golly, Miss Molly*, Roy Orbison's *Oh, Pretty Woman*, and Stevie Wonder's *Superstition*.

TOP 10 DJ REQUESTS IN THE US

	SONG	ARTIST OR GROUP
1	Electric Boogie (Slide)	Marcia Griffiths
2	Y.M.C.A.	Village People
3	Cha Cha Slide	DJ Casper
4	Love Shack	B52s
5	Get the Party Started	Pink
6	Old Time Rock and Roll	Bob Seger
7	Brown Eyed Girl	Van Morrison
8	I Will Survive	Gloria Gaynor
9	Brick House	The Commodores
10	Celebration	Kool & the Gang

Source: Mobile Beat Magazine, *2003*

This Top 10 was compiled by a nationwide poll of mobile DJs. The survey results produced a list that extended to 101 songs, among them, and just outside the Top 10, such long-established hits as Chubby Checker's *Twist*, the Bee Gees' *Stayin' Alive*, and the Beatles' *Twist and Shout*.

TOP 10 WEDDING SONGS IN THE US

	SONG	ARTIST OR GROUP
1	From This Moment On	Shania Twain/Bryan White
2	At Last	Etta James
3	Power of Love	Celine Dion
4	I Cross My Heart	George Strait
5	Unchained Melody	Righteous Brothers
6	Amazed	Lonestar
7	Wonderful Tonight	Eric Clapton
8	Always and Forever	Heatwave
9	I Don't Want to Miss a Thing	Aerosmith
10	If You Say My Eyes Are Beautiful	Whitney Houston/Janet Jackson

Source: *Wedding Zone*

Outside the Top 10, the list of the most popular wedding songs continues with such favorites as Elvis Presley's *Can't Help Falling in Love* and Louis Armstrong's *What a Wonderful World*. Some sources itemize songs that are played to accompany specific stages in the reception, from the first dance to garter-tossing.

Record Firsts

THE 10 ALBUMS IN THE FIRST US ALBUMS TOP 10*

	TITLE	ARTIST
1	Al Jolson (Volume III)	Al Jolson
2	A Presentation of Progressive Jazz	Stan Kenton
3	Emperor's Waltz	Bing Crosby
4	Songs of Our Times	Carmen Cavallaro
5	Wizard at the Organ	Ken Griffin
6	Glenn Miller Masterpieces	Glen Miller
7	Busy Fingers	Three Suns
8	Songs of Our Times	B. Grant Orchestra
9	Glenn Miller	Glenn Miller
10	Theme Songs	Various artists

Source: Billboard

September 3, 1948

THE 10 FIRST GRAMMY RECORDS OF THE YEAR

YEAR	RECORD	ARTIST
1958	Nel Blu Dipinto di Blu (Volare)	Domenico Modugno
1959	Mack the Knife	Bobby Darin
1960	Theme from A Summer Place	Percy Faith
1961	Moon River	Henry Mancini
1962	I Left My Heart in San Francisco	Tony Bennett
1963	The Days of Wine and Roses	Henry Mancini
1964	The Girl from Ipanema	Stan Getz & Astrud Gilberto
1965	A Taste of Honey	Herb Alpert & the Tijuana Brass
1966	Strangers in the Night	Frank Sinatra
1967	Up Up and Away	5th Dimension

◄ **The King rules**
Elvis Presley's *Heartbreak Hotel*, his first single to sell a million copies, was the biggest-selling single of 1956. In that year, he sold a record total of 10 million discs.

THE 10 SINGLES IN THE FIRST US TOP 10

	TITLE	ARTIST
1	I'll Never Smile Again	Tommy Dorsey
2	The Breeze and I	Jimmy Dorsey
3	Imagination	Glenn Miller
4	Playmates	Kay Kyser
5	Fools Rush In	Glenn Miller
6	Where Was I	Charlie Barnet
7	Pennsylvania 6-5000	Glenn Miller
8	Imagination	Tommy Dorsey
9	Sierra Sue	Bing Crosby
10	Make-Believe Island	Mitchell Ayres

Source: Billboard

This was the first "Best Sellers In Store" chart compiled by *Billboard* magazine, for its issue dated July 20, 1940. Since the 7-inch 45-rpm single was still the best part of a decade in the future, all these would have been 10-inch 78-rpm discs. Note the almost total domination of big-name bands more than a half century ago—and spare a thought for Mitchell Ayres, who crept in at the bottom of this very first chart, and then never had a hit again.

THE 10 FIRST FEMALE SINGERS TO HAVE A NO. 1 HIT IN THE US DURING THE ROCK ERA

	ARTIST/TITLE	DATE AT NO. 1
1	**Joan Weber,** Let Me Go Lover	Jan. 1, 1955
2	**Georgia Gibbs,** Dance With Me Henry (Wallflower)	May 14, 1955
3	**Kay Starr,** Rock and Roll Waltz	Feb. 18, 1956
4	**Gogi Grant,** The Wayward Wind	June 16, 1956
5	**Debbie Reynolds,** Tammy	Aug. 19, 1957
6	**Connie Francis,** Everybody's Somebody's Fool	June 27, 1960
7	**Brenda Lee,** I'm Sorry	July 18, 1960
8	**Shelley Fabares,** Johnny Angel	Apr. 7, 1962
9	**Little Eva,** The Loco-motion	Aug. 25, 1962
10	**Little Peggy March,** I Will Follow Him	Apr. 27, 1963

Source: *Music Information Database*

By the time Little Peggy March had her first No. 1, Connie Francis had had two more and Brenda Lee one.

THE 10 FIRST GOLD ALBUMS IN THE US

	TITLE/ARTIST	CERTIFICATION DATE
1	**Oklahoma!,** Soundtrack	July 8, 1958
2	**Hymns,** Tennessee Ernie Ford	Feb. 20, 1959
3	**Johnny's Greatest Hits,** Johnny Mathis	June 1, 1959
4 =	**Sing Along with Mitch,** Mitch Miller	Nov. 16, 1959
=	**The Music Man,** Original Cast	Nov. 16, 1959
6	**South Pacific,** Soundtrack	Dec. 18, 1959
7	**Peter Gunn,** Henry Mancini	Dec. 31, 1959
8	**The Student Prince,** Mario Lanza	Jan. 19, 1960
9	**Pat's Great Hits,** Pat Boone	Feb. 12, 1960
10	**Elvis,** Elvis Presley	Feb. 17, 1960
=	**60 Years of Music,** Various Artists	Feb. 17, 1960

Source: *RIAA*

THE 10 FIRST MILLION-SELLING ROCK 'N' ROLL SINGLES IN THE US

	TITLE/ARTIST	YEAR
1	**(We're Gonna) Rock Around the Clock,** Bill Haley & His Comets	1954
2	**Shake, Rattle and Roll,** Bill Haley & His Comets	1954
3	**Maybellene,** Chuck Berry	1955
4	**Ain't it a Shame,** Fats Domino	1955
5	**Ain't That a Shame,** Pat Boone	1955
6	**Seventeen,** Boyd Bennett	1955
7	**I Hear You Knocking,** Gale Storm	1955
8	**See You Later Alligator,** Bill Haley & His Comets	1955
9	**Tutti Frutti,** Little Richard	1955
10	**Heartbreak Hotel,** Elvis Presley	1956

Widely regarded as the first rock 'n' roll hit, (*We're Gonna) Rock Around the Clock* saw the dawn of a new musical era, a hybrid of R & B and country that would explode as its own genre in the mid-1950s

FIRST MILLION-SELLERS

The RIAA (Recording Industry Association of America) started certifying records in the US in 1958 by introducing its Gold Awards for sales of over 500,000 copies. The RIAA's first Gold Award for an album went to *Oklahoma!* The soundtrack recorded by Gordon MacRae and the cast of the movie had been released in 1955, stayed in the chart for 255 weeks, and sold a million copies by 1959. When the disco boom of the 1970s made million-sellers commonplace, the RIAA introduced the Platinum Award for sales of one million. The first recipient was *The Eagles: Their Greatest Hits 1971–1975*, which was certified on February 24, 1976—and has since sold over 26 million copies in the US.

FIRST FACT

Stars of the Decades

TOP 10 SOLO SINGERS OF THE 1970s IN THE US

	SINGER	TOTAL HITS*
1	James Brown	33
2	Neil Diamond	29
3	Elvis Presley	26
4 =	John Denver	25
=	Elton John	25
6	Aretha Franklin	21
7 =	Olivia Newton-John	20
=	Linda Ronstadt	20
=	Rod Stewart	20
=	Stevie Wonder	20

* Includes only records that entered the charts in the 1970s

Source: *Music Information Database*

While none of James Brown's singles of the 1970s achieved a chart position higher than No. 13, he had at least one in the US Top 100 every year until 1977, when *Body Heat* peaked at No. 88. A run of setbacks curtailed his output until 1986, when *Living in America* hit No. 4.

▲ **Material girl**
Since her first chart hit, *Holiday*, in 1983, Madonna has achieved more chart hits than any other female artist.

TOP 10 SOLO SINGERS OF THE 1980s IN THE US

	SINGER	TOTAL HITS*
1	Billy Joel	21
2	John Cougar Mellencamp	20
3 =	Elton John	19
=	Madonna	19
=	Rod Stewart	19
6	Sheena Easton	17
7 =	Pat Benatar	16
=	Michael Jackson	16
=	Diana Ross	16
=	Rick Springfield	16
=	Donna Summer	16

* Includes only records that entered the charts in the 1980s

Source: *Music Information Database*

Billy Joel's all-time total of sales of over 77 million discs in the US alone ranks him in third place among solo singers (after Garth Brooks and Elvis Presley).

TOP 10 SOLO SINGERS OF THE 1990s IN THE US

	SINGER	TOTAL HITS*
1	Madonna	24
2	Mariah Carey	17
3	Whitney Houston	16
4 =	Mary J. Blige	15
=	Gloria Estefan	15
=	R. Kelly	15
7 =	Celine Dion	14
=	Elton John	14
9	Janet Jackson	13
10 =	Tevin Campbell	12
=	LL Cool J	12
=	Michael Bolton	12

* Includes only records that entered the charts in the 1990s

Source: *Music Information Database*

TOP 10 GROUPS OF THE 1970s IN THE US

	GROUP	TOTAL HITS*
1	Chicago	28
2	The Carpenters	26
3	The Bee Gees	24
4 =	The Isley Brothers	22
=	The Jackson 5/The Jacksons	22
6 =	Gladys Knight & the Pips	21
=	The Spinners	21
8 =	Dawn	20
=	Earth, Wind & Fire	20
10 =	The Chi-Lites	19
=	The Doobie Brothers	19

* Includes only records that entered the charts in the 1970s

Source: *Music Information Database*

TOP 10 GROUPS OF THE 1980s IN THE US

	GROUP	TOTAL HITS*
1	The Pointer Sisters	20
2	Journey	19
3 =	Kool & the Gang	18
=	Survivor	18
5 =	Chicago	17
=	Huey Lewis & the News	17
=	Jefferson Starship#	17
8 =	Duran Duran	15
=	Genesis	15
=	Heart	15
=	REO Speedwagon	15

* Includes only records that entered the charts in the 1980s

Jefferson Starship dropped the "Jefferson" and became Starship in 1985

Source: *Music Information Database*

ROCK 'N' ROLL

THE ROCK 'N' ROLL ERA is generally dated from the release of Bill Haley and his Comets' single (*We're Gonna*) *Rock Around the Clock*. Recorded in New York's Pythian Temple Studios on April 12, 1954, it was first released later that year, but became a smash hit only after it appeared in the teen film *Blackboard Jungle*, which opened in the US on March 25, 1955. On July 9 it became the first rock record to top the US chart, where it stayed for eight weeks, and on October 14 became the first rock record ever to top the UK chart.

▶ **All the right moves**
Led by Michael Stipe, American band R.E.M., named after the Rapid Eye Movement dream phase of the sleep cycle, was among the most successful of the 1990s.

TOP 10 GROUPS OF THE 1990s IN THE US

	GROUP	TOTAL HITS*
1	Boyz II Men	16
2	R.E.M.	13
3 =	SWV	12
=	TLC	12
5 =	Aerosmith	11
=	En Vogue	11
=	Jodeci	11
=	U2	11
9	Metallica	10
10 =	Depeche Mode	9
=	Prince & the New Power Generation	9

* Includes only records that entered the charts in the 1990s

Source: *Music Information Database*

All-Time Greats

TOP 10 SINGLES OF ALL TIME

	TITLE/ARTIST OR GROUP/YEAR	SALES EXCEED
1	Candle in the Wind (1997)/Something About the Way You Look Tonight, Elton John, 1997	37,000,000
2	White Christmas, Bing Crosby, 1945	30,000,000
3	Rock Around the Clock, Bill Haley and His Comets, 1954	17,000,000
4	Want to Hold Your Hand, The Beatles, 1963	12,000,000
5 =	Hey Jude, The Beatles, 1968	10,000,000
=	It's Now or Never, Elvis Presley, 1960	10,000,000
=	I Will Always Love You, Whitney Houston, 1992	10,000,000
8 =	Hound Dog/Don't Be Cruel, Elvis Presley, 1956	9,000,000
=	Diana, Paul Anka, 1957	9,000,000
10 =	I'm a Believer, The Monkees, 1966	8,000,000
=	(Everything I Do) I Do it for You, Bryan Adams, 1991	8,000,000

Global sales are notoriously difficult to calculate, since for many decades, little statistical research on record sales was done in a large part of the world. "Worldwide" is thus usually taken to mean the known minimum "Western world" sales. It took 55 years for a record to overtake Bing Crosby's 1942 *White Christmas*, although the song, as also recorded by others and sold as sheet music, has achieved such enormous total sales that it would still appear in first position in any list of best-selling songs.

TOP 10 ALBUMS OF ALL TIME IN THE US

	TITLE/ARTIST OR GROUP/YEAR	SALES
1	Their Greatest Hits, 1971–1975, The Eagles, 1976	28,000,000
2	Thriller, Michael Jackson, 1982	26,000,000
3	Led Zeppelin IV, Led Zeppelin, 1971	22,000,000
4 =	Back In Black, AC/DC, 1980	19,000,000
=	Come On Over, Shania Twain, 1997	19,000,000
6	Rumours, Fleetwood Mac, 1977	18,000,000
7	The Bodyguard, Soundtrack, 1992	17,000,000
8 =	Boston, Boston, 1976	16,000,000
=	Cracked Rear View, Hootie & the Blowfish, 1994	16,000,000
=	Jagged Little Pill, Alanis Morissette, 1995	16,000,000
=	No Fences, Garth Brooks, 1990	16,000,000

Source: *RIAA*

Certain double albums, such as Pink Floyd's *The Wall* and Billy Joel's *Greatest Hits*, have been excluded: according to the RIAA's certification procedures, each component of a double album is counted separately, so an apparent sale of 20 million units is in reality 10 million. All the singers and groups represented here are an elite who have achieved sales of at least 20 million albums overall—over 100 million in the case of Led Zeppelin and Garth Brooks.

TOP 10 "GREATEST HITS" ALBUMS IN THE US

	TITLE/ARTIST OR GROUP	YEAR
1	Their Greatest Hits, 1971–1975, The Eagles	1976
2	Greatest Hits, Elton John	1974
3	Simon & Garfunkel's Greatest Hits, Simon & Garfunkel	1972
4	Greatest Hits, Kenny Rogers	1980
5	James Taylor's Greatest Hits, James Taylor	1976
6	Eagles Greatest Hits Volume 2, The Eagles	1982
7	Greatest Hits Volumes I & II, Billy Joel	1985
8	The Immaculate Collection, Madonna	1990
9	The Hits, Garth Brooks	1994
10	Best of The Doobies, The Doobie Brothers	1976

Source: *Music Information Database*

All of the above have sold in excess of 10 million copies each, with the Eagles' album the biggest-selling of all-time, with sales of 28 million. Released in February 1976, it went to #1, where it stayed for six weeks, and resided in the chart for precisely two years.

TOP 10 NORTH AMERICAN CONCERT TOURS

	ARTIST OR GROUP	TOUR/YEAR	GROSS ($)
1	The Rolling Stones	Voodoo Lounge, 1994	121,200,000
2	U2	Elevation, 2001	109,700,000
3	Pink Floyd	The Division Bell, 1994	103,500,000
4	Paul McCartney	Driving USA, 2002	103,300,000
5	The Rolling Stones	Steel Wheels, 1989	98,000,000
6	The Rolling Stones	Bridges to Babylon, 1997	89,300,000
7	The Rolling Stones	Licks, 2002	87,900,000
8	*NSYNC	Popodyssey, 2001	86,800,000
9	The Backstreet Boys	Black and Blue, 2001	82,100,000
10	Tina Turner	Twenty-Four Seven, 2000	80,200,000

Source: Fortune/*Pollstar*

The most recent member of this elite is Paul McCartney, who beat the Rolling Stones into second place during 2002—the first time during the past 20 years that the Stones failed to top the list in a year when they have toured. While the Rolling Stones' 2002–03 *Licks* world tour was in progress, it was estimated that the group had earned more than $1 billion from ticket sales alone since its 1989 sell-out *Steel Wheels* tour.

 ## ARTISTS WITH THE MOST GRAMMY AWARDS

	ARTIST	YEARS	AWARDS*
1	Sir Georg Solti	1962–97	38
2	Pierre Boulez	1969–2001	29
3 =	Vladimir Horowitz	1962–92	26
=	Quincy Jones	1963–93	26
5	Stevie Wonder	1973–2002	22
6 =	Leonard Bernstein	1961–2001	20
=	Henry Mancini	1958–70	20
8	John T. Williams	1975–2000	18
9 =	Eric Clapton	1972–2001	16
=	Itzhak Perlman	1977–95	16

* Excludes *Lifetime Achievements*

The Grammy Awards are considered to be the most prestigious in the music industry. The proliferation of classical artists reflects the number of classical award categories at the Grammys, which have only latterly been overshadowed by pop and rock.

 ## SINGERS WITH THE MOST POSTHUMOUS HITS IN THE US

	SINGER	TOTAL POTHUMOUS CHART HITS
1 =	2Pac	8
=	Otis Redding	8
3	Jim Reeves	7
4 =	Sam Cooke	6
=	Jim Croce	6
6	John Lennon	5
7 =	Aaliyah	4
=	Elvis Presley	4
9 =	Patsy Cline	2
=	Jimi Hendrix	2
=	Roy Orbison	2
=	Ritchie Valens	2

Source: *Music Information Database*

ARTISTS WITH THE MOST WEEKS ON THE US SINGLES CHART

	ARTIST	TOTAL WEEKS*
1	Elvis Presley	1,203
2	Elton John	979
3	Madonna	814
4	Stevie Wonder	768
5	Rod Stewart	692
6	Michael Jackson	684
7	James Brown	681
8	Aretha Franklin	659
9	Janet Jackson	653
10	Whitney Houston	622

* To December 2002

Source: *Music Information Database*

▼ Bell ringer

Along with the majority of the top-earning concert tours, the dramatic stage set for Pink Floyd's 1994 *The Division Bell* tour was designed by British architect Mark Fisher.

Today's Stars

TOP 10 ALBUMS OF 2002 IN THE US

	ALBUM	ARTIST OR GROUP
1	The Eminem Show	Eminem
2	Nellyville	Nelly
3	Let Go	Avril Lavigne
4	Home	Dixie Chicks
5	8 Mile	Soundtrack
6	M!ssundaztood	Pink
7	Ashanti	Ashanti
8	Drive	Alan Jackson
9	Up	Shania Twain
10	O Brother, Where Art Thou?	Various Artists

Source: *Nielsen Soundscan*

The Eminem Show sold 1.32 million units in the first week of its release.

TOP 10 SINGLES OF 2002 IN THE US

	SINGLE	ARTIST OR GROUP
1	Before Your Love/ A Moment Like This	Kelly Clarkson
2	Uh Huh	B2K
3	Lights Camera Action!	Mr. Cheeks
4	Hush Lil' Lady	Corey
5	Girlfriend	*NSYNC remix featuring Nelly
6	A Thousand Miles	Vanessa Carlton
7	Die Another Day	Madonna
8	A Little Less Conversation	Elvis Presley vs. JXL
9	Long Time Gone	Dixie Chicks
10	Can't Fight the Moonlight	LeAnn Rimes

Source: *Nielsen Soundscan*

THE 10 LATEST GRAMMY RECORDS OF THE YEAR

YEAR	RECORD	ARTIST OR GROUP
2002	Don't Know Why	Norah Jones
2001	Walk On	U2
2000	Beautiful Day	U2
1999	Smooth	Santana featuring Rob Thomas
1998	My Heart Will Go On	Celine Dion
1997	Sunny Came Home	Shawn Colvin
1996	Change The World	Eric Clapton
1995	Kiss from a Rose	Seal
1994	All I Wanna Do	Sheryl Crow
1993	I Will Always Love You	Whitney Houston

The Grammys are awarded retrospectively, thus the 45th awards were presented in 2003 in recognition of musical accomplishment during 2002.

THE 10 LATEST GRAMMY NEW ARTISTS OF THE YEAR

YEAR	ARTIST
2002	Norah Jones
2001	Alicia Keys
2000	Shelby Lynne
1999	Christina Aguilera
1998	Lauryn Hill
1997	Paula Cole
1996	LeeAnn Rimes
1995	Hootie & the Blowfish
1994	Sheryl Crow
1993	Toni Braxton

Most recent winner Norah Jones swept the Grammys, winning an unprecedented five awards at the 45th annual ceremony (held on February 23, 2003, honoring 2002 releases). The week after the event, her Grammy-winning Album of the Year *Come Away With Me* sold 621,000 units, rocketing to No. 1.

THE 10 LATEST GRAMMY POP VOCALISTS OF THE YEAR (FEMALE)

YEAR	VOCALIST	SONG
2002	Norah Jones	Don't Know Why
2001	Nelly Furtado	I'm Like a Bird
2000	Macy Gray	I Try
1999	Sarah McLachlan	I Will Remember You
1998	Celine Dion	My Heart Will Go On
1997	Sarah McLachlan	Building a Mystery
1996	Toni Braxon,	Un-Break My Heart
1995	Annie Lennox	No More "I Love You"s
1994	Sheryl Crow	All I Wanna Do
1993	Whitney Houston	I Will Always Love You

Norah Jones's *Don't Know Why*, a track from her award-winning *Come Away With Me* album, also won Song of the Year for songwriter Jesse Harris and Record of the Year, as well as accolades from veteran singer Tony Bennett, who remarked at the event, "She's not good, she's great! She's phenomenal!"

THE 10 LATEST GRAMMY POP VOCALISTS OF THE YEAR (MALE)

YEAR	VOCALIST	SONG
2002	John Mayer	Your Body is a Wonderland
2001	James Taylor	Don't Let Me Be Lonely Tonight
2000	Sting	She Walks this Earth (Soberana Rosa)
1999	Sting	Brand New Day
1998	Eric Clapton	My Father's Eyes
1997	Elton John	Candle in the Wind (1997)
1996	Eric Clapton	Change the World
1995	Seal	Kiss from a Rose
1994	Elton John	Can You Feel the Love Tonight
1993	Sting	If I Ever Lose My Faith in You

Latest winner John Mayer's track comes from his debut major-label album *Room for Squares*. His win was an exceptional achievement when viewed alongside those of his predecessors, all of whom are long-established artists.

TOP 10 | BEST-PAID ROCK AND POP STARS

	STAR	EST. EARNINGS (2001–02*) ($)
1	U2	69,000,000
2	Mariah Carey	58,000,000
3	Dave Matthews Band	50,000,000
4	Madonna	43,000,000
5	*NSYNC	42,300,000
6	Britney Spears	39,200,000
7	Jennifer Lopez	37,000,000
8	Backstreet Boys	36,800,000
9	Elton John	30,000,000
10	Aerosmith	25,000,000

For the period June 2001–June 2002

Source: Forbes

THE 10 | LATEST GRAMMY AWARDS FOR BEST HARD ROCK PERFORMANCE

YEAR	ARTIST OR GROUP	TITLE
2002	Foo Fighters	All My Life
2001	Linkin Park	Crawling
2000	Rage Against the Machine	Guerrilla Radio
1999	Metallica	Whiskey in the Jar
1998	Robert Plant & Jimmy Page	Most High
1997	Smashing Pumpkins	The End is the Beginning is the End
1996	Smashing Pumpkins,	Bullet with Butterfly Wings
1995	Pearl Jam	Spin the Black Circle
1994	Soundgarden	Black Hole Sun
1993	Stone Temple,	Plush

▶ **Pro Bono**
The combined revenue from record sales and concert tours has propelled U2 to the head of the rock star earnings league.

US Chart Toppers

TOP 10 | ARTISTS WITH THE MOST NO. 1 SINGLES

	ARTIST OR GROUP	NO. 1 SINGLES
1	The Beatles	20
2	Elvis Presley	18
3	Mariah Carey	15*
4	Michael Jackson	13
5 =	Madonna	12
=	The Supremes	12
7	Whitney Houston	11
8 =	Janet Jackson	10
=	Stevie Wonder	10
10 =	The Bee Gees	9
=	Elton John	9
=	Paul McCartney/Wings	9

* Including duets with Boyz II Men, Joe and 98 Degrees, and Jay-Z

Source: *Music Information Database*

TOP 10 | ALBUMS WITH THE MOST CONSECUTIVE WEEKS AT NO. 1 IN THE CHARTS

	ALBUM	ARTIST OR GROUP	DATES	WEEKS AT NO. 1
1	Love Me or Leave Me (Soundtrack)	Doris Day	Aug. 6, 1955–Jan. 21, 1956	25
2 =	Calypso	Harry Belafonte	Jan. 12, 1957–May 25, 1957	24
=	Purple Rain (Soundtrack)	Prince	Aug. 4, 1984–Jan. 12, 1985	24
=	Saturday Night Fever	Soundtrack	Jan. 21, 1978–July 1, 1978	24
5	Blue Hawaii (Soundtrack)	Elvis Presley	Dec. 16, 1961–Apr. 28, 1961	20
6	Rumours	Fleetwood Mac	July 23, 1977–Nov. 26, 1977	19
=	More of the Monkees	The Monkees	Feb. 11, 1967–June 10, 1967	18
=	Please Hammer Don't Hurt 'Em	MC Hammer	July 7, 1990–Nov. 3, 1990	18
9 =	Thriller	Michael Jackson	Feb. 26, 1983–July 18, 1983	17
=	Thriller	Michael Jackson	Dec. 24, 1983–Apr. 14, 1984	17
=	Some Gave All	Billy Ray Cyrus	June 13, 1992–Oct. 3, 1992	17

Source: *Music Information Database*

TOP 10 LONGEST GAPS BETWEEN NO. 1 HIT SINGLES

	ARTIST OR GROUP	PERIOD	(YRS)	GAP (MTHS)	(DAYS)
1	Cher	Mar. 23, 1974–Mar. 19, 1999	24	11	27
2	Elton John	Nov. 11, 1975–Oct. 11, 1997	21	11	0
3	The Beach Boys	Dec. 10, 1966–Nov. 5, 1988	21	10	26
4	Paul Anka	July 13, 1959–Aug. 24, 1974	15	1	11
5	George Harrison	June 30, 1973–Jan. 16, 1988	14	6	16
6	Neil Sedaka	Aug. 11, 1962–Feb. 1, 1975	12	5	21
7	The Four Seasons	July 18, 1964–Mar. 13, 1976	11	7	26
8	Herb Alpert	June 22, 1968–Oct. 20, 1979	11	3	28
9	Frank Sinatra	July 9, 1955–July 2, 1966	10	11	24
10	Stevie Wonder	Aug. 10, 1963–Jan. 27, 1973	9	5	17

Source: *The Music Information Database*

TOP 10 SINGLES THAT STAYED THE LONGEST AT NO. 1*

	TITLE	ARTIST OR GROUP	YEAR RELEASED	WEEKS AT NO. 1
1	One Sweet Day	Mariah Carey and Boyz II Men	1995	16
2	= I Will Always Love You	Whitney Houston	1992	14
	= I'll Make Love to You	Boyz II Men	1994	14
	= Macarena (Bayside Boys Mix)	Los Del Rio	1995	14
	= Candle in the Wind (1997)/ Something About the Way You Look Tonight	Elton John	1997	14
6	= End of the Road	Boyz II Men	1992	13
	= The Boy is Mine	Brandy and Monica	1998	13
8	= Don't be Cruel/ Hound Dog	Elvis Presley	1956	11
	= I Swear	All-4-One	1994	11
	= Un-break My Heart	Toni Braxton	1996	11
	= Independent Women Part 1	Destiny's Child	2000	11

* Based on Billboard charts

Source: *Music Information Database*

◀ **Wings over America**
As a member of The Beatles, with Wings (pictured here), and solo, Paul McCartney has totalled more weeks at US No. 1 than any other artist.

TOP 10 OLDEST ARTISTS TO HAVE A NO. 1 SINGLE*

	ARTIST/YEAR	TITLE	(YRS)	AGE* (MTHS)	(DAYS)
1	Louis Armstrong, 1964	Hello Dolly!	63	9	5
2	Lawrence Welk, 1961	Calcutta	57	11	14
3	Morris Stoloff, 1956	Moonglow and Theme from Picnic	57	10	8
4	Cher, 1999	Believe	52	9	15
5	Frank Sinatra#, 1967	Somethin' Stupid	51	4	24
6	Lorne Greene, 1964	Ringo	50	9	3
7	Elton John, 1997	Candle in the Wind (1997)/ Something about the Way You Look Tonight	50	9	21
8	Rod Stewart, 1994	All For Love	49	0	12
9	Bill Medley†, 1987	(I've Had) the Time of My Life	47	2	9
10	Dean Martin, 1964	Everybody Loves Somebody	47	2	8

* During last week of No. 1 US single

Duet with Nancy Sinatra

† Duet with Jennifer Warnes

Source: *The Popular Music Database*

TOP 10 YOUNGEST SOLO ARTISTS TO HAVE A NO. 1 SINGLE

	ARTIST/YEAR	TITLE	YEAR	AGE* (YRS)	(MTHS)
1	Jimmy Boyd	I Saw Mommy Kissing Santa Claus	1952	12	11
2	Stevie Wonder	Fingertips	1963	13	1
3	Donny Osmond	Go Away Little Girl	1971	13	7
4	Michael Jackson	Ben	1972	13	11
5	Laurie London	He's Got the Whole World in His Hands	1958	14	2
6	Little Peggy March	I Will Follow Him	1963	15	0
7	Brenda Lee	I'm Sorry	1960	15	5
8	Paul Anka	Diana	1957	16	0
9	Tiffany	I Think We're Alone Now	1987	16	10
10	Lesley Gore	It's My Party	1963	17	0

* During first week of debut No. 1 US single

Source: *The Popular Music Database*

If group members were eligible for the list, all three Hanson brothers would be in the Top 10. Isaac was 16 years and 6 months, Taylor 14 years and 2 months, and Zachary 11 years and 7 months when *Mmmbop* topped the charts in 1997.

Gold & Platinum

TOP 10 GROUPS WITH THE MOST PLATINUM ALBUMS IN THE US

	GROUP	PLATINUM ALBUMS*
1	The Beatles	92
2	The Eagles	81
3	Led Zeppelin	80
4	AC/DC	60
5	Aerosmith	59
6	Pink Floyd	54
7	Van Halen	50
8	U2	45
9 =	Alabama	44
=	Fleetwood Mac	44

By number of album awards, rather than number of albums qualifying for awards; double/triple albums counted once

► **They just keep rolling along**
The Rolling Stones' tally of gold albums spans the period from 1973, with *Goats Head Soup*, to 2002, with *40 Licks*.

TOP 10 GROUPS WITH THE MOST GOLD ALBUMS IN THE US

	GROUP	GOLD ALBUMS
1	The Beatles	41
2	The Rolling Stones	38
3 =	Kiss	23
=	Aerosmith	23
5 =	Alabama	22
=	Chicago	22
=	Rush	22
8 =	The Beach Boys	20
=	Jefferson Airplane/Starship	20
10	AC/DC	19

The RIAA's Gold Awards have been presented since 1958 to artists who have sold 500,000 units of a single, album, or multidisc set. Multiple Gold Awards were presented up to 1976, when Platinum Awards, honoring million-selling discs, were introduced.

TOP 10 MALE SOLO ARTISTS WITH THE MOST GOLD ALBUMS IN THE US

	ARTIST	GOLD ALBUMS
1	Elvis Presley	73*
2	Neil Diamond	35
3	Elton John	34
4	Bob Dylan	32#
5 =	Frank Sinatra	28
=	George Strait	28
7	Kenny Rogers	25†
8	Hank Williams Jr.	21
9 =	Eric Clapton	20§
=	Rod Stewart	20

Excluding 16 gold albums for EPs

Excluding three gold albums with the Grateful Dead

† *Excluding one gold album with Dolly Parton and two with Dottie West*

§ *Excluding one gold album with B.B. King*

TOP 10 FEMALE SOLO ARTISTS WITH THE MOST GOLD ALBUMS IN THE US

	ARTIST	GOLD ALBUMS
1	Barbra Streisand	42*
2	Reba McEntire	20
3	Linda Ronstadt	17#
4 =	Madonna	14
=	Olivia Newton-John	14†
6	Aretha Franklin	13
=	Anne Murray	13
8 =	Amy Grant	12
=	Tanya Tucker	12
10 =	Natalie Cole	11
=	Donna Summer	11

Excluding one with Kris Kristofferson

Excluding two with Dolly Parton and Emmylou Harris

† *Excluding two with John Travolta and the Electric Light Orchestra*

TOP 10 MALE ARTISTS WITH THE MOST PLATINUM ALBUMS IN THE US

	ARTIST	PLATINUM ALBUMS*
1	Garth Brooks	97
2	Elvis Presley	71
3	Billy Joel	62
4	Elton John	59
5	Michael Jackson	56
6	George Strait	49
7	Bruce Springsteen	46
8	Kenny G	45
9	Kenny Rogers	43
10	Neil Diamond	36

* By number of album awards, rather than number of albums qualifying for awards

Source: *RIAA*

Platinum singles and albums in the US are those that have achieved sales of one million units. The award has been made by the Recording Industry Association of America (RIAA) since 1976, when it was introduced in response to escalating music sales.

TOP 10 FEMALE ARTISTS WITH THE MOST PLATINUM ALBUMS IN THE US

	ARTIST	PLATINUM ALBUMS*
1	Madonna	59
2 =	Whitney Houston	52
=	Barbra Streisand	52#
4	Mariah Carey	49
5	Celine Dion	42
6	Reba McEntire	33
7	Shania Twain	32
8	Linda Ronstadt	28†
9	Janet Jackson	22
10	Alanis Morissette	20

* By number of album awards, rather than number of albums qualifying for awards

 # Excluding four with Kris Kristofferson

† Excluding one with Dolly Parton and Emmylou Harris

Winning Whitney
Including her two soundtrack albums, Whitney Houston has sold over 53 million albums in the US alone. Worldwide her total is some 100 million.

Music Genres

TOP 10 RAP SINGLES IN THE US, 2002

	TITLE	ARTIST OR GROUP
1	Hot in Herre	Nelly
2	Always on Time	Ja Rule featuring Ashanti
3	Dilemma	Nelly featuring Kelly Rowland
4	What's Luv?	Fat Joe featuring Ashanti
5	I Need a Girl (Part Two)	P. Diddy & Ginuwine featuring Loon, Mario Winans & Tammy Ruggeri
6	Oh Boy	Cam'ron featuring Juelz Santana
7	Nothin'	N.O.R.E.
8	I Need a Girl (Part One)	P. Diddy featuring Usher & Loon
9	Gangsta Lovin'	Eve featuring Alicia Keys
10	Move B***h	Ludacris featuring Mystikal & Infamous 2.0

Source: Billboard

▼ Always first
Taken from his *Pain is Love* album, Ja Rule with Ashanti's hit single *Always on Time* was a global chart-topper in 2002.

TOP 10 R&B/HIP-HOP ALBUMS IN THE US, 2002

	TITLE	ARTIST OR GROUP
1	The Eminem Show	Eminem
2	Word of Mouf	Ludacris
3	Nellyville	Nelly
4	Ashanti	Ashanti
5	Stillmatic	Nas
6	Pain Is Love	Ja Rule
7	8701	Usher
8	Invincible	Michael Jackson
9	Genesis	Busta Rhymes
10	P. Diddy & Bad Boy Records Present... We Invented the Remix	Various Artists

Source: Billboard

Within four months of its release, Eminem's third album *The Eminem Show* had achieved sales of 5.4 million, placing it midway between his first release *The Marshall Mathers LP* (8.9 million) and *The Slim Shady LP* (4.3 million).

TOP 10 ROCK ALBUMS IN THE US

	TITLE/ARTIST OR GROUP	YEAR OF ENTRY
1	Their Greatest Hits 1971–1975, The Eagles	1976
2	Led Zeppelin IV, Led Zeppelin	1973
3	Back in Black, AC/DC	1980
4	Rumours, Fleetwood Mac	1977
5	Cracked Rear View, Hootie & the Blowfish	1994
6	Boston, Boston	1976
7	Hotel California, The Eagles	1976
8	Physical Graffiti, Led Zeppelin	1975
9	Born In the USA, Bruce Springsteen	1984
10	Appetite For Destruction, Guns 'N Roses	1987

Source: *Music Information Database*

At the end of 2002, sales of list-toppers The Eagles' *Their Greatest Hits* were certified as having attained 28 million, while even the 10th entry had sold a remarkable 15 million.

TOP 10 MUSIC GENRES IN THE US

GENRE	MARKET SHARE PERCENTAGE (2000)
1 Rock	24.8
2 Pop	11.0
3 Country	10.7
4 Rap	10.3
5 R&B/urban	9.7
6 Religious	4.8
7 Jazz	2.9
8 Classical	2.7
9 Hip hop	2.6
10 Oldies	0.9

Source: *Recording Industry Association of America*

The market breaks down into CD sales, representing 89.3 percent of the market, cassettes (4.9 percent), singles (2.5 percent), music videos (0.8 percent), and vinyl LPs (0.5 percent). The largest age group by far was 45 and older, with male buyers edging out female buyers by 1.2 percent.

TOP 10 COUNTRY SINGLES IN THE US

	TITLE/ARTIST OR GROUP	YEAR
1	**How Do I Live,** LeAnn Rimes	1997
2	**Islands in the Stream,** Kenny Rogers and Dolly Parton	1983
3	**This Kiss,** Faith Hill	1998
4	**You're Still the One,** Shania Twain	1998
5	**Elvira,** Oak Ridge Boys	1981
6	**Achy Breaky Heart,** Billy Ray Cyrus	1992
7	**The Devil Went Down to Georgia,** Charlie Daniels Band	1979
8	**Always on My Mind,** Willie Nelson	1982
9	**I Hope You Dance,** Lee Ann Womack	2000
10	**Behind Closed Doors,** Charlie Rich	1973

Source: *Music Information Database*

▶ **High-profile J-Lo**
The remix of Jennifer Lopez's *Alive*, originally featured on her film *Enough*, was one of the top dance singles of 2002.

TOP 10 DANCE MAXI-SINGLES IN THE US, 2002

	TITLE	ARTIST OR GROUP
1	**Die Another Day** (remixes)	Madonna
2	**Heaven**	DJ Sammy & Yanou featuring Do
3	**Song for the Lonely**	Cher
4	**Lifetime** (Ben Watt remix)	Maxwell
5	**Alive** (Thunderpuss remix)	Jennifer Lopez
6	**U Don't Have to Call** (remixes)	Usher
7	**Where the Party At** (remixes)	Jagged Edge with Nelly
8	**By Your Side** (remixes)	Sade
9	**Thank You** (Deep Dish remix)	Dido
10	**Yes**	Amber

Source: Billboard

MOST PROLIFIC CLASSICAL COMPOSERS

	COMPOSER/NATIONALITY/DATES	HOURS OF MUSIC
1	Joseph Haydn (Austrian; 1732–1809)	340
2	George Handel (German-English; 1685–1759)	303
3	Wolfgang Amadeus Mozart (Austrian; 1756–91)	202
4	Johann Sebastian Bach (German; 1685–1750)	175
5	Franz Schubert (German; 1797–1828)	134
6	Ludwig van Beethoven (German; 1770–1827)	120
7	Henry Purcell (English; 1659–95)	116
8	Giuseppe Verdi (Italian; 1813–1901)	87
9	Anton Dvorák (Czech; 1841–1904)	79
10 =	Franz Liszt (Hungarian; 1811–86)	76
=	Peter Tchaikovsky (Russian; 1840–93)	76

Based on a survey by *Classical Music* magazine, which ranked classical composers by the total number of hours of music each composed. If the length of the composer's working life is taken into account, Schubert wins: his 134 hours were composed in a career of 18 years—an average of 7 hours 27 minutes per annum. The method puts Tchaikovsky ahead of Liszt: although both composed 76 hours, Tchaikovsky worked for 30 years, Liszt for 51, giving them annual averages of 2 hours 32 minutes and 1 hour 29 minutes respectively.

THE FIRST ENGLISH OPERA

THE IDENTITY OF THE FIRST OPERA in English is the subject of debate. It may have been Richard Flecknoe's *Ariadne* (1654), or *The Siege of Rhodes* by English Poet Laureate Sir William D'Avenant (1606–68), performed at Rutland House, London in September 1656. The latter was described by John Evelyn in his Diary as "…a new opera after the Italian way, in recitative music and scenes." It was the first theatrical production with painted perspective stage sets, and the first with a female performer, Mrs. Coleman, as Ianthe.

FIRST FACT

CITIES WITH THE MOST OPERAS

	CITY/COUNTRY	PRODUCTIONS*
1	Vienna, Austria	32
2	Berlin, Germany	21
3	Prague, Czech Republic	20
4	Paris, France	16
5	Hamburg, Germany	13
6 =	London, UK	12
=	Zurich, Switzerland	12
8 =	New York, US	11
=	Munich, Germany	11
10	Hanover, Germany	10

* Sample during a 12-month period

LARGEST OPERA THEATERS

	THEATER/LOCATION	CAPACITY*
1	Arena di Verona# Verona, Italy	16,663
2	Municipal Opera Theater# St. Louis, MO	11,745
3	Teatro alla Scala Milan, Italy	3,600
4	Civic Opera House Chicago, IL	3,563
5 =	The Metropolitan, Lincoln Center New York, NY	3,500
=	Teatro San Carlo Naples, Italy	3,500
6	Music Hall Cincinnati, OH	3,417
8 =	The Hummingbird Center Toronto, Canada	3,200
=	Teatro Massimo Palermo, Italy	3,200
10	Halle aux Grains, Toulouse, France	3,000

* Indoor venues—seating capacity only given, although capacity is often larger when standing capacity is included

Open-air venue

Although there are many more venues in the world where opera is regularly performed, the above list is limited to those where the principal performances are opera.

MOST PERFORMED OPERA COMPOSERS

	COMPOSER/NATIONALITY/DATES	PRODUCTIONS*
1	Giuseppe Verdi (Italian; 1813–1901)	68
2	Giacomo Puccini (Italian; 1858–1924)	44
3	Wolfgang Amadeus Mozart (Austrian; 1756–91)	40
4 =	Gioacchino Rossini (Italian; 1792–1868)	13
=	Richard Strauss (German; 1864–1949)	13
6	Richard Wagner (German; 1813–83)	12
7	Gaetano Donizetti (Italian; 1797–1848)	11
8 =	Leos Janáček (Czech; 1854–1928)	10
=	Jacques Offenbach (German; 1819–80)	10
10	Georges Bizet (French; 1838–75)	9

* International sample during a 12-month period

MOST PERFORMED OPERAS

	OPERA	PRODUCTIONS	PERFORMANCES*
1	La Bohème	11	52
2	Tosca	12	48
3	Madama Butterfly	9	42
4	Die Zauberflöte	11	37
5	Un Ballo in Maschera	8	35
6	Don Giovanni	9	31
7	Otello	9	30
8	Les Contes d'Hoffmann	7	29
9	Il Barbiere di Siviglia	9	27
10 =	La Traviata	8	24
=	Salome	6	24

* Based on a sample of 180 international productions

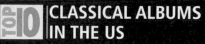

CLASSICAL ALBUMS IN THE US

	PERFORMER(S)/ORCHESTRA	TITLE	YEAR
1	José Carreras, Placido Domingo, Luciano Pavarotti	The Three Tenors In Concert	1990
2	Andrea Bocelli	Romanza	1997
3	Andrea Bocelli	Sogno	1999
4	Charlotte Church	Voice of an Angel	1999
5	Benedictine Monks of Santo Domingo De Silos	Chant	1994
6	José Carreras, Placido Domingo, Luciano Pavarotti	The Three Tenors—In Concert 1994	1994
7	Andrea Bocelli	Sacred Arias	1999
8	Van Cliburn	Tchaikovsky: Piano Concerto No. 1	1958
9	Soundtrack (Philadelphia Orchestra)	Fantasia (50th Anniversary Edition)	1990
10	Placido Domingo	Perhaps Love	1981

Source: *The Music Information Database*

The 1990s saw a huge increase in sales of classical and opera music, a change that owes much to the influence of tenors such as Placido Domingo and Luciano Pavarotti, whose amazing rise to international stardom has led to opera music becoming a far more accessible genre.

OPERAS MOST FREQUENTLY PERFORMED AT THE METROPOLITAN OPERA HOUSE, NEW YORK

	OPERA	COMPOSER	PERFORMANCES*
1	La Bohème	Giacomo Puccini	1,126
2	Aïda	Giuseppi Verdi	1,066
3	Carmen	Georges Bizet	908
4	La Traviata	Giuseppi Verdi	881
5	Tosca	Giacomo Puccini	839
6	Madama Butterfly	Giacomo Puccini	768
7	Rigoletto	Giuseppi Verdi	753
8	Faust	Charles Gounod	713
9	Pagliacci	Ruggero Leoncavallo	688
10	Cavalleria Rusticana	Pietro Mascagni	648

* As of end of 2002–03 season

Source: *Metropolitan Opera*

▶ **Nights at the opera**
Tosca, here sung by Luciano Pavarotti with Carole Vanes, is one of the most performed productions at the principal opera houses on both sides of the Atlantic.

Broadcast Music

THE10 LATEST RECIPIENTS OF THE MTV VMA "BEST VIDEO" AWARD

YEAR	ARTIST OR GROUP	TITLE
2002	Eminem	Without Me
2001	Christina Aguilera, Lil' Kim, Mya, Pink, featuring Missy "Misdeameanor" Elliott	Lady Marmalade
2000	Eminem	The Real Slim Shady
1999	Lauryn Hill	Doo Wop (That Thing)
1998	Madonna	Ray of Light
1997	Jamiroquai	Virtual Insanity
1996	The Smashing Pumpkins	Tonight, Tonight
1995	TLC	Waterfalls
1994	Aerosmith	Cryin'
1993	Pearl Jam	Jeremy

THE10 LATEST RECIPIENTS OF THE MTV VMA "BEST GROUP VIDEO" AWARD

YEAR	ARTIST OR GROUP	TITLE
2002	No Doubt (featuring Bounty Killer)	Hey Baby
2001	*NSYNC	POP
2000	Blink 182	All the Small Things
1999	TLC	No Scrubs
1998	Backstreet Boys	Everybody (Backstreet's Back)
1997	No Doubt	Don't Speak
1996	Foo Fighters	Big Me
1995	TLC	Waterfalls
1994	Aerosmith	Cryin'
1993	Pearl Jam	Jeremy

TOP10 SINGLES OF TV THEME TUNES IN THE US

	TITLE/ARTIST OR GROUP	PROGRAM
1	Welcome Back, John Sebastian	Welcome Back Kotter
2	T.S.O.P., MFSB	Soul Train
3	Theme from S.W.A.T., Rhythm Heritage	S.W.A.T.
4	Theme from "The Greatest American Hero" (Believe It Not), Joey Scarbury	The Greatest American Hero
5	Theme from "The Dukes of Hazzard", Waylon Jennings	The Dukes of Hazzard
6	Makin' It, David Naughton	Makin' It
7	Nadia's Theme (The Young & the Restless), Barry DeVorzon & Perry Botkin, Jr.	The Young and the Restless
8	How Do You Talk to an Angel, Heights	The Heights
9	Miami Vice Theme, Jan Hammer	Miami Vice
10	Hawaii Five-0, Ventures	Hawaii Five-0

Former member of the Lovin' Spoonful John Sebastian wrote *Welcome Back* for the 1970s TV series *Kotter* (duly renamed *Welcome Back Kotter*). Sebastian's expanded version of the theme song topped the chart and became his first million-seller.

 **No Doubt about It**

The video of *Hey Baby*, co-written by Dave Stewart and performed by Gwen Stefani of No Doubt, received the accolade as MTV's "Best Group Video."

THE10 LATEST NAB MARCONI ROCK STATIONS OF THE YEAR

YEAR*	STATION	LOCATION
2002	KOZT	Fort Bragg, California
2001	WEBN	Cincinnati, Ohio
2000	WFBQ	Indianapolis, Indiana
1999	WEBN,	Cincinnati, Ohio
1998	WFBQ-FM	Indianapolis, Indiana
1997	WDVE-FM	Pittsburg, Pennsylvania
1996	WFBQ-FM	Indianapolis, Indiana
1995	KROQ-FM	Los Angeles, California
1994	KQRS-AM/FM	El Paso, Texas
1993	WXRT-FM	Chicago, Illinois

* In 1993 and previous years, the award was for AOR/Classic rock

THE10 LATEST RECIPIENTS OF THE MTV VMA "BEST FEMALE VIDEO" AWARD

YEAR	ARTIST	TITLE
2002	Pink	Get the Party Started
2001	Eve (featuring Gwen Stefani)	Let Me Blow Ya Mind
2000	Aaliyah	Try Again
1999	Lauryn Hill	Doo Wop (That Thing)
1998	Madonna	Ray of Light
1997	Jewel	You Were Meant for Me
1996	Alanis Morissette	Ironic
1995	Madonna	Take a Bow
1994	Janet Jackson	If
1993	k.d. lang	Constant Crying

Launched in 1981 as a cable channel, MTV started presenting its Video Music Awards (VMA) in 1984.

LATEST RECIPIENTS OF THE MTV VMA "BEST MALE VIDEO" AWARD

YEAR	ARTIST OR GROUP	TITLE
2002	Eminem	Without Me
2001	Moby (featuring Gwen Stefani)	South Side
2000	Eminem	The Real Slim Shady
1999	Will Smith	Miami
1998	Will Smith	Just the Two of Us
1997	Beck	The Devil's Haircut
1996	Beck	Where It's At
1995	Tom Petty and the Heartbreakers	You Don't Know How it Feels
1994	Tom Petty and the Heartbreakers	Mary Jane's Last Dance
1993	Lenny Kravitz	Are You Gonna Go My Way

▼ The real Slim Shady

Eminem's award-winning video of his single *Without Me* depicts the rap star both as himself and in a diverse range of provocative personae, from a fat Elvis to Osama bin Laden.

MUSIC SHOWS ON US TELEVISION, 2001–02

	TITLE	NETWORK	HOUSEHOLD VIEWERS
1	Michael Jackson 30th Anniversary	CBS	12,353,000
2	New Year's Rockin' Eve Part 1	ABC	11,330,000
3	Jennifer Lopez in Concert	NBC	7,804,000
4	Concert for America	NBC	6,756,000
5	Garth Brooks Live! 2	CBS	6,403,000
6	Garth Brooks Live! 3	CBS	6,120,000
7	Garth Brooks Live! 1	CBS	5,920,000
8	Celine Dion: A New Day	CBS	5,910,000
9	New Year's Rockin' Eve '02	ABC	5,907,000
10	Ultimate Manilow!	CBS	4,709,000

Source: *Nielsen Media Research*

It was estimated that more than 25 million individuals watched the November 16, 2001 screening of the concert celebrating the 30 years since Michael Jackson's first solo single, *Got to Be There*, the largest audience for a music special since the *Beatles Anthology* in 1995.

Movie Music

MUSICAL FILMS

	FILM	YEAR
1	Grease	1978
2	Saturday Night Fever	1977
3	The Sound of Music	1965
4	Evita	1996
5	The Rocky Horror Picture Show	1975
6	Staying Alive	1983
7	American Graffiti	1973
8	Mary Poppins	1964
9	Flashdance	1983
10	Fantasia 2000	2000

Traditional musicals (films in which the cast actually sing) and films in which a musical soundtrack is a major component of the film are included here. The era of the blockbuster musical film may be over, but in recent years animated films with an important musical content appear to have taken over from them—*Beauty and the Beast*, *Aladdin*, *The Lion King*, *Pocahontas*, *The Prince of Egypt*, and *Tarzan* all won "Best Original Song" Oscars—while the film soundtrack album of *Titanic* is the best-selling of all time.

SOUNDTRACK ALBUMS IN THE US

	TITLE	YEAR OF RELEASE	EST. SALES
1	The Bodyguard	1992	17,000,000
2	Purple Rain	1984	13,000,000
3	Forrest Gump	1994	12,000,000
4	= Dirty Dancing	1987	11,000,000
	= Titanic	1997	11,000,000
6	The Lion King	1994	10,000,000
7	= Top Gun	1986	9,000,000
	= Footloose	1984	9,000,000
9	Grease	1978	8,000,000
10	Saturday Night Fever	1977	7,500,000

Source: *RIAA*

FILMS WITH TITLES DERIVED FROM SONG TITLES

	FILM		YEAR*
1	American Pie	1972	1999
2	Sweet Home Alabama	1976	2002
3	Bad Boys	1983	1995
4	Sea of Love	1959	1989
5	One Fine Day	1963	1996
6	My Girl	1965	1991
7	Something To Talk About	1991	1995
8	When a Man Loves a Woman	1966	1994
9	The Crying Game	1964	1992
10	Addicted to Love	1986	1997

* Release of first hit version

Remarkably, the first film with a title derived from a song title was *How Would You Like to Be the Ice Man?*, released on April 21, 1899!

Grease is the word
Although it has celebrated its 25th anniversary, *Grease*, starring John Travolta as Danny and Olivia Newton-John as Sandy, remains unbeaten as the highest-earning musical film.

THE 10 LATEST "BEST SONG" OSCAR WINNERS

YEAR	TITLE	FILM
2002	Lose Yourself	8 Mile
2001	If I Didn't Have You	Monsters, Inc.
2000	Things Have Changed	Wonder Boys
1999	You'll Be in My Heart	Tarzan
1998	When You Believe	The Prince of Egypt
1997	My Heart Will Go On	Titanic
1996	You Must Love Me	Evita
1995	Colors of the Wind	Pocahontas
1994	Can You Feel the Love Tonight	The Lion King
1993	Streets of Philadelphia	Philadelphia

The "Best Song" Oscar was instituted at the 1934 Academy Awards ceremony, when it was won by "The Continental" from the film *The Gay Divorcee*. Songs from animated Disney films have been especially successful, winning on eight occasions since 1940, when "When You Wish Upon a Star" from *Pinocchio* received the award. "Zip-a-Dee-Doo-Dah" from part-animated *Song of the South* (1947) and "Chim Chim Cher-ee" from *Mary Poppins* (1964), along with songs from live-action films, bring the overall Disney total to 12.

TOP 10 JAMES BOND FILM THEMES IN THE US

	TITLE	ARTIST(S)	YEAR
1	A View to a Kill	Duran Duran	1985
2	Nobody Does It Better*	Carly Simon	1977
3	Live and Let Die	Paul McCartney and Wings	1973
4	For Your Eyes Only	Sheena Easton	1981
5	Goldfinger	Shirley Bassey	1965
6	Thunderball	Tom Jones	1966
7	All Time High#	Rita Coolidge	1983
8	You Only Live Twice	Nancy Sinatra	1967
9	Diamonds are Forever	Shirley Bassey	1972
10	Die Another Day	Madonna	2002

* from The Spy Who Loved Me

 # from Octopussy

By no means have all the James Bond themes been major US hits, especially those from the later movies, some of which failed to register at all. Every song listed here reached the Top 100, but only the first seven made the Top 40, and only Duran Duran had a Bond-associated US No. 1 hit.

TOP 10 FILM MUSICALS ADAPTED FROM STAGE VERSIONS

	FILM MUSICAL	THEATER OPENING	FILM RELEASE
1	Grease	1972	1978
2	The Sound of Music	1959	1965
3	Evita	1978	1996
4	The Rocky Horror Picture Show	1973	1975
5	Chicago	1975	2002
6	Fiddler on the Roof	1964	1971
7	My Fair Lady	1956	1964
8	The Best Little Whorehouse in Texas	1978	1982
9	Annie	1977	1982
10	West Side Story	1957	1961

The adapting of stage musicals as films has a long history, with these the most successful cinematic versions of, in most instances, long-running theatrical productions. Some followed an even longer progress from stage to screen, having been non-musical theatrical productions before being adapted as stage musicals, among them the recent success *Chicago*, which started life in 1926 as a play by Maurine Dallas Watkins and was made into two films, *Chicago* (1927) and *Roxie Hart* (1942), before Bob Fosse wrote the 1975 musical.

TOP 10 POP STAR FILM DEBUTS

	POP STAR(S)	FILM	YEAR
1	Whitney Houston	The Bodyguard	1992
2	Eminem	8 Mile	2002
3	Meatloaf	Rocky Horror Picture Show	1975
4	Dolly Parton	Nine to Five	1980
5	The Spice Girls	Spice World	1998
6	Jennifer Lopez	Money Train	1995
7	Aaliyah	Romeo Must Die	2000
8	Britney Spears	Crossroads	2002
9	Ice Cube	Boyz N the Hood	1991
10	Barbra Streisand	Funny Girl	1968

Since Al Jolson's debut role in the pioneering talkie *The Jazz Singer* (1927), many popular vocalists have made the transition to films, with those listed representing the most successful (although some had minor parts, often uncredited, in films before starring in these). Since the 1930s this catalog has included artists of the caliber of Bing Crosby, Marlene Dietrich, Elvis Presley, The Beatles, David Bowie, Sting, Madonna, and Björk.

STAGE &
SCREEN

The Play's the Thing

THE 10 | LATEST DRAMA DESK AWARDS FOR AN ACTRESS

YEAR	ACTRESS	PLAY
2002	Lindsay Duncan	Private Lives
2001	Mary-Louise Parker	Proof
2000	Eileen Heckart	The Waverly Gallery
1999	Kathleen Chalfant	Wit
1998	Cherry Jones	Pride's Crossing
1997	Janet McTeer	A Doll's House
1996	Zoë Caldwell	Master Class
1995	Glenn Close	Sunset Boulevard
1994	Myra Carter	Three Tall Women
1993	Jane Alexander	The Sisters Rosensweig

Source: *New York Drama Desk*

THE 10 | LATEST DRAMA DESK AWARDS FOR AN ACTOR

YEAR	ACTOR	PLAY
2002	Alan Bates	Fortune's Fool
2001	Richard Easton	The Invention of Love
2000	Stephen Dillane	The Real Thing
1999	Brian Dennehy	Death of a Salesman
1998	Anthony LaPaglia	A View from the Bridge
1997	= David Morse	How I Learned to Drive
	= Christopher Plummer	Barrymore
1996	Frank Langella	The Father
1995	Ralph Fiennes	Hamlet
1994	Stephen Spinella	Angels in America Part II: Perestroika

Source: *New York Drama Desk*

THE 10 | LATEST TONY AWARDS FOR A DIRECTOR

YEAR	DIRECTOR	PLAY
2002	Mary Zimmerman	Metamorphoses
2001	Daniel Sullivan	Proof
2000	Michael Blakemore	Copenhagen
1999	Robert Falls	Death of a Salesman
1998	Garry Hynes	The Beauty Queen of Leenane
1997	Anthony Page	A Doll's House
1996	Gerald Gutierrez	A Delicate Balance
1995	Gerald Gutierrez	The Heiress
1994	Stephen Daldry	An Inspector Calls
1993	George C. Wolfe	Angels in America Part I: Millennium Approaches

The Tony Awards, established by the American Theater Wing in 1947, honor outstanding Broadway actors, directors, and others. They are named for actress and director Antoinette Perry (1888–1946), who headed the American Theater Wing.

◀ **Class comedy**
Seen here with co-star Alan Rickman, Lindsay Duncan won the New York Drama Desk Award for her role in *Private Lives*.

TOP 10 | MOST PRODUCED SHAKESPEARE PLAYS ON BROADWAY

	PLAY	PRODUCTIONS
1	Hamlet	61
2	The Merchant of Venice	46
3	Macbeth	40
4	Romeo and Juliet	32
5	Twelfth Night	29
6	As You Like It	22
7	Othello	20
8	= Julius Caesar	19
	= Richard III	19
	= The Taming of the Shrew	19

Source: *The League of American Theaters and Producers*

The least popular have been *The Two Gentlemen of Verona* (never produced—except as a musical written by the composers of *Hair*), *All's Well That Ends Well*, *The Comedy of Errors, Timon of Athens, Coriolanus, Henry IV Part I,* and *Henry IV Part II,* which have all been produced just once.

TOP 10 LONGEST-RUNNING NON-MUSICALS ON BROADWAY

SHOW/YEARS RUNNING	PERFORMANCES
1 Oh! Calcutta! (1976–89)	5,959
2 Life with Father (1939–47)	3,224
3 Tobacco Road (1933–41)	3,182
4 Abie's Irish Rose (1922–27)	2,327
5 Gemini (1977–81)	1,819
6 Deathtrap (1978–82)	1,793
7 Harvey (1944–49)	1,775
8 Born Yesterday (1946–49)	1,642
9 Mary, Mary (1961–64)	1,572
10 The Voice of the Turtle (1943–48)	1,557

Source: *The League of American Theaters and Producers*

More than half the longest-running non-musical shows on Broadway began their runs before World War II; the others all date from the period up to the 1970s, before the long-running musical completely dominated the Broadway stage.

TOP 10 LONGEST-RUNNING THRILLERS ON BROADWAY

SHOW/YEARS RUNNING	PERFORMANCES
1 Deathtrap (1978–82)	1,793
2 Arsenic and Old Lace (1941–44)	1,444
3 Angel Street (1941–1944)	1,295
4 Sleuth (1970–73)	1,222
5 Dracula (1977–80)	925
6 Witness for the Prosecution (1954–56)	645
7 Dial M for Murder (1952–54)	556
8 Sherlock Holmes (1974–76)	471
9 An Inspector Calls (1994–95)	454
10 Ten Little Indians (1944–45)	426

Source: *The League of American Theaters and Producers*

Ira Levin's record-breaking *Deathtrap* ran at the Music Box Theater before transferring to the Biltmore Theater. Marian Seldes played the same part in almost every performance, for which she won a Best Supporting Actress Tony Award.

TOP 10 LATEST PULITZER DRAMA AWARDS

YEAR*	PLAYWRIGHT	PLAY
2003	Nilo Cruz	Anna in the Tropics
2002	Suzan-Lori Parks	Topdog/Underdog
2001	David Auburn	Proof
2000	Jhumpa Lahiri	Dinner with Friends
1999	Margaret Edson	Wit
1998	Paula Vogel	How I Learned to Drive
1996	Jonathan Larson	Rent
1995	Horton Foote	The Young Man from Atlanta
1994	Edward Albee	Three Tall Women
1993	Tony Kushner	Angels in America Part I: Millennium Approaches

* No award in 1997

The Pulitzer Drama Award is made for "an American play, preferably original and dealing with American life." Regarded as the most prestigious of all drama awards, it is presented to playwrights; the first winner, in 1918, was Jesse Lynch Williams for *Why Marry?*

TOP 10 LONGEST-RUNNING MUSICALS ON BROADWAY

SHOW/YEARS RUNNING	PERFORMANCES
1 Cats (1982–2000)	7,485
2 Les Misérables (1987–2003)	6,684
3 The Phantom of the Opera (1988–)	6,231*
4 A Chorus Line (1975–90)	6,137
5 Miss Saigon (1991–2001)	4,095
6 Beauty and the Beast (1994–)	3,556*
7 42nd Street (1980–89)	3,486
8 Grease (1972–80)	3,388
9 Fiddler on the Roof (1964–72)	3,242
10 Hello, Dolly! (1964–71)	2,844

* Still running; total as of January 1, 2003

Source: *The League of American Theaters and Producers*

▶ **The cats' whiskers**
Cats made theater history by topping the long-running musicals chart on both sides of the Atlantic.

Blockbusters

TOP 10 HIGHEST-GROSSING FILMS WORLDWIDE

	FILM	YEAR	US	GROSS INCOME ($) OVERSEAS	WORLD TOTAL
1	Titanic*	1997	600,800,000	1,234,600,000	1,835,400,000
2	Harry Potter and the Sorcerer's Stone	2001	317,600,000	649,400,000	967,000,000
3	Star Wars: Episode I—The Phantom Menace	1999	431,100,000	492,000,000	923,100,000
4	Jurassic Park	1993	334,800,000	547,000,000	881,800,000
5	The Lord of the Rings: The Two Towers	2002	333,600,000	533,000,000	866,600,000
6	Harry Potter and the Chamber of Secrets	2002	261,700,000	604,000,000	865,700,000
7	The Lord of the Rings: The Fellowship of the Ring	2001	313,400,000	547,200,000	860,600,000
8	Independence Day	1996	306,300,000	505,000,000	811,200,000
9	Spider-Man	2002	403,700,000	402,000,000	805,700,000
10	Star Wars: Episode IV—A New Hope	1977	461,000,000	337,000,000	798,000,000

* Winner of "Best Picture" Academy Award

In March 2003, *Harry Potter and the Chamber of Secrets* became only the third film ever (after *Titanic* and *Harry Potter and the Sorcerer's Stone*) to make more than $600 million at the international box office—a remarkable feat, since only four films have ever made more than $500 million and three over $400 million outside the US.

TOP 10 FILM BUDGETS

	FILM	YEAR	BUDGET ($)
1	Titanic	1997	200,000,000
2	= Waterworld	1995	175,000,000
	= Wild, Wild West	1999	175,000,000
4	Terminator 3: Rise of the Machines	2003	170,000,000
5	Tarzan*	1999	145,000,000
6	Die Another Day	2002	142,000,000
7	= Armageddon	1998	140,000,000
	= Lethal Weapon 4	1998	140,000,000
	= Men in Black II	2002	140,000,000
	= Pearl Harbor	2001	140,000,000
	= Treasure Planet	2002	140,000,000

* Animated

The two most expensive films ever made are water-based, with large-scale special effects being major factors in escalating budgets. The two blockbusters of 2001, *Harry Potter and the Sorcerer's Stone* and *Lord of the Rings: The Fellowship of the Ring*, had budgets of $125 million and $109 million, and their sequels, *Harry Potter and the Chamber of Secrets* and *The Lord of the Rings: The Two Towers*, $100 million and $94 million respectively, and so do not make the Top 10.

▼ **Star quality**
Queen Padmé Amidala, played by Natalie Portman in *Star Wars: Episode I—The Phantom Menace*, which was second only to *Titanic* as the highest-grossing film of the 20th century.

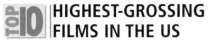

TOP 10 HIGHEST-GROSSING FILMS IN THE US

	FILM	YEAR	GROSS US INCOME ($)
1	Titanic*	1997	600,800,000
2	Star Wars#	1977	461,000,000
3	E.T. the Extra-Terrestrial	1982	435,000,000
4	Star Wars: Episode I—The Phantom Menace	1999	431,100,000
5	Spider-Man	2002	403,700,000
6	Jurassic Park	1993	357,100,000
7	The Lord of the Rings: The Two Towers	2002	334,800,000
8	Forrest Gump*	1994	329,700,000
9	Harry Potter and the Sorcerer's Stone	2001	317,600,000
10	The Lord of the Rings: The Fellowship of the Ring	2001	313,400,000

* Winner of "Best Picture" Academy Award

Later retitled Star Wars: Episode IV—A New Hope

Only 14 films have ever earned more than $300 million in the US. The four former members of this premier league, The Lion King (1994), Star Wars: Episode II— Attack of the Clones (2002), Star Wars: Episode VI—Return of the Jedi (1983), and Independence Day (1996), have recently been deposed by the Harry Potter and Lord of the Rings films.

TOP 10 FILM FRANCHISES

	FRANCHISE	FILMS	YEARS	TOTAL WORLD GROSS ($)*
1	James Bond	20	1963–2002	3,630,559,554
2	Star Wars	5	1977–2002	3,471,554,580
3	Jurassic Park	3	1993–2001	1,901,027,106
4	Harry Potter	2	2001–02	1,832,722,908
5	The Lord of the Rings	2	2001–02	1,742,399,971
6	Batman	4	1989–97	1,268,376,929
7	Indiana Jones	3	1981–89	1,211,716,531
8	Star Trek	10	1979–2002	1,053,666,245
9	Men in Black	2	1997–2002	1,013,409,342
10	Mission: Impossible	2	1996–2000	1,012,391,875

* Cumulative global earnings of the original film and all its sequels to March 31, 2003

A successful film does not guarantee a successful sequel: although their total income earns them a place just outside the Top 10. Each of the four Superman films actually earned less than the previous one, with Superman IV earning just one-tenth of the original. Smokey and the Bandit Part III earned just one-seventeenth of the original, and Grease 2 less than one-tenth of the original Grease. Sometimes the situation is reversed. Terminator 2: Judgment Day earned more than six times as much as its "prequel."

TOP 10 MOST PROFITABLE FILMS OF ALL TIME*

	FILM	YEAR	BUDGET ($)	WORLD GROSS ($)	PROFIT RATIO
1	The Blair Witch Project	1999	35,000	248,662,839	7,104.65
2	American Graffiti	1973	750,000	115,000,000	153.33
3	Snow White and the Seven Dwarfs#	1937	1,488,000	187,670,866	126.12
4	The Rocky Horror Picture Show	1975	1,200,000	139,876,417	116.56
5	Rocky†	1976	1,100,000	117,235,147	106.58
6	Gone With the Wind†	1939	3,900,000	390,555,278	100.14
7	The Full Monty	1997	3,500,000	256,950,122	73.41
8	Star Wars§	1977	11,000,000	797,998,007	72.55
9	E.T. the Extra-Terrestrial	1982	10,500,000	756,774,579	72.07
10	My Big Fat Greek Wedding	2002	5,000,000	353,906,779	70.78

* Minimum entry $100 million world gross

Animated

† Academy Award for "Best Picture"

§ Later retitled Star Wars: Episode IV—A New Hope

It should be noted that the budget for The Blair Witch Project represents only the cost of making the film: further post-production costs, for example to enhance the sound quality, were incurred prior to theatrical release.

TOP 10 FILMS IN THE US, 2002

	FILM	US BOX OFFICE ($)
1	Spider-Man	403,706,375
2	Star Wars: Episode II—Attack of the Clones	310,308,606
3	The Lord of the Rings: The Two Towers	268,666,211
4	Harry Potter and the Chamber of Secrets	253,040,825
5	My Big Fat Greek Wedding	228,774,165
6	Signs	227,791,166
7	Austin Powers in Goldmember	213,117,789
8	Men in Black II	190,418,803
9	Ice Age*	176,387,405
10	Die Another Day	154,666,799

* Animated

While this represents the highest-earning movies of 2002, certain films remained on release and continued to attract audiences in 2003, most notably among them The Lord of the Rings: The Two Towers, thus elevating it to second place among the year's releases.

World Movies

TOP 10 FILMS IN INDIA

	FILM	YEAR	TOTAL INDIA GROSS (IRs)
1	Gadar	2001	650,000,000
2	Hum Aapke Hai Kaun	1994	600,000,000
3	Dilwale Dulhania Le Jayenge	1995	500,000,000
4	Raja Hindustani	1996	450,000,000
5	Kuch Kuch Hota Hai	1998	425,000,000
6	Kabhi Khushi Kabhie Gham	2001	380,500,000
7	Kaho Na Pyaar Hai	2000	350,000,000
8	Karan Arjun	1995	320,000,000
9 =	Border	1997	300,000,000
=	Lagaan	2001	300,000,000

▼ Bollywood blockbuster
Aditya Chopra's popular directorial debut, *Dilwale Dulhania Le Jayenge* (*The Brave-Hearted Will Take the Bride*), starring Shahrukh Khan and Kajol, was a huge hit.

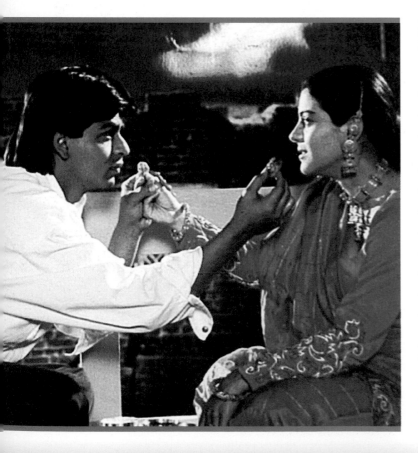

TOP 10 FILMS IN FRANCE

	FILM*	YEAR	TOTAL FRANCE GROSS (US$)
1	Titanic	1998	138,928,349
2	Astérix & Obélix: Mission Cleopatra (France)	2002	75,846,048
3	Taxi 2 (France)	2000	63,703,757
4	Astérix & Obélix contre César (France)	1999	59,154,242
5	Star Wars: Episode I—The Phantom Menace	1999	55,825,511
6	The Fifth Element	1997	54,080,230
7	Les Visiteurs II: Les couloirs du temps (France)	1998	53,898,537
8	Le Dîner de Cons (France)	1998	53,155,025
9	Harry Potter and the Chamber of Secrets	2002	53,141,000
10	Harry Potter and the Sorcerer's Stone	2001	48,745,200

* All from US unless otherwise specified

France's all-time Top 10 films mirrors the country's cosmopolitan movie tastes, with half the films among Hollywood blockbusters and half from the homegrown output.

TOP 10 FILMS IN AUSTRALIA

	FILM*	YEAR	TOTAL AUSTRALIA GROSS (AUS$)
1	Titanic	1997	57,642,943
2	Crocodile Dundee (Australia)	1986	47,707,045
3	The Lord of the Rings: The Fellowship of The Ring	2001	46,851,327
4	The Lord of the Rings: The Two Towers	2002	45,183,872
5	Harry Potter and the Sorcerer's Stone	2001	42,310,037
6	Star Wars: Episode I—The Phantom Menace	1999	38,828,310
7	Harry Potter and the Chamber of Secrets	2002	37,009,842
8	Babe (Australia/US)	1995	36,776,544
9	Star Wars: Episode II—Attack of the Clones	2002	33,811,334
10	Jurassic Park	1993	33,002,776

* All from US unless otherwise specified

Australia's most popular films reflect the international box office, but with a distinct Antipodean bias: *Crocodile Dundee* is the most successful Australian film ever, earning over US$300 million worldwide, while *Babe* was an Australian/US co-production filmed in Australia with an Australian director (Chris Noonan). Australian films earned AUS$ 48.1 million, 4.9 percent of the total, at the Australian box office in 2002.

TOP 10 FILMS IN JAPAN

	FILM*	YEAR	TOTAL JAPAN GROSS (US$)
1	Sen to Chihiro no Kamikakushi (Spirited Away)# (Japan)	2001	228,612,367
2	Harry Potter and the Chamber of Secrets	2002	142,786,414
3	Harry Potter and the Sorcerer's Stone	2001	127,687,138
4	Titanic	1997	101,800,644
5	The Lord of the Rings: The Two Towers	2002	59,156,943
6	Star Wars: Episode I—The Phantom Menace	1999	50,812,345
7	Mononoke Hime (Princess Mononoke)# (Japan)	1997	49,959,609
8	Kindaichi Shonen no Jikenbo (The Case Book of Young Kindaichi)# (Japan)	1997	47,637,131
9	Armageddon	1998	45,533,387
10	Independence Day	1996	44,239,833

All from US unless otherwise specified

 # Animated

The Japanese Top 10 features a number of global successes while representing the local enthusiasm for *anime*—animation, often with a fantasy element, aimed to appeal to adults.

 **High spirits**
The popular Japanese *anime* production *Spirited Away* was the first film ever to earn more than $200 million before it opened in the US and won the "Best Animated Feature" Oscar.

TOP 10 FOREIGN LANGUAGE FILMS IN THE US

	FILM	YEAR	ORIGINAL LANGUAGE*	TOTAL US GROSS ($)
1	Crouching Tiger, Hidden Dragon	2000	Mandarin	128,078,872
2	Life is Beautiful	1998	Italian	57,600,759
3	Amélie	2001	French	33,225,499
4	The Gods Must Be Crazy	1984	Afrikaans	30,031,783
5	Il Postino (The Postman)	1995	Italian	21,845,977
6	Like Water for Chocolate	1993	Spanish	21,665,468
7	La Dolce Vita	1966	Italian	19,500,000
8	Brotherhood of the Wolf	2002	French	18,828,863
9	I am Curious (Yellow)	1969	Swedish	18,570,318
10	La Cage aux Folles	1979	French	17,921,489

Some dubbed in English, others subtitled

TOP 10 FILMS IN SPAIN

	FILM*	YEAR	TOTAL SPAIN GROSS (US$)
1	Titanic	1997	43,672,525
2	The Lord of the Rings: The Two Towers	2002	32,840,128
3	The Lord of the Rings: The Fellowship of the Ring	2001	28,925,390
4	The Sixth Sense	1999	27,305,275
5	Harry Potter and the Chamber of Secrets	2002	25,890,767
6	Star Wars: Episode I—The Phantom Menace	1999	25,808,403
7	Harry Potter and the Sorcerer's Stone	2001	24,685,592
8	The Others	2001	24,599,316
9	Mortadelo y Filemón (Spain)	2003	24,102,774
10	Spider-Man	2002	22,074,731

All from US unless otherwise specified

Movie Genres

WAR FILMS

	FILM	YEAR
1	Saving Private Ryan	1998
2	Pearl Harbor	2001
3	Schindler's List	1993
4	The English Patient	1996
5	Life is Beautiful (La vita è bella)	1997
6	Braveheart	1995
7	Black Hawk Down	2001
8	U-571	2000
9	Three Kings	1999
10	Enemy at the Gates	2001

In recent years, until the hugely successful *Saving Private Ryan*, surprisingly few war films appeared in the high-earning bracket, which led some to consider that the days of big-budget films in this genre were over. However, excluding military-themed but non-war films, recent blockbusters, including "historical" war films such as Mel Gibson's two notable successes, *Braveheart* and *The Patriot*, and *Pearl Harbor*, appear to have disproved this prediction.

SUPERHERO FILMS

	FILM	YEAR
1	Spider-Man	2002
2	Batman	1989
3	Batman Forever	1995
4	The Mask	1994
5	Superman	1978
6	X-Men	2000
7	Batman Returns	1992
8	Batman & Robin	1997
9	Teenage Mutant Ninja Turtles	1990
10	Blade II	2002

Superman makes a single showing in this Top 10, since it is in the unusual situation where the first film made a large amount (in excess of $300 million) at the world box office, while each of its three sequels made progressively less.

▼ Worldwide web
With global earnings of over $800 million, *Spider-Man* confirmed its place as the most successful superhero film ever.

SCIENCE-FICTION FILMS

	FILM	YEAR
1	Star Wars: Episode I— The Phantom Menace	1999
2	Jurassic Park	1993
3	Independence Day	1996
4	Spider-Man	2002
5	Star Wars	1977
6	E.T. the Extra-Terrestrial	1982
7	Star Wars: Episode II— Attack of the Clones	2002
8	The Lost World: Jurassic Park	1997
9	Men in Black	1997
10	Star Wars: Episode VI— Return of the Jedi	1983

The first five films in this list are also in the all-time Top 10 films, and all 10 are among the 18 most successful films ever, having earned over $570 million each—a total of more than $7.4 billion at the worldwide box office.

TOP 10 MAGIC, WITCHES, AND WIZARDS FILMS

	FILM	YEAR
1	Harry Potter and the Sorcerer's Stone	2001
2	The Lord of the Rings: The Two Towers	2002
3	The Lord of the Rings: The Fellowship of the Ring	2001
4	Harry Potter and the Chamber of Secrets	2002
5	Shrek*	2001
6	Beauty and the Beast*	1991
7	The Blair Witch Project	1999
8	Sleepy Hollow	1999
9	Snow White and the Seven Dwarfs*	1937
10	Fantasia/2000*	1999

* Animated

▶ **Golden ring**
The second of the *Lord of the Rings* trilogy, *The Two Towers* has outearned its predecessor to become the fifth highest-earning film of all time.

TOP 10 DINOSAUR FILMS

	FILM	YEAR
1	Jurassic Park	1993
2	The Lost World: Jurassic Park	1997
3	Godzilla	1998
4	Jurassic Park III	2001
5	Dinosaur*	2000
6	Fantasia*#	1940
7	T-Rex: Back to the Cretaceous	1998
8	The Flintstones in Viva Rock Vegas	2000
9	The Land Before Time*	1988
10	Super Mario Bros.	1993

* Animated; others live-action with mechanical or computer-generated animation sequences

 # Igor Stravinsky's "Rite of Spring" sequence

The animated *Gertie the Dinosaur* (1914) was the first notable example in a catalog of well over 100 films featuring prehistoric monsters.

TOP 10 JAMES BOND FILMS

	FILM	BOND ACTOR	YEAR
1	Die Another Day	Pierce Brosnan	2002
2	The World Is Not Enough	Pierce Brosnan	1999
3	GoldenEye	Pierce Brosnan	1995
4	Tomorrow Never Dies	Pierce Brosnan	1997
5	Moonraker	Roger Moore	1979
6	The Living Daylights	Timothy Dalton	1987
7	For Your Eyes Only	Roger Moore	1981
8	The Spy Who Loved Me	Roger Moore	1977
9	Octopussy	Roger Moore	1983
10	License to Kill	Timothy Dalton	1990

Ian Fleming wrote 12 James Bond novels, only two of which, *Moonraker* (1955) and *The Spy Who Loved Me* (1962), figure in this Top 10. After his death in 1964, *For Your Eyes Only*, *Octopussy*, *The Living Daylights*, and *GoldenEye* were developed by other writers from his short stories, while subsequent releases were written without reference to Fleming's writings. *Casino Royale* (book 1953, film 1967), featuring 56-year-old David Niven as the retired spy Sir James Bond, is an oddity in that it was presented as a comedy. This and *Never Say Never Again* (1983), effectively a remake of *Thunderball*, are not considered "official" Bond films, making the 2002 release *Die Another Day* the 20th in the canonical series.

Leading Men

TOP 10 ACTORS AT THE US BOX OFFICE

ACTOR*	FILMS	TOTAL ($)
1 Harrison Ford	30	3,187,215,057
2 Samuel L. Jackson	56	2,832,308,762
3 Tom Hanks	30	2,805,563,647
4 Tom Cruise	25	2,389,498,678
5 James Earl Jones	36	2,326,924,965
6 Eddie Murphy	27	2,300,000,784
7 Mel Gibson	31	2,285,154,698
8 Robin Williams	41	2,230,226,135
9 Jim Cummings	24	2,193,119,817
10 Rance Howard	38	2,190,866,163

Appeared in or provided voice in animated film

Although a volatile list, this presents a snapshot of the actors who, to date, have appeared in the films or provided the voice of a character in an animated film that cumulatively have earned the most in the US. Such is the box office appeal of Harrison Ford that US distributors voted him "Star of the Century."

TOP 10 RUSSELL CROWE FILMS

FILM	YEAR
1 Gladiator*	2000
2 A Beautiful Mind	2001
3 L.A. Confidential	1997
4 The Insider	1999
5 The Quick and the Dead	1995
6 Proof of Life	2000
7 Virtuosity	1995
8 Mystery, Alaska	1999
9 The Sum of Us	1994
10 Proof	1991

Won Academy Award for "Best Actor"

After appearing in Australian TV series including *Neighbours* (1987), New Zealand-born Russell Crowe gained his first Hollywood role with *The Quick and the Dead* (1995).

TOP 10 PIERCE BROSNAN FILMS

FILM	YEAR
1 Mrs. Doubtfire	1993
2 Die Another Day	2002
3 The World Is Not Enough	1999
4 GoldenEye	1995
5 Tomorrow Never Dies	1997
6 Dante's Peak	1997
7 The Thomas Crown Affair	1999
8 Mars Attacks!	1996
9 The Mirror Has Two Faces	1996
10 The Lawnmower Man	1992

Pierce Brosnan, now best known as James Bond, provided the voice of King Arthur in the animated *Quest for Camelot* (1998). If included, it would be ranked ninth. Each of the eight leading films in his Top 10 has earned in excess of $100 million worldwide.

TOP 10 BRAD PITT FILMS

FILM	YEAR
1 Ocean's Eleven	2001
2 Se7en	1995
3 Interview with the Vampire: The Vampire Chronicles	1994
4 Sleepers	1996
5 Twelve Monkeys	1995
6 Legends of the Fall	1994
7 The Devil's Own	1997
8 Meet Joe Black	1998
9 Seven Years in Tibet	1997
10 Spy Game	2001

Brad Pitt is a member of an elite group of actors all of whose 10 highest-earning films have made more than $100 million in total at the world box office, with runners-up *The Mexican* (2001) and *Fight Club* (1999) also falling into this high-earning league.

FIRST $1M STAR

FIRST FACT

In 1921—after ironically appearing in a film called *The Dollar a Year Man*—silent film star Roscoe ("Fatty") Arbuckle (1887–1933) signed a three-year contract with Paramount that would have made him the first film star ever to earn $1 million a year. However, at a party to celebrate his success, a starlet called Virginia Rappe was injured and later died, and he was charged with her manslaughter. Although he was acquitted, the scandal meant Arbuckle became the first star to be banned from acting. He began working as a director under the pseudonym William Goodrich and in 1933 agreed a deal with Warner Bros. but died, aged 46, the day he signed the contract that would have enabled his return to the screen.

TOP 10 BRUCE WILLIS FILMS

FILM	YEAR
1 The Sixth Sense	1999
2 Armageddon	1998
3 Die Hard: With a Vengeance	1995
4 The Fifth Element	1997
5 Unbreakable	2000
6 Die Hard 2	1990
7 Pulp Fiction	1994
8 Twelve Monkeys	1995
9 The Jackal	1997
10 Death Becomes Her	1992

Although discounted here, it is somewhat ironic to consider that the fourth most successful film role of an actor whose screen persona is of a tough guy would otherwise be that of a baby in *Look Who's Talking* (1989)—and that consisting only of Willis's dubbed voice.

TOP 10 LEONARDO DiCAPRIO FILMS

	FILM	YEAR
1	Titanic	1997
2	Catch Me If You Can	2002
3	Gangs of New York	2002
4	The Man in the Iron Mask	1998
5	The Beach	2000
6	Romeo + Juliet	1996
7	The Quick and the Dead	1995
8	Marvin's Room	1996
9	What's Eating Gilbert Grape	1993
10	Celebrity	1998

A film career of less than 10 years has seen Leonardo DiCaprio star in six $100 million-plus earning films, including the biggest blockbuster of all time. His role in *What's Eating Gilbert Grape* also gained him an Oscar nomination.

TOP 10 TOM CRUISE FILMS

	FILM	YEAR
1	Mission: Impossible II	2000
2	Mission: Impossible	1996
3	Rain Man	1988
4	Top Gun	1986
5	Minority Report	2002
6	Jerry Maguire	1996
7	The Firm	1993
8	A Few Good Men	1992
9	Interview with the Vampire: The Vampire Chronicles	1994
10	Vanilla Sky	2001

Few actors have matched Tom Cruise's commercial success: every one of his Top 10 films has earned more than $200 million worldwide, a total of $3.3 billion.

▼ **Leonardo masterpiece**
Leonardo DiCaprio stars as conman Frank Abagnale Jr. in *Catch Me If You Can*, which has netted over $300 million worldwide.

Leading Women

TOP 10 ACTRESSES AT THE US BOX OFFICE

	ACTRESS*	FILMS	TOTAL ($)
1	Julia Roberts	27	1,889,883,547
2	Carrie Fisher	25	1,760,869,785
3	Whoopi Goldberg	41	1,683,352,258
4	Kathy Bates	31	1,447,092,182
5	Drew Barrymore	27	1,303,932,619
6	Cameron Diaz	21	1,289,627,290
7	Maggie Smith	20	1,286,055,060
8	Bonnie Hunt	16	1,270,837,762
9	Sally Field	20	1,237,398,519
10	Glenn Close	28	1,236,979,789

Appeared in or provided voice in animated film

As with the actor counterpart list, these are the actresses whose films (and voice-only parts in animated films) have earned the most cumulatively in the US. Julia Roberts has appeared in nine films that have made over $100 milion in the US, and 13 that have netted more than that amount worldwide.

TOP 10 JULIANNE MOORE FILMS

	FILM	YEAR
1	The Lost World: Jurassic Park	1997
2	The Fugitive	1993
3	Hannibal	2001
4	Nine Months	1995
5	The Hand that Rocks the Cradle	1992
6	Evolution	2001
7	Assassins	1995
8	The Hours*	2002
9	Magnolia	1999
10	Boogie Nights	1997

Nominated for Academy Award for "Best Actress"

Julianne Moore's early appearances were in TV series and TV films. Following her break into mainstream movies, her relatively minor role in *The Fugitive* so impressed Steven Spielberg that he cast her in *The Lost World: Jurassic Park*, both of which top her personal Top 10.

TOP 10 MERYL STREEP FILMS

	FILM	YEAR
1	Out of Africa	1985
2	The Bridges of Madison County	1995
3	Death Becomes Her	1992
4	Kramer vs. Kramer	1979
5	The River Wild	1994
7	The Hours	2002
6	The Deer Hunter	1978
8	Manhattan	1979
9	Postcards from the Edge	1990
10	Silkwood	1983

Meryl Streep has been nominated for Academy Awards on a total of 13 occasions, winning for her supporting role in *Kramer vs. Kramer*, and "Best Actress" for *Sophie's Choice* (1982), which scores outside her personal Top 10. She provided the voice of the Blue Fairy in *A.I.: Artificial Intelligence* (2001), which, were it taken into account, would be in second place.

TOP 10 NICOLE KIDMAN FILMS

	FILM	YEAR
1	Batman Forever	1995
2	Moulin Rouge!*	2001
3	The Others	2001
4	Days of Thunder	1990
5	Eyes Wide Shut	1999
6	The Peacemaker	1997
7	Practical Magic	1998
8	Far and Away	1992
9	The Hours#	2002
10	Malice	1993

Nominated for Academy Award for "Best Actress"

Winner of Academy Award for "Best Actress"

Honolulu-born Nicole Kidman was raised in Australia, where she acted on TV before her break into film, in which she has pursued a highly successful career: more than half her Top 10 films have earned over $100 million worldwide.

TOP 10 GWYNETH PALTROW FILMS

	FILM	YEAR
1	Se7en	1995
2	Hook	1991
3	Shakespeare in Love*	1998
4	Shallow Hal	2001
5	A Perfect Murder	1998
6	The Talented Mr. Ripley	1999
7	The Royal Tenenbaums	2001
8	Sliding Doors	1998
9	Great Expectations	1998
10	Malice	1993

Winner of "Best Actress" Academy Award

Noted for her faultless English accent in her Academy Award-winning role in *Shakespeare in Love* and other movies – and for her tearful Oscar acceptance speech – in little over a decade Gwyneth Paltrow's Top 10 films have cumulatively earned more than $1.5 billion globally.

TOP 10 CAMERON DIAZ FILMS

	FILM	YEAR
1	There's Something About Mary	1998
2	The Mask	1994
3	My Best Friend's Wedding	1997
4	Charlie's Angels	2000
5	Vanilla Sky	2001
6	Gangs of New York	2002
7	Any Given Sunday	1999
8	Being John Malkovich	1999
9	The Sweetest Thing	2002
10	A Life Less Ordinary	1997

Cameron Diaz's Top 10 films include several that are among the highest earning of recent years. She also provided the voice of Princess Fiona in *Shrek* (2001)—which has outearned all of them. Her uncredited cameo role as "woman on metro" in *Minority Report* (2002) has not been included, but would be in second place.

TOP 10 | CATHERINE ZETA-JONES FILMS

	FILM	YEAR
1	The Mask of Zorro	1998
2	Entrapment	1999
3	Traffic	2000
4	Chicago	2002
5	The Haunting	1999
6	America's Sweethearts	2001
7	High Fidelity	2000
8	The Phantom	1996
9	Christopher Columbus: The Discovery	1992
10	Splitting Heirs	1993

After a debut as Sheherezade in the French film *Les Mille et Une Nuits* (1990), Welsh-born Catherine Zeta-Jones rose to prominence as Mariette Larkin in the British TV series *The Darling Buds of May* before her first Hollywood screen role in *Christopher Columbus: The Discovery* (1992).

▶ Two Zee's

Catherine Zeta-Jones took the Oscar for "Best Supporting Actress" as Velma Kelly in *Chicago*. Actress Renée Zellweger was also nominated for an award.

TOP 10 | RENEE ZELLWEGER FILMS

	FILM	YEAR
1	Bridget Jones's Diary	2001
2	Jerry Maguire	1996
3	Chicago	2002
4	Me, Myself & Irene	2000
5	Nurse Betty	2000
6	One True Thing	1998
7	The Bachelor	1999
8	Reality Bites	1994
9	8 Seconds	1994
10	White Oleander	2002

Apart from some unmemorable early parts in films such as *The Return of the Texas Chainsaw Massacre* (1994), Renée Zellweger has followed an ever-upward trajectory in her film career. Her title role in *Bridget Jones's Diary* and *Nurse Betty* earned her two Golden Globe awards, and she was nominated for the "Best Actress" Oscar for her performance in *Chicago*.

Oscar-Winning Films

THE 10 LATEST "BEST PICTURE" OSCAR WINNERS

YEAR	FILM	DIRECTOR
2002	Chicago	Rob Marshall*
2001	A Beautiful Mind	Ron Howard
2000	Gladiator	Ridley Scott*
1999	American Beauty	Sam Mendes
1998	Shakespeare in Love	John Madden*
1997	Titanic	James Cameron
1996	The English Patient	Anthony Minghella
1995	Braveheart	Mel Gibson
1994	Forrest Gump	Robert Zemeckis
1993	Schindler's List	Steven Spielberg

* Did not also win "Best Director" Academy Award

The first picture to be honored at the first-ever Academy Awards ceremony, held on May 16, 1929, was *Wings*, a silent World War I epic.

TOP 10 HIGHEST-EARNING "BEST PICTURE" OSCAR WINNERS*

	FILM	YEAR#
1	Titanic	1997
2	Forrest Gump	1994
3	Gladiator	2000
4	Dances With Wolves	1990
5	Rain Man	1988
6	Gone With the Wind	1939
7	American Beauty	1999
8	Schindler's List	1993
9	A Beautiful Mind	2001
10	Shakespeare in Love	1998

* Ranked by world box-office income

 # Of release; Academy Awards are awarded the following year

THE 10 LATEST BLACK-AND-WHITE FILMS TO WIN "BEST PICTURE" OSCARS

	FILM	YEAR
1	Schindler's List	1993
2	The Apartment	1960
3	Marty	1955
4	On the Waterfront	1954
5	From Here to Eternity	1953
6	All About Eve	1950
7	All the King's Men	1949
8	Hamlet	1948
9	Gentleman's Agreement	1947
10	The Best Years of Our Lives	1946

TOP 10 STUDIOS WITH THE MOST "BEST PICTURE" OSCARS

	STUDIO	AWARDS
1 =	Columbia	12
=	United Artists	12
3	Paramount	11
4	MGM	9
5	20th Century Fox	7
6 =	Universal	6
=	Warner Bros.	6
8	Orion	4
9 =	DreamWorks	3
=	Miramax	3

In the 75 years of the Academy Awards up to the 2003 ceremony, these, along with RKO Radio Pictures with two wins (1931 and 1946), are the only studios to have won a "Best Picture" Oscar.

◀ **Top Gere**
Richard Gere as astute lawyer Billy Flynn in *Chicago*. The film, an adaptation of a stage musical, won "Best Picture" and five other Academy Awards.

TOP 10 FILMS TO WIN THE MOST OSCARS*

	FILM	YEAR	NOMINATIONS	AWARDS
1 =	Ben-Hur	1959	12	11
=	Titanic	1997	14	11
3	West Side Story	1961	11	10
4 =	Gigi	1958	9	9
=	The Last Emperor	1987	9	9
=	The English Patient	1996	12	9
7 =	Gone With the Wind	1939	13	8#
=	From Here to Eternity	1953	13	8
=	On the Waterfront	1954	12	8
=	My Fair Lady	1964	12	8
=	Cabaret	1972	10	8
=	Gandhi	1982	11	8
=	Amadeus	1984	11	8

* Oscar® is a Registered Trade Mark

 # Plus two special awards

Ten other films have won seven Academy Awards each: *Going My Way* (1944), *The Best Years of Our Lives* (1946), *The Bridge on the River Kwai* (1957), *Lawrence of Arabia* (1962), *Patton* (1970), *The Sting* (1973), *Out of Africa* (1985), *Dances With Wolves* (1991), *Schindler's List* (1993), and *Shakespeare in Love* (1998). *Titanic* (1997) matched the previous record of 14 nominations of *All About Eve* (1950), but outshone it by winning 11, compared with the latter's six.

TOP 10 FILMS WITH THE MOST NOMINATIONS WITHOUT A SINGLE WIN

	FILM	YEAR	NOMINATIONS
1 =	The Turning Point	1977	11
=	The Color Purple	1985	11
3	Gangs of New York	2002	10
4 =	The Little Foxes	1941	9
=	Peyton Place	1957	9
6 =	Quo Vadis	1951	8
=	The Nun's Story	1959	8
=	The Sand Pebbles	1966	8
=	The Elephant Man	1980	8
=	Ragtime	1981	8
=	The Remains of the Day	1993	8

Gangs of New York is the latest of a number of films to have received an impressive tally of nominations, but no wins in any category. *Mutiny on the Bounty* (1935) was the last to win "Best Picture" but no other awards.

TOP 10 FILMS NOMINATED FOR THE MOST OSCARS

	FILM	YEAR	AWARDS	NOMINATIONS
1 =	All About Eve	1950	6	14
=	Titanic	1997	11	14
3 =	Gone With the Wind	1939	8*	13
=	From Here to Eternity	1953	8	13
=	Mary Poppins#	1964	5	13
=	Who's Afraid of Virginia Woolf?#	1966	5	13
=	Forrest Gump	1994	6	13
=	Shakespeare in Love	1998	7	13
=	The Lord of the Rings: The Fellowship of the Ring	2001	4	13
=	Chicago	2002	6	13

* Plus two special awards

 # Did not win "Best Picture" Academy Award

Thirteen is clearly not unlucky where Oscar nominations are concerned, no fewer than nine films having received that number. They and the two with 14 are those that received the greatest share of votes from Academy members using a system that creates a shortlist of five nominees in each of 24 categories other than special, honorary, and technical awards. However, eliminating such specialist categories as "Best Foreign Language," "Live Action Short," and "Animated Feature" reduces the potential number of awards for which a film may be nominated, while those that are eligible may be nominated in one category but not another—screenplays, for example, are separately nominated according to whether they are based on material previously produced or published or written directly for the screen.

THE 10 LATEST "BEST FOREIGN LANGUAGE FILM" OSCAR WINNERS

YEAR	FILM	COUNTRY
2002	Nowhere in Africa (Nirgendwo in Afrika)	Germany
2001	No Man's Land (Nicija zemlja)	Bosnia and Herzegovina/ Slovenia/Italy/France/UK/Belgium
2000	Crouching Tiger, Hidden Dragon (Wo hu cang long)	Hong Kong/China/ Taiwan/US
1999	All About My Mother (Todo sobre mi madre)	Spain/France
1998	Life Is Beautiful (La Vita è bella)	Italy
1997	Character (Karakter)	Belgium/Netherlands
1996	Kolya	Czech Republic
1995	Antonia's Line (Antonia)	Netherlands/Belgium/UK
1994	Burnt by the Sun (Utomlyonnye solntsem)	France/Russia
1993	The Age of Beauty (Belle époque)	Spain/Portugal/France

Prior to 1956, when *La Strada* won this award, foreign language films received awards in special or honorary categories.

Oscar-Winning Stars

THE 10 LATEST "BEST ACTRESS" OSCAR WINNERS

YEAR	ACTRESS	FILM
2002	Nicole Kidman	The Hours
2001	Halle Berry	Monster's Ball
2000	Julia Roberts	Erin Brockovich
1999	Hilary Swank	Boys Don't Cry
1998	Gwyneth Paltrow	Shakespeare in Love*
1997	Helen Hunt	As Good As It Gets
1996	Frances McDormand	Fargo
1995	Susan Sarandon	Dead Man Walking
1994	Jessica Lange	Blue Sky
1993	Holly Hunter	The Piano

* Won "Best Picture" Academy Award

Only one actress has ever won the "Best Actress in a Leading Role" Academy Award in consecutive years—Katharine Hepburn in 1967 and 1968 (shared with Barbra Streisand), with further wins in 1933 and 1981. Just 10 other actresses have won twice: Ingrid Bergman, Bette Davis, Olivia De Havilland, Sally Field, Jane Fonda, Jodie Foster, Glenda Jackson, Vivien Leigh, Luise Rainer, and Elizabeth Taylor.

▶ **Unafraid of Virginia Woolf**
Nicole Kidman gained her first "Best Actress" Oscar nomination for *Moulin Rouge!* (2001), winning with her role as Virginia Woolf in *The Hours* (2002).

THE 10 LATEST "BEST ACTOR" OSCAR WINNERS

YEAR	ACTOR	FILM
2002	Adrien Brody	The Pianist
2001	Denzel Washington	Training Day
2000	Russell Crowe	Gladiator*
1999	Kevin Spacey	American Beauty*
1998	Roberto Benigni	Life Is Beautiful
1997	Jack Nicholson	As Good As It Gets
1996	Geoffrey Rush	Shine
1995	Nicolas Cage	Leaving Las Vegas
1994	Tom Hanks	Forrest Gump*
1993	Tom Hanks	Philadelphia

* Won "Best Picture" Academy Award

Tom Hanks shares the honor of two consecutive wins with Spencer Tracy (1937: *Captains Courageous*, and 1938: *Boys Town*). Only four other actors have ever won twice: Marlon Brando (1954; 1972), Gary Cooper (1941; 1952), Dustin Hoffman (1977; 1988), and Jack Nicholson (1975; 1997).

THE 10 LATEST WINNERS OF AN OSCAR FOR THEIR DEBUT FILM*

	ACTOR/ACTRESS	FILM	FILM YEAR
1	Anna Paquin#	The Piano	1993
2	Marlee Matlin†	Children of a Lesser God	1986
3	Haing S. Ngor#	The Killing Fields	1984
4	Timothy Hutton#	Ordinary People	1980
5	Tatum O'Neal#	Paper Moon	1973
6	Barbra Streisand†	Funny Girl	1968
7 =	Julie Andrews†	Mary Poppins	1964
=	Lila Kedrova#	Zorba the Greek	1964
9	Miyoshi Umeki#	Sayonara	1957
10	Anna Magnani†	The Rose Tattoo	1955

* In a film eligible for a "Best" or "Best Supporting Actor/Actress" Academy Award win (hence excluding previous TV movies, etc.)

"Best Actor/Actress in a Supporting Role"

† "Best Actor/Actress in a Leading Role"

TOP 10 ACTRESSES WITH THE MOST OSCAR NOMINATIONS*

	ACTRESS	WINS SUPPORTING	BEST	NOMINATIONS
1	Meryl Streep	1	1	13
2	Katharine Hepburn	0	4	12
3	Bette Davis	0	2	10
4	Geraldine Page	0	1	8
5 =	Ingrid Bergman	1	2	7
=	Jane Fonda	0	2	7
=	Greer Garson	0	1	7
8 =	Ellen Burstyn	0	1	6
=	Deborah Kerr	0	0	6
=	Jessica Lange	1	1	6
=	Vanessa Redgrave	1	0	6
=	Thelma Ritter	0	0	6
=	Norma Shearer	0	0	6
=	Maggie Smith	1	1	6
=	Sissy Spacek	0	1	6

* In all acting categories

TOP 10 ACTORS WITH THE MOST OSCAR NOMINATIONS*

	ACTOR	WINS SUPPORTING	BEST	NOMINATIONS
1	Jack Nicholson	1	3	12
2	Laurence Olivier	0	1	10
3 =	Paul Newman	0	1	9
=	Spencer Tracy	0	2	9
5 =	Marlon Brando	0	2	8
=	Jack Lemmon	1	1	8
=	Al Pacino	0	1	8
8 =	Richard Burton	0	0	7
=	Dustin Hoffman	0	2	7
=	Peter O'Toole	0	0	7

* In all acting categories

Several of the actors listed here were also nominated for and won awards in non-acting categories: Laurence Olivier won "Best Actor" for his leading role but also "Best Picture" as the producer of *Hamlet* (1948), for which he was also nominated as "Best Director," while Paul Newman was nominated as producer of "Best Picture" nominee *Rachel, Rachel* (1968). In 2003, Peter O'Toole initially declined an honorary award on the ground that, as his career was not yet over, he retained hopes of winning one for an acting role.

THE 10 LATEST ACTORS AND ACTRESSES TO RECEIVE THREE OR MORE CONSECUTIVE NOMINATIONS

	ACTOR/ACTRESS	NOMINATIONS	YEARS
1	Russell Crowe	3	1999–2001
2	William Hurt	3	1985–87
3	Glenn Close	3	1982–84
4	Meryl Streep	3	1981–83
5	Jane Fonda	3	1977–79
6 =	Jack Nicholson	3	1973–75
=	Al Pacino	4	1972–75
8	Richard Burton	3	1964–66
9	Elizabeth Taylor	4	1957–60
10	Deborah Kerr	3	1956–58

In the earlier years of the Academy Awards, two actresses were nominated for "Best Actress" Oscars on a record five consecutive occasions: Bette Davis (1938–52), with wins in 1935 and 1939, and Greer Garson (1941–45), who never won.

THE 10 LATEST NOMINATIONS FOR ACTORS AND ACTRESSES FOR NON-ENGLISH-LANGUAGE PERFORMANCES

	ACTOR/ACTRESS	FILM	LANGUAGE	YEAR
1	Javier Bardem	Before Night Falls	Spanish	2000
2 =	Roberto Benigni*	Life Is Beautiful	Italian	1998
=	Fernanda Montenegro	Central Station	Portuguese	1998
4	Massimo Troisi	Il Postino	Italian	1995
5	Catherine Deneuve	Indochine	French	1992
6	Gérard Depardieu	Cyrano de Bergerac	French	1990
7	Isabelle Adjani	Camille Claudel	French	1989
8	Max von Sydow	Pelle the Conqueror	Swedish	1988
9	Marcello Mastroianni	Dark Eyes	Italian	1987
10	Marlee Matlin*	Children of a Lesser God	American sign language	1986

* Won Academy Award

And the Winner Is...

THE 10 LATEST WINNERS OF THE CANNES PALME D'OR FOR BEST FILM

YEAR	FILM	COUNTRY
2002	The Pianist	UK/France/Germany/Netherlands/Poland
2001	The Son's Room (La Stanza del figlio)	Italy/France
2000	Dancer in the Dark	Denmark/etc.
1999	Rosetta	France
1998	Eternity and a Day (Mia aioniotita kai mia mera)	Greece/France/Italy
1997	= The Eel (Unagi)	Japan
	= The Taste of Cherry (Ta`m e guilass)	Iran
1996	Secrets and Lies	UK
1995	Underground (Bila jednom jedna zemlja)	Yugoslavia/France/Germany/Hungary
1994	Pulp Fiction	US

In its early years, there was no single "Best Film" award at the Cannes Film Festival, several films being honored jointly. A "Grand Prize," first awarded in 1949, has been known since 1955 as the "Palme d'Or."

THE 10 LATEST GOLDEN GLOBE AWARDS FOR "BEST FOREIGN LANGUAGE" FILM

YEAR	FILM	COUNTRY
2002	Talk to Her (Habla con Ella)	Spain
2001	Amélie	France/Germany
2000	Crouching Tiger, Hidden Dragon (Wo hu cang long)	Hong Kong/China/Taiwan/US
1999	All About My Mother (Todo sobre mi madre)	Spain
1998	Central Station (Central do Brasil)	Brazil/France
1997	My Life in Pink (Ma Vie en Rose)	France/Belgium/UK
1996	Kolya	Czech Republic
1995	Les Misérables	France
1994	Farinelli	Italy/Belgium/France
1993	Farewell My Concubine (Ba wang bie ji)	China/Hong Kong

▲ **Palme winner**
Adrien Brody, in the title role in *The Pianist*, the latest winner of the prestigious Cannes Film Festival Palme d'Or.

THE 10 LATEST GOLDEN GLOBE AWARDS FOR "BEST MOTION PICTURE—DRAMA"

YEAR	FILM
2002	The Hours
2001	A Beautiful Mind
2000	Billy Elliott
1999	American Beauty
1998	Saving Private Ryan
1997	Titanic
1996	The English Patient
1995	Sense and Sensibility
1994	Forrest Gump
1993	Schindler's List

THE 10 LATEST GOLDEN GLOBE AWARDS FOR "BEST PERFORMANCE BY AN ACTRESS IN A MOTION PICTURE—DRAMA"

YEAR	ACTRESS	FILM
2002	Nicole Kidman	The Hours
2001	Sissy Spacek	In the Bedroom
2000	Julia Roberts	Erin Brockovich
1999	Hilary Swank	Boys Don't Cry
1998	Cate Blanchett	Elizabeth
1997	Judi Dench	Mrs. Brown
1996	Brenda Blethyn	Secrets and Lies
1995	Sharon Stone	Casino
1994	Jessica Lange	Blue Sky
1993	Holly Hunter	The Piano

Jennifer Jones received the first-ever "Best Actress" Golden Globe for *The Song of Bernadette* (1943), for which she also won an Academy Award.

THE 10 LATEST GOLDEN GLOBE AWARDS FOR "BEST DIRECTOR"

YEAR	DIRECTOR	FILM
2002	Martin Scorsese	Gangs of New York
2001	Robert Altman	Gosford Park
2000	Ang Lee	Crouching Tiger, Hidden Dragon (Wo hu cang long)
1999	Sam Mendes	American Beauty
1998	Steven Spielberg	Saving Private Ryan
1997	James Cameron	Titanic
1996	Milos Foreman	The People vs. Larry Flynt
1995	Mel Gibson	Braveheart
1994	Robert Zemeckis	Forrest Gump
1993	Steven Spielberg	Schindler's List

The Golden Globe awards, which take place a month before the Academy Awards, are often seen as predictions of Oscars to come. In this category, *American Beauty, Saving Private Ryan, Titanic, Braveheart, Forrest Gump,* and *Schindler's List* were all mirrored by the subsequent winners of "Best Director" Academy Awards.

THE 10 LATEST RECIPIENTS OF THE AMERICAN FILM INSTITUTE LIFE ACHIEVEMENT AWARD

YEAR	RECIPIENT
2003	Robert de Niro
2002	Tom Hanks
2001	Barbra Streisand
2000	Harrison Ford
1999	Dustin Hoffman
1998	Robert Wise
1997	Martin Scorsese
1996	Clint Eastwood
1995	Steven Spielberg
1994	Jack Nicholson

The first recipient of the American Film Institute's Life Achievement Award was veteran director and actor John Ford, who was honored in 1973, the year he died. Subsequent winners have included many of the most illustrious figures in the film world, including Orson Welles, Alfred Hitchcock, and, in 1977, Bette Davis, the first female winner.

THE 10 LATEST GOLDEN GLOBE AWARDS FOR "BEST PERFORMANCE BY AN ACTOR IN A MOTION PICTURE—DRAMA"

YEAR	ACTOR	FILM
2002	Jack Nicholson	About Schmidt
2001	Russell Crowe	A Beautiful Mind
2000	Tom Hanks	Cast Away
1999	Denzel Washington	The Hurricane
1998	Jim Carrey	The Truman Show
1997	Peter Fonda	Ulee's Gold
1996	Geoffrey Rush	Shine
1995	Nicolas Cage	Leaving Las Vegas
1994	Tom Hanks	Forrest Gump
1993	Tom Hanks	Philadelphia

THE 10 LATEST WINNERS OF THE GOLDEN RASPBERRY AWARD FOR WORST PICTURE

YEAR	FILM
2002	Swept Away
2001	Freddy Got Fingered
2000	Battlefield Earth
1999	Wild Wild West
1998	An Alan Smithee Film: Burn, Hollywood, Burn!
1997	The Postman
1996	Striptease
1995	Showgirls
1994	Color of Night
1993	Indecent Proposal

The Golden Raspberry Award Foundation™, founded by film critic John J. B. Wilson, has been presenting its annual "anti-accolades," popularly known as the "Razzies," since 1980.

FIRST FILM AWARDS

PRE-DATING THE ACADEMY AWARDS by almost a decade and the Golden Globes by more than two, the Photoplay Medal of Honor was the first-ever annual film award. Presented by the US film magazine *Photoplay,* which had been founded in 1911, it was initially based on a poll of its readers, who in its debut year voted for *Humoresque,* a drama directed by Frank Borzage, later the winner of two Academy Awards. After 1930, when *All Quiet on the Western Front* won both the *Photoplay* Medal and the "Best Picture" Academy Award, the winners often coincided. "Most Popular Star" and other categories were later added to the *Photoplay* awards, the last of which were presented in 1968.

FIRST FACT

Funny Business

TOP 10 COMEDY FILMS*

FILM	YEAR
1 Forrest Gump	1994
2 Men in Black	1997
3 Home Alone	1990
4 Ghost	1990
5 Pretty Woman	1990
6 Men in Black II	2002
7 Mrs. Doubtfire	1993
8 Ocean's Eleven	2001
9 What Women Want	2001
10 Notting Hill	1999

Excluding animated

▼ Sky-high pie
American Pie 2 figures among the recent wave of popular gross-out comedies designed to appeal to the young and repel older audiences.

TOP 10 GROSS-OUT COMEDY FILMS

FILM	YEAR
1 There's Something About Mary	1998
2 Austin Powers: The Spy Who Shagged Me	1999
3 Austin Powers in Goldmember	2002
4 Scary Movie	2000
5 American Pie 2	2001
6 Dumb & Dumber	1994
7 Big Daddy	1999
8 American Pie	1999
9 The Waterboy	1998
10 Nutty Professor II: The Klumps	2000

"Gross-out" films represent a new wave of films featuring outrageous and extreme juvenile comedy for teens and young adults, generally revolving round disgusting behaviour and often involving bodily functions.

THE 10 LATEST WINNERS OF THE PRIMETIME EMMY "OUTSTANDING COMEDY SERIES" AWARD

YEAR*	PROGRAM
2002	Friends
2001	Sex and the City
2000	Will and Grace
1999	Ally McBeal
1998	Frasier
1997	Frasier
1996	Frasier
1995	Frasier
1994	Frasier
1993	Seinfeld

Season ending

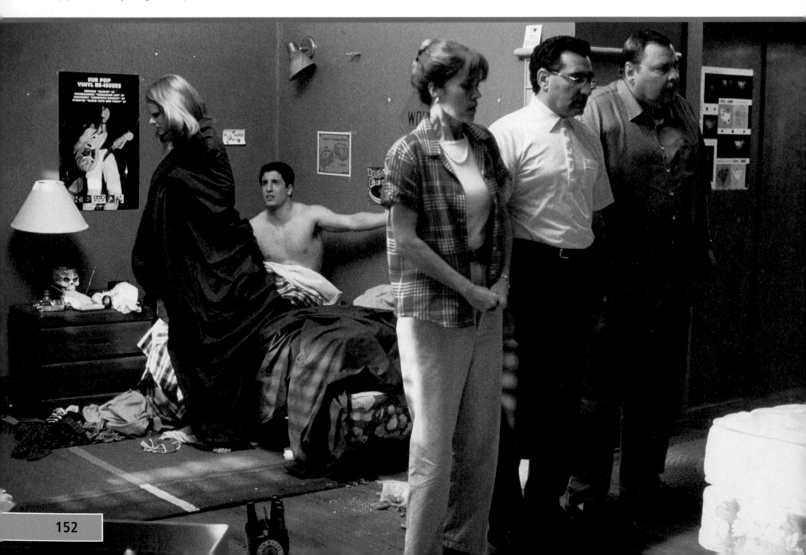

TOP 10 LONGEST-RUNNING STAGE COMEDIES OF ALL TIME ON BROADWAY

COMEDY/YEARS RUNNING	PERFORMANCES
1 Life with Father (1939–47)	3,224
2 Abie's Irish Rose (1922–27)	2,327
3 Gemini (1977–81)	1,819
4 Harvey (1944–49)	1,775
5 Born Yesterday (1946–49)	1,642
6 Mary, Mary (1961–64)	1,572
7 The Voice of the Turtle (1943–48)	1,557
8 Barefoot in the Park (1963–67)	1,530
9 Same Time Next Year (1975–78)	1,454
10 Brighton Beach Memoirs (1983–86)	1,299

Source: *The League of American Theaters and Producers*

Shown at the Empire Theater, Howard Lindsay and Russel Crouse's *Life with Father*, adapted from stories in *New Yorker*, owed its success in part to the show's nostalgic view of bygone America that appeared under threat as it opened on the eve of World War II. Runner-up *Abie's Irish Rose*, a Jewish-Catholic comedy by Anne Nichols, was a long-runner despite receiving poor reviews. Following its five-year Broadway run, *Harvey* was re-created as a popular film starring James Stewart.

TOP 10 MOST WATCHED TELEVISION COMEDY/VARIETY SHOWS OF ALL TIME

SHOW	AIR DATE	RATING
1 M*A*S*H Special	Feb. 28, 1983	60.2
2 Bob Hope Christmas Show	Jan. 15, 1970	46.6
3 Cheers	May 20, 1993	45.5
4 Ed Sullivan	Feb. 9, 1964	45.3
5 Bob Hope Christmas Show	Jan. 14, 1971	45.0
6 The Beverly Hillbillies	Jan. 8, 1964	44.0
7 Ed Sullivan	Feb. 16, 1964	43.8
8 Academy Awards	Apr. 7, 1970	43.4
9 The Beverly Hillbillies	Jan. 15, 1964	42.8
10 The Beverly Hillbillies	Feb. 26, 1964	42.4

Source: *Nielsen Media Research*

The three-hour *M*A*S*H Special*, the farewell episode also known as "Goodbye, Farewell and Amen," depicted the events surrounding the 4,077th M*A*S*H unit in the closing stages of the Korean War. It had been running since 1972 and attracted consistently high audiences, with this final program registering an estimated 50,150,000 out of a then total of 83,300,000 "TV households" in the US, thereby producing the highest-ever rating for a comedy show.

TOP 10 HORROR SPOOF FILMS

FILM	YEAR
1 Scary Movie	2000
2 Scream	1996
3 Scream 2	1997
4 Scream 3	2000
5 Scary Movie 2	2001
6 Young Frankenstein	1974
7 Love at First Bite	1979
8 An American Werewolf in London	1981
9 An American Werewolf in Paris	1997
10 Fright Night	1985

While many films combine comedy and horror elements—among them *Ghoulies* (1985), the two *Gremlins* movies (1984 and 1990), *Little Shop of Horrors* (1986), and *Arachnophobia* (1990)—those in this Top 10 represent the most successful of a species of parodies of classic horror films that began more than half a century ago with such examples as *Abbott and Costello Meet Frankenstein* (1948). Such has been the success of the most recent crop that each movie in the *Scream* and *Scary Movie* franchise has earned more than $100 million globally.

TOP 10 FUNNIEST MOVIES VOTED FOR BY THE AMERICAN FILM INSTITUTE

MOVIE	YEAR
1 Some Like It Hot	1959
2 Tootsie	1982
3 Dr. Strangelove, or: How I Learned to Stop Worrying and Love the Bomb	1964
4 Annie Hall	1977
5 Duck Soup	1933
6 Blazing Saddles	1974
7 M*A*S*H	1970
8 It Happened One Night	1934
9 The Graduate	1967
10 Airplane!	1980

Source: *American Film Institute*

This list is the cream of the 500 titles nominated and 100 selected by a panel of 1,500 film experts for the AFI's "100 Years 100 Laughs" list, published on June 13, 2000. The Top 100 includes comedy movies that range in time from Buster Keaton's 1924 silent *The Navigator* (in 84th place) to 1998 box office hit *There's Something About Mary* (27th).

Animation

ANIMATED FILMS

FILM	US RELEASE	WORLWIDE TOTAL GROSS ($)
1 The Lion King*	1994	771,900,000
2 Monsters, Inc.*	2001	529,000,000
3 Aladdin*	1992	502,400,000
4 Toy Story 2*	1999	485,800,000
5 Shrek	2001	477,000,000
6 Tarzan*	1999	449,400,000
7 Ice Age	2002	366,300,000
8 A Bug's Life*	1998	363,400,000
9 Toy Story*	1995	361,500,000
10 Dinosaur*	2000	356,100,000

* Disney

▼ Towering success
One of the most successful movies derived from a TV series, *Rugrats in Paris*, the $30 million-budget sequel to *The Rugrats Movie* (1988), has made over $100 million worldwide.

BUDGETS FOR ANIMATED FILMS

FILM	DATE	BUDGET ($)
1 = Tarzan	1999	150,000,000
= The Polar Express	2004	150,000,000
3 Treasure Planet	2002	140,000,000
4 Final Fantasy: The Spirits Within	2001	137,000,000
5 Dinosaur	2000	128,000,000
6 Monsters, Inc.	2001	115,000,000
7 The Emperor's New Groove	2000	100,000,000
8 The Road to El Dorado	2000	95,000,000
9 Finding Nemo	2003	94,000,000
10 The Incredibles	2004	92,000,000

Animated film budgets have come a long way since *Snow White and the Seven Dwarfs* (1937) established a then record of $1.49 million. The $2.6 million budget for *Pinocchio* (1940), and $2.28 million for the original *Fantasia* (1940) were the two biggest of the 1940s, while *Sleeping Beauty* (1959) at $6 million was the highest of the 1950s. *Robin Hood* (1973) had a budget of $15 million, a record that remained unbroken until 1985, when *The Black Cauldron* (1985) became the first to break the $25 million barrier. Since the 1990s budgets of $50 million to $100 million or more have become commonplace.

TOP 10 PART ANIMATION/PART LIVE-ACTION FILMS

	FILM	YEAR
1	Who Framed Roger Rabbit	1988
2	Casper	1995
3	Space Jam	1996
4	9 to 5	1980
5	Mary Poppins	1964
6	Fantasia/2000	2000
7	Small Soldiers	1998
8	Song of the South	1946
9	James and the Giant Peach	1996
10	Pete's Dragon	1977

Many recent movies, from *Jurassic Park* to *Stuart Little*, contain computer-generated three-dimensional images with live action, but these stand out as the highest-earning that combine the traditional animation of imaginary characters alongside live action as a key element. *Fantasia* (1940) may arguably warrant a place in the list, but the only combination sequence is a brief encounter between Mickey Mouse and the conductor Leopold Stokowski in what is otherwise an animated film. *The Adventures of Rocky and Bullwinkle* (2000) fails to make the grade, since it earned no more than a fraction of its reputed $76 million budget.

THE 10 LATEST OSCAR-WINNING ANIMATED FILMS*

YEAR	FILM	DIRECTOR/COUNTRY
2002	The ChubbChubbs!	Eric Armstrong, Canada
2001	For the Birds	Ralph Eggleston, US
2000	Father and Daughter	Michael Dudok de Wit, Netherlands
1999	The Old Man and the Sea	Aleksandr Petrov, US
1998	Bunny	Chris Wedge, US
1997	Geri's Game	Jan Pinkava, US
1996	Quest	Tyron Montgomery, UK
1995	Wallace & Gromit: A Close Shave	Nick Park, UK
1994	Bob's Birthday	David Fine and Alison Snowden, UK
1993	Wallace & Gromit: The Wrong Trousers	Nick Park, UK

* In the category "Short Films (Animated)"

An Oscar was first awarded in the category "Short Subjects (Cartoons)"—later "Short Subjects (Animated Films)" and "Short Films (Animated)"—in 1932, when it was won by Walt Disney for *Flowers and Trees*, the first-ever color animated short. During the award's first decade, and with few exceptions up to 1968, it was won annually by Walt Disney. The new category "Best Animated Feature" has existed only since 2001 (when it was won by *Shrek*); prior to this, films such as *Snow White and the Seven Dwarfs* (1937) and *Fantasia* (1940) received honorary Oscars.

TOP 10 ANIMATED FILMS BASED ON TV SERIES

	FILM	TV SERIES*	YEAR
1	Pokémon: The First Movie	1997	1999
2	The Rugrats Movie	1991	1998
3	Rugrats in Paris: The Movie—Rugrats II	1991	2000
4	Beavis and Butt-Head Do America	1993	1996
5	South Park: Bigger, Longer & Uncut	1997	1999
6	Pokémon: The Movie 2000	1997	2000
7	Recess: School's Out	1997	2001
8	Jetsons: The Movie	1962	1990
9	Doug's 1st Movie	1991	1999
10	The Smurfs and the Magic Flute	1981	1983

* Launched on TV in US

Such is the fan following of many TV animated series that when they reach the big screen, they attract huge audiences: the first three movies in this list each earned in excess of $100 million, and the others have all made respectable eight-figure sums.

TOP 10 ANIMATED FILM OPENING WEEKENDS IN THE US

	FILM	US RELEASE	OPENING WEEKEND GROSS ($)
1	Monsters, Inc.	Nov. 2, 2001	62,577,067
2	Toy Story 2*	Nov. 26, 1999	57,388,839
3	Ice Age	Mar. 15, 2002	46,312,454
4	Shrek	May 18, 2001	42,347,760
5	The Lion King	June 24, 1994	40,888,194
6	Dinosaur	May 19, 2000	38,854,851
7	Lilo & Stitch	June 21, 2002	35,260,212
8	Tarzan	June 18, 1999	34,221,968
9	A Bug's Life*	Nov. 28, 1998	33,258,052
10	Pokémon: The First Movie	Nov. 12, 1999	31,036,678

* Second weekend; opening weekend release in limited number of theaters only

The popularity of animated feature films in recent years has initiated the new phenomenon of the $20 million-plus opening weekend, with these high earners closely trailed by successes including *Pocahontas* (1995), *Toy Story* (1995), *The Rugrats Movie* (1998), and *Mulan* (1998).

▲ The price of fame
Youngest-ever Oscar winner Shirley Temple said, "I stopped believing in Santa Claus when my mother took me to see him in a department store and he asked for my autograph."

TOP 10 BEST-SELLING CHILDREN'S VIDEOS IN THE US, 2002

	VIDEO
1	Cinderella II—Dreams Come True
2	The Land Before Time—The Big Freeze
3	Mickey's Magical Christmas—Snowed In The House Of Mouse
4	Tarzan & Jane
5	Barbie in the Nutcracker
6	Peter Pan—Return to Neverland
7	Mary-Kate & Ashley—Holiday in the Sun
8	The Hunchback of Notre Dame II
9	Spider-Man—The Ultimate Villain Showdown
10	Scooby-Doo and the Reluctant Werewolf

Source: Billboard

TOP 10 YOUNGEST OSCAR WINNERS

	ACTOR/ACTRESS	AWARD	AWARD YEAR	AGE YRS	MTHS	DAYS
1	Shirley Temple	Special Award (outstanding contribution during 1934)	1934	6	10	4
2	Vincent Winter	Special Award (*The Little Kidnappers*)	1954	7	3	1
3	Margaret O'Brien	Special Award (outstanding child actress of 1944)	1944	8	2	0
4	Jon Whiteley	Special Award (*The Little Kidnappers*)	1954	10	1	11
5	Tatum O'Neal	Best Supporting Actress (*Paper Moon*)	1973	10	4	27
6	Anna Paquin	Best Supporting Actress (*The Piano*)	1993	11	7	28
7	Ivan Jandl	Special Award (*The Search*)	1948	12	0	27
8	Claude Jarman Jr.	Special Award (*The Yearling*)	1946	12	5	16
9	Bobby Driscoll	Special Award (outstanding juvenile actor)	1949	13	0	20
10	Hayley Mills	Special Award (outstanding juvenile performance)	1960	13	11	29

The Academy Awards ceremony usually takes place in March the year after the film was released, so winners are generally at least a year older when they receive their Oscars than when they acted in their films. Hayley Mills, the 12th and last winner of the "Special Award" miniature Oscar (presented to her by its first winner, Shirley Temple), won her award one day before her 14th birthday. Subsequent winners have had to compete on the same basis as adult actors and actresses for the major awards. Tatum O'Neal is the youngest winner of—as well as the youngest ever nominee for—an "adult" Oscar. The youngest winner of the "Best Actor" award is Richard Dreyfuss (for *The Goodbye Girl* in the 1977 Awards). The youngest winner in the "Best Supporting Actor" category is Timothy Hutton, who was aged 20 when he won in the 1980 Awards for his role in *Ordinary People*.

TOP 10 MOST WATCHED CHILDREN'S PROGRAMS ON US TELEVISION, 2001–02

	PROGRAM	AVERAGE VIEWERS PERCENTAGE	TOTAL
1	Barbie in the Nutcracker	3.1	3,250,000
2	Pokémon	2.6	2,739,000
3	Ozzy & Drix	2.5	2,696,000
4	Yu-Gi-Oh2	2.5	2,628,000
5	Jackie Chan	2.3	2,476,000
6	X-Men	2.3	2,434,000
7	What's New Scooby-Doo	2.0	2,178,000
8	Jimmy Neutron	2.0	2,163,000
9	Rocket Power TV movie	1.9	2,035,000
10	The Proud Family	1.8	1,972,000

* *Highest rated showing of each program only included in ranking*

Barbie in the Nutcracker, featuring the popular doll as the central character, with Tim Curry providing the voice of the Mouse King, in a made-for-TV computer-animated adaptation of the traditional *Nutcracker* ballet, was not only the most-watched children's program of the year when screened by CBS, but also won the Video Premier Award for "Best Animated Video Premiere Movie." There is a clear trend for popular TV programs to generate major Hollywood movies: as well as the past smash *Pokémon*, *Scooby-Doo* and *Jimmy Neutron* have both recently transferred from the small to the big screen.

TOP 10 FILMS WITH CHILD STARS

	FILM	YEAR
1	Harry Potter and the Sorcerer's Stone	2001
2	Star Wars: Episode I—The Phantom Menace	1999
3	Jurassic Park	1993
4	Harry Potter and the Chamber of Secrets	2002
5	E.T. the Extra-Terrestrial	1982
6	The Sixth Sense	1999
7	Home Alone	1990
8	Mrs. Doubtfire	1993
9	Signs	2002
10	Jurassic Park III	2001

Family films, especially those with child stars, are among the highest-earning of all time: all those in the Top 10 have earned upwards of $365 million each worldwide. Several of those appearing here featured children early in careers, with Drew Barrymore's one of the most notable. Having appeared in *Altered States* (1980) at the age of four, she took the role of Gertie in *E.T. the Extra-Terrestrial* while still only six, going on to pursue a successful adult career in such films as *Batman Forever* (1995) and *Charlie's Angels* (2000).

▲ **Secret success**
Child stars Ron and Harry take to the air in a flying Ford Anglia in box-office smash *Harry Potter and the Chamber of Secrets.*

THE 10 LATEST WINNERS OF THE DAYTIME EMMY "OUTSTANDING CHILDREN'S ANIMATED PROGRAM" AWARD

YEAR*	PROGRAM
2002	Madeline
2001	Arthur
2000	Steven Spielberg Presents: Pinky, Elmyra and the Brain
1999	Steven Spielberg Presents: Pinky and the Brain
1998	Arthur
1997	Animaniacs
1996	Animaniacs
1995	Where on Earth Is Carmen Santiago
1994	Rugrats
1993	Tiny Toon Adventures

* Season ending

These award-winning programs feature the voices of a diverse range of artists: *Madeline* contains contributions from actor Christopher Plummer and former British rock star Long John Baldry, while several characters in *Pinky, Elmyra and the Brain* and *Animaniacs* are voiced by Nancy Cartwright, who also provides the voice of Bart Simpson in *The Simpsons*.

THE 10 LATEST WINNERS OF THE DAYTIME EMMY "OUTSTANDING CHILDREN'S SERIES" AWARD

YEAR*	PROGRAM
2002	Sesame Street
2001	Reading Rainbow
2000	Bill Nye the Science Guy
1999	Sesame Street (pre-school); Bill Nye the Science Guy (school age)
1998	Sesame Street
1997	Sesame Street (pre-school); Reading Rainbow (school age)
1996	Reading Rainbow
1995	Nick News
1994	Sesame Street
1993	Reading Rainbow

* Season ending

Several of the multiple award winners are not only among the most popular children's series but also some of the longest runners: *Sesame Street* was first screened in 1969, *Reading Rainbow* in 1983, and *Bill Nye the Science Guy* in 1993. *Reading Rainbow* host LeVar Burton gained additional kudos by appearing in the show while also starring in *StarTrek: The Next Generation*.

DVD & Video

TOP 10 VIDEO COUNTRIES

	COUNTRY	DVD %	TOTAL SPENDING (2001) ($)
1	US	34	20,549,000,000
2	Japan	35	4,768,000,000
3	UK	36	2,857,000,000
4	France	41	1,681,000,000
5	Canada	34	1,666,000,000
6	Germany	39	1,027,000,000
7	Australia	29	595,000,000
8	South Korea	3	556,000,000
9	Italy	23	540,000,000
10	Spain	31	405,000,000

Source: Screen Digest

The availability of comparative international statistics lags behind the rapidly moving video (VHS and DVD) business, but figures for the US for 2002 revealed that the home-video industry in the US—DVD and VHS rentals and sales—was worth $20.3 billion, more than double the $9.37 billion generated by domestic movie releases.

THE 10 WORST COUNTRIES FOR VIDEO PIRACY

	COUNTRY	PIRACY RATE (%)	EST. LOSSES (2002*) ($)
1	Russia	80	250,000,000
2	China	91	168,000,000
3	Italy	20	140,000,000
4	Brazil	35	120,000,000
5	India	60	75,000,000
6	Turkey	45	50,000,000
7	= Malaysia	75	42,000,000
	= Taiwan	44	42,000,000
9	= Colombia	90	40,000,000
	= Saudi Arabia	35	40,000,000
	= Ukraine	90	40,000,000

* Preliminary figures

Source: International Intellectual Property Alliance (IIPA)

Despite international attempts to curb video piracy by both legal and technological means, it has reached epidemic proportions in many territories.

TOP 10 VIDEOS RENTED IN THE US

	TITLE	YEAR*	REVENUE ($)
1	Titanic	1997	324,430,000
2	Star Wars	1977	270,920,000
3	E.T. the Extra-Terrestrial	1982	228,170,000
4	Jurassic Park	1993	212,950,000
5	Star Wars: Episode VI— Return of the Jedi	1983	191,650,000
6	Independence Day	1996	177,190,000
7	Star Wars: Episode V— The Empire Strikes Back	1980	173,810,000
8	The Lion King	1994	173,060,000
9	Forrest Gump	1994	156,000,000
10	Batman	1989	150,500,000

* Of cinema release

Video rentals have declined since the arrival of DVD in 1997. Total DVD and VHS rentals in 2002 were $8.2 billion, compared with $12.1 billion for sales.

TOP 10 BESTSELLING VIDEOS IN THE US

	TITLE	YEAR*	SALES#($)
1	Shrek	2001	228,000,000
2	Tarzan	2000	210,000,000
3	Dr. Seuss's How the Grinch Stole Christmas	2001	192,000,000
4	Dinosaur	2001	153,000,000
5	Toy Story 2	2000	145,300,000
6	Monsters, Inc.	2002	145,200,000
7	Star Wars: Episode I— The Phantom Menace	2000	133,400,000
8	Harry Potter and the Sorcerer's Stone	2002	131,300,000
9	Pearl Harbor	2001	119,200,000
10	Lady and the Tramp II: Scamp's Adventure	2001	119,100,000

* Of video release in US; 21st century only

In release year

Source: VSDA VidTrac

TOP 10 BESTSELLING VIDEOS IN THE US, 2002

	TITLE	SALES*($)
1	Monsters, Inc.	145,200,000
2	Harry Potter and the Sorcerer's Stone	131,300,000
3	Spider-Man	84,000,000
4	Lilo & Stitch	81,700,000
5	Cinderella II: Dreams Come True	76,500,000
6	The Lord of the Rings— The Fellowship of the Ring	72,800,000
7	Atlantis: The Lost Empire	70,400,000
8	Miss Congeniality	63,000,000
9	Spirit: Stallion of the Cimarron	58,000,000
10	Snow Dogs	52,700,000

* In release year

Source: VSDA VidTrac

Monsters, Inc. also earned some $202 million from DVD, reflecting the shift in the ratio between the two, with just $23.5 million from VHS and $14.36 from DVD rentals as increasing numbers of people prefer to own rather than rent their favorite movies.

TOP 10 VIDEOS RENTED IN THE US, 2002

	TITLE
1	Don't Say a Word
2	Training Day
3	Ocean's Eleven
4	The Fast and the Furious
5	American Pie 2
6	The Others
7	Shallow Hal
8	Rat Race
9	Domestic Disturbance
10	Black Hawk Down

Source: VSDA VidTrac

In 2002, each of the Top 10 most rented videos generated revenue of $37 million or more, a total of $434 million. However, during the year, as DVD gained momentum, VHS rentals dwindled by 25 percent to an overall total of $5.3 billion.

TOP 10 — DVDs RENTED IN THE US, 2002

	TITLE
1	Ocean's Eleven
2	Training Day
3	Don't Say a Word
4	Mr. Deeds
5	The Others
6	Spy Game
7	Insomnia
8	John Q.
9	Panic Room
10	The Sum of All Fears

Source: *VSDA VidTrac*

Since DVD rentals have increased every year, and every one of the Top 10 earned more than the highest earner of any previous year, the most-rented DVDs of 2002 are synonymous with the most-rented videos of all time.

TOP 10 — BESTSELLING DVDs IN THE US, 2002

	TITLE	SALES*($)
1	The Lord of the Rings: The Fellowship of the Ring	257,300,000
2	Spider-Man	215,300,000
3	Monsters, Inc.	202,000,000
4	Harry Potter and the Sorcerer's Stone	166,700,000
5	Star Wars: Episode II— Attack of the Clones	144,800,000
6	The Fast and the Furious	132,000,000
7	Ice Age	124,800,000
8	Lilo & Stitch	116,100,000
9	Austin Powers in Goldmember	92,700,000
10	Band of Brothers	84,400,000

* In release year

Source: *VSDA VidTrac*

TOP 10 — DVD RENTAL GENRES IN THE US, 2002

	GENRE	FILMS IN TOP 500 RENTALS
1	Comedy	155
2	Drama	96
3	Action	95
4	Suspense	59
5	Horror	27
6	Family	17
7	Children's	16
8	Science fiction	14
9	Romance	11
10	Western	2

Source: *VSDA VidTrac*

▼ Ocean wave
Ocean's Eleven, the most-rented DVD of 2002, made a total of $192.2 million from DVD and VHS sales and rentals.

Top TV

THE 10 LATEST EMMY AWARDS FOR "OUTSTANDING LEAD ACTOR IN A DRAMA SERIES"

YEAR*	ACTOR	SERIES
2002	Michael Chiklis	The Shield
2001	James Gandolfini	The Sopranos
2000	James Gandolfini	The Sopranos
1999	Dennis Franz	NYPD Blue
1998	Andre Braugher	Homicide: Life on the Street
1997	Dennis Franz	NYPD Blue
1996	Dennis Franz	NYPD Blue
1995	Mandy Patinkin	Chicago Hope
1994	Dennis Franz	NYPD Blue
1993	Tom Skerritt	Picket Fences

* Season ending

▼ TV age
The proliferation of terrestrial and satellite television in recent years has transformed both the industry and the skylines of today's cities.

THE 10 LATEST EMMY AWARDS FOR "OUTSTANDING LEAD ACTRESS IN A DRAMA SERIES"

YEAR*	ACTRESS	SERIES
2002	Allison Janney	The West Wing
2001	Edie Falco	The Sopranos
2000	Sela Ward	Once and Again
1999	Edie Falco	The Sopranos
1998	Christine Lahti	Chicago Hope
1997	Gillian Anderson	The X-Files
1995	Kathy Baker	Picket Fences
1994	Sela Ward	Sisters
1993	Kathy Baker	Picket Fences

* Season ending; no award in 1996

FIRST TV BROADCASTS

ALTHOUGH THERE HAD BEEN earlier low-definition experimental transmissions, the world's first daily high-definition public broadcasting television service was launched in the UK by the BBC on November 2, 1936. Television's debut in the US dates from April 30, 1939, when NBC showed an outside broadcast of the opening of the New York World's Fair by Franklin D. Roosevelt – who thereby became the first US President ever to appear on television.

FIRST FACT

TOP 10 SATELLITE TELEVISION COUNTRIES

	COUNTRY	HOME SATELLITE ANTENNAE (2000)
1	US	16,000,000
2	Germany	12,900,000
3	Japan	10,620,000
4	UK	5,200,000
5	France	4,300,000
6	Indonesia	3,900,000
7	Algeria	3,500,000
8	Poland	2,500,000
9	Saudi Arabia	1,914,000
10	Spain	1,840,000

Source: *International Telecommunication Union*, World Telecommunication Development Report, 2002

TOP 10 TELEVISION-OWNING COUNTRIES

	COUNTRY	TVs PER 1,000 POPULATION (2000)
1	Qatar	869
2	US	854
3	Denmark	807
4	Latvia	789
5	Australia	738
6	Japan	725
7	Canada	715
8	Finland	692
9	Norway	669
10	UK	653
	World	270

Source: *International Telecommunication Union*, World Telecommunication Development Report, 2002

TOP 10 | PRIMETIME PROGRAMS ON NETWORK TELEVISION, 2001–02

	PROGRAM*	%	AVERAGE VIEWERS TOTAL
1	The Academy Awards	25.4	26,832,000
2	Friends (Special)	17.2	18,154,000
3	On Red Carpet: The Oscars 2002	17.1	17,999,000
4	Friends	16.6	17,462,000
5	The Golden Globe Awards	14.9	15,718,000
6	The Emmy Awards	13.5	14,397,000
7	Survivor: Thailand Special	13.2	14,124,000
8	Survivor: Marquesas Finale	13.4	14,122,000
9	Law and Order: Criminal Intent	12.9	13,628,000
10	CSI	12.9	13,588,000

* Excluding sports; highest-ranked screening only listed

Source: Nielsen Media Research

TOP 10 | TALK SHOWS ON US TELEVISION, 2001–02

	TALK SHOW*	ORIGINATOR	AVERAGE AUDIENCE TOTAL
1	The Oprah Winfrey Show	Kingworld Media Sales	5,810,000
2	The Dr. Phil Show	Kingworld Media Sales	4,698,000
3	Live with Regis and Kelly	Buena Vista Television	3,762,000
4	Maury	Studios USA	3,317,000
5	Jerry Springer	Studios USA	2,905,000
6	The Montel Williams Show	Paramount	2,702,000
7	The Rosie O'Donnell Show	Warner Bros. TV	2,324,000
8	Jerry Springer	Universal TV	2,226,000
9	The Jenny Jones Show	Warner Bros. TV	1,968,000
10	Blind Date	Tribune/Universal TV	1,948,000

* Highest-rated shows only—i.e., excludes alternative originators

Source: Nielsen Media Research

TOP 10 | DAYTIME DRAMAS ON US TELEVISION, 2001–02

	DRAMA	NETWORK	%	AVERAGE VIEWERS TOTAL
1	The Young and the Restless	CBS	5.0	5,293,000
2	The Bold and the Beautiful	CBS	3.9	4,103,000
3	Days of Our Lives	NBC	3.6	3,804,000
4	General Hospital	ABC	3.4	3,611,000
5	As the World Turns	CBS	3.3	3,448,000
6	All My Children	ABC	3.3	3,443,000
7	One Life to Live	ABC	3.2	3,336,000
8	Guiding Light	CBS	2.9	3,076,000
9	Passions	NBC	2.1	2,185,000
10	Port Charles	ABC	1.8	1,854,000

* Excludes specials

Source: Nielsen Media Research

TOP 10 | MOVIES ON US TELEVISION, 2001–02

	FILM	%	AVERAGE VIEWERS TOTAL
1	ABC Premiere Event: Stephen King's Rose Red (Pt. 1)	11.8	12,419,000
2	CBS Tuesday Movie Special: Living with the Dead (Pt. 2)	11.1	11,725,000
3	ABC Premiere Event: Saving Private Ryan	11.1	11,691,000
4	ABC Premiere Event: Stephen King's Rose Red (Pt. 3)	9.8	10,299,000
5	CBS Wednesday Movie Special: Diagnosis Murder: Town without Pity	9.1	9,569,000
6	Dinotopia (Pt. 1)	8.4	8,840,000
7	9/11	8.0	8,554,000
8	NBC Movie of the Week (Monday): Uprising	8.1	8,520,000
9	Dinotopia (Pt. 2)	8.0	8,419,000
10	CBS Tuesday Movie: Jack and the Beanstalk (Pt. 2)	7.7	8,294,000

Source: Nielsen Media Research

Radio Days

TOP 10 | RADIO-OWNING COUNTRIES

	COUNTRY	RADIOS PER 1,000 POPULATION (2000)
1	US	2,118
2	Australia	1,908
3	Finland	1,623
4	UK	1,432
5	Denmark	1,349
6	Estonia	1,096
7	Canada	1,047
8	South Korea	1,033
9	Switzerland	1,002
10	New Zealand	997
	World	*419*

Source: *World Bank,* World Development Indicators 2002/*UNESCO*

THE 10 | LATEST NAB NETWORK/SYNDICATED PERSONALITIES OF THE YEAR

YEAR	PERSONALITIES/PROGRAM	NETWORK
2002	**Paul Harvey,** Paul Harvey News and Comment	ABC Radio Networks
2001	**Rick Dees**	Premiere Radio Networks
2000	**Rush Limbaugh,** The Rush Limbaugh Show	Premiere Radio Networks
1999	**Bob Kevoian and Tom Griswold,** The Bob & Tom Show	AMFM Radio Networks
1998	**Paul Harvey**	ABC Radio Networks
1997	**Dr. Laura Schlessinger**	Synergy Broadcasting
1996	**Paul Harvey**	ABC Radio Networks
1995	**Rush Limbaugh**	EFM Media Management
1994	**Don Imus**	Westwood One Radio Networks
1993	**Charles Osgood**	CBS Radio Networks

The US National Association of Broadcasters presents annual awards in 22 different categories. They are known as the Marconi Awards in honor of radio pioneer, inventor, and 1909 Nobel Physics Prize winner Guglielmo Marconi. Latest winner Paul Harvey also won the first Award, in 1989.

TOP 10 LONGEST-RUNNING PROGRAMS ON NATIONAL PUBLIC RADIO

	PROGRAM	FIRST BROADCAST
1	All Things Considered	1971
2	Weekend All Things Considered	1974
3	Fresh Air with Terry Gross	1977
4	Marian McPartland's Piano Jazz	1978
5	Morning Edition	1979
6	Weekend Edition/Saturday with Scott Simon	1985
7	Performance Today	1987
8	Weekend Edition/Sunday with Liane Hansen	1987
9	Car Talk	1987
10	Talk of the Nation	1991

Source: *National Public Radio*

All Things Considered, the longest-running NPR program, was first broadcast on May 3, 1971. The first show broadcast covered antiwar demonstrations in Washington, DC. In 1993, it became the first public radio program inducted into the Radio Hall of Fame.

TOP 10 RADIO STATIONS IN THE US

	STATION	CITY	FORMAT	AQH*
1	WLTW-FM	New York	Soft adult contemporary	153,900
2	WQHT-FM	New York	Black/urban	146,000
3	WHTZ-FM	New York	CHR	106,900
4	WCBS-FM	New York	Oldies	101,300
5	WKTU-FM	New York	Dance/CHR	96,800
6	WSKQ-FM	New York	Hispanic CHR	94,700
7	WABC-AM	New York	Talk	94,000
8 =	KROQ-FM	Los Angeles	Modern rock	86,500
=	WBLS-FM	New York	Black/urban	86,500
10	WINS-AM	New York	News	84,700

* Average Quarter Hour statistic based on number of listeners aged 12+ listening between Monday and Sunday 6:00 am to midnight, from Arbitron data

Source: *Duncan's American Radio*

THE 10 LATEST NAB HALL OF FAME INDUCTEES

YEAR	INDUCTEE
2003	**Scott Shannon,** radio personality and program director
2002	**Dick Orkin,** radio personality and creative producer
2001	**Bruce Morrow,** radio personality
2000	**Tom Joyner,** radio personality
1999	**Wolfman Jack,** radio personality
1998	**Rush Limbaugh,** radio personality
1997	**Wally Phillips,** radio personality
1996	**Don Imus,** radio personality
1995	**Gary Owens,** radio personality
1994	**Harry Caray,** radio sportscaster

Since 1977, the National Association of Broadcasters' Hall of Fame has been honoring radio personalities and programs that have earned a place in US broadcasting history. Ronald Reagan, a former radio sportscaster, was inducted in 1981.

◀ **Radio head**
Radio listeners maintain loyalty for their favorite stations, ensuring multimillion audiences for the leading broadcasters.

THE 10 LATEST GEORGE FOSTER PEABODY AWARDS FOR BROADCASTING WON BY NATIONAL PUBLIC RADIO*

	PROGRAM	YEAR
1	The Yiddish Radio Project	2002
2 =	Coverage of September 11, 2001	2001
=	Jazz Profiles	2001
4	The NPR 100	2000
5 =	Lost & Found Sound	1999
=	Morning Edition with Bob Edwards	1999
7 =	Coverage of Africa	1998
=	I Must Keep Fightin': The Art of Paul Robeson	1998
=	Performance Today	1998
10	Jazz from Lincoln Center	1997

* Includes only programs made or co-produced by NPR

Source: *Peabody Awards*

RADIO BROADCAST

ALTHOUGH WIRELESS MESSAGES had been broadcast earlier using Morse code, the first ever to transmit sound and music took place on Christmas Eve 1906. Canadian physicist and inventor Reginald Fessenden (1866–1932) set up a radio station and 420-ft (128-m) mast at Brant Rock Station in Massachusetts. He opened the broadcast with an explanation of what he proposed to do, followed by a phonograph recording of Handel's *Largo*, after which he sang and played violin. This first radio show was repeated on New Year's Eve and received as far afield as Norfolk, Virginia, the West Indies, and by ships at sea. Over the years, radio continued as a means of telecommunications between ships, but did not become established as a popular medium until the 1920s.

FIRST FACT

COMMERCIAL
WORLD

World Finance

TOP 10 GLOBAL INDUSTRIAL COMPANIES

	COMPANY	SECTOR	REVENUE (2001) ($)
1	**Wal-Mart Stores, Inc.,** US	Retailing	219,812,000,000
2	**Exxon Mobil,** US	Oil, gas, fuel	191,581,000,000
3	**General Motors Corp,** US	Transport	177,260,000,000
4	**BP plc,** UK	Oil, gas	174,218,000,000
5	**Ford Motor Co.,** US	Transport	162,412,000,000
6	**Enron Corp.*,** US	Gas, electricity	138,718,000,000
7	**DaimlerChrysler AG,** Germany	Transport	136,897,300,000
8	**Royal Dutch/Shell Group,** Netherlands/UK	Oil, gas, chemicals	135,211,000,000
9	**General Electric,** US	Electronics, electrical equipment	125,913,000,000
10	**Toyota Motor,** Japan	Transport	120,814,400,000

Revenue for nine months January–September 2001; filed for bankruptcy December 2 , 2001.

Source: Fortune *magazine,* The 2002 Global 500, 22 July 2002

Sam Walton opened his first Wal-Mart store in Rogers, Arkansas, in 1962. It has undergone phenomenal growth in the past 40 years to become the world's No. 1 company. On the day after Thanksgiving, 2001, it achieved the largest single day's sales in retail history, taking $1.25 billion.

TOP 10 RICHEST COUNTRIES

	COUNTRY	GDP* PER CAPITA (2000) ($)
1	**Luxembourg**	50,061
2	**US**	34,142
3	**Norway**	29,918
4	**Ireland**	29,866
5	**Iceland**	29,581
6	**Switzerland**	28,769
7	**Canada**	27,840
8	**Denmark**	27,627
9	**Belgium**	27,178
10	**Austria**	26,765
	World	7,446

* *Gross Domestic Product*

Source: *United Nations,* Human Development Report 2002

▼ Retail giant
Wal-Mart was founded in 1962. By 1979 it was achieving sales of over $1 billion a year; by 1993 it did so in a week, and can now sell that amount in a single day.

TOP 10 MOST EXPENSIVE COUNTRIES IN WHICH TO BUY A BIG MAC

	COUNTRY	COST OF A BIG MAC ($)*
1	Iceland	5.5
2	Switzerland	4.56
3	Sweden	3.46
4	UK	3.19
5	Malta	3.03
6	Euro area	2.87
7	South Korea	2.73
8	US	2.65
9	United Arab Emirates	2.45
10	Saudi Arabia	2.40

* As of Jan. 16, 2003; of those countries surveyed

Source: The Economist/McDonald's price data

The Economist's Big Mac index assesses the value of countries' currencies against the standard US price of a Big Mac, by assuming that an identical amount of goods and services should cost the same in all countries. By this reckoning, all of the countries in the Top 10 are above the US, which means that they have over-valued currencies. Conversely, all those below the US (in Argentina a Big Mac costs just $1.18) are under-valued.

TOP 10 FASTEST-GROWING ECONOMIES

	COUNTRY	GDP* PER CAPITA (2000) ($)	GROWTH RATE (1990–2000) (%)
1	Equatorial Guinea	15,073	18.9
2	China	3,976	9.2
3	Ireland	29,866	6.5
4	Vietnam	1,996	6.0
5	Sudan	1,797	5.6
6	Maldives	4,485	5.4
7	Chile	9,417	5.2
8	Guyana	3,963	5.0
9	Myanmar	1,500	4.8
10 =	St. Kitts and Nevis	12,510	4.7
=	Singapore	23,356	4.7
=	South Korea	17,380	4.7
	World	*7,446*	*1.2*
	US	*34,142*	*2.2*

* Gross Domestic Product

Source: *United Nations,* Human Development Report 2002

THE 10 POOREST COUNTRIES

	COUNTRY	GDP* PER CAPITA (2000) ($)
1	Sierra Leone	490
2	Tanzania	523
3	Burundi	591
4	Malawi	615
5	Ethiopia	668
6	Niger	746
7	Guinea-Bissau	755
8	Dem. Rep. of Congo	765
9	Mali	797
10	Congo	825

* Gross Domestic Product

Source: *United Nations,* Human Development Report 2002

GDP is an indicator of a country's comparative economic performance, but the scale of extreme poverty is graphically revealed in statistics that show the proportion of the population with an income of under $1 a day: a figure as high as 72.8 percent in Mali, while that for people earning less than $2 a day rises to 90.6 percent.

THE 10 COUNTRIES MOST IN DEBT

	COUNTRY	TOTAL EXTERNAL DEBT (2000) ($)
1	Brazil	237,953,000,000
2	Russia	160,300,000,000
3	Mexico	150,288,000,000
4	China	149,800,000,000
5	Argentina	146,172,000,000
6	Indonesia	141,803,000,000
7	South Korea	134,417,000,000
8	Turkey	116,209,000,000
9	India	100,367,000,000
10	Thailand	79,675,000,000

Source: *World Bank,* World Development Indicators 2002

TOP 10 BIGGEST EXPORTERS

	COUNTRY	EXPORTS (2000) ($)
1	US	1,065,740,000,000
2	Germany	633,052,000,000
3	Japan	528,751,000,000
4	UK	401,385,000,000
5	France	377,274,000,000
6	Canada	321,693,000,000
7	Italy	294,852,000,000
8	China	279,562,000,000
9	Netherlands	258,951,000,000
10	Hong Kong (China)	244,004,000,000

Source: *World Bank,* World Development Indicators 2002

TOP 10 NOBEL ECONOMIC SCIENCES PRIZE-WINNING COUNTRIES

	COUNTRY	ECONOMIC SCIENCES PRIZES
1	US	32
2	UK	7
3 =	Canada	2
=	Norway	2
=	Sweden	2
6 =	France	1
=	Germany	1
=	India	1
=	Israel	1
=	Netherlands	1
=	USSR	1

Workers of the World

THE 10 COUNTRIES WITH THE HIGHEST PROPORTION OF CHILD WORKERS

	COUNTRY	TOTAL	10–14 YEAR OLDS AT WORK (2000) PERCENTAGE*
1	Mali	726,000	51.14
2	Bhutan	136,000	51.10
3	Burundi	445,000	48.50
4	Uganda	1,343,000	43.79
5	Niger	609,000	43.62
6	Burkina Faso	686,000	43.45
7	Ethiopia	3,277,000	42.45
8	Nepal	1,154,000	42.05
9	Rwanda	413,000	41.35
10	Kenya	1,699,000	39.15

Excludes unpaid work

Source: *International Labor Organization*

It is estimated that there are some 21 million children aged from five to 14 working around the world, including as many as 111 million who are involved in tasks that are hazardous.

THE 10 COUNTRIES WITH THE HIGHEST PROPORTION OF ELDERLY PEOPLE AT WORK*

	COUNTRY	EST. PERCENTAGE OF OVER-64 YEAR OLDS ECONOMICALLY ACTIVE* (2000)
1	Mozambique	77.24
2	Malawi	74.85
3	Ghana	71.30
4	Central African Republic	70.91
5	Tanzania	69.80
6	Gambia	61.60
7	Uganda	61.01
8	Congo	60.07
9	Madagascar	57.92
10	Solomon Islands	57.91

Excludes unpaid work

Source: *International Labor Organization*

The concept of retirement is a Western phenomenon that is unavailable to many, especially subsistence farmers in Africa.

TOP 10 COUNTRIES WITH THE LOWEST PROPORTION OF ELDERLY PEOPLE AT WORK*

	COUNTRY	EST. PERCENTAGE OF OVER-64 YEAR OLDS ECONOMICALLY ACTIVE* (2000)
1	Hungary	0.46
2	Belgium	0.93
3	Netherlands	1.14
4	Luxembourg	1.16
5	Austria	1.26
6	France	1.52
7	Spain	2.04
8	Germany	2.30
9	Finland	2.35
10	Martinique	3.00
	World	18.77
	US	9.93

Excludes unpaid work

Source: *International Labor Organization*

THE 10 COUNTRIES WITH THE MOST STRIKES AND LOCKOUTS, 2000

	COUNTRY	WORKERS INVOLVED	DAYS LOST	STRIKES AND LOCKOUTS
1	Denmark	75,656	124,800	1,081
2	Italy	687,000	884,100	966
3	Russia	31,000	236,400	817
4	Spain	2,067,287	3,616,907	750
5	Australia	325,400	469,100	698
6	India	689,592	16,720,762	656
7	Morocco	43,619	395,703	484
8	Tunisia	35,886	47,549	411
9	Canada	143,570	1,661,620	377
10	Guyana	no data	56,175	268
	US	393,700	20,419,400	39

Source: *International Labor Organization*

Strikes are temporary work stoppages precipitated by workers attempting, for example, to enforce their demands, while lockouts involve the closure of workplaces.

TOP 10 COUNTRIES WITH THE HIGHEST PROPORTION OF FARMERS

	COUNTRY	WORKERS IN AGRICULTURE (2000) TOTAL	PERCENTAGE OF WORK FORCE
1	Bhutan	942,000	93
2 =	Burkina Faso	5,062,000	92
=	Nepal	10,109,000	92
4 =	Burundi	3,022,000	90
=	Rwanda	3,734,000	90
6	Niger	4,388,000	87
7 =	Ethiopia	22,891,000	82
=	Guinea Bissau	454,000	82
9 =	Mali	4,500,000	80
=	Uganda	9,130,000	80

Source: *Food and Agriculture Organization of the United Nations*

Despite a global trend toward urbanization, a very high proportion of the populations of many Asian and African countries depend on farming for their livelihoods.

TOP 10 COUNTRIES WITH THE HIGHEST PROPORTION OF WOMEN WORKING IN SERVICE INDUSTRIES

	COUNTRY	% FEMALE LABOR FORCE IN SERVICES* (1998–2000)
1	Argentina	89
2 =	Hong Kong (China)	88
=	Norway	88
=	Panama	88
5 =	Canada	87
=	Sweden	87
=	UK	87
8 =	Australia	86
=	Belgium	86
=	France	86
=	Israel	86
=	Peru	86
=	US	86

* Service industries include wholesale and retail trade, restaurants and hotels; transportation, storage, and communications; financing, insurance, real estate, and business services; and community, social, and personal services

Source: *World Bank*, World Development Indicators 2002

TOP 10 COUNTRIES WITH THE HIGHEST PROPORTION OF MEN WORKING IN SERVICE INDUSTRIES

	COUNTRY	% MALE LABOR FORCE IN SERVICES* (1998–2000)
1 =	Columbia	71
=	Hong Kong (China)	71
3 =	Peru	67
=	Singapore	67
5	Argentina	65
6 =	Australia	64
=	US	64
8 =	Canada	63
=	Ecuador	63
=	France	63
=	Morocco	63
=	Netherlands	63

* Service industries include wholesale and retail trade, restaurants and hotels; transportation, storage, and communications; financing, insurance, real estate, and business services; and community, social, and personal services

Source: *World Bank*, World Development Indicators 2002

▶ **Leading the field**
The Himalayan kingdom of Bhutan tops the list of countries with the highest percentage of its people involved in agriculture, mainly growing rice, vegetables, and fruit.

THE 10 COUNTRIES WITH THE HIGHEST UNEMPLOYMENT

	COUNTRY	EST. % LABOR FORCE UNEMPLOYED (2001*)
1	Liberia	70
2	Zimbabwe	60
3 =	Djibouti	50
=	East Timor	50
=	Zambia	50
6	Senegal	48
7	Nepal	47
8	Lesotho	45
9 =	Bosnia and Herzegovina	40
=	Botswana	40
=	Kenya	40
	US	5.7

* Or latest year/those countries for which data available

Source: *CIA*, The World Factbook 2002

Hazards at Home & Work

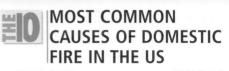

THE 10 MOST COMMON CAUSES OF DOMESTIC FIRE IN THE US

	MAJOR CAUSE	FIRES (1998)
1	Cooking	97,797
2	Incendiary/suspicious	51,894
3	Heating	50,998
4	Electrical	40,459
5	Appliances	31,715
6	Open flame	29,544
7	Smoking	23,121
8	Exposure	16,885
9	Children playing	16,402
10	Natural	9,557

Source: *National Fire Data Center, US Fire Administration, Federal Emergency Management Agency*

During the five-year period 1994–98, an annual average of 406,400 home fires were recorded in the US.

THE 10 MOST COMMON CAUSES OF UNNATURAL DEATH IN THE US

	TYPE OF ACCIDENT	DEATHS (2000) TOTAL	RATE PER 100,000
1	Traffic accident	46,259	16.76
2	Suicide—firearm	16,586	6.01
3	Falling	13,322	4.83
4	Unintentional poisoning	12,757	4.62
5	Homicide—firearm	10,801	3.91
6	Fire—burns and flames	6,864	2.48
7	Suicide—suffocation	5,688	2.06
8	Unintentional suffocation	5,648	2.05
9	Suicide—poisoning	4,859	1.76
10	Drowning	3,482	1.26
	Total deaths from injury and adverse effects	*146,781*	*53.84*

Source: *National Center for Injury Prevention and Control*

◀ **Kitchen conflagration**
Kitchen fires are the most common among almost 400,000 annual incidents. Domestic fires cause over 3,000 deaths, 15,000 injuries, and cost $5.5 billion in property damage.

THE 10 COUNTRIES WITH THE MOST FATAL INJURIES AT WORK

	COUNTRY	FATAL INJURIES PER 100,000 WORKERS (2000)
1	Austria	39.0
2	Canada	31.2
3	India	31.0
4	Turkey	24.6
5	Argentina	18.6
6	Tunisia	15.1
7	= Chile	14.0
	= Mexico	14.0*
9	Togo	11.7
10	Brazil	11.5
	US	4.0

* Partial data

Source: *International Labor Organization*

THE 10 WORST INDUSTRIAL DISASTERS*

	LOCATION/DATE	INCIDENT	NO. KILLED
1	**Bhopal,** India, December 3, 1984	Methyl isocyanate gas escape at Union Carbide plant	up to 3,849
2	**Jesse,** Nigeria, October 17, 1998	Oil pipeline explosion	more than 700
3	**Oppau,** Germany, September 21, 1921	Chemical plant explosion	561
4	**San Juanico,** Mexico, November 19, 1984	Explosion at a PEMEX liquified petroleum gas plant	540
5	**Cubatão,** Brazil, February 25, 1984	Oil pipeline explosion	508
6	**Durunkah,** Egypt, November 2, 1994	Fuel storage depot fire	more than 500
7	**Novosibirsk,** USSR, precise date unknown, April 1979	Anthrax infection following an accident at a biological and chemical warfare plant	up to 300
8	**Adeje,** Nigeria, July 10, 2000	Oil pipeline explosion	250
9	**Guadalajara,** Mexico, April 22, 1992	Explosions caused by a gas leak into sewers	230
10	**Ludwigshafen,** Germany, July 28, 1948	Dimethyl ether explosion in a lacquer plant	184

* Including industrial sites, factories, and fuel depots and pipelines; excluding military, munitions, bombs, mining, marine and other transport disasters, dam failures, and mass poisonings

THE 10 COUNTRIES WITH THE MOST INJURIES AT WORK

	COUNTRY	NONFATAL INJURIES PER 100,000 WORKERS (2000)
1	Costa Rica	15,994
2	Chile	7,964
3	Argentina	7,747
4	Spain	7,549
5	Portugal	5,471
6	Slovenia	5,091
7	Nicaragua	4,150
8	Italy	4,030
9	Germany	4,001
10	Tunisia	3,962
	US	181

Source: *International Labor Organization*

Work injuries are those sustained during the course of employment, including acts of violence, but excluding long-term occupational diseases or accidents while traveling to and from work.

THE 10 MOST DANGEROUS OCCUPATIONS IN THE US

	OCCUPATION	ACCIDENTAL DEATHS (2001)
1	**Truck drivers**	799
2	**Construction trades** (except supervisors)	567
3	**Sales occupations**	388
4	**Management/administrative executives**	378
5	**Construction laborers**	349
6	**Other farm workers,** including supervisors	327
7	**Farmers and farm managers**	321
8	= **Mechanics and repairers**	287
	= **Protective services** (police, firefighters, guards)	287
10	**Machine operators, assemblers, and inspectors**	208

Source: *US Department of Labor, Bureau of Labor Statistics*

Of the total of 5,900 occupational fatalities reported, those involving transportation and material-moving occupations are the most hazardous: as well as the 799 truck drivers heading the list, taxicab drivers and chauffeurs, railroad and other workers comprised a total of 1,185 who met their deaths in these activities, while fatalities resulting from transportation incidents represent the highest incidence—up to 100 percent in some of those in some occupations. Among construction trades, carpenters were the leading group, with 112 fatalities, followed by electricians with 109.

Advertising & Brands

TOP 10 ADVERTISING CATEGORIES

CATEGORY	EST. GLOBAL ADVERTISING EXPENDITURE (2001) ($)
1 Automotives	19,334,400,000
2 Food	11,220,700,000
3 Personal care	10,300,200,000
4 Electronics, computers	6,557,500,000
5 Media and entertainment	6,285,400,000
6 Pharmaceuticals	5,655,800,000
7 Fast food	2,989,400,000
8 Household cleaners	2,203,500,000
9 Telecommunications	1,733,000,000
10 Financial services, credit	1,156,300,000

Source: Ad Age Special Report, *Novembe 11, 2002*

TOP 10 BRANDS ADVERTISED IN THE US

BRAND	MEASURED US AD SPEND (2001) ($)
1 AT&T telephone Services	996,600,000
2 Verizon telecommunications	824,400,000
3 Chevrolet vehicles	780,400,000
4 Ford vehicles	655,900,000
5 McDonald's restaurants	635,100,000
6 Sprint telecommunications	620,400,000
7 Toyota vehicles	568,300,000
8 Sears department stores	511,500,000
9 Dodge vehicles	499,200,000
10 Chrysler vehicles	474,400,000

Source: *Taylor Nelson Sofre's* Competitive Media Reporting/Advertising Age

FIRST FACT

FIRST TV SOAP AD!

THE FIRST TELEVISION BROADCAST of a live Major League baseball game was also the occasion of the first screening of a soap advertisement. The two events took place on August 21, 1939, when the Brooklyn Dodgers met the Cincinnati Reds at Ebbets Field, Brooklyn, New York. TV station W2XBS broadcast the event, but since television was in its infancy, barely 400 people, all in New York, were able to tune in. Those who did saw an advertisement for Procter & Gamble's Ivory Soap.

TOP 10 GLOBAL MARKETERS

COMPANY/BASE	MEASURED MEDIA SPEND* (2001) ($)
1 Procter & Gamble Company, US	3,820,100,000
2 General Motors Corporation, US	3,028,900,000
3 Unilever, Netherlands/UK	3,005,500,000
4 Ford Motor Company, US	2,309,000,000
5 Toyota Motor Corporation, Japan	2,213,300,000
6 AOL Time Warner, US	2,099,800,000
7 Philip Morris Companies, US	1,934,600,000
8 DaimlerChrysler, Germany/US	1,835,300,000
9 Nestlé, Switzerland	1,798,500,000
10 Volkswagen, Germany	1,574,100,000

* Includes magazines, newspapers, outdoor, television, radio, Internet, and Yellow Pages

Source: Ad Age Global

◀ **Automobile production**
As one of the costliest of all items of consumer expenditure, advertising budgets for automobiles figure prominently among the highest for any products.

TOP 10 CORPORATE ADVERTISERS IN THE US

CORPORATION/HEADQUARTERS	MEASURED MEDIA* SPEND (2001) ($)
1 **General Motors Corp.,** Detroit	2,206,900,000
2 **Proctor & Gamble Co.,** Cincinnati	1,702,200,000
3 **AOL Time Warner,** New York	1,564,800,000
4 **DaimlerChrysler,** Auburn Hills, Michigan/Stuttgart, Germany	1,399,600,000
5 **Philip Morris Cos.,** New York	1,325,500,000
6 **Ford Motor Co.,** Dearborn, Michigan	1,269,800,000
7 **Walt Disney Co.,** Burbank, California	1,054,400,000
8 **Johnson & Johnson,** New Brunswick, New Jersey	881,800,000
9 **Verizon Communications,** New York	847,700,000
10 **Pfizer,** New York	804,600,000

Includes magazines, newspapers, outdoor, television, radio, internet, and Yellow Pages

Source: *Taylor Nelson Sofre's* Competitive Media Reporting *and Yellow Pages Integrated Media Association*/Advertising Age

TOP 10 MOST VALUABLE GLOBAL BRANDS

BRAND NAME*	INDUSTRY	BRAND VALUE (2002) ($)
1 Coca-Cola	Beverages	69,637,000,000
2 **Microsoft**	Technology	64,091,000,000
3 **IBM**	Technology	51,188,000,000
4 **General Electric**	Diversified	41,311,000,000
5 **Intel**	Technology	30,861,000,000
6 **Nokia,** Finland	Technology	29,970,000,000
7 **Disney**	Leisure	29,256,000,000
8 **McDonald's**	Food retail	26,375,000,000
9 **Marlboro**	Tobacco	24,151,000,000
10 **Mercedes,** Germany	Automobiles	21,010,000,000

All US-owned unless otherwise stated

Source: *Interbrand*/Business Week

Brand consultants Interbrand use a method of estimating value that takes into account the profitability of individual brands within a business (rather than the companies that own them), as well as such factors as their potential for growth. Well over half of the 75 most valuable global brands surveyed by Interbrand are US-owned, with Europe accounting for another 30 percent.

▶ **Things go better...**
The Coca-Cola brand stands alone as a symbol of American culture, the most valued international beverage and one of the best-selling products in the world.

Shopping Lists

TOP 10 GLOBAL RETAILERS

	COMPANY/COUNTRY	RETAIL SALES IN 2001* ($)
1	**Wal-Mart**, US	217,799,000,000
2	**Carrefour**, France	61,565,000,000
3	**Ahold**, Netherlands	57,976,000,000
4	**Home Depot**, US	53,553,000,000
5	**Kroger Co.**, US	50,098,000,000
6	**METRO AG**, Germany	43,357,000,000
7	**Target**, US	39,455,000,000
8	**Albertson's**, US	37,931,000,000
9	**Kmart**, US	36,151,000,000
10	**Sears, Roebuck**, US	35,843,000,000

* Financial year

Source: Stores *magazine* Top 200 Global Retailers

Formed in 1887, Sears Roebuck flourished to become the world's largest mail-order company, before opening its first stores in the 1920s.

TOP 10 COUNTRIES WITH THE MOST SHOPS

	COUNTRY	SHOPS IN 2000
1	**China**	19,306,800
2	**India**	10,537,080
3	**Brazil**	1,595,062
4	**Japan**	1,240,237
5	**Mexico**	1,087,995
6	**Spain**	780,247
7	**Vietnam**	727,268
8	**South Korea**	704,032
9	**Italy**	697,853
10	**US**	685,367
	World	*44,443,840*

Source: *Euromonitor*

Less developed countries tend to have a high ratio of small stores to population: China has 1 store per 67 people whereas the ratio in the US is 1 to 400.

▶ **Street trader**
India's tradition of entrepreneurship and trade has given rise to a culture in which small stores play a prominent part.

TOP 10 SUPERMARKET COUNTRIES

	COUNTRY	SPENDING PER CAPITA IN 2000 ($)
1	**US**	1,600.2
2	**UK**	1,366.5
3	**Sweden**	1,339.2
4	**Switzerland**	1,318.9
5	**Australia**	1,301.7
6	**Norway**	1,234.6
7	**Japan**	1,229.4
8	**Netherlands**	1,087.9
9	**Canada**	1,077.9
10	**Belgium**	1,051.0
	World	*244.6*

Source: *Euromonitor*

TOP 10 WORLD RETAIL SECTORS

	SECTOR	NO. OF COMPANIES*
1	**Specialty**	96
2	**Supermarket**	81
3	**Department**	54
4	**Hypermarket**	42
5	**Discount**	39
6	**Convenience**	26
7	**Superstore**	24
8	**= Mail order**	21
	= DIY	21
10	**Food service**	20

* Of those listed in Stores' Top 200 Global Retailers; stores can operate in more than one area

Source: *Stores magazine*

INTERNET RETAILERS

	COMPANY	WEBSITE	EST. US SALES ($)*
1	eBay	eBay.com	3,500–3,700,000,000
2	Amazon.com	amazon.com	1,700–1,900,000,000
3	Dell	dell.com	1,100–1,300,000,000
4	buy.com	buy.com	700–800,000,000
5 =	Egghead.com (formerly) OnSale.com	Egghead.com	500–600,000,000
=	Gateway	Gateway.com	500–600,000,000
7	Quixtar	Quixtar.com	400–450,000,000
8 =	Barnes & Noble	bn.com	275–325,000,000
=	uBid.com	uBid.com	275–325,000,000
10 =	Cyberian Outpost	Outpost.com	200–250,000,000
=	MicroWarehouse	MicroWarehouse.com	200–250,000,000
=	Value America#	va.com	200–250,000,000

* In latest financial year surveyed   # Ceased retail operations

Source: *Stores/Verifone and Russell Reynold Associates'* Top 100 Internet Retailers, Sept 2001 © NRF Enterprises, Inc.

SPECIALTY RETAILERS

	COMPANY/HEADQUARTERS	SPECIALITY	RETAIL SALES IN 2001 ($)
1	Home Depot, Inc., US	Home improvement supplies	53,553,000,000
2	Lowe's Companies, Inc., US	Home improvement supplies	22,111,000,000
3	AutoNation, Inc., US	Car dealers	19,989,000,000
4	Best Buy Co. Inc., US	Consumer electronics	19,597,000,000
5	The Gap, Inc., US	Clothing	13,848,000,000
6	Circuit City Stores, Inc., US	Consumer electronics	12,791,000,000
7	TJX Companies, Inc., US	Clothing and accessories	10,709,000,000
8	Toys "R" Us, Inc., US	Toys	11,019,000,000
9	IKEA, Sweden	Home furnishing	10,359,000,000
10	Staples, Inc., US	Office supplies	10,100,000,000

Source: Stores *magazine* Top 200 Global Retailers

MAIL-ORDER COUNTRIES

	COUNTRY	SPENDING PER CAPITA IN 2000 ($)
1	US	520.6
2	Germany	228.6
3	UK	198.6
4	Denmark	171.7
5	Switzerland	149.1
6	Austria	137.4
7	France	111.7
8	Norway	109.2
9	Sweden	102.8
10	Finland	56.5

Source: *Euromonitor*

Despite a general global market slowdown, driven by new technologies such as the Internet, the mail order sector in many countries is growing: in the US, for example, it expanded by 9 percent between 1999 and 2000 (the latest year for which comparative country data are available) to reach a value of almost $142.7 billion.

Rich Lists

TOP 10 RICHEST AMERICAN MEN

	NAME	SOURCE	NET WORTH ($)
1	William H. Gates III	Microsoft	40,700,000,000
2	Warren Edward Buffett	Berkshire Hathaway	30,500,000,000
3	Paul Gardner Allen	Microsoft	20,100,000,000
4	Lawrence Joseph Ellison	Oracle	16,600,000,000
5 =	Jim C. Walton	Wal-Mart	16,500,000,000
=	John T. Walton	Wal-Mart	16,500,000,000
=	S. Robson Walton	Wal-Mart	16,500,000,000
8	Steven Anthony Ballmer	Microsoft	11,100,000,000
9	John Werner Kluge	Metromedia	10,500,000,000
10 =	Forrest E. Mars Jr.	Mars Inc.	10,000,000,000
=	John F. Mars	Mars Inc.	10,000,000,000

Source: Forbes *magazine*, The World's Richest People, *February 27, 2003*

TOP 10 RICHEST NON-AMERICAN MEN*

	NAME/COUNTRY	SOURCE	NET WORTH ($)
1	Karl and Theo Albrecht, Germany	Retail	25,600,000,000
2	Prince Alwaleed Bin Talal Alsaud, Saudi Arabia	Investments	17,700,000,000
3	Kenneth Thomson and family, Canada	Publishing	14,000,000,000
4	Ingvar Kamprad, Sweden	Ikea	13,000,000,000
5	Amancio Ortega, Spain	Clothing	10,300,000,000
6	Mikhail B. Khodorkovsky, Russia	Banking and oil	8,000,000,000
7	Li Ka-shing, Hong Kong	Diversified	7,800,000,000
8	Hans Rausing, Sweden	Packaging	7,700,000,000
9	Gerald Cavendish Grosvenor (Duke of Westminster), UK	Land and property	7,500,000,000
10	Carlos Slim Helu, Mexico	Telecom	7,400,000,000

* Excluding rulers

Source: Forbes *magazine*, The World's Richest People, *February 27, 2003*

TOP 10 US STATES WITH THE MOST BILLIONAIRES

	STATE	NET WORTH OF BILLIONAIRES ($)	BILLIONAIRES
1	California	139,255,000,000	90
2	New York	89,100,000,000	48
3	Texas	75,130,000,000	37
4	Florida	24,855,000,000	22
5	Illinois	38,540,000,000	16
6	Pennsylvania	17,195,000,000	15
7	Washington	87,350,000,000	13
8 =	Colorado	35,195,000,000	12
=	Michigan	12,255,000,000	12
10	Massachusetts	32,800,000,000	11

Source: Forbes *magazine*, 400 Richest Americans by State, *August 16, 2002*

◀ **World's richest**
Microsoft founder Bill Gates III has led both the list of the richest Americans and that of the world's richest people for the past 10 years.

 **RICHEST WOMEN***

	NAME/COUNTRY#	SOURCE	NET WORTH ($)
1 =	Alice L. Walton	Wal-Mart	16,500,000,000
=	Helen R. Walton	Wal-Mart	16,500,000,000
3	Liliane Bettencourt, France	L'Oréal	14,500,000,000
4	Birgit Rausing and family, Sweden	Inheritance/Packaging	12,900,000,000
5 =	Barbara Cox Anthony	Media	10,300,000,000
=	Anne Cox Chambers	Media	10,300,000,000
7	Jacqueline Mars	Mars Inc.	10,000,000,000
8	Abigail Johnson	Mutual funds	8,200,000,000
9	Susanne Klatten, Germany	Inheritance	5,300,000,000
10	Maria-Elisabeth and Georg Schaeffler (mother and son)	Roller bearings	3,800,000,000

Excluding rulers

All from US unless otherwise specified

Source: Forbes *magazine*, The World's Richest People, *February 27, 2003*

 **BEST-PAID CELEBRITIES**

	CELEBRITY	PROFESSION	EARNINGS (2001–02*) ($)
1	George Lucas	Film producer/director	200,000,000
2	Oprah Winfrey	TV host/producer	150,000,000
3	Steven Spielberg	Film producer/director	100,000,000
4 =	Tiger Woods	Golfer	69,000,000
=	U2	Rock band	69,000,000
6	Michael Schumacher	Race car driver	67,000,000
7	Mariah Carey	Pop singer	58,000,000
8	Stephen King	Writer/director	52,100,000
9	Dave Matthews Band	Rock band	50,000,000
10	Tom Clancy	Writer	47,800,000

June 2001–June 2002

Source: Forbes *magazine*, The Celebrity 100

BEST-PAID CEOS IN THE US

	NAME	COMPANY	EARNINGS* ($)
1	Lawrence Joseph Ellison	Oracle	706,077,000
2	Michael Dell	Dell Computer	201,287,000
3	Jozef Straus	JDS Uniphase	150,817,000
4	Howard Solomon	Forest Labs	148,498,000
5	Richard D. Fairbank	Capital One Financial	142,231,000
6	Eugune M. Isenberg	Nabors Industries	123,778,000
7	Richard S. Fuld Jr.	Lehman Bros. Holdings	115,582,000
8	Joseph P. Nacchio	Qwest Communications	101,891,000
9	Landon H. Rowland	Stilwell Financial	93,289,000
10	Thomas M. Siebel	Siebel Systems	88,383,000

Data as of April 6, 2002, based on earnings for latest financial year available; includes earnings from company stocks

Source: Forbes *magazine*

▶ **Super celebrity**
Oprah Winfrey has consistently figured among—sometimes topping—the list of highest-earning celebrities since the 1980s.

Energy & Environment

TOP 10 | PAPER-RECYCLING COUNTRIES

	COUNTRY	PRODUCTION PER 1,000 PEOPLE (2001) (TONS)
1	Switzerland	184.48
2	Sweden	181.45
3	Austria	173.91
4	Netherlands	171.18
5	US	158.88
6	Germany	154.92
7	Finland	148.59
8	Japan	128.47
9	Norway	108.31
10	France	103.19

Source: *Food and Agriculture Organization of the United Nations*

TOP 10 | COUNTRIES WITH THE GREATEST CRUDE OIL RESERVES

	COUNTRY	2001 RESERVES (TONS)
1	Saudi Arabia	39,700,000,000
2	Iraq	16,600,000,000
3	Kuwait	14,700,000,000
4	United Arab Emirates	14,300,000,000
5	Iran	13,600,000,000
6	Venezuela	12,300,000,000
7	Russia	7,400,000,000
8	= Libya	4,200,000,000
	= Mexico	4,200,000,000
10	US	4,100,000,000

Source: *BP Amoco* Statistical Review of World Energy 2002

TOP 10 | CARBON DIOXIDE-EMITTING COUNTRIES

	COUNTRY	CO_2 EMISSIONS PER CAPITA (2001) (TONS OF CARBON)
1	Qatar	15.06
2	United Arab Emirates	14.67
3	Bahrain	10.44
4	Kuwait	9.17
5	Singapore	8.34
6	Trinidad and Tobago	6.89
7	Luxembourg	6.18
8	US	6.07
9	Guam	5.71
10	Canada	5.75

Source: *Energy Information Administration*

TOP 10 | ENERGY-CONSUMING COUNTRIES

	COUNTRY	ENERGY CONSUMPTION (2001*)					
		OIL	GAS	COAL	NUCLEAR	HEP#	TOTAL
1	US	987.2	611.3	612.6	201.9	53.2	2,466.2
2	China	255.6	27.4	573.9	4.4	64.3	925.6
3	Russia	134.8	369.7	126.3	34.1	43.9	708.8
4	Japan	272.5	78.4	113.5	80.1	22.5	567.1
5	Germany	145.1	82.2	93.0	42.7	6.4	369.5
6	India	78.4	26.1	191.3	4.9	17.7	346.9
7	Canada	97.0	72.1	31.9	19.2	82.7	302.7
8	France	105.6	40.3	12.0	104.6	20.0	282.6
9	UK	83.9	94.7	44.4	22.5	1.7	246.9
10	South Korea	113.6	22.9	50.4	28.0	1.0	215.9
	World	3,869.8	2,385.7	2,485.8	662.7	655.3	10,058.4

* Millions of tons of oil equivalent

Hydroelectric power

Source: *BP Amoco* Statistical Review of World Energy 2002

◀ **Paper chase**
Every ton of recycled paper uses 64 percent less energy and 50 percent less water, causes 74 percent less air pollution, and saves 17 trees compared with the same quantity derived from new wood pulp.

TOP 10 COUNTRIES WITH THE MOST RELIANCE ON NUCLEAR POWER

	COUNTRY	NUCLEAR ELECTRICITY AS PERCENTAGE OF TOTAL ELECTRICITY (2001)
1	Lithuania	78
2	France	77
3	Belgium	58
4	Slovakia	53
5	Ukraine	46
6	Sweden	44
7	Bulgaria	42
8 =	Hungary	39
=	Slovenia	39
=	South Korea	39
	US	20

Source: *International Atomic Energy Agency*

TOP 10 ALTERNATIVE POWER*-CONSUMING COUNTRIES

	COUNTRY	KW/HR CONSUMPTION (2001)
1	US	84,800,000,000
2	Germany	22,600,000,000
3	Japan	19,100,000,000
4	Brazil	14,800,000,000
5	Philippines	12,200,000,000
6	Spain	9,200,000,000
7	Finland	8,400,000,000
8 =	Italy	7,800,000,000
=	Luxembourg	7,800,000,000
10	Canada	7,200,000,000
	World	251,100,000,000

* Includes geothermal, solar, wind, wood, and waste electric power

Source: *Energy Information Administration*

◀ **Wind power**
Some countries have taken the lead in the amount of electricity they generate by wind turbines: Germany's capacity is now double that of the US.

Science & Technology

TOP 10 INTERNATIONAL COMPANIES FOR RESEARCH AND DEVELOPMENT

	COMPANY/COUNTRY	INDUSTRY	R&D SPENDING (2001) ($)
1	**Ford Motor,** US	Automobiles and parts	7,400,000,000
2	**General Motors,** US	Automobiles and parts	6,200,000,000
3	**Siemens,** Germany	Electronic and electrical	5,980,550,000
4	**DaimlerChrysler,** Germany	Automobiles and parts	5,231,880,000
5	**Pfizer,** US	Pharmaceuticals	4,847,000,000
6	**IBM,** US	Software and IT services	4,620,000,000
7	**Ericsson,** Sweden	IT hardware	4,410,410,000
8	**Microsoft,** US	Software and IT services	4,379,000,000
9	**Motorola,** US	IT hardware	4,318,000,000
10	**Matsushita Electric,** Japan	Electronic and electrical	4,310,440,000

Source: *The Financial Times Ltd., 2002*

The 300 international companies featured in the *Financial Times'* survey spent a total of $267.6 trillion on research and development. Of them, some 70 firms spent in excess of $1 billion a year, with automobile manufacturers representing the most prominent among the world's biggest R&D spenders.

TOP 10 INDUSTRIES FOR RESEARCH AND DEVELOPMENT

	INDUSTRY	R&D SPENDING (2001) ($)
1	**IT hardware**	69,687,090,000
2	**Automobiles and parts**	47,877,160,000
3	**Pharmaceuticals**	46,553,340,000
4	**Electronic and electrical**	28,751,540,000
5	**Software and IT services**	15,925,250,000
6	**Chemicals**	11,725,580,000
7	**Aerospace and defense**	11,367,060,000
8	**Engineering and machinery**	5,941,040,000
9	**Telecommunications**	5,898,190,000
10	**Health**	4,727,640,000

Source: *The Financial Times Ltd., 2002*

▼ Trading place
With one computer for every 10 people in the world, the workplace has undergone a transformation, although the true "paperless office" remains a rarity.

THE 10 FIRST PATENTS IN THE US

	PATENT	PATENTEE	DATE
1	**Making pot and pearl ash**	Samuel Hopkins	July 31, 1790
2	**Candle making**	Joseph S. Sampson	Aug. 6, 1790
3	**Flour and meal making**	Oliver Evans	Dec. 18, 1790
4 =	**Punches for type**	Francis Bailey	Jan. 29, 1791
=	**Improvement in distilling**	Aaron Putnam	Jan. 29, 1791
6	**Driving piles**	John Stone	Mar. 10, 1791
7 =	**Threshing machine**	Samuel Mullikin	Mar. 11, 1791
=	**Breaking hemp**	Samuel Mullikin	Mar. 11, 1791
=	**Polishing marble**	Samuel Mullikin	Mar. 11, 1791
=	**Raising nap on cloth**	Samuel Mullikin	Mar. 11, 1791

America's first patent, issued to Samuel Hopkins of Vermont, was for a process for manufacturing potash, or potassium carbonate, which was used in such industries as glass-, gunpowder-, and soap-making. For every ton produced, an acre of trees was cut down and burned, and the potash extracted from the resulting ashes. This group of pioneer patentees was followed in 1791 by others with devices reflecting the diversity of American inventiveness, and included improvements in making nails, bedsteads, manufacturing boats, and propelling boats by cattle-power.

TOP 10 COUNTRIES WITH THE HIGHEST PROPORTION OF COMPUTER USERS

	COUNTRY	TOTAL	COMPUTERS (2001) PER 100 INHABITANTS
1	US	178,000,000	62.25
2	Sweden	5,000,000	56.12
3	Australia	10,000,000	51.71
4	Luxembourg	230,000	51.45
5	Singapore	2,100,000	50.83
6	Norway	2,300,000	50.80
7	Switzerland	3,600,000	49.97
8	Denmark	2,300,000	43.15
9	Netherlands	6,900,000	42.85
10	Finland	2,200,000	42.35
	World	455,366,000	7.74

Source: *International Telecommunication Union*, World Telecommunication Development Report, 2002

TOP 10 COUNTRIES REGISTERING THE MOST PATENTS

	COUNTRY	PATENTS REGISTERED (2000)
1	US	157,496
2	Japan	125,880
3	Germany	41,585
4	France	36,404
5	South Korea	34,956
6	UK	33,756
7	Italy	19,652
8	Russia	17,592
9	Netherlands	17,052
10	Spain	15,809

Source: *World Intellectual Property Organization*

This international list provides a yardstick of the state of each nation's technological development. A further 35,357 patents were granted by the European Patent Office, which has no national affiliation.

TOP 10 MOST VALUABLE TECHNOLOGY BRANDS*

	BRAND NAME/COUNTRY	BRAND VALUE (2002) ($)
1	Microsoft, US	64,091,000,000
2	IBM, US	51,188,000,000
3	Intel, US	30,861,000,000
4	Nokia, Finland	29,970,000,000
5	Hewlett-Packard, US	16,780,000,000
6	Cisco, US	16,220,000,000
7	AT&T, US	16,060,000,000
8	Sony, Japan	13,900,000,000
9	Oracle, US	11,510,000,000
10	Compaq, US	9,800,000,000

* Includes computer, telecommunications, and consumer electronics brands

Source: *Interbrand*/Business Week

Brand consultants Interbrand uses a method of estimating value that takes account of the profitability of individual brands within a business (rather than the companies that own them), as well as such factors as their potential for growth.

TOP 10 NOBEL PHYSICS PRIZE-WINNING COUNTRIES

	COUNTRY	PHYSICS PRIZES
1	US	73
2 =	Germany	21
=	UK	21
4	France	12
5	Netherlands	8
6	USSR	7
7 =	Japan	4
=	Sweden	4
9 =	Austria	3
=	Denmark	3
=	Italy	3

World Wide Web

MOST WIRED CITIES

	CITY/COUNTRY	COUNTRIES CONNECTED	INTERNATIONAL INTERNET BANDWIDTH (MBPS) (2001)
1	**London,** UK	61	237,389.2
2	**Paris,** France	48	179,064.8
3	**New York,** USA	71	173,098.6
4	**Amsterdam,** Holland	27	170,371.8
5	**Frankfurt,** Germany	28	160,459.0
6	**Brussels,** Belgium	17	76,246.4
7	**Stockholm,** Sweden	18	60,349.0
8	**Copenhagen,** Denmark	13	43,456.0
9	**Milan,** Italy	15	29,701.8
10	**Toronto,** Canada	6	24,942.3

Source: *TeleGeography*

These are the top cities in the world for connection to the Internet. New York has direct connections with 71 countries, and has the highest bandwidth capacity of any city in the world

INTERNET FRAUDS, 2002

	CATEGORY	% ALL COMPLAINTS*
1	**Online auctions**	90
2	**General merchandise**	5
3	**Nigerian money offers**	4
4	**Computer equipment/software**	0.5
5	**Internet access services**	0.4
6 =	**Work-at-home plans**	more than 0.1
=	**Information/adult services**	more than 0.1
=	**Advance-fee loans**	more than 0.1
=	**Travel/vacations**	more than 0.1
=	**Prizes/sweepstakes**	more than 0.1

Source: *National Fraud Information Center, National Consumers League*

The overall loss in the US to Internet fraud in 2002 was $14,647,933, with an average loss (per victim of Internet fraud) of $468

TOP 10 COUNTRIES WITH THE MOST INTERNET USERS

	COUNTRY	INTERNET USERS*
1	US	168,600,000
2	Japan	56,000,000
3	China	45,800,000
4	Germany	41,800,000
5	UK	30,400,000
6	Italy	25,300,000
7	France	23,000,000
8	Brazil	19,700,000
9	Spain	17,000,000
10	Canada	16,840,000
	World total	580,000,000

* Estimate, as at March 14, 2003

Source: *CyberAtlas/Nielsen/NetRatings*

◀ **Cyber café**
The arrival of Internet cafés in 1984 heralded a new era of communications and information gathering for people on the move, those lacking personal Internet access, or as a social activity.

TOP 10 COUNTRIES WITH THE HIGHEST DENSITY OF INTERNET HOSTS

	COUNTRY	INTERNET HOSTS PER 1,000 PEOPLE (2001)
1	US	371.40
2	Tonga	209.00
3	Iceland	190.48
4	Finland	170.72
5	Netherlands	163.47
6	Australia	118.34
7	New Zealand	104.95
8	Denmark	104.53
9	Canada	93.19
10	Sweden	82.51

Source: *International Telecommunication Union*, World Telecommunciation Development Report, 2002

An Internet host is a computer system connected to the Internet—either a single terminal directly connected, or a computer that allows multiple users to access network services through it. The ratio of hosts to population is a crude measure of how "wired" a country is.

TOP 10 WEBSITE BRANDS IN THE US

	WEBSITE	UNIQUE VISTORS IN US*
1	Yahoo!	80,745,000
2	Microsoft	75,228,000
3	MSN	74,270,000
4	AOL	69,721,000
5	Google	40,310,000
6	Amazon	34,518,000
7	Real	34,182,000
8	eBay	34,109,000
9	Lycos Networks	30,116,000
10	About Network	23,275,000

* Estimated number of unique visitors during month of February 2003

Source: *Nielsen/NetRatings Audience Measurement Service*

It is generally accepted that the best way of assessing a website's popularity is to count how many separate individuals visit the site. This makes it possible to rank a website according to the number of people who visit it, rather than the number of times it is visited, since this will count each separate visit by the same individual.

WORLD WIDE WORDS

FIRST FACT

BOTH THE INTERNET AND ITS language have evolved over the past 40 years. "Hypertext" was first proposed as early as 1965 by Ted Nelson. Ray Tomlinson pioneered and named e-mail in 1971 and the following year advocated the use of the "@" sign. The first "smiley" [:-)]or emoticon was used by Scott E. Fahlman on a Carnegie Mellon University Bulletin Board in 1982, the same year that William Gibson invented the term "cyberspace" in his novel *Neuromancer*. The "World Wide Web," and its name, were devised by Tim Berners-Lee in 1990, and the description "surfing the internet" was coined in 1992 by Jean Armour Polly.

TOP 10 MOST SEARCHED TERMS OF ALL TIME ON LYCOS

	TERM	WEEKS ON LIST*
1	= Pamela Anderson	188
	= Britney Spears	188
	= Dragonball	188
	= Las Vegas	188
	= Tattoos	188
	= Jennifer Lopez	188
	= WWF	188
8	Final Fantasy	186
9	The Bible	185
10	Harry Potter	143

* Continuous runs only; as at March 22, 2003

Source: *Lycos 50*

TOP 10 SEARCH ENGINES

	SEARCH ENGINE	SEARCHES PER DAY*
1	Google	112,000,000
2	AOL Search	93,000,000
3	Yahoo	42,000,000
4	MSN Search	32,000,000
5	Ask Jeeves	14,000,000
6	InfoSpace	7,000,000
7	= AltaVista	5,000,000
	= Overture	5,000,000
9	Netscape	4,000,000
10	Earthlink	3,000,000

* As of Januaray 2003, US traffic only; estimated by dividing search hours per month by 30 to get the number of minutes per day, and assuming that a typical search takes 20 seconds

Source: SearchEngineWatch.com

Keep in Touch

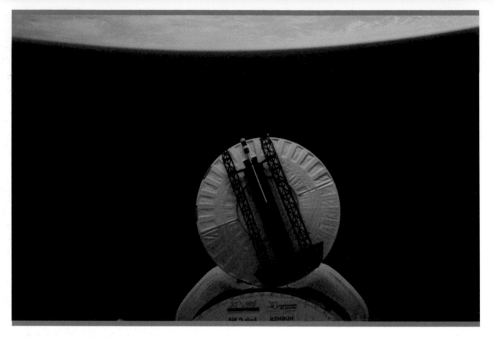

▲ **Syncom IV (LEASAT) satellite**
Since the mid-1960s, satellites launched into geostationary orbit have enabled international telecommunications to become one of the fastest growing industries on Earth—and beyond.

TOP 10 COUNTRIES MAKING THE MOST INTERNATIONAL PHONE CALLS

	COUNTRY	MINUTES (2000) CALL PER HEAD	TOTAL
1	US	125.9	34,640,700,000
2	Germany	112.1	9,223,000,000
3	UK	133.5	7,981,000,000
4	Canada	234.9	7,224,000,000
5	France	84.1	4,952,000,000
6	Hong Kong	466.8	3,142,400,000
7	Netherlands	177.0	2,830,000,000
8	Italy	47.8	2,740,000,000
9	Japan	20.3	2,575,000,000
10	Spain	64.1	2,570,000,000

Source: *International Telecommunication Union*, World Telecommunication Development Report, *2002*

Dividing international call minutes by the number of inhabitants provides a somewhat different picture, in which Bermuda leads the world with 944.1 minutes per capita, compared with the USA's 125.9.

TOP 10 INTERNATIONAL TELECOMMUNICATIONS CARRIERS

	COMPANY/ORIGIN COUNTRY	OUTGOING TRAFFIC (2001) (MINUTES)
1	AT&T Corp, US	12,006,800,000
2	WorldCom, US	11,454,700,000
3	Sprint, US	5,384,400,000
4	Deutsche Telekom, Germany	5,025,100,000
5	France Télécom, France	4,592,000,000
6	BT, UK	4,233,500,000
7	Cable & Wireless, UK	3,113,800,000
8	Telefónica, Spain	3,084,800,000
9	Telecom Italia, Italy	3,042,000,000
10	China Telecom, China	2,600,000,000

Source: *TeleGeography*

In 2001, the Top 10 and other international telecommunications carriers handled an estimated total of 144 billion minutes of outgoing traffic—equivalent to more than 23 minutes for every person on the planet.

TOP 10 COUNTRIES WITH THE MOST POST OFFICES

	COUNTRY	AVERAGE NO. OF PEOPLE SERVED PER OFFICE	TOTAL NO. OF POST OFFICES (2001*)
1	India	6,568	154,919
2	China	22,490	57,135
3	Russia	3,546	41,052
4	US	7,471	38,123
5	Japan	5,143	24,760
6	Indonesia	10,806	19,881
7	UK	3,377	17,633
8	France	3,469	17,067
9	Ukraine	3,282	14,963
10	Italy	4,203	13,788

* Or latest year for which data available

Source: *Universal Postal Union*

There are some 770,000 post offices worldwide, ranging from major city post offices offering a wide range of services to small establishments providing only basic facilities, such as the sale of stamps.

TOP 10 LETTER-MAILING COUNTRIES

	COUNTRY	AVERAGE NO. OF LETTER POST ITEMS MAILED PER INHABITANT (2001*)
1	Vatican City	6,500.00
2	US	706.11
3	Norway	561.72
4	Liechtenstein	556.00
5	Austria	467.10
6	Luxembourg	449.21
7	France	447.57
8	Finland	344.58
9	Belgium	344.05
10	Slovenia	272.74

* Or latest year for which data available

Source: *Universal Postal Union*

The Vatican's statistics are partly explained by the number of official missives sent by the Holy See, and partly by the fact that mail sent within the Vatican, and bearing its stamps, is treated as priority.

TOP 10 COUNTRIES WITH THE MOST TELEPHONES PER 100 PEOPLE

	COUNTRY	TOTAL	TELEPHONE LINES PER 100 INHABITANTS (2001)
1	Guernsey	55,000	87.50
2	Bermuda	56,300	87.15
3	Jersey	73,000	84.79
4	Luxembourg	350,900	78.30
5	Sweden	6,585,000	73.91
6	Denmark	3,882,000	72.33
7	Norway	3,262,000	72.04
8	Switzerland	5,183,000	71.79
9	US	190,000,000	66.45
10	Iceland	190,600	66.39

Source: *International Telecommunications Union*, World Telecommunication Development Report, *2002*

TOP 10 COUNTRIES WITH THE HIGHEST RATIO OF CELLULAR MOBILE PHONE USERS

	COUNTRY	SUBSCRIBERS	CELL PHONES PER 100 INHABITANTS (2001)
1	Luxembourg	432,400	96.73
2	Taiwan	21,633,000	96.55
3	Hong Kong	5,701,700	84.35
4	Italy	48,698,000	83.94
5	Norway	3,737,000	82.53
6	Iceland	235,400	82.02.
7	Israel	5,260,000	80.82
8	Austria	6,565,900	80.66
9	UK	47,026,000	78.28
10	Finland	4,044,000	77.84

Source: *International Telecommunications Union*, World Telecommunication Development Report, *2002*

THE 10 FIRST CITIES AND COUNTRIES TO ISSUE POSTAGE STAMPS

	CITY OR COUNTRY	STAMPS ISSUED
1	Great Britain	May 1840
2	New York, NY	Feb. 1842
3	Zurich, Switzerland	Mar. 1843
4	Brazil	Aug. 1843
5	Geneva, Switzerland	Oct. 1843
6	Basle, Switzerland	July 1845
7	US	July 1847
8	Mauritius	Sept. 1847
9	Bermuda	Unknown 1848
10	France	Jan. 1849

The first adhesive postage stamps issued in Great Britain were the Penny Blacks that went on sale on May 1, 1840. The first issued in the US were designed for local delivery (as authorized by an 1836 Act of Congress) and produced by the City Despatch Post, New York City, inaugurated on February 15, 1842, and incorporated into the US Post Office Department later that year.

► **Phone home**
The adoption of cell phones has revolutionized telecommunications worldwide, with Scandinavian countries standing out among those with the highest density of users.

Food Favorites

TOP 10 BAKED BEAN CONSUMERS

| | COUNTRY | EST. CONSUMPTION PER CAPITA (2004) | | |
		(LB)	(OZ)	(KG)
1	Ireland	12	5	5.6
2	UK	10	9	4.8
3	New Zealand	5	1	2.3
4	US	4	6	2.0
5	Australia	4	3	1.9
6 =	France	3	8	1.6
=	Saudi Arabia	3	8	1.6
8	Switzerland	3	5	1.5
9	Ukraine	2	13	1.3
10 =	Canada	2	10	1.2
=	Mexico	2	10	1.2

Source: *Euromonitor*

Canned baked beans originated in New England. Brand leader Heinz's baked beans were test-marketed in the North of England in 1901. They were imported from the US up to 1928, when they were first canned in the UK.

TOP 10 POTATO CHIP CONSUMERS

| | COUNTRY | EST. CONSUMPTION PER CAPITA (2004) | | |
		(LB)	(OZ)	(KG)
1	UK	6	9	3.0
2 =	Australia	5	15	2.7
=	Ireland	5	15	2.7
4	New Zealand	5	12	2.6
5 =	Norway	4	14	2.4
=	US	4	14	2.4
7	Finland	4	10	2.1
8	Sweden	3	15	1.8
9	Israel	3	11	1.7
10	Canada	3	8	1.6

Source: *Euromonitor*

◀ **Full of beans**
Although baked beans originated in the US, the British have adopted them as a staple dish to become the world's foremost consumers.

TOP 10 FROZEN FOOD CONSUMERS

| | COUNTRY | EST. CONSUMPTION PER CAPITA (2004) | | |
		(LB)	(OZ)	(KG)
1	Denmark	104	7	47.4
2	Norway	76	15	34.9
3	Sweden	54	7	24.7
4	Finland	51	12	23.5
5	UK	49	2	22.3
6	Ireland	45	3	20.5
7	Switzerland	36	9	16.6
8	Israel	36	2	16.4
9	New Zealand	34	6	15.6
10	US	31	4	14.2

Source: *Euromonitor*

Having studied Eskimos' methods of preserving food by freezing, Clarence Birdseye established the first frozen food company in 1924 in Gloucester, Massachusetts. The Birds Eye company sold its first individual frozen meals—chicken fricassée and steak—in 1939.

TOP 10 MEAT CONSUMERS

| | COUNTRY | EST. CONSUMPTION PER CAPITA (2000) | | |
		(LB)	(OZ)	(KG)
1	US	269	10	122.3
2	Denmark	253	1	114.8
3	Spain	250	14	113.8
4	Australia	243	6	110.4
5	New Zealand	235	7	106.8
6	Austria	235	0	106.6
7	Cyprus	234	2	106.2
8	Mongolia	228	9	103.7
9	France	220	3	99.9
10	Canada	220	0	99.8
	World	83	15	38.1

Source: *Food and Agriculture Organization of the United Nations*

Worldwide, meat consumption ranges from 220 pounds or more for countries in the Top 10, to less than 12 pounds per head in countries such as India.

TOP 10 FAST FOOD COMPANIES

	COMPANY/COUNTRY	FAST FOOD MARKET SHARE (1999) (%)
1	McDonald's Corporation, US	21.9
2	Tricon Global Restaurants, Inc., US	10.7
3	Diageo plc, UK	7.1
4	Wendy's International, Inc., US	3.8
5 =	Allied Domecq plc, UK	2.3
=	Doctor's Associates, Inc., US	2.3
7	CKE Restaurants, Inc.	2.0
8	Domino's Pizza, Inc., US	1.8
9	Berkshire Hathaway, Inc., US	1.5
10	Triarc Corporation, US	1.3

Source: *Euromonitor*

The world's leading fast food company, McDonald's, began in Des Plaines, Illinois, in 1955, with the opening of Ray Kroc's first restaurant. Today more than 30,000 restaurants serve 46 million people a day in 121 countries; the one in Pushkin Square, Russia, is the busiest of all.

TOP 10 CANNED FOOD CONSUMERS

	COUNTRY	(LB)	(OZ)	(KG)
1	Sweden	73	10	33.4
2	UK	51	12	23.5
3	Portugal	51	2	23.2
4	France	49	2	22.3
5	Belgium	47	2	21.4
6	US	46	11	21.2
7	New Zealand	36	6	16.5
8	Norway	36	2	16.4
9	Czech Republic	35	11	16.2
10	Australia	35	4	16.0

EST. CONSUMPTION PER CAPITA (2004)

Source: *Euromonitor*

Bryan Donkin and John Hall of Bermondsey, London, were the first to can food in tinplate cans, originally designed for military use during the Napoleonic wars, but sold to the public from 1814 onward.

TOP 10 VEGETABLE CONSUMERS

	COUNTRY	(LB)	(OZ)	(KG)
1	United Arab Emirates	694	0	314.8
2	Lebanon	679	0	308.0
3	Greece	646	2	293.1
4	Israel	527	12	239.4
5	South Korea	511	14	232.2
6	Turkey	463	3	210.1
7	Macedonia	461	10	209.4
8	Libya	456	5	207.0
9	Albania	451	8	204.8
10	China	448	10	203.5
	World	224	10	101.9
	US	277	5	125.8

EST. CONSUMPTION PER CAPITA (2000)

Source: *Food and Agriculture Organization of the United Nations*

▶ **Fruits and veggies**
Although apples and bananas remain among the US's favorite fruits, the modern shopping basket contains a far more diverse range of products than in the past.

Sweet Success

TOP 10 CONFECTIONERY MANUFACTURERS

	MANUFACTURER/COUNTRY OF ORIGIN	PERCENTAGE SHARE OF CONFECTIONERY MARKET (2001)
1	**Philip Morris Company Inc.,** US	4.5
2 =	**Nestlé SA,** Switzerland	4.0
=	**Perfetti Van Melle Group,** Italy/Netherlands	4.0
4	**Hershey Foods Corporation,** US	3.3
5	**Pfizer Inc.,** US	3.1
6	**Cadbury-Schweppes plc,** UK	3.0
7 =	**CSM nv,** Netherlands	2.7
=	**Mars Inc.,** US	2.7
9	**August Storck KG,** Germany	2.4
10	**Haribo GmbH & Co. KG,** Germany	2.1

Source: *Euromonitor*

Global sales of confectionery in 2001 were estimated at 14 million tons, an average of 4 lb 6 oz (2.1 kg) for everyone on Earth – although per capita consumption in many countries is much higher – with a total value of just under $100 billion.

TOP 10 CHOCOLATE CONFECTIONERY CONSUMERS

	COUNTRY	CONSUMPTION PER CAPITA (2000) (LB)	(OZ)	(KG)
1	**Switzerland**	25	6	11.5
2	**Liechtenstein**	22	15	10.4
3	**Luxembourg**	22	11	10.3
4	**UK**	21	10	9.8
5	**Belgium**	18	15	8.6
6	**Norway**	17	3	7.8
7 =	**Germany**	17	0	7.7
=	**Ireland**	17	0	7.7
9	**Iceland**	16	12	7.6
10	**Austria**	13	14	6.3
	World	2	3	1.0

Source: *Euromonitor*

World chocolate confectionery consumption is around 6.5 million tons a year, just under 2 lb 3 oz (1 kg) per capita, with a total value of some $53 billion.

◀ **Taking the cake**
The world's passion for chocolate and sugar-based products grows annually—as do the waistlines of its consumers....

TOP 10 SUGAR CONSUMERS

	COUNTRY	CONSUMPTION PER CAPITA* (2000) (LB)	(OZ)	(KG)
1	**Macedonia**	162	12	73.8
2	**Belize**	144	6	65.5
3	**Swaziland**	125	8	56.9
4	**Cuba**	124	15	56.6
5	**Trinidad and Tobago**	122	0	55.3
6	**Barbados**	116	4	52.7
7	**Brazil**	114	1	51.7
8	**Costa Rica**	111	8	50.6
9	**New Zealand**	108	9	49.2
10	**St. Kitts and Nevis**	108	0	49.0
	World	41	5	18.75
	US	66	10	30.24

* *Refined equivalent*

Source: *Food and Agriculture Organization of the United Nations*

In the past decade, Cuba has lost its former role as the world's leading sugar consumer.

CHEWING GUM CONSUMERS
TOP 10

| COUNTRY | CONSUMPTION PER CAPITA (2000) | | |
	(LB)	(OZ)	(G)
1 = Andorra	2	0	900
= Iceland	2	0	900
= Norway	2	0	900
4 = Israel	1	9	700
= Liechtenstein	1	9	700
= Switzerland	1	9	700
= US	1	9	700
8 = St. Kitts and Nevis	1	5	600
= Spain	1	5	600
= Turkey	1	5	600
World	*0*	*3*	*100*

Source: *Euromonitor*

Worldwide chewing gum consumption in 2000 was estimated as 877,000 tons, and that of the US 218,400 tons, or just under 25 percent of the total.

ICE CREAM CONSUMERS
TOP 10

| COUNTRY | CONSUMPTION PER CAPITA (2000) | |
	(PINTS)	(LITERS)
1 Australia	31.1	17.7
2 US	24.1	13.7
3 New Zealand	23.4	13.3
4 Sweden	20.5	11.7
5 Ireland	17.9	10.2
6 = Denmark	16.3	9.3
= Israel	16.3	9.3
8 Canada	16.0	9.1
9 Finland	14.9	8.5
10 Norway	14.7	8.4

Source: *Euromonitor*

Just under 4 percent of the world's total expenditure on packaged food is devoted to ice cream, the 10th largest sector in the global market, which was worth a total of $43 billion in 2000.

▶ **Knickerbocker glory**
Invented in the 1930s, this over-the-top concoction was named after Diedrich Knickerbocker, fictitious author of Washington Irving's *History of New York*.

CANDY MANUFACTURERS IN THE US
TOP 10

MANUFACTURER	PERCENTAGE SHARE OF MARKET (2001)*
1 Hershey Foods Corp.	23.6
2 Mars Inc.	18.2
3 Nestlé USA Inc.	4.6
4 William Wrigley Jr. Co.	4.5
5 Warner-Lambert Co.	2.9
6 Kraft Foods Inc.	2.3
7 Russell Stover Candies	2.1
8 Favorite Brands International Inc.	1.9
9 Brach & Brock Confections Inc.	1.8
10 Tootsie Roll Industries Inc.	1.4

* Based on $ sales volume

Source: *Euromonitor*

CHOCOLATE CANDY BARS IN THE US
TOP 10

BRAND/MANUFACTURER	SALES* ($)
1 M&Ms, Mars	97,404,576
2 Hershey's Milk Chocolate, Hershey Chocolate	81,296,784
3 Reese's Peanut Butter Cups, Hershey Chocolate	54,391,268
4 Snickers, Mars	53,695,428
5 KitKat, Hershey Chocolate (under license from Nestlé)	38,168,580
6 Twix, Mars	33,174,400
7 York Peppermint Patty, York Cone Company	25,494,038
8 Peter Paul Almond Joy, Hershey Chocolate	23,721,998
9 Butterfinger, Nestlé	22,804,380
10 Three Musketeers, Mars	19,834,244
Total (including those not in Top 10)	*773,904,832*

* 3.5 oz candy bars only; 52 weeks to January 27, 2002

Source: *Information Resources, Inc.*

Drink Up

CARBONATED SOFT DRINK CONSUMERS

	COUNTRY	CONSUMPTION PER CAPITA (2000)	
		(GALLONS)	(LITERS)
1	US	42.7	161.8
2	Mexico	30.2	114.2
3	Norway	26.9	102.0
4	Canada	22.6	85.6
5	Australia	21.7	82.3
6	Belgium	21.1	79.8
7	Chile	21.0	79.5
8	Argentina	19.2	72.8
9	UK	19.2	72.7
10	Saudi Arabia	19.0	72.2

Source: *Euromonitor*

◀ Café society
The world's most enthusiastic coffee drinkers are all Europeans—led by the Scandinavians, who each consume two or more cups a day.

BOTTLED WATER CONSUMERS

	COUNTRY	CONSUMPTION PER CAPITA (2000)	
		(GALLONS)	(LITERS)
1	France	34.3	130.0
2	Italy	30.6	115.7
3	Spain	24.6	93.1
4	Belgium	22.4	84.8
5	Germany	19.8	74.7
6	Switzerland	18.0	68.0
7	Austria	16.2	61.2
8	Czech Republic	16.0	60.4
9	Slovakia	10.5	39.6
10	Poland	9.1	34.6
	US	6.0	22.9

Source: *Euromonitor*

French bottled mineral water consumption began in the 19th century. Leading sources such as Evian, Perrier, and Vittel supply the domestic market as well as exporting billions of bottles annually to the rest of the world.

BEER CONSUMERS

	COUNTRY	CONSUMPTION PER CAPITA (2001)	
		(GALLONS)	(LITERS)
1	Czech Republic	34.8	158.1
2	Ireland	33.2	150.8
3	Germany	27.1	123.1
4	Austria	23.5	106.9
5	Luxembourg	22.2	100.9
6	Denmark	21.7	98.6
7	Belgium	21.6	98.0
8	UK	21.4	97.1
9	Australia	20.5	93.0
10	Slovak Republic	19	86.4*
	US	18.3	83.2*

* *Estimated from beer production due to lack of consumption data*

Source: *Commission for Distilled Spirits*

While no African countries appear in this list, this does not mean that people in Africa do not drink beer. Bottled beer is often prohibitively expensive, so people drink homemade beers sold in local markets.

CARBONATED DRINKS

THE FIRST ARTIFICIAL MINERAL WATER—"soda water"—was made by English chemist Joseph Priestley in 1767. His process, which he called "Impregnating Water with Fixed Air," was improved by others. Various manufacturers, including Jacob Schweppe in Europe, began bottling water, while in Philadelphia, Pennsylvania, Townsend Speakman supplied carbonated water to a local doctor, Philip Syng Physick, who administered it to his patients as a medicine. In 1807 Speakman mixed fruit juice with it to create the first flavored carbonated drink, to which he gave the name "Nephite Julep."

FIRST FACT

TOP 10 COFFEE CONSUMERS

	COUNTRY	CONSUMPTION PER CAPITA (2001)			
		(LB)	(OZ)	(KG)	(CUPS*)
1	Finland	24	4	11.01	1,652
2	Denmark	21	9	9.79	1,469
3	Norway	20	13	9.46	1,419
4	Sweden	18	13	8.55	1,283
5	Austria	15	9	7.08	1,062
6	Germany	15	3	6.90	1,035
7	Switzerland	14	15	6.80	1,020
8	Netherlands	13	15	6.34	951
9	Belgium and Luxembourg	12	3	5.53	830
10	Italy	11	15	5.44	816
	US	9	5	4.23	635

* Based on 150 cups per kg (2 lb 3 oz)

Source: *International Coffee Organization*

TOP 10 TEA CONSUMERS

	COUNTRY	ANNUAL CONSUMPTION PER CAPITA*			
		(LB)	(OZ)	(KG)	(CUPS#)
1	Ireland	5	15	2.71	1,192
2	Libya	5	13	2.65	1,166
3	Kuwait	5	1	2.29	1,007
4	UK	5	0	2.28	1,003
5	Qatar	4	14	2.23	981
6	Iraq	4	13	2.20	968
7	Turkey	4	12	2.17	954
8	Iran	3	2	1.43	629
9	Hong Kong	3	0	1.36	598
10	Morocco	2	15	1.34	589

* 1999–2001

Based on 440 cups per kg (2 lb 3 oz)

Source: *International Tea Committee Ltd., London*

TOP 10 WINE PRODUCERS

	COUNTRY	PRODUCTION (1999)	
		(GALLONS)	(LITERS)
1	France	1,340,375,000	6,093,500,000
2	Italy	1,278,237,500	5,811,000,000
3	Spain	809,525,000	3,680,200,000
4	US	455,137,500	2,069,100,000
5	Argentina	349,487,500	1,588,800,000
6	Germany	269,325,000	1,224,400,000
7	Australia	187,212,500	851,100,000
8	South Africa	175,262,500	796,800,000
9	Portugal	171,700,000	780,600,000
10	Romania	143,062,500	650,400,000

Source: *Commission for Distilled Spirits*

▶ **Wine lovers**
The world's vineyards produce a total of
55 billion pints (26 billion litres) of wine
annually – more than five bottles for
every inhabitant on the planet.

TRANSPORT & TOURISM

On the Road

BESTSELLING CARS OF ALL TIME

	MODEL	YEARS IN PRODUCTION	EST. NO. MADE*
1	Toyota Corolla	1966–	29,000,000
2	Volkswagen Golf	1974–	21,517,415[#]
3	Volkswagen Beetle	1937–	21,517,414[#]
4	Lada Riva	1972–97	19,000,000
5	Ford Model T	1908–27	16,536,075
6	Honda Civic	1972–	14,920,000
7	Nissan Sunny/Pulsar	1966–94	13,571,100
8	Honda Accord	1976–	12,520,000
9	Ford Escort/Orion	1967–2000	12,000,000
10	Volkswagen Passat	1959–	11,509,165

* *To 1 January, 2003, except where otherwise indicated*

[#] *To June 2002 (when production of the Golf officially overtook that of the original Beetle – which is still produced in Mexico)*

Estimates of manufacturers' output of their bestselling models vary from the vague to the unusually precise 16,536,075 of the Model T Ford, with 15,007,033 produced in the US and the rest in Canada and the UK, between 1908 and 1927. However, certain models have undergone such radical modification during their lifespans that they are only distantly related to their predecessors.

▼ **The road ahead**
For better or for worse, in barely 100 years the coming of the automobile has changed the landscape of vast areas of our planet.

BESTSELLING CARS IN THE US, 2002

	CAR	SALES (2002)
1	Toyota Camry	434,145
2	Honda Accord	398,980
3	Ford Taurus	332,690
4	Honda Civic	313,159
5	Ford Focus	243,199
6	Chevrolet Cavalier	238,225
7	Nissan Altima	201,822
8	Chevrolet Impala	198,918
9	Toyota Corolla	195,606
10	Chevrolet Malibu	169,377

Source: *Ward's AutoInfoBank*

Sales of the redesigned Toyota Camry increased by 11 percent in the US in 2002, enabling it to reclaim its place as the nation's best-selling car from the former No. 1, the Honda Accord, while for the 21 consecutive year a Ford truck, the F-Series, with sales of 813,701, remained the US's top-selling vehicle.

PRODUCTION CARS WITH THE FASTEST 0–60 MPH TIMES

	MODEL*	COUNTRY	SECONDS TAKEN[#]
1	Caterham 7 Superlight R500	UK	3.4
2	Westfield 317 FW400	UK	3.5
3	Lamborghini Murcielago	Italy	3.7
4	TVR Tuscan 4.5	UK	3.8
5	Noble M12 GTO3	UK	3.9
6	AC Cobra 3.5	UK	4.0
7	Porsche 911 GT2	Germany	4.1
8	Ferrari 575M	Italy	4.2
9	= Audi A6 4.2RS6	Germany	4.7
	= BMW Z8	Germany	4.7
	= Mercedes-Benz E-Class E55AMG	Germany	4.9

* *Currently in production; highest achiever per make*

[#] *May vary according to specification modifications to meet national legal requirements*

[†] *Also achieved by the Mercedes-Benz SL55AMG*

THE FIRST 200-MPH CAR

SUPERCARS CAPABLE OF 200 MPH (322 KM/H) are rare even today, so it is remarkable to consider that the first car to break this barrier did so as long ago as 1927. The vehicle was a British-built Sunbeam, powered by two 22.5-liter 12-cylinder aero engines capable of delivering a total of 1,000 horsepower. On 29 March in Daytona Beach, Florida, in front of a crowd of over 30,000, the US-born British racer, Major Henry Segrave (1896–1930), took the car on two runs at an average speed of 203.79 mph (327.97 km/h), establishing a new land speed record. Segrave was knighted for his achievement, but in 1930 he was killed making an attempt on the water speed record.

FIRST FACT

TOP 10 MOTOR VEHICLE MANUFACTURERS

	MANUFACTURER	MOTOR VEHICLE PRODUCTION* (2001)
1	General Motors	7,582,561
2	Ford	6,575,491
3	Toyota-Daihatsu-Hino	6,054,968
4	Volkswagen Group	5,108,982
5	DaimlerChrysler	4,364,492
6	PSA Peugeot Citroën	3,102,449
7	Honda	2,673,671
8	Hyundai-Kia	2,578,443
9	Nissan-Nissan diesel	2,558,979
10	Fiat-Iveco	2,409.016

Includes cars, light trucks, heavy trucks, and buses

Source: *OICA Correspondents Survey*

TOP 10 COUNTRIES WITH THE LONGEST ROAD NETWORKS

		LENGTH	
	COUNTRY	(MILES)	(KM)
1	US	3,958,191	6,370,031
2	India	2,062,731	3,319,644
3	Brazil	1,230,315	1,980,000
4	China	869,919	1,400,000
5	Japan	715,948	1,152,207
6	Russia	591,545	952,000
7	Australia	567,312	913,000
8	Canada	560,416	901,902
9	France	554,822	892,900
10	Italy	415,491	668,669

Source: *CIA*, The World Factbook, 2002

THE 10 WORST MOTOR VEHICLE AND ROAD DISASTERS

LOCATION/DATE/INCIDENT	NO. KILLED
1 Afghanistan, November 3, 1982 Following a collision with a Soviet army truck, a fuel tanker exploded in the 1.7-mile (2.7-km) Salang Tunnel. Some authorities have put the death toll from the explosion, fire, and fumes as high as 3,000.	over 2,000
2 Colombia, August 7, 1956 Seven army ammunition trucks exploded at night in the center of Cali, destroying eight city blocks, including a barracks where 500 soldiers were sleeping.	1,200
3 Thailand, February 15, 1990 A dynamite truck exploded.	over 150
4 Nigeria, November 4, 2000 A fuel tanker collided with a line of parked cars on the Ile-Ife-Ibadan Expressway, exploding and burning many to death. Some 96 bodies were recovered, but some estimates put the final toll as high as 200.	150
5 Nepal, November 23, 1974 Hindu pilgrims were killed when a suspension bridge over the Mahahali River collapsed.	148
6 Egypt, August 9, 1973 A bus drove into an irrigation canal.	127
7 Togo, December 6, 1965 Two trucks collided with dancers during a festival in Sotouboua.	125
8 Spain, July 11, 1978 A liquid gas tanker exploded in a camping site in San Carlos de la Rapita.	120
9 South Korea, April 28, 1995 An undergound explosion destroyed vehicles and caused about 100 cars and buses to plunge into the pit it created.	110
10 Kenya, early December 1992 A bus carrying 112 skidded, hit a bridge, and plunged into a river.	106

The worst-ever motor racing accident occurred on June 13, 1955, in Le Mans, France, when, in attempting to avoid other cars, French driver Pierre Levegh's Mercedes-Benz 300 SLR went out of control, hit a wall, and exploded in midair, showering wreckage into the crowd and killing a total of 82. The worst single US highway disaster occurred on December 15, 1967, when the Silver Bridge, spanning the Ohio River from Kanauga, Ohio, to Point Pleasant, West Virginia, collapsed during heavy pre-Christmas afternoon rush-hour traffic, plunging some 60 vehicles into the river, resulting in 46 deaths and many injuries. It is believed that the worst-ever accident involving a single car occurred on December 17, 1956, when eight adults and four children were killed when the overcrowded car in which they were traveling was hit by a train near Phoenix, Arizona. Although she was injured, 20-month-old Crucita Alires survived after being hurled into a tree by the impact.

Track Records

TOP 10 FASTEST RAIL JOURNEYS*

	JOURNEY/COUNTRY	TRAIN	DISTANCE (MILES)	DISTANCE (KM)	SPEED (MPH)	SPEED (KM/H)
1	**Hiroshima–Kokura,** Japan	15 Nozomi	119.3	192.0	162.7	261.8
2	**Valence TGV–Avignon TGV,** France	TGV 5102	80.6	129.7	161.2	259.4
3	**Brussels Midi–Valence TGV,** International	ThalysSoleil	516.5	831.3	150.4	242.1
4	**Madrid–Seville,** Spain	5 AVE	292.4	470.5	129.9	209.1
5	**Stendal–Wolfsburg,** Germany	2 ICE	47.3	76.2	118.3	190.4
6	**York–Stevenage,** UK	Tees Tyne Pullman	160.3	258.0	113.6	182.8
7	**Skövde–Södertälje,** Sweden	X2000 436	172.1	277.0	107.6	173.1
8	**Rome–Florence,** Italy	ES 9548	162.2	261.0	103.5	166.6
9	**Baltimore–Wilmington,** US	9 Acela Express	68.4	110.1	102.6	165.1
10	**Salo–Karjaa,** Finland	Pandollno S126	33.0	53.1	94.3	151.7

* *Fastest journey for each country; all those in the Top 10 have other similarly or equally fast services*

Source: Railway Gazette International

▲ **Bullet train**
The Shinkansen "bullet trains" were introduced in Japan in 1964 and have been constantly improved: the Nozomi 500 is capable of 186 mph (300 km/h).

TOP 10 LONGEST UNDERGROUND RAILROAD NETWORKS

	CITY/COUNTRY	OPENED	STATIONS	TOTAL RAIL LENGTH (MILES)	(KM)
1	**London,** UK	1863	267	244	392
2	**New York,** NY	1904	468	231	371
3	**Moscow,** Russia	1935	160	163	262
4	**Paris,** France*	1900	297	125	201
5 =	**Mexico City,** Mexico	1969	154	111	178
=	**Tokyo,** Japan#	1927	164	111	178
7	**Chicago,** IL	1943	140	107	173
8	**Copenhagen,** Denmark†	1934	80	106	170
9 =	**Berlin,** Germany	1902	170	89	144
=	**Seoul,** South Korea	1974	114	89	144

* *Metro and RER*

Through-running extensions raise total to 391 miles (683 km), with 502 stations

† *Only partly underground*

Source: Tony Pattison, Center for Environmental Initiatives Researcher

TOP 10 OLDEST UNDERGROUND RAILROAD SYSTEMS

	CITY/COUNTRY	OPENED
1	**London,** UK	1863
2	**Budapest,** Hungary	1896
3	**Glasgow,** UK	1896
4	**Boston,** MA	1897
5	**Paris,** France	1900
6	**Berlin,** Germay	1902
7	**New York,** NY	1904
8	**Philadelphia,** PA	1907
9	**Hamburg,** Germany	1912
10	**Buenos Aires,** Argentina	1913

The Metropolitan Line, opened in London on January 10, 1863, and the Circle Line, completed in 1884, operated with steam trains equipped with a device to absorb smoke so that passengers did not suffocate in their gaslit carriages. The "cut-and-cover" method of digging trenches and arching them over was used on these lines, but in built-up areas tunnels were dug. The service could not be electrified until all necessary inventions came together during the 1890s, prompting the construction of underground networks worldwide.

TOP 10 LONGEST RAILROAD NETWORKS

	COUNTRY	TOTAL RAIL LENGTH (MILES)	(KM)
1	**US**	132,000	212,433
2	**Russia**	54,157	87,157
3	**China**	41,957	67,524
4	**India**	39,576	63,693
5	**Germany**	25,368	44,000
6	**Canada**	22,440	36,114
7	**Australia**	21,014	33,819
8	**Argentina**	20,967	33,744
9	**France**	19,846	31,939
10	**Japan**	14,698	23,654

Source: *CIA, The World Factbook, 2002*

The total of all world networks is today estimated to be 746,476 miles (1,201,337 km). Of this, some 118,061–121,167 miles (190,000–195,000 km) is electrified.

THE 10 WORST RAIL DISASTERS

LOCATION/DATE/INCIDENT	NO. KILLED
1 **Bagmati River,** India, June 6, 1981	c.800

The cars of a train traveling from Samastipur to Banmukhi in Bihar plunged off a bridge over the Bagmati River near Mansi when the driver braked, apparently to avoid hitting a sacred cow. Although the official death toll was said to have been 268, many authorities have claimed that the train was so massively overcrowded that the actual figure was in excess of 800, making it probably the worst rail disaster of all time.

| 2 **Chelyabinsk,** Russia, June 3, 1989 | up to 800 |

Two passenger trains, laden with vacationers heading to and from Black Sea resorts, were destroyed when liquid gas from a nearby pipeline exploded.

| 3 **Guadalajara,** Mexico, January 18, 1915 | over 600 |

A train derailed on a steep incline, but political strife in the country meant that full details of the disaster were suppressed.

| 4 **Modane,** France, December 12, 1917 | 573 |

A troop-carrying train ran out of control and was derailed. It has been claimed that it was overloaded and that as many as 1,000 may have died.

| 5 **Balvano,** Italy, March 2, 1944 | 521 |

A heavily laden train stalled in the Armi Tunnel, and many passengers were asphyxiated. Like the disaster at Torre (No. 6), wartime secrecy prevented full details from being published.

| 6 **Torre,** Spain, January 3, 1944 | over 500 |

A double collision and fire in a tunnel resulted in many deaths—some have put the total as high as 800.

| 7 **Awash,** Ethiopia, January 13, 1985 | 428 |

A derailment hurled a train laden with some 1,000 passengers into a ravine.

| 8 **Cireau,** Romania, January 7, 1917 | 374 |

An overcrowded passenger train crashed into a military train and was derailed.

| 9 **Reqa al-Gharbiya,** Egypt, February 20, 2002 | 372 |

A fire on the Cairo–Luxor train engulfed the carriages. The driver was unaware and continued while passengers were burned or leaped from the train to their deaths.

| 10 **Quipungo,** Angola, May 31, 1993 | 355 |

A trail was derailed by UNITA guerrilla action.

Casualty figures for rail accidents are often extremely imprecise, especially during wartime—and no fewer than half of the 10 worst disasters occurred during the two World Wars. Further vague incidents, such as one in Kalish, Poland, in December 1914, for example, with "400 dead," one in November 1918 in Norrköpping, Sweden, wihch was alleged to have killed 300, and certain other similarly uncertain cases have been omitted.

▶ First stop
London's Baker Street was one of the stations on the world's first ever underground railroad system.

Water Ways

LONGEST SHIP CANALS

	CANAL	COUNTRY	OPENED	LENGTH (MILES)	(KM)
1	Grand Canal	China	283*	1,114	1,795
2	Erie Canal	US	1825	363	584
3	Göta Canal	Sweden	1832	240	386
4	St. Lawrence Seaway	Canada/US	1959	180	290
5	Canal du Midi	France	1692	149	240
6	Main-Danube	Germany	1992	106	171
7	Suez	Egypt	1869	101	162
8 =	Albert	Belgium	1939	80	129
=	Moscow-Volga	Russia	1937	80	129
10	Kiel	Germany	1895	62	99

Extended (605–10) and rebuilt (1958–72)

THE 10 **LARGEST PASSENGER SHIPS EVER SUNK**

	SHIP	LOCATION	DATE	TONNAGE
1	Seawise University*	Hong Kong	Jan. 9, 1972	83,763
2	Titanic	off Newfoundland	Apr. 14, 1912	46,328
3	Paris	Le Havre, France	Apr. 19, 1939	34,569
4	Lusitania	off Ireland	May 7, 1915	31,550
5	Andrea Doria	off US coast	July 25, 1956	29,083
6	Angelina	Pacific	Sept. 24, 1979	24,377
7	Lakonia	Atlantic	Dec. 29, 1963	20,314
8	Mikhail Lermontov	off New Zealand	Feb. 16, 1986	20,027
9	Rasa Sayang	Kynosoura, Greece	Aug. 27, 1980	18,739
10	Bianca C.	off Grenada	Oct. 22, 1961	18,427

* *Formerly* Queen Elizabeth

▼ **Suez Canal**
The strategically and economically important Suez Canal, connecting the Mediterranean with the Red Sea, was built over the course of 10 years, from 1859 to 1869.

TOP 10 LARGEST CRUISE SHIPS

	SHIP/COUNTRY BUILT/YEAR	PASSENGER CAPACITY	GROSS TONNAGE
1	**Queen Mary 2**, France, 2004*	2,800	142,200
2	**Explorer of the Seas**, Finland, 2000	3,840	137,308
3 =	**Adventure of the Seas**, Finland, 2001	3,840	137,276
=	**Mariner of the Seas**, Finland, 2003*	3,840	137,276
=	**Navigator of the Seas**, Finland, 2002	3,807	137,276
=	**Voyager of the Seas**, Finland, 1999	3,840	137,276
7 =	**Diamond Princess**, Japan, 2004*	2,600	113,000
=	**Sapphire Princess**, Japan 2004*	3,100	113,000
9 =	**Carnival Conquest**, Italy, 2002	3,783	110,239
=	**Carnival Glory**, Italy, 2003*	3,783	110,000
=	**Carnival Valor**, Italy, 2004*	3,783	110,000
=	**Crown Princess**, Italy, 2004*	3,100	110,000

* Still under construction as of January 14, 2003

Source: *Lloyd's Register-Fairplay Ltd. www.lrfairplay.com*

The latest addition to the Cunard fleet, the 1,132-ft (345-m) *Queen Mary 2*, is scheduled to make her maiden voyage in 2004. Like her predecessor *Queen Mary* (1934), she will be the longest, tallest, and widest cruise ship in the world.

TOP 10 LARGEST OIL TANKERS*

	TANKER/COUNTRY BUILT/YEAR	GROSS TONNAGE#	DEADWEIGHT TONNAGE†
1	**Jahre Viking**, Japan, 1976	260,851	564,650
2	**Sea Giant**, France, 1979	261,453	555,051
3	**Sea World**, Sweden, 1978	237,768	491,120
4	**Arctic Blue**, Japan, 1975	234,287	484,276
5	**Folk II**, Taiwan, 1978	218,593	457,927
6	**Folk I**, Taiwan, 1977	218,593	457,841
7 =	**Hellespont Fairfax**, South Korea, 2002	238,700	442,500
=	**Hellespont Metropolis**, South Korea, 2002	238,700	442,500
=	**Hellespont Tara**, South Korea, 2002	238,700	442,500
10	**Hellespont Alhambra**, South Korea, 2002	235,000	441,893

* As of January 1, 2003

 # The weight of the ship when empty

† The total weight of the vessel, including its cargo, crew, passengers, and supplies

Source: *Lloyd's Register-Fairplay Ltd. www.lrfairplay.com*

The 1,504-ft (485.45-m) long *Jahre Viking* (formerly called *Happy Giant* and *Seawise Giant*) is the longest vessel ever built—as long as more than 20 tennis courts end-to-end and 226 ft (68.86 m) wide. It was extensively damaged during the Iran–Iraq War, but was salvaged, refitted, and relaunched in 1991.

TOP 10 LARGEST MERCHANT SHIPPING FLEETS

	COUNTRY	SHIPS IN FLEET*
1	Japan	3,962
2	Greece	3,032
3	Germany	2,321
4	China	1,999
5	US	1,963
6	Russia	1,872
7	Norway	1,458
8	Singapore	1,122
9	Netherlands	1,016
10	UK	957
	All countries (inc. those not in the Top 10)	35,213

* Ships over 1,000 DWT (deadweight tonnage—total weight of the vessel, including cargo, crew, passengers, and supplies) in service December 2002

Source: *Lloyd's Register-Fairplay Ltd. www.lrfairplay.com*

THE 10 WORST OIL TANKER SPILLS

	TANKER/LOCATION	DATE	APPROX. SPILLAGE (TONS)
1	**Atlantic Empress** and **Aegean Captain**, Trinidad	July 19, 1979	301,900
2	**Castillio de Bellver**, Cape Town, South Africa	Aug. 6, 1983	281,225
3	**Olympic Bravery**, Ushant, France	Jan. 24, 1976	275,575
4	**Amoco Cadiz**, Finistère, France	Mar. 16, 1978	246,125
5	**Odyssey**, Atlantic, off Canada	Nov. 10, 1988	154,400
6	**Haven**, off Genoa, Italy	Apr. 11, 1991	150,475
7	**Torrey Canyon**, Scilly Isles, UK	Mar. 18, 1967	136,850
8	**Sea Star**, Gulf of Oman	Dec. 19, 1972	135,775
9	**Irenes Serenade**, Pilos, Greece	Feb. 23, 1980	131,125
10	**Texaco Denmark**, North Sea, off Belgium	Dec. 7, 1971	112,850

Source: *Environmental Technology Center, Oil Spill Intelligence Report*

In addition to these major slicks, it is estimated that an average of 2 million tons of oil is spilled into the world's seas every year. The grounding of the *Exxon Valdez* in Prince William Sound, Alaska, on March 24, 1989 ranks outside the 10 worst at about 35,000 tons, but resulted in major ecological damage. All these accidents were caused by collision, grounding, fire, or explosion; worse tanker oil spills have been caused by military action: in 1991, during the Gulf War, various tankers were sunk in the Persian Gulf, spilling a total of more than 1 million tons of oil.

100 Years of Flight

BIGGEST AIRSHIPS EVER BUILT

	AIRSHIP	COUNTRY	YEAR	VOLUME (CU FT)	(CU M)	LENGTH (FT)	(M)
1 =	Hindenburg	Germany	1936	7,062,934	200,000	804	245
=	Graf Zeppelin II	Germany	1938	7,062,934	200,000	804	245
3 =	Akron	US	1931	6,500,000	184,060	785	239
=	Macon	US	1933	6,500,000	184,060	785	239
5	R101	UK	1930	5,500,000	155,744	777	237
6	Graf Zeppelin	Germany	1928	3,708,040	105,000	776	237
7	L72	Germany	1920	2,419,055	68,500	743	226
8	R100	UK	1929	5,500,000	155,744	709	216
9	R38	UK*	1921	2,724,000	77,136	699	213
10 =	L70	Germany	1918	2,418,700	62,200	694	212
=	L71	Germany	1918	2,418,700	62,200	694	212

* UK-built, but sold to US Navy

Although several of the giant airships in this list traveled long distances carrying thousands of passengers, they all ultimately suffered unfortunate fates: six (the *Hindenburg, Akron, Macon, R101, L72,* and *R38*) crashed with the loss of many lives, the *L70* was shot down, and the *L71*, both *Graf Zeppelins* and the *R100* were broken up for scrap. The *Hindenburg* was the victim of one of the most spectacular of all aviation disasters when, after several successful transatlantic crossings, she flew from Frankfurt, Germany, to Lakehurst, New Jersey, arriving on May 6, 1937. As she moored, she caught fire and turned into an inferno, the last moments of which remain among the most haunting sights ever captured on newsreel, with commentator Herb Morrison describing the horrific scene through floods of tears. Amazingly, 61 of the 97 on board survived, but the day of the airship was over.

FIRST ROCKET AND JET AIRCRAFT

	AIRCRAFT	COUNTRY	FIRST FLIGHT
1	Heinkel He 176*	Germany	June 20, 1939
2	Heinkel He 178	Germany	Aug. 27, 1939
3	DFS 194*	Germany	Aug. 1940#
4	Caproni-Campini N-1	Italy	Aug. 28, 1940
5	Heinkel He 280V-1	Germany	Apr. 2, 1941
6	Gloster E.28/39	UK	May 15, 1941
7	Messerschmitt Me 163 Komet*	Germany	Aug. 13, 1941
8	Messerschmitt Me 262V-3	Germany	July 18, 1942
9	Bell XP-59A Airacomet	US	Oct. 1, 1942
10	Gloster Meteor F Mk 1	UK	Mar. 5, 1943

* Rocket-powered

Precise date unknown

▼ **Graf Zeppelin**
When built, the *Graf Zeppelin* was the biggest airship in the world. It was the first to circumnavigate the globe, and carried a total of 16,000 passengers before being broken up in 1940.

THE 10 FIRST PEOPLE TO FLY IN HEAVIER-THAN-AIR AIRCRAFT

PILOT/DATES/COUNTRY	AIRCRAFT	FLIGHT DATE
1 Orville Wright (1871–1948), US	Wright Flyer I	Dec. 17, 1903
2 Wilbur Wright (1867–1912), US	Wright Flyer I	Dec. 17, 1903
3 Alberto Santos-Dumont (1873–1932), Brazil	No. 14-bis	Oct. 23, 1906
4 Charles Voisin (1882–1912), France	Voisin-Delagrange I	Mar. 30, 1907
5 Henri Farman (1874–1958), UK, later France	Voisin-Farman I-bis	Oct. 7, 1907
6 Léon Delagrange (1873–1910), France	Voisin-Delagrange I	Nov. 5, 1907
7 Robert Esnault-Pelterie (1881–1957), France	REP No.1	Nov. 16, 1907
8 Charles W. Furnas* (1880–1941), US	Wright Flyer III	May 14, 1908
9 Louis Blériot (1872–1936), France	Blériot VIII	June 29, 1908
10 Glenn Hammond Curtiss (1878–1930), US	AEA June Bug	July 4, 1908

* Furnas was a passenger in a plane piloted by Wilbur Wright

While most of the fliers listed flew on numerous subsequent occasions and broke their first time records, most other "flights" of the 1906–08 period, other than those of the Wright Brothers, were uncontrolled or no more than short hops of a few seconds' duration. Meanwhile, the Wrights were so far in advance of their competitors that they were flying under full control for more than an hour and over distances of 50 miles (80 km).

▲ The first to fly

In 1903, Orville Wright became the first person ever to fly a powered aircraft. He was followed by his brother Wilbur 45 minutes later.

THE 10 FIRST AROUND-THE-WORLD FLIGHTS

PILOT(S)/COUNTRY/AIRCRAFT	ROUTE (START/END LOCATION)	TOTAL DISTANCE (MILES)	(KM)	FLIGHT DATES
1 Lt. Lowell H. Smith/Lt. Leslie P. Arnold (US) Douglas World Cruiser *Chicago*	Seattle, WA	26,345	42,398	Apr. 6–Sept. 28, 1924
2 Lt. Erik H. Nelson/Lt. John Harding Jr. (US) Douglas World Cruiser *New Orleans*	Seattle, WA	27,553	44,342	Apr. 6–Sept. 28, 1924
3 Dr. Hugo Eckener, Ernst Lehmann, and crew (Germany) Airship *Graf Zeppelin*	Lakehurst, NJ	20,373	37,787	Apr. 8–29, 1929
4 Wiley Post and Harold Gatty (US) Lockheed Vega *Winne Mae*	Roosevelt Field, Long Island, NY	15,474	24,903	June 23–July 1, 1931
5 Wiley Post (US) Lockheed Vega *Winne Mae* (first solo)	Floyd Bennett Field, NY	15,596	25,093	July 15–22, 1933
6 Howard Hughes, Lt. Thomas Thurlow, Henry P. McClean Conner, Richard Stoddart, and Eddie Lund (US) Lockheed 14 *New York World's Fair 1939*	Floyd Bennett Field, NY	14,672	23,612	July 10–14, 1938
7 = Clifford Evans (US) Piper PA-12 *City of Washington*	Teterboro, NJ	25,162	40,494	Aug. 9–Dec. 10, 1947
= George Truman (US) Piper PA-12 *City of the Angels*	Teterboro, NJ	25,162	40,494	Aug. 9–Dec. 10, 1947
9 Capt. James Gallagher and crew of 13 (US) Boeing B-50A *Lucky Lady II* (first nonstop with in-flight refueling)	Fort Worth, TX	23,452	37,742	Feb. 26–Mar. 2, 1949
10 Peter Mack (US) Bonanza A35 *Friendship Flame*	Springfield, Il.	33,789	54,378	Oct. 7, 1951–Apr. 19, 1952

Air Ways

BUSIEST INTERNATIONAL AIRPORTS

	AIRPORT	LOCATION	INTERNATIONAL PASSENGERS (2001)
1	London Heathrow	London, UK	53,796,000
2	Charles de Gaulle	Paris, France	43,352,000
3	Frankfurt	Frankfurt, Germany	39,975,000
4	Schiphol	Amsterdam, Netherlands	39,167,000
5	Hong Kong	Hong Kong, China	32,027,000
6	London Gatwick	Gatwick, UK	28,114,000
7	Singapore International	Singapore	26,542,000
8	Narita International	Tokyo, Japan	22,241,000
9	Bankok International	Bangkok, Thailand	21,394,000
10	Kloten	Zurich, Switzerland	19,968,000

Source: *Air Transport Intelligence at www.rati.com*

BUSIEST AIRPORTS IN THE US

	AIRPORT	LOCATION	TOTAL PASSENGERS (2001)*
1	Atlanta Hartsfield International	Atlanta, GA	75,859,000
2	Chicago O'Hare International	Chicago, IL	67,448,000
3	Los Angeles International	Los Angeles, CA	61,606,000
4	Dallas/Fort Worth International	Irving, TX	55,151,000
5	Denver International	Denver, CO	36,093,000
6	Phoenix Sky Harbor International	Phoenix, AR	35,439,000
7	McCarran International	Las Vegas, NV	35,181,000
8	San Francisco International	San Francisco, CA	34,632,000
9	Minneapolis/St. Paul International	St. Paul, MN	34,308,000
10	Detroit Metropolitan Wayne County	MI	32,294,000

* Includes international, domestic, and in transit

Source: *Air Transport Intelligence at www.rati.com*

▼ **Flying start**
Despite recent fluctuations in response to safety and economic concerns, worldwide passenger numbers in 2002 remained stable, at around 1.6 billion.

HEATHROW'S FIRST FLIGHTS

ON JANUARY 1, 1946, a BSAA (British South American Airways) Lancastrian took off from Heathrow en route for Buenos Aires, Argentina. The airport was officially opened on May 31, and the following day a Pan Am Constellation became the first transatlantic airliner to land there. At this stage the former RAF air base was no more than a field with wooden duckboards to keep passengers out of the mud and a check-in that had seen service as a military tent.

FIRST FACT

TOP 10 LARGEST AIRLINERS

AIRCRAFT MODEL	MAXIMUM NO. OF PASSENGERS
1 Boeing B-747-300	660
2 Airbus A-380-800	656
3 Boeing B-777-300	550
4 Airbus A340-600	485
5 Airbus A330-300	440
6 Boeing MD-11	410
7 Lockheed L-1011 TriStar	400
8 McDonnell Douglas DC-10-10	380
9 = Boeing 767-400ER	375
= Ilyushin Il-96	375

* Largest of each type listed

Source: Air Transport Intelligence at www.rati.com

TOP 10 AIRLINES WITH THE MOST AIRCRAFT

AIRLINE/COUNTRY*	FLEET SIZE (2001)
1 American Airlines	834
2 United Airlines	554
3 Delta Airlines	551
4 Northwest Airlines	437
5 Continental Airlines	370
6 Southwest Airlines	367
7 US Airways	295
8 Air France, France	247
9 British Airways, UK	236
10 Air Canada, Canada	224

* All from the US unless otherwise stated

Source: Airline Business/Air Transport Intelligence at www.rati.com

TOP 10 AIRLINES WITH THE MOST PASSENGER TRAFFIC

AIRLINE/COUNTRY	PASSENGER MILES FLOWN (2001)*
1 United Airlines, US	116,643,800,200
2 American Airlines, US	108,359,679,465
3 Delta Airlines, US	101,758,853,300
4 Northwest Airlines, US	73,155,894,575
5 British Airways, UK	66,033,116,600
6 Continental Airlines, US	61,126,148,300
7 Air France, France	58,923,387,400
8 Lufthansa German Airlines, Germany	53,869,775,500
9 Japan Airlines, Japan	49,313,881,930
10 US Airways, US	45,997,623,875

* Total distance traveled by aircraft of these airlines multiplied by number of passengers carried

Source: Airline Business/Air Transport Intelligence at www.rati.com

World Tourism

TOP 10 TOURIST DESTINATIONS

	COUNTRY	INTERNATIONAL VISITORS (2001)
1	France	76,500,000
2	Spain	49,500,000
3	US	45,500,000
4	Italy	39,000,000
5	China	33,200,000
6	UK	23,400,000
7	Russia	21,200,000*
8	Mexico	19,800,000
9	Canada	19,700,000
10	Austria	18,200,000

* 2000 data

Source: *World Tourism Organization*

The World Tourism Organization's estimate for 2001 puts the total number of international tourists at just under 693 million, down over five million on the record high of 698 million set in the previous year.

TOP 10 COUNTRIES OF ORIGIN OF OVERSEAS VISITORS TO THE US

	COUNTRY*	OVERSEAS VISITORS TO THE US (2001)	(2002)
1	UK	4,097,258	3,816,736
2	Japan	4,082,661	3,627,264
3	Germany	1,313,756	1,189,856
4	France	875,854	734,260
5	South Korea	617,892	638,697
6	Australia	425,934	407,130
7	Italy	472,348	406,160
8	Brazil	551,406	405,094
9	Venezuela	555,292	395,913
10	Netherlands	411,742	384,367

Source: *US Department of Commerce, International Trade Administration, Office of Travel and Tourism Industries*

TOP 10 TOURIST EARNING COUNTRIES

	COUNTRY	INTERNATIONAL TOURISM RECEIPTS IN 2001 ($)
1	US	72,300,000,000
2	Spain	32,900,000,000
3	France	29,600,000,000
4	Italy	25,900,000,000
5	China	17,800,000,000
6	Germany	17,200,000,000
7	UK	15,900,000,000
8	Austria	12,000,000,000
9	Canada	10,700,000,000*
10	Greece	9,200,000,000*

* 2000 data

Source: *World Tourism Organization*

▼ **Super duper roller coaster**
Built at a cost of $20 million, Superman The Escape held the record as the world's fastest and highest thrill ride for four years.

TOP 10 WORLDWIDE AMUSEMENT AND THEME PARKS

	PARK/LOCATION	EST. ATTENDANCE IN 2002
1	The Magic Kingdom at Walt Disney World, Lake Buena Vista, Florida	14,044,800
2	Tokyo Disneyland, Tokyo, Japan	13,000,000
3	Disneyland, Anaheim, California	12,720,500
4	Disneysea, Tokyo, Japan	12,000,000
5	Disneyland Paris, Marne-La-Vallée, France	10,300,000
6	Everland, Kyonggi-Do, South Korea	9,335,000
7	Lotte World, Seoul, South Korea	9,100,000
8	Epcot at Walt Disney World, Lake Buena Vista, Florida	8,289,000
9	Disney-MGM Studios at Walt Disney World, Lake Buena Vista, Florida	8,031,360
10	Universal Studios Japan, Osaka, Japan	8,010,000

Source: Amusement Business

Although there had been earlier amusement parks and fun fairs, Disneyland was the first modern theme park. The inspiration of filmmaker Walt Disney, it was built in less than a year on a site in Anaheim, California and opened on July 17 1955. About 6,000 journalists and other guests were invited, but admission tickets were forged and an estimated 28,000 people turned up, causing chaoes as rides broke under the strain and visitors' shoes sunk into the un-set asphalt of Main Street. After overcoming these initial problems, it rapidly became one of American's most popular tourist attractions.

TOP 10 FASTEST ROLLER COASTERS

	ROLLER COASTER/LOCATION	YEAR OPENED	SPEED MPH	SPEED KM/H
1	Top Thrill Dragster, Cedar Point, Sandusky, Ohio	2003	120	193
2	Dodonpa, Fuji-Q Highlands, ShinNishihara, FujiYoshida-shi, Yamanashi, Japan	2001	106.9	172
3 =	Superman The Escape, Six Flags Magic Mountain, Valencia, California	1997	100	161
=	Tower of Terror, Dreamworld, Coomera, Queensland, Australia	1997	100	161
5	Steel Dragon 2000, Nagashima Spa Land, Nagashima, Mie, Japan	2000	95	153
6	Millennium Force, Cedar Point, Sandusky, Ohio	2000	93	149
7 =	Goliath, Six Flags Magic Mountain, Valencia, California	2000	85	137
=	Titan, Six Flags Over Texas, Arlington, Texas	2001	85	137
9	Phantom's Revenge, Kennywood Park, West Mifflin, Pennsylvania	2001	82	132
=	Xcelerator, Knott's Berry Farm, Buena Park, California	2002	82	132

The newly constructed Top Thrill Dragster breaks all previous roller coaster records, with a length of 2,800 ft (853 m), height of 420 ft (128 m), and a drop of 400 ft (122 m). It can accelerate from 0–120 mph in approximately 4 seconds.

TOP 10 TOURISM CITIES IN THE US

	CITY/STATE	ESTIMATED OVERSEAS VISITORS (2001)
1	New York City, New York	4,803,000
2	Los Angeles, California	2,816,000
3	Miami, Florida	2,554,000
4	Orlando, Florida	2,467,000
5	San Francisco, California	1,965,000
6	Oahu/Honolulu, Hawaii	1,747,000
7	Las Vegas, Nevada	1,506,000
8	Washington, DC (Metro)	1,201,000
9 =	Boston, Massachussetts	1,070,000
=	Chicago, Illinois	1,070,000

Source: *US Department of Commerce, International Trade Administration, Office of Travel and Tourism Industries*

In the months following the terrorist attacks of September 11, 2001, the number of overseas visitors to the US declined dramatically, but 2002 saw signs of recovery.

TOP 10 MOST VISITED NATIONAL PARKS IN THE US

	PARK/RECREATION	RECREATION VISITS (2002)
1	Great Smoky Mountains National Park, North Carolina/Tennessee	9,316,420
2	Grand Canyon National Park, Arizona	4,001,974
3	Olympic National Park, Washington	3,691,310
4	Yosemite National Park, California	3,361,867
5	Cuyahoga Valley National Park, near Cleveland and Akron, Ohio	3,217,935
6	Rocky Mountain National Park, Colorado	2,988,475
7	Yellowstone National Park, Wyoming	2,973,677
8	Grand Teton National Park, Wyoming	2,612,629
9	Zion National Park, Utah	2,592,545
10	Acadia National Park, Maine	2,558,572

SPORT & LEISURE

Summer Olympics

FIRST INDIVIDUALS TO WIN GOLD IN THE SAME EVENT AT FOUR SUMMER OLYMPICS

	INDIVIDUAL/COUNTRY	SPORT	EVENT	YEARS
1 =	**Aladár Gerevich***, Hungary	Fencing	Team saber	1932–52
=	**Pál Kovács**, Hungary	Fencing	Team saber	1932–52
3	**Paul Elvstrøm**, Denmark	Sailing	Finn	1948–60
4	**Edoardo Mangiarotti**, Italy	Fencing	Team epee	1936–60
5	**Rudolf Kárpáti**, Hungary	Fencing	Team saber	1948–60
6	**Al Oerter**, US	Track & field	Discus	1956–68
7	**Hans–Günther Winkler**, Germany	Show jumping	Team	1956–72
8	**Reiner Klimke#**, West Germany	Dressage	Team	1964–84
9	**Carl Lewis**, US	Track & field	Long jump	1984–96
10	**Teresa Edwards**, US	Basketball	Women's	1984–2000

* Also won gold in the same event in 1956 and 1960

 # Also won gold in the same event in 1988

Few Olympic competitors have succeeded in attaining gold over a span of 16 years or more. When, after becoming the first person to do so, 50-year-old Aldár Gerevich was refused a place on the Hungarian fencing squad at the 1960 Games, he promptly challenged the entire team, defeating them all.

COUNTRIES WITH THE MOST SUMMER OLYMPICS MEDALS, 1896–2000

	COUNTRY	GOLD	MEDALS SILVER	BRONZE	TOTAL
1	**US**	872	659	581	2,112
2	**USSR***	485	395	354	1,234
3	**UK**	188	245	232	665
4	**France**	189	195	217	601
5	**Germany#**	165	198	210	573
6	**Italy**	179	144	155	478
7	**Sweden**	138	157	176	471
8	**Hungary**	150	134	158	442
9	**East Germany**	153	130	127	410
10	**Australia**	103	110	139	352

* Includes Unified Team of 1992; does not include Russia since then

 # Not including West/East Germany 1968–88

The host nations at the first two Modern Olympics—Greece in 1896 and France in 1900—both led the medal table, with the US achieving its first commanding total of 72 medals at the 1904 St. Louis Games. Other hosts, the US and USSR, vied for first place in subsequent Olympics, with the US the ultimate victor.

▶ **Record leap**
Carl Lewis's long jump victory at the 1996 Atlanta Olympics gained him his ninth gold at four consecutive Games.

TOP 10 MEDAL WINNERS IN A SUMMER OLYMPICS CAREER

	WINNER/COUNTRY	SPORT	YEARS	GOLD	SILVER	BRONZE	TOTAL
1	**Larissa Latynina**, USSR	Gymnastics	1956–64	9	5	4	18
2	**Nikolay Andrianov**, USSR	Gymnastics	1972–80	7	5	3	15
3 =	**Edoardo Mangiarotti**, Italy	Fencing	1936–60	6	5	2	13
=	**Takashi Ono**, Japan	Gymnastics	1952–64	5	4	4	13
=	**Boris Shakhlin**, USSR	Gymnastics	1956–64	7	4	2	13
6 =	**Sawao Kato**, Japan	Gymnastics	1968–76	8	3	1	12
=	**Paavo Nurmi**, Finland	Track & Field	1920–28	9	3	0	12
8 =	**Viktor Chukarin**, USSR	Gymnastics	1952–56	7	3	1	11
=	**Vera Cáslavská**, Czechoslovakia	Gymnastics	1964–68	7	4	0	11
=	**Carl Osburn**, US	Shooting	1912–24	5	4	2	11
=	**Mark Spitz**, US	Swimming	1968–72	9	1	1	11
=	**Matt Biondi**, US	Swimming	1984–92	8	2	1	11

Larissa Latynina won six medals at each of three Games between 1956 and 1964. The only discipline at which she did not win a medal was on the beam in 1956. An achievement that rivals those of the individuals represented by this Top 10 was that of Ray C. Ewry (US), a competitor at the Games from 1900 to 1908, who won 10 medals, all in jumping events (and hence does not make this list)—but all of them were gold.

TOP 10 MEDAL-WINNING COUNTRIES AT THE SUMMER PARALYMPICS*

	COUNTRY	GOLD	SILVER	BRONZE	TOTAL
1	**US**	576	523	522	1,621
2	**UK**	389	401	387	1,177
3	**Germany/ West Germany**	404	385	361	1,150
4	**Canada**	311	250	262	823
5	**France**	279	264	241	784
6	**Australia**	240	248	228	716
7	**Netherlands**	219	179	153	551
8	**Poland**	194	184	148	526
9	**Sweden**	197	190	135	522
10	**Spain**	156	137	152	445

* Excluding medals won at the 1960 Rome and 1968 Tel Aviv Games—the International Paralympic Committee has not kept records of medals won at these Games

The first international games for the disabled were at Stoke Mandeville, England, in 1952, when 130 athletes from the UK and the Netherlands competed.

TOP 10 MOST SUCCESSFUL COUNTRIES AT ONE SUMMER OLYMPICS

	COUNTRY	VENUE	YEAR	GOLD	SILVER	BRONZE	TOTAL
1	**US**	St. Louis	1904	80	84	76	242
2	**USSR**	Moscow	1980	80	69	46	195
3	**US**	Los Angeles	1984	83	61	30	174
4	**Great Britain**	London	1908	56	50	39	145
5	**USSR**	Seoul	1988	55	31	46	132
6	**East Germany**	Moscow	1980	47	37	42	126
7	**USSR**	Montreal	1976	49	41	35	125
8	**EUN***	Barcelona	1992	45	38	29	112
9	**US**	Barcelona	1992	37	34	37	108
10	**US**	Mexico City	1968	45	28	34	107

* Unified Team, Commonwealth of Independent States, 1992

The Soviet Union's total at Seoul in 1988 is the highest by a country not competing on home soil. East Germany's 126 in 1980 is the highest total of a country not heading the medal list, although the US boycotted the Games that year, enabling Eastern Bloc countries to achieve their greatest-ever medal haul. The only other nations with 100 medals at one Games are East Germany (1988, Seoul) with 102, and France (1900, Paris) with 100 exactly. The US gained 97 medals (39 gold, 25 silver, and 33 bronze) at the 2000 Sydney Olympics, the most of any nation.

TOP 10 SPORTS AT WHICH THE MOST GOLD MEDALS HAVE BEEN WON AT THE OLYMPIC GAMES, 1896–2002

	SPORT	GOLD MEDALS
1	**Track and field**	818
2	**Swimming/diving**	527
3	**Wrestling**	340
4	**Gymnastics**	291
5	**Shooting**	229
6	**Boxing**	204
7	**Rowing**	203
8	**Fencing**	179
9	**Cycling**	166
10	**Canoeing**	161

Winter Olympics

▲ Salt Lake City celebration
Olympic medal-winning German, Norwegian, and Swiss ski teams celebrate their respective victories at Salt Lake City, 2002.

TOP 10 GOLD MEDALISTS AT THE WINTER OLYMPICS (MEN)

	MEDALLIST/COUNTRY	SPORT	GOLD MEDALS
1	**Bjørn Dählie,** Norway	Nordic skiing	8
2 =	**Eric Heiden,** US	Speed skating	5
=	**Clas Thunberg,** Norway	Speed skating	5
4 =	**Ivar Ballangrud,** Norway	Speed skating	4
=	**Yevgeny Grishin,** Soviet Union	Speed skating	4
=	**Sixten Jernberg,** Sweden	Nordic skiing	4
=	**Johann Olav Koss,** Norway	Speed skating	4
=	**Matti Nykänen,** Finland	Ski jumping	4
=	**Alexander Tikhonov,** Soviet Union	Biathlon	4
=	**Thomas Wassberg,** Sweden	Nordic skiing	4
=	**Nikolai Zimyatov,** Soviet Union	Nordic skiing	4
=	**Gunde Svan,** Sweden	Nordic skiing	4

TOP 10 GOLD MEDALISTS AT THE WINTER OLYMPICS (WOMEN)

	MEDALLIST/COUNTRY	SPORT	GOLD MEDALS
1 =	**Lydia Skoblikova,** Soviet Union	Speed skating	6
=	**Lyubov Egorova,** EUN*/Russia	Nordic skiing	6
3 =	**Bonnie Blair,** US	Speed skating	5
=	**Larissa Lazutina,** EUN*/Russia	Nordic skiing	5
5 =	**Galina Kulakova,** Soviet Union	Nordic skiing	4
=	**Lee-Kyung Chun,** South Korea	Short track speed skating	4
=	**Claudia Pechstein,** Germany	Speed skating	4
=	**Raisa Smetanina,** EUN*/Russia	Nordic skiing	4
9 =	**Claudia Boyarskikh,** Soviet Union	Nordic skiing	3
=	**Marja-Liisa Kirvesniemi** (née Hämäläinen), Finland	Nordic skiing	3
=	**Sonja Henie,** Norway	Figure skating	3
=	**Karin Kania** (née Enke), East Germany	Speed skating	3
=	**Gunda Niemann-Stirnemann,** Germany	Speed skating	3
=	**Anfisa Reztsova,** Soviet Union/EUN*	Nordic skiing/biathlon	3
=	**Irina Rodnina,** Soviet Union	Figure skating	3
=	**Vreni Schneider,** Switzerland	Alpine skiing	3
=	**Katja Seizinger,** Germany	Alpine skiing	3
=	**Elena Valbe,** EUN*/Russia	Nordic skiing	3
=	**Yvonne van Gennip,** Netherlands	Speed skating	3

Unified Team, Commonwealth of Independent States, 1992

TOP 10 MEDAL-WINNING COUNTRIES AT THE 2002 SALT LAKE WINTER OLYMPICS

	COUNTRY	GOLD	SILVER	BRONZE	TOTAL
1	**Germany**	12	16	7	35
2	**US**	10	13	11	34
3	**Norway**	11	7	6	24
4	**Canada**	6	3	8	17
5 =	**Austria**	2	4	10	16
=	**Russia**	6	6	4	16
7	**Italy**	4	4	4	12
8 =	**France**	4	5	2	11
=	**Switzerland**	3	2	6	11
10 =	**China**	2	2	4	8
=	**Netherlands**	3	5	0	8

TOP 10 WINTER OLYMPICS MEDAL-WINNING COUNTRIES, 1924–2002*

COUNTRY	GOLD	MEDALS SILVER	BRONZE	TOTAL
1 Soviet Union#	113	82	78	273
2 Norway	94	93	73	260
3 US	70	70	51	191
4 Austria	41	57	65	163
5 Germany†	54	51	37	142
6 Finland	41	51	49	141
7 East Germany	39	37	35	111
8 Sweden	36	28	38	102
9 Switzerland	32	33	36	101
10 Canada	30	28	37	95

* Includes medals won at figure skating and ice hockey included in the Summer Games prior to the launch of the Winter Olympics in 1924

 # Includes Unified Team of 1992; excludes Russia since then

† Not including East/West Germany, 1968–88

The Winter Olympics have been staged on 19 occasions since the first, with the 20th scheduled for Turin, Italy, February 10–26, 2006. The Soviet Union first competed at the seventh Games in Cortina d'Ampezzo, Italy, where it succeeded in leading the medal table with seven gold, three silver, and six bronze medals

TOP 10 COMPETITOR-ATTENDED WINTER OLYMPICS

HOST CITY/COUNTRY	YEAR	COMPETITORS
1 Salt Lake City, US	2002	2,399
2 Nagano, Japan	1998	2,177
3 Albertville, France	1992	1,801
4 Lillehammer, Norway	1994	1,736
5 Calgary, Canada	1988	1,425
6 Sarajevo, Yugoslavia	1984	1,274
7 Grenoble, France	1968	1,158
8 Innsbruck, Austria	1976	1,123
9 Innsbruck, Austria	1964	1,091
10 Lake Placid, US	1980	1,072

The first Winter Games in Chamonix, France, in 1924 were attended by 258 competitors (of whom 13 were women), representing 16 countries. The second Winter Games, held in St. Moritz, Switzerland, in 1928, saw the number of competitors and countries increase to 464 (including 26 women) and 25 respectively. The third Games in 1932, in Lake Placid, New York, were affected by the Depression, which saw the numbers reduced to 252 competitors (with 21 women) from 17 countries. Since the fourth Games, in 1936 in Garmisch-Partenkirchen, Germany (668 competitors, with 80 women, from 28 countries), the number of competitors and countries represented have generally increased: a total of 2,399 competitors (886 women) from 77 countries took part in the 19th Games in Salt Lake City, Utah.

▼ **Red hot team**
The German four-man bobsleigh hurtles to Olympic gold at the 2002 Winter Games.

Winter Sports

TOP 10 ALPINE SNOW-BOARDERS (MALE)

	SNOWBOARDER/COUNTRY	TOTAL POINTS*
1	**Tony Albrecht,** Switzerland	2,221.48
2	**Gilles Jaquet,** Switzerland	2,213.60
3	**Cyrill Buehler,** Switzerland	2,194.53
4	**Urs Eiselin,** Switzerland	2,166.30
5	**Simon Schoch,** Switzerland	2,131.04
6	**Philippe Schoch,** Switzerland	2,080.01
7	**Martin Bolt,** Switzerland	1,888.93
8	**Nicolas Wolken,** Switzerland	1,815.41
9	**Roland Haldi,** Switzerland	1,792.86
10	**Antonin Cip,** Czech Republic	1,788.22

* Ranked by best four results in 52-week period to January 29, 2003

Source: *World Snowboarding Federation*

Snowboarding was invented in 1965 by Sherman Poppen (US), and the sport became an Olympic event in 1998.

TOP 10 ALPINE SNOW-BOARDERS (FEMALE)

	SNOWBOARDER/COUNTRY	TOTAL POINTS*
1	**Daniela Meuli,** Switzerland	1,172.30
2	**Perrine Buehler,** Switzerland	1,064.44
3	**Ursula Bruhin,** Switzerland	1,049.06
4	**Blanka Isielonis,** Poland	986.82
5	**Malgorzata Kukcz,** Poland	985.68
6	**Nadia Livers,** Switzerland	913.33
7	**Petra Elsterova,** Czech Republic	911.72
8	**Milena Meisser,** Switzerland	828.13
9	**Fraenzi Kohli,** Switzerland	776.09
10	**Rebekka von Kaenel,** Switzerland	773.97

* Ranked by best four results in 52-week period to January 29, 2003

Source: *World Snowboarding Federation*

The World Snowboarding Federation was constituted in Munich, Germany, in 2002 and is now the international governing body for the sport.

TOP 10 SKIERS IN THE 2002/03 ALPINE WORLD CUP (FEMALE)

	SKIER/COUNTRY	OVERALL POINTS*
1	**Janica Kostelic,** Croatia	1,570
2	**Karen Putzer,** Italy	1,100
3	**Anja Paerson,** Sweden	1,042
4	**Michaela Dorfmeister,** Austria	972
5	**Martina Ertl,** Germany	922
6	**Carole Montillet,** France	869
7	**Renate Goetschl,** Austria	830
8	**Alexandra Meissnitzer,** Austria	776
9	**Kirsten L. Clark,** US	661
10	**Nicole Hosp,** Austria	558

* Awarded for performances in slalom, giant slalom, super giant, downhill, and combination disciplines

Source: *International Ski Federation*

Downhill racer
Swiss snowboarder Gilles Jaquet is among the world's leading competitors in a sport dominated by his compatriots.

TOP 10 | SKI-JUMPERS IN THE 2002/03 SKI-JUMPING WORLD CUP

	SKIER/COUNTRY	OVERALL POINTS
1	Adam Malysz, Poland	1,357
2	Sven Hannawald, Germany	1,235
3	Andreas Widhoelzl, Austria	1,028
4	Janne Ahonen, Finland	1,016
5	Florian Liegl, Austria	986
6	Martin Hoellwarth, Austria	925
7	Primoz Peterka, Slovenia	805
8	Matti Hautamaeki, Finland	797
9	Roar Ljoekelsoey, Norway	757
10	Sigurd Pettersen, Norway	747

Source: *International Ski Federation*

▶ A jump ahead

German ski-jumper Sven Hannawald gained his fifth World Cup victory at Bad Mittendorf, Austria, but lost out to overall points leader Adam Malysz.

TOP 10 | SKIERS IN THE 2002/03 ALPINE WORLD CUP (MALE)

	SKIER/COUNTRY	OVERALL POINTS*
1	Stephen Eberharter, Austria	1,333
2	Bode Miller, US	1,100
3	Kjetil Andre Aamodt, Norway	940
4	Kalle Palander, Finland	718
5	Didier Cuche, Switzerland	709
6	Daron Rahlves, US	647
7	Ivica Kostelic, Croatia	632
8	Benjamin Raich, Austria	622
9	Michael Walchhofer, Austria	600
10	Hans Knauss, Austria	596

* *Awarded for performances in slalom, giant slalom, super giant, downhill, and combination disciplines*

Source: *International Ski Federation*

TOP 10 | FASTEST SPEED-SKATERS

	SKATER*/COUNTRY	LOCATION	DATE	TIME FOR 500 M (SECS)
1	Hiroyasu Shimizu, Japan	Salt Lake City, US	Mar. 10, 2001	34.32
2	Jeremy Wotherspoon, Canada	Salt Lake City	Jan. 11, 2003	34.41
3	Casey FitzRandolph, US	Salt Lake City	Feb. 11, 2002	34.42
4	Gerard van Velde, Netherlands	Calgary, Canada	Jan. 18, 2003	34.61
5	Toyoki Takeda, Japan	Calgary	Dec. 9, 2001	34.62
6 =	Joey Cheek, US	Salt Lake City	Dec. 19, 2001	34.66
=	Michael Ireland, Canada	Calgary	Mar. 18, 2000	34.66
8	Kip Carpenter, US	Salt Lake City	Feb. 11, 2002	34.68
9	Jan Bos, Netherlands	Salt Lake City	Feb. 12, 2002	34.72
10	Lee Kyu-Hyuk, South Korea	Salt Lake City	Feb. 11, 2002	34.74

* *Skater's fastest time only included*

Source: *International Skating Union*

Track & Field

LATEST MARATHON RECORD BREAKERS (MALE)

	ATHLETE/COUNTRY	VENUE	YEAR	TIME
1	**Khalid Khannouchi,** US	London, UK	2002	2:05:38
2	**Khalid Khannouchi**	Chicago, IL	1999	2:05:42
3	**Ronaldo da Costa,** Brazil	Berlin, Germany	1998	2:06:05
4	**Belayneh Dinsamo,** Ethiopia	Rotterdam, Netherlands	1988	2:06:50
5	**Carlos Lopes,** Portugal	Rotterdam, Netherlands	1985	2:07:12
6	**Steve Jones,** UK	Chicago, IL	1984	2:08:05
7	**Rob de Castella,** Australia	Fukuoka, Japan	1981	2:08:18
8	**Derek Clayton,** Australia	Antwerp, Belgium	1969	2:08:34
9	**Derek Clayton**	Fukuoka, Japan	1967	2:09:36
10	**Abebe Bikila,** Ethiopia	Tokyo, Japan	1964	2:12:11

The Marathon commemorates the run of Pheidippides from Marathon to Athens in 490 BC, bringing news of a victory over the invading Persians. The distance of 26 miles 385 yards (42.195 km) was set at the 1908 London Olympics.

LATEST MARATHON RECORD BREAKERS (FEMALE)

	ATHLETE/COUNTRY	VENUE	YEAR	TIME
1	**Paula Radcliffe,** UK	London, UK	2003	2:15:35
2	**Paula Radcliffe,** UK	Chicago, IL	2002	2:17:18
3	**Catherine Ndereba,** Kenya	Chicago, IL	2001	2:18:47
4	**Naoko Takahashi,** Japan	Berlin, Germany	2001	2:19:46
5	**Tegla Loroupe,** Kenya	Berlin, Germany	1999	2:20:43
6	**Tegla Loroupe**	Rotterdam, Netherlands	1998	2:20:47
7	**Ingrid Christensen-Kristiansen,** Norway	London, UK	1985	2:21:06
8	**Greta Waitz,** Norway	London, UK	1983	2:25:29
9	**Greta Waitz**	New York, NY	1980	2:25:41
10	**Greta Waitz**	New York, NY	1979	2:27:33

▼ **London Marathon**
Khalid Khannouchi (No. 2) broke his own world record at the 2002 London Marathon. In the past 100 years, the time has been trimmed by more than 50 minutes.

TOP 10 LATEST 100-METER RECORD BREAKERS (MALE)

	ATHLETE/COUNTRY	YEAR	TIME
1	**Tim Montgomery,** US	2002	9.78
2	**Maurice Greene,** US	1999	9.79
3	**Donovan Bailey,** Canada	1996	9.84
4	**Leroy Burrell,** US	1994	9.85
5	**Carl Lewis,** US	Aug. 1991	9.86
6	**Leroy Burrell**	June 1991	9.90
7	**Carl Lewis**	1988	9.92
8	**Calvin Smith,** US	July 1983	9.93
9	**Carl Lewis**	May 1983	9.97
10	**Silvio Leonard,** Cuba	19/7	9.98

In a discipline where the winners and runners-up are separated by hundredths of a second, it is worth noting that the world record time has been cut by more than a second in the past 100 years. The 10.8 sec record set by Luther Cary in 1891 remained unbroken until 1906.

▲ **Pole position**
Russian pole vaulter, Svetlana Feofanova, won gold at the 2002 European championships and set a new indoor world record in 2003.

TOP 10 FASTEST WOMEN EVER*

	ATHLETE/COUNTRY	YEAR	TIME
1	**Florence Griffith Joyner,** US	1988	10.49
2	**Marion Jones,** US	1998	10.65
3	**Christine Arron,** France	1998	10.73
4	**Merlene Ottey,** Jamaica	1996	10.74
5	**Evelyn Ashford,** US	1984	10.76
6	**Irina Privalova,** Russia	1994	10.77
7	**Dawn Sowell,** US	1989	10.78
8 =	**Xuemei Li,** China	1997	10.79
=	**Inger Miller,** US	1999	10.79
10	**Marlies Oelsner-Göhr,** East Germany	1983	10.81

* Based on fastest time for the 100 meters

The late Florence Griffith Joyner's world record for the 100 meters has stood since she set it in Indianapolis on July 16, 1988. In the same year at the Seoul Olympics, she also set the still unbroken 200-meter record (21.34 secs).

TOP 10 FIELD ATHLETES (MALE)

	ATHLETE/COUNTRY	EVENT	SCORE*
1	**Jonathan Edwards,** UK	Triple jump	1,378
2	**Christian Olsson,** Sweden	Triple jump	1,377
3	**Róbert Fazekas,** Hungary	Discus throw	1,362
4	**Adrián Annus,** Hungary	Hammer throw	1,350
5	**Roman Sebrle,** Czech Republic	Decathlon	1,348
6	**Adam Nelson,** US	Shot put	1,346
7	**Jeff Hartwig,** US	Pole vault	1,342
8	**Koji Murofushi,** Japan	Hammer throw	1,341
9 =	**Walter Davis,** US	Triple jump	1,334
=	**Sergey Makarov,** Russia	Javelin throw	1,334

* As of March 10, 2003

Source: *International Association of Athletics Federations*

These athletes have been ranked by the IAAF according to their Ranking Score. After each competition, athletes' Performance Scores are calculated, which consist of points awarded for results and placing; athletes are then ranked by taking the average of their top five Performance Scores. The system was established in 2000 and currently takes account of 35 different events.

TOP 10 FIELD ATHLETES (FEMALE)

	ATHLETE/COUNTRY	EVENT	SCORE*
1	**Kajsa Bergqvist,** Sweden	High jump	1,363
2	**Tatyana Kotova,** Russia	Long jump	1,345
3	**Hestrie Cloete,** South Africa	High jump	1,327
4	**Svetlana Feofanova,** Russia	Pole vault	1,324
5	**Maurren Higa Maggi,** Brazil	Long jump	1,320
6	**Osleidys Menendez,** Cuba	Javelin throw	1,313
7	**Marina Kuptsova,** Russia	High jump	1,305
8	**Ashia Hansen,** UK	Triple jump	1,298
9	**Francoise Mbango Etone,** Cameroon	Long jump, triple jump	1,292
10	**Natalya Sadova,** Russia	Discus throw	1,290

* As of March 10, 2003

Source: *International Association of Athletics Federations*

Rankings require a minimum of six performances, four of which must be main events. Result scores take account of wind speed (according to whether it aids or hinders an athlete) and the awarding of a world record, which confers bonus points.

Football

TOP 10 PLAYERS WITH THE MOST CAREER TOUCHDOWNS

	PLAYER	TOUCHDOWNS
1	Jerry Rice*	192
2	Emmitt Smith*	164
3	Marcus Allen	145
4	Cris Carter*	130
5	Jim Brown	126
6	Walter Payton	125
7	Marshall Faulk*	120
8	John Riggins	116
9	Lenny Moore	113
10	Barry Sanders	109

* Still active at end of 2002 season

Source: National Football League

TOP 10 PLAYERS WITH THE MOST CAREER POINTS

	PLAYER	POINTS
1	Gary Anderson*	2,223
2	Morten Andersen*	2,153
3	George Blanda	2,002
4	Norm Johnson	1,736
5	Nick Lowery	1,711
6	Jan Stenerud	1,699
7	Eddie Murray	1,594
8	Al Del Greco	1,584
9	Jim Carney*	1,541
10	Pat Leahy	1,470

* Still active at end of 2002 season

Source: National Football League

TOP 10 PLAYERS WITH THE MOST CAREER PASSING YARDS

	PLAYER	PASSING YARDS
1	Dan Marino	61,361
2	John Elway	51,475
3	Warren Moon	49,325
4	Fran Tarkenton	47,003
5	Dan Fouts	43,040
6	Brett Favre*	42,285
7	Joe Montana	40,551
8	Johnny Unitas	40,239
9	Vinny Testaverde*	39,558
10	Dave Krieg	38,147

* Still active at end of 2002 season

Source: National Football League

◀ **Rice records**
Wide receiver Jerry Rice, considered one of the greatest players of all time, has held numerous NFL career records during his time with the San Francisco 49ers (1985–2000) and Oakland Raiders (2001–).

TOP 10 COACHES WITH THE MOST CAREER WINS

	COACH	GAMES WON
1	Don Shula	347
2	George Halas	324
3	Tom Landry	270
4	Curly Lambeau	229
5	Chuck Noll	209
6	Dan Reeves*	195
7	Chuck Knox	193
8	Paul Brown	170
9	Bud Grant	168
10	Marv Levy	154

* Still active at end of 2002 season

Source: National Football League

▲ **Giants Stadium**
The first game played at Giants Stadium was on October 10, 1976, when the New York Giants were beaten by the Dallas Cowboys 24–14.

TOP10 | MOST SUCCESSFUL SUPER BOWL TEAMS

	TEAM	WINS	SUPER BOWL GAMES RUNNERS-UP	POINTS*
1	Dallas Cowboys	5	3	13
2	San Francisco 49ers	5	0	10
3	Pittsburgh Steelers	4	1	9
4 =	Oakland/Los Angeles Raiders	3	2	8
=	Washington Redskins	3	2	8
6	Denver Broncos	2	4	8
7	Green Bay Packers	3	1	7
8	Miami Dolphins	2	3	7
9	New York Giants	2	1	5
10 =	Buffalo Bills	0	4	4
=	Minnesota Vikings	0	4	4

* *Based on two points for a Super Bowl win, and one for the runner-up; wins take precedence over runners up in determining ranking*

Source: *National Football League*

TOP10 | LARGEST NFL STADIUMS

	STADIUM	HOME TEAM	CAPACITY
1	Giants Stadium	New York Giants/Jets	80,242
2	FedExField	Washington Redskins	80,116
3	Arrowhead Stadium	Kansas City Chiefs	79,451
4	Invesco Stadium	Denver Broncos	76,125
5	Pro Player Stadium	Miami Dolphins	75,540
6	Ralph Wilson Stadium	Buffalo Bills	73,967
7	Ericsson Stadium	Carolina Panthers	73,367
8	Sun Devil Stadium	Arizona Cardinals	73,273
9	Cleveland Browns Stadium	Cleveland Browns	73,200
10	Alltel Stadium	Jacksonville Jaguars	73,000

Source: *National Football League*

The seating capacity of most stadiums varies according to the event. The Giants Stadium reached a capacity of 82,948 on October 5, 1995 when Pope John Paul II celebrated Mass there.

Basketball Bests

TOP 10 POINT-SCORERS IN AN NBA CAREER

	PLAYER	TOTAL POINTS*
1	Kareem Abdul-Jabbar	38,387
2	Karl Malone#	36,374
3	Michael Jordan#	32,292
4	Wilt Chamberlain	31,419
5	Moses Malone	27,409
6	Elvin Hayes	27,313
7	Hakeem Olajuwon#	26,946
8	Oscar Robertson	26,710
9	Dominique Wilkins	26,668
10	John Havlicek	26,395

* Regular season games only

 # Still active at end of 2002–03 season

Source: *National Basketball Association*

The greatest points-scorer in NBA history, Kareem Abdul-Jabbar was born Lew Alcindor but adopted a new name when he converted to Islam in 1969. He began his career in 1970, turning professional with Milwaukee, and played 20 seasons before retiring at the end of 1989. Despite scoring an NBA record of 38,387 points, he could not emulate Wilt Chamberlain by scoring 100 points in a game, which Chamberlain achieved for Philadelphia against New York at Hershey, Pennsylvania, on March 2, 1962. Chamberlain also scored 70 points in a game six times, a feat Abdul-Jabbar never succeeded in rivaling.

TOP 10 FREE THROW PERCENTAGES

	PLAYER	ATTEMPTS	MADE	%
1	Mark Price	2,362	2,135	.904
2	Rick Barry	4,243	3,818	.900
3	Calvin Murphy	3,864	3,445	.892
4	Scott Skiles	1,741	1,548	.889
5	= Larry Bird	4,471	3,960	.886
	= Reggie Miller*	6,593	5,841	.886
7	Bill Sharman	3,559	3,143	.883
8	Ray Allen*	2,215	1,954	.882
9	Jeff Hornacek	3,390	2,973	.877
10	Ricky Pierce	3,871	3,389	.875

* Still active at end of 2002–03 season

Source: *National Basketball Association*

Air Jordan
The holder of numerous basketball records, Michael Jordan's astonishing skill has earned him both a reputation and a personal fortune from the game.

TOP 10 — BEST-PAID PLAYERS IN THE NBA, 2002–03

	PLAYER/TEAM	EARNINGS ($)
1	Kevin Garnett, Minnesota Timberwolves	25,200,000
2	Shaquille O'Neal, Los Angeles Lakers	24,000,000
3	Alonzo Mourning, Miami Heat	20,600,000
4	Juwan Howard, Denver Nuggets	20,300,000
5	Scottie Pippen, Portland Trail Blazers	19,730,000
6	Karl Malone, Utah Jazz	19,250,000
7	Rasheed Wallace, Portland Trail Blazers	16,185,000
8	Dikembe Mutombo, Philadelphia 76ers	16,110,000
9	Chris Webber, Sacramento Kings	14,344,000
10	Allan Houston, New York Knicks	14,340,000

Source: *InsideHoops.com*

Born in Mauldin, South Carolina, on May 19, 1976, Kevin Garnett turned pro in 1995 after being selected out of Farragut Academy High School (IL) in the Draft by Minnesota Timberwolves (fifth pick on the first round). In 1997 he signed a six-year contract worth over $126 million. In his seven-year career he has been selected six times to play on the NBA All Star selection and won the MVP in 2003. Garrett has twice had 40-point games in his career, but in the time he has been playing for the Timberwolves, they have not enjoyed notable success at team level, failing to get past the first round of the Conference play-offs in the seven seasons up to 2001–02. Even with his massive salary of over $25 million, Kevin Garnett is still well short of the NBA record of $33.14 million earned by Michael Jordan in the 1997–98 season.

TOP 10 — TEAMS WITH THE MOST NBA TITLES

	TEAM*	TITLES
1	Boston Celtics	16
2	Minneapolis/Los Angeles Lakers	14
3	Chicago Bulls	6
4 =	Philadelphia/Golden State Warriors	3
=	Syracuse Nationals/Philadelphia 76ers	3
6 =	Baltimore/Washington Bullets	2
=	Detroit Pistons	2
=	Houston Rockets	2
=	New York Knicks	2
10 =	Milwaukee Bucks	1
=	Portland Trail Blazers	1
=	Rochester Royals#	1
=	St. Louis Hawks†	1
=	Seattle Supersonics	1

* *Teams separated by / indicate change of franchise and mean they have won the championship under both names*

\# *Now the Sacramento Kings*

† *Now the Atlanta Hawks*

Source: *National Basketball Association*

TOP 10 — PLAYERS WITH THE HIGHEST POINTS AVERAGE

	PLAYER	GAMES PLAYED	POINTS SCORED	POINTS AVERAGE
1 =	Wilt Chamberlain	1,045	31,419	30.1
=	Michael Jordan*	1,072	32,292	30.1
3	Shaquille O'Neal*	742	20,475	27.6
4	Elgin Baylor	846	23,149	27.4
5 =	Allen Iverson*	487	13,170	27.0
=	Jerry West	932	25,192	27.0
7	Bob Pettit	792	20,880	26.4
8	George Gervin	791	20,708	26.2
9	Oscar Robertson	1,040	26,710	25.7
10	Karl Malone*	1,434	36,374	25.4

* *Still active at end of 2002–03 season*

Source: *National Basketball Association*

TOP 10 — BIGGEST NBA ARENAS

	ARENA/LOCATION	TEAM	CAPACITY
1	The Palace of Auburn Hills, Auburn Hills	Detroit Pistons	22,076
2	United Center, Chicago	Chicago Bulls	21,711
3	MCI Center, Washington	Washington Wizards	20,674
4	Gund Arena, Cleveland	Cleveland Cavaliers	20,562
5	First Union Center, Philadelphia	Philadelphia 76ers	20,444
6	Continental Airlines Arena, East Rutherford	New Jersey Nets	20,049
7	The Rose Garden, Portland	Portland Trail Blazers	19,980
8	Delta Center, Salt Lake City	Utah Jazz	19,911
9	Air Canada Centre, Toronto	Toronto Raptors	19,800
10	Madison Square Garden, New York	New York Knicks	19,763

Source: *National Basketball Association*

Baseball Teams

TOP 10 TEAMS WITH THE MOST WORLD SERIES WINS

	TEAM*	WINS
1	New York Yankees	26
2 =	Philadelphia/Kansas City/Oakland Athletics	9
=	St. Louis Cardinals	9
4	Brooklyn/Los Angeles Dodgers	6
5 =	Boston Red Sox	5
=	Cincinnati Reds	5
=	New York/San Francisco Giants	5
=	Pittsburgh Pirates	5
9	Detroit Tigers	4
10 =	Boston/Milwaukee/Atlanta Braves	3
=	St. Louis/Baltimore Orioles	3
=	Washington Senators/Minnesota Twins	3

* Teams separated by / indicate changes of franchise and are regarded as the same team for Major League record purposes

Source: *Major League Baseball*

Major League Baseball started in the US with the formation of the National League in 1876. The rival American League was started in 1901.

TOP 10 LATEST WINNERS OF THE WORLD SERIES

YEAR*	WINNER/LEAGUE	LOSER/LEAGUE	SCORE
2002	Anaheim Angels (AL)	San Francisco Giants (NL)	4–3
2001	Arizona Diamondbacks (NL)	New York Yankees (AL)	4–3
2000	New York Yankees (AL)	New York Mets (NL)	4–1
1999	New York Yankees (AL)	Atlanta Braves (NL)	4–0
1998	New York Yankees (AL)	San Diego Padres (NL)	4–0
1997	Florida Marlins (NL)	Cleveland Indians (AL)	4–3
1996	New York Yankees (AL)	Atlanta Braves (NL)	4–2
1995	Atlanta Braves (NL)	Cleveland Indians (AL)	4–2
1993	Toronto Blue Jays (AL)	Philadelphia Phillies (NL)	4–2
1992	Toronto Blue Jays (AL)	Atlanta Braves (NL)	4–2

* The 1994 event was canceled due to a players' strike

AL = American League

NL = National League

Source: *Major League Baseball*

The Angels won their first World Series in 2002 in dramatic style. They lost the first game to the Giants, then went 2–1 up before trailing 3–2 after a 16–4 defeat in game 5, but the Angels won the last two games to snatch victory.

TOP 10 TEAMS WITH THE MOST HOME RUNS, 2002

	TEAM	HOME RUN TOTAL
1	Texas Rangers	230
2	New York Yankees	223
3	Chicago White Sox	217
4	Oakland Athletics	205
5	Chicago Cubs	200
6	San Francisco Giants	198
7	Cleveland Indians	191
8	Toronto Blue Jays	187
9	Boston Red Sox	177
10	St. Louis Cardinals	175

Source: *Major League Baseball*

The Rangers also led the MLB in 2002 in extra base hits (561) and total bases (2,558). They scored 800 runs (843) for the seventh straight season, but on the other side of the coin, their ERA of 5.15 was one of the highest in the MBL. They finished the season in fourth place in AL (West).

TOP 10 TEAMS WITH THE WORST ERA, 2002

	TEAM	ERA
1	Tampa Bay Devil Rays	5.29
2	Kansas City Royals	5.21
3	Colorado Rockies	5.20
4	Texas Rangers	5.15
5	Detroit Tigers	4.92
6	Cleveland Indians	4.91
7	Toronto Blue Jays	4.80
8	Milwaukee Brewers	4.73
9	San Diego Padres	4.62
10	Chicago White Sox	4.53

Source: *Major League Baseball*

The Colorado Rockies are the only team on the list to have had an ERA in excess of 5 in each of the past four seasons: in 2001 it was 5.29, in 2000, 5.27, and in 1999, 6.10. In those years, their only winning season was in 2000, when they had an 82–80 record.

TOP 10 TEAMS WITH THE BEST ERA, 2002

	TEAM	ERA
1	Atlanta Braves	3.13
2	San Francisco Giants	3.54
3	Oakland Athletics	3.68
4 =	Anaheim Angels	3.69
=	Los Angeles Dodgers	3.69
6	St. Louis Cardinals	3.70
7	Boston Red Sox	3.75
8	New York Yankees	3.87
9	New York Mets	3.89
10	Arizona Diamondbacks	3.92

Source: *Major League Baseball*

The Atlanta Braves have had a great record in recent years. They had the best ERA in the National League in three consecutive years—2000, 2001, and 2002—and in that period also topped the MBL list, with the exception of 2001, when they finished tied second with Oakland behind the leaders, Seattle.

TOP 10 LARGEST MAJOR LEAGUE BALLPARKS*

	STADIUM	HOME TEAM	CAPACITY
1	Qualcomm Stadium	San Diego Padres	63,480
2	Veterans Stadium	Philadelphia Phillies	62,418
3	Dodger Stadium	Los Angeles Dodgers	56,000
4	Shea Stadium	New York Mets	55,300
5	Yankee Stadium	New York Yankees	55,070
6	SkyDome	Toronto Blue Jays	50,516
7	Coors Field	Colorado Rockies	50,445
8	Turner Field	Atlanta Braves	49,831
9	Busch Stadium	St. Louis Cardinals	49,814
10	The Ballpark in Arlington	Texas Rangers	49,115

* By capacity

Source: *Major League Baseball*

Stadium capacities vary constantly, some being adjusted according to the event: Veterans Stadium, for example, holds fewer people for baseball games than for football matches.

TOP 10 BASEBALL TEAM PAYROLLS, 2003

	TEAM	TOTAL PAYROLL (2003) ($)
1	New York Yankees	149,710,995
2	New York Mets	116,868,613
3	Los Angeles Dodgers	105,897,619
4	Atlanta Braves	104,622,210
5	Texas Rangers	104,526,470
6	Boston Red Sox	96,631,677
7	Seattle Mariners	87,184,500
8	St. Louis Cardinals	83,150,895
9	San Francisco Giants	82,352,167
10	Chicago Cubs	80,743,333

Source: *Associated Press*

Yankees owner George Steinbrenner pushed their payroll up to an all-time MBL record in an effort to improve performances on the field, increasing wages by over $20 million on 2002. Top Yankee earners were Cuban pitcher Jose Contreras and Japanese slugger Hideki Matsui, who signed contracts in December 2002 worth $32 million over four years and $21 million over three years, respectively.

TOP 10 BASEBALL TEAM SALES

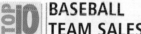

	TEAM	BUYER	YEAR	COST ($)
1	Boston Red Sox	John Henry	2001	700,000,000
2	Cleveland Indians	Larry Dolan	2000	323,000,000
3	Los Angeles Dodgers	News Corp.	1998	311,000,000
4	Texas Rangers	Tom Hicks	1998	250,000,000
5	Baltimore Orioles	Peter Angelos	1993	173,000,000
6 =	Florida Marlins	John Henry	1999	150,000,000
=	St. Louis Cardinals	William DeWitt Jr.	1995	150,000,000
8 =	Arizona Diamondbacks	Jerry Colangelo	1995	130,000,000
=	Tampa Bay Devil Rays	Vincent Naimoli	1995	130,000,000
10	Houston Astros	Drayton McLane Jr.	1992	115,000,000

Source: *Bonham Group*

While the deal for John Henry and his ownership group to purchase the major shares in the Red Sox was started in 2001, it was not finalized until February 27, 2002, and a new era in the long history of the Boston Red Sox began. General Manager Dan Duquette was fired and Joe Kerrigan was replaced as manager by Grady Little, who had formerly been a coach in Boston under Jimy Williams.

TOP 10 NEWEST MAJOR LEAGUE TEAMS

	TEAM	LEAGUE	1ST SEASON
1 =	Arizona Diamondbacks	NL	1998
=	Tampa Bay Devil Rays	AL	1998
3 =	Colorado Rockies	NL	1993
=	Florida Marlins	NL	1993
5 =	Seattle Mariners	AL	1977
=	Toronto Blue Jays	AL	1977
7 =	Kansas City Royals	AL	1969
=	Montreal Expos	NL	1969
=	Seattle Pilots/Milwaukee Brewers	AL	1969
10 =	Houston Astros	NL	1962
=	New York Mets	NL	1962

AL = *American League*

NL = *National League*

Source: *Major League Baseball*

The Arizona Diamondbacks played their first MLB game on March 31, 1998, in front of 50,179 fans at their Bank One Ballpark. Andy Benes delivered the Diamondbacks' first pitch, but the new team lost 9–2 to Colorado.

Baseball Stars

PLAYERS WITH THE BIGGEST CONTRACTS

	PLAYER/CLUB	PERIOD OF CONTRACT	TOTAL ($)
1	**Alex Rodriguez,** Texas Rangers	2001–10	252,000,000
2	**Derek Jeter,** New York	2001–10	189,000,000
3	**Manny Ramirez,** Boston Red Sox	2001–08	160,000,000
4	**Todd Helton,** Colorado Rockies	2003–11	141,500,000
5	**Mike Hampton,** Colorado Rockies	2001–08	121,000,000
6	**Jason Giambi,** New York Yankees	2002–09	120,000,000
7	**Ken Griffey Jr.,** Cincinnati Reds	2000–08	116,500,000
8	**Kevin Brown,** Los Angeles Dodgers	1999–2005	105,000,000
9	**Mike Piazza,** New York Mets	1999–2005	91,000,000
10 =	**Barry Bonds,** San Francisco Giants	2000–06	90,000,000
=	**Chipper Jones,** Atlanta Braves	2000–06	90,000,000

Source: *Major League Baseball*

After seven seasons with the Seattle Mariners, New Yorker Alex Rodriguez joined the Texas Rangers in 2001, when his salary went up from $4,362,500 to $22,000,000. This is a considerable increase on his first salary of $442,333 as an 18-year-old with the Mariners in 1994. A right-handed batter, Rodriguez's best season was in 1996, when he hit 141 runs and topped the leader board in batting averages, with .358.

LATEST WINNERS OF THE CY YOUNG AWARD

	AMERICAN LEAGUE PLAYER/TEAM	NATIONAL LEAGUE PLAYER/TEAM
2002	**Barry Zito,** Oakland Athletics	**Randy Johnson,** Arizona Diamondbacks
2001	**Roger Clemens,** New York Yankees	**Randy Johnson,** Arizona Diamondbacks
2000	**Pedro Martínez,** Boston Red Sox	**Randy Johnson,** Arizona Diamondbacks
1999	**Pedro Martínez,** Boston Red Sox	**Randy Johnson,** Arizona Diamondbacks
1998	**Roger Clemens,** Toronto Blue Jays	**Tom Glavine,** Atlanta Braves
1997	**Roger Clemens,** Toronto Blue Jays	**Pedro Martínez,** Montreal Expos
1996	**Pat Hentgen,** Toronto Blue Jays	**John Smoltz,** Atlanta Braves
1995	**Randy Johnson,** Seattle Mariners	**Greg Maddux,** Atlanta Braves
1994	**David Cone,** Kansas City Royals	**Greg Maddux,** Atlanta Braves
1993	**Jack McDowell,** Chicago White Sox	**Greg Maddux,** Atlanta Braves

Source: *Major League Baseball*

At 6 ft 10 in, Randy Johnson is the tallest man to play Major League Baseball, and with the scowl he delivers to batters, he is also one of the most intimidating men in the game. Johnson made his debut with the Montreal Expos in 1988 but was traded to the Seattle Mariners in 1989, and it was then that his true talent emerged. He won the first of four consecutive strikeout titles in 1992, including a Mariners record 308 in 1993. In 1995 he won the first of five Cy Young Awards, after finishing second to Jack McDowell in 1993 and third behind David Cone and Jimmy Key in 1994. When Johnson won the Cy Young Award in 1999, he became only the third man to do so in both leagues.

PLAYERS WITH THE MOST CONSECUTIVE GAMES PLAYED

	PLAYER	YEARS	GAMES
1	**Cal Ripken Jr.**	1981–2001	2,632
2	**Lou Gehrig**	1923–39	2,130
3	**Everett Scott**	1914–26	1,307
4	**Steve Garvey**	1969–87	1,207
5	**Billy Williams**	1959–76	1,117
6	**Joe Sewell**	1920–33	1,103
7	**Stan Musial**	1941–63	895
8	**Eddie Yost**	1944–62	829
9	**Gus Suhr**	1930–40	822
10	**Nellie Fox**	1947–65	798

Source: *Major League Baseball*

Cal Ripken took himself out of the starting line-up on September 21, 1998, in a game between the Orioles and the Yankees, having played in every game since May 30, 1982.

PLAYERS WITH THE MOST HOME RUNS IN A CAREER

	PLAYER	YEARS	HOME RUNS
1	**Hank Aaron**	1954–76	755
2	**Babe Ruth**	1914–35	714
3	**Willie Mays**	1951–73	660
4	**Barry Bonds**	1986–*	613
5	**Frank Robinson**	1956–76	586
6	**Mark McGwire**	1986–2001	583
7	**Harmon Killebrew**	1954–75	573
8	**Reggie Jackson**	1967–87	563
9	**Mike Schmidt**	1972–89	548
10	**Mickey Mantle**	1951–68	536

* Still active 2002 season

Source: *Major League Baseball*

George Herman "Babe" Ruth's career (1914–35) home run record was unbroken until Henry Louis "Hank" Aaron overtook him in 1974. His total of 714 came from 8,399 at-bats, which represents an average of 8.5 percent—considerably better than the next man in the averages, Harmon Killebrew, at 7.0 percent.

TOP 10 LATEST PERFECT GAMES

	PLAYER	MATCH	DATE
1	David Cone	New York Yankees vs. Montreal Expos	July 18, 1999
2	David Wells	New York Yankees vs. Minnesota Twins	May 17, 1998
3	Kenny Rogers	Texas Rangers vs. California Angels	July 28, 1994
4	Dennis Martinez	Montreal Expos vs. Los Angeles Dodgers	July 28, 1991
5	Tom Browning	Cincinnati Reds vs. Los Angeles Dodgers	Sept. 16, 1988
6	Mike Witt	California Angels vs. Texas Rangers	Sept. 30, 1984
7	Len Barker	Cleveland Indians vs. Toronto Blue Jays	May 15, 1981
8	Catfish Hunter	Oakland Athletics vs. Minnesota Twins	May 8, 1968
9	Sandy Koufax	Los Angeles Dodgers vs. Chicago Cubs	Sept. 9, 1965
10	Jim Bunning	Philadelphia Phillies vs. New York Mets	June 21, 1964

Source: *Major League Baseball*

Seventeen pitchers have thrown perfect games; that is, they have pitched in all nine innings, dismissing 27 opposing batters, and without conceding a run. The first player to pitch a perfect game was Lee Richmond, for Worcester against Cleveland, on June 12, 1880, while the first player to pitch a perfect game in American League history was Ty Cobb in the Red Sox win over Connie Mack's Philadelphia Athletics on May 5, 1904.

TOP 10 PLAYERS WITH THE MOST CAREER STRIKEOUTS

	PLAYER	YEARS	STRIKEOUTS
1	Nolan Ryan	1966–93	5,714
2	Steve Carlton	1965–88	4,136
3	Roger Clemens	1983–*	3,909
4	Randy Johnson	1985–*	3,746
5	Bert Blyleven	1970–92	3,701
6	Tom Seaver	1967–86	3,640
7	Don Sutton	1966–88	3,574
8	Gaylord Perry	1962–83	3,534
9	Walter Johnson	1907–27	3,508
10	Phil Niekro	1964–87	3,342

* Still active

Source: *Major League Baseball*

Nolan Ryan was known as the "Babe Ruth of strikeout pitchers," pitching faster (a record 101 mph) and longer (27 seasons—1966 and 1968–93) than any previous player. As well as his 5,714 strikeouts, including 383 in one season, he walked 2,795 batters and allowed the fewest hits (6.55) per nine innings.

TOP 10 PITCHERS WITH THE MOST CAREER WINS

	PLAYER	YEARS	WINS
1	Cy Young	1890–1911	511
2	Walter Johnson	1907–27	417
3 =	Grover Alexander	1911–30	373
=	Christy Mathewson	1900–16	373
5	Jim Galvin	1875–92	365
6	Warren Spahn	1942–65	363
7	Kid Nichols	1890–1906	361
8	Tim Keefe	1880–93	342
9	Steve Carlton	1965–88	329
10	John Clarkson	1882–94	328

Source: *Major League Baseball*

Denton True "Cy" Young won almost 100 games more than the sport's next-best pitcher, Walter Johnson. Young topped 30 game wins five times and 20 game wins 15 times. He was a member of the Boston Red Sox team that played in the first World Series in 1903, winning two games in a 6–3 series win. Born in Gilmore, Ohio, in 1867, Young played for the Cleveland Spiders, St. Louis Perfectos, St. Louis Cardinals, Boston Americans/Somersets/Pilgrims/Red Sox, Cleveland Naps (later the Indians), and Boston Braves. In 1904 he pitched the first perfect game in American League history, against Philadelphia Athletics.

TOP 10 PLAYERS WITH THE HIGHEST CAREER BATTING AVERAGES

	PLAYER	AT BAT	HITS	AVERAGE*
1	Ty Cobb	11,434	4,189	.366
2	Rogers Hornsby	8,173	2,930	.358
3	Joe Jackson	4,981	1,772	.356
4	Ed Delahanty	7,505	2,596	.346
5	Tris Speaker	10,195	3,514	.345
6 =	Billy Hamilton	6,269	2,159	.344
=	Ted Williams	7,706	2,654	.344
8 =	Dan Brouthers	6,711	2,296	.342
=	Harry Heilmann	7,787	2,660	.342
=	Babe Ruth	8,399	2,873	.342

* Calculated by dividing the number of hits by the number of times a batter was at bat

Source: *Major League Baseball*

Second only to the legendary Ty Cobb, Rogers Hornsby stands as the all-time best-hitting second baseman, topping the .400 mark in three seasons. Baseball's greatest right-handed hitter, slugging 20-plus homers on seven occasions, he achieved a career average of .358. Hornsby collected seven batting titles, including six in a row. Known as "The Rajah," he was the player-manager of the Cardinals when they won their first World Series in 1926. He was elected to the Baseball Hall of Fame in 1942.

International Soccer

TOP 10 TRANSFERS IN WORLD SOCCER

	PLAYER/COUNTRY	FROM	TO	YEAR	FEE ($)*
1	**Zinedine Zidane**, France	Juventus, Italy	Real Madrid, Spain	2001	67,100,000
2	**Luis Figo**, Portugal	Barcelona, Spain	Real Madrid, Spain	2000	56,700,000
3	**Hernan Crespo**, Argentina	Parma, Italy	Lazio, Italy	2000	54,100,000
4	**Rio Ferdinand**, UK	Leeds United, England	Manchester United, England	2002	47,400,000
5	**Gianluigi Buffon**, Italy	Parma, Italy	Juventus, Italy	2001	46,200,000
6	**Gaizka Mendieta**, Spain	Valencia, Spain	Lazio, Italy	2001	40,600,000
7	**Juan Sebastian Veron**, Argentina	Lazio, Italy	Manchester United, England	2001	39,600,000
8	**Rui Costa**, Portugal	Fiorentina, Italy	AC Milan, Italy	2001	39,400,000
9	**Christian Vieri**, Italy	Lazio, Italy	Inter Milan, Italy	1999	38,500,000#
10	**Nicolas Anelka**, France	Arsenal, England	Real Madrid, Spain	1999	37,400,000

* Figures vary slightly from source to source, depending on whether local taxes, agents' fees, and player's commission are included

Vieri's transfer was part of a package deal with Nicola Ventola, who was valued at $11.2 million. Vieri was valued at $38.5 million

The $2 million barrier was broken in 1975, when Giuseppe Savoldi moved from Bologna (Italy) to Napoli (Italy). Gianluigi Lentini's June 1992 transfer from Torino (Italy) to AC Milan (Italy) hit a new record of $18.6 million, while Brazilian player Denilson's move from São Paolo (Brazil) to Real Betis (Spain) in 1998 cost the club $33 million – a figure that, has since become eclipsed by the huge sums paid for international-class players.

TOP 10 COUNTRIES THAT HAVE PLAYED THE MOST MATCHES IN THE FINAL STAGES OF THE WORLD CUP

	COUNTRY	TOURNAMENTS	MATCHES PLAYED
1	**Brazil**	17	87
2	**Germany/West Germany**	15	85
3	**Italy**	15	70
4	**Argentina**	13	60
5	**England**	11	50
6	**Spain**	11	45
7	**France**	11	44
8	**Sweden**	10	41
9	**Uruguay**	10	40
10	= **Yugoslavia**	9	37
	= **Russia/USSR**	9	37

Brazil is the only country to appear in the final stages of all 17 competitions.

TOP 10 GOAL-SCORERS IN INTERNATIONAL SOCCER

	PLAYER/COUNTRY	YEARS	GOALS
1	**Ferenc Puskás**, Hungary/Spain	1945–56	84
2	= **Ali Daei**, Iran	1993–2002	77
	= **Pelé**, Brazil	1957–71	77
4	**Sándor Kocsis**, Hungary	1948–56	75
5	**Gerd Müller**, West Germany	1966–74	68
6	**Majed Abdullah**, Saudi Arabia	1978–94	67
7	**Jassem Al-Houwaidi,*** Kuwait	1992–*	63
8	= **Hossam Hassan,*** Egypt	1985–*	60
	= **Imre Schlosser**, Hungary	1906–27	60
10	**Kiatisuk Senamuang,*** Thailand	1993–*	59

* Still active in 2003

Source: Roberto Mamrud, Karel Stokkermans, and RSSSF 1998/2003

Puskás played for Hungary 84 times, and for Spain on four occasions. For all his exploits, his only international honor with Hungary came in 1952, when he captained his country to the Olympic title. He had made his international debut against Austria as an 18 year old in 1945, but rose to world prominence when Hungary demolished England 6–3 at Wembley, England, in November 1953.

TOP 10 GOAL-SCORERS IN THE FINAL STAGES OF THE WORLD CUP

	PLAYER/COUNTRY	YEARS	GOALS
1	**Gerd Müller**, West Germany	1970–74	14
2	**Just Fontaine**, France	1958	13
3	= **Pelé**, Brazil	1958–70	12
	= **Ronaldo**, Brazil	1998–2002	12
5	= **Jürgen Klinsman**, Germany	1990–98	11
	= **Sándor Kocsis**, Hungary	1954	11
7	= **Gabriel Batistuta**, Argentina	1994–2002	10
	= **Teófilo Cubillas**, Peru	1970–82	10
	= **Grzegorz Lato**, Poland	1974–82	10
	= **Gary Lineker**, England	1986–90	10
	= **Helmut Rahn**, West Germany	1954–58	10

Source: Jaroslaw Owsianski and RSSSF 2002

Gerd Muller scored his first goal in the World Cup finals at Leon, Mexico, on June 3, 1970—just 12 minutes from time—to save West Germany from embarrassment, beating Morocco 2–1 in their opening match. He had already scored ten goals in the qualifying tournament and added ten more in the 1970 final stages, including two hat-tricks. Just Fontaine's 13 goals in 1958 is a record for one tournament.

TOP 10 RICHEST SOCCER CLUBS

	CLUB/COUNTRY	TURNOVER ($)
1	**Manchester United,** England	189,400,000
2	**Real Madrid,** Spain	167,800,000
3	**Bayern Munich,** Germany	148,200,000
4	**AC Milan,** Italy	145,200,000
5	**Juventus,** Italy	143,000,000
6	**SS Lazio,** Italy	128,500,000
7	**Chelsea,** England	124,100,000
8	**Barcelona,** Spain	121,700,000
9	**Inter Milan,** Italy	111,500,000
10	**AS Roma,** Italy	103,700,000

Compiled from Deloitte & Touche Sport data

The latest Deloitte & Touche/SportBusiness International Rich List compares the incomes of the world's top soccer clubs during the 1999–2000 season. It reveals the extent to which soccer has become a major business enterprise, with many clubs generating considerably more revenue from commercial activities such as the sale of merchandise and income from TV rights than they receive from admissions to games.

TOP 10 COUNTRIES WITH THE MOST REGISTERED SOCCER CLUBS

	COUNTRY	REGISTERED CLUBS*
1	**South Africa**	51,944
2	**Russia**	43,700
3	**England**	42,000
4	**Germany**	26,760
5	**France**	21,629
6	**Italy**	20,961
7	**Uzbekistan**	15,000
8	**Japan**	13,047
9	**Brazil**	12,987
10	**Spain**	10,240

* Registered with FIFA through national associations

◀ **World class**
One of the foremost goal-scorers of the World Cup, Ronaldo shows off his skills during the 2002 tournament.

Hockey Highlights

TOP 10 GOAL-SCORING ROOKIES IN THE NHL, 2002–03

	PLAYER	TEAM	GAMES PLAYED	GOALS
1	Henrik Zetterberg	Detroit Red Wings	79	22
2	Ales Kotalik	Buffalo Sabres	68	21
3	Tyler Atnason	Chicago Blackhawks	82	19
4	Rick Nash	Columbus Blue Jackets	74	17
5	Adam Hall	Nashville Predators	79	16
6 =	Jason Chimera	Edmonton Oilers	66	14
=	Alexander Frolov	Los Angeles Kings	79	14
8 =	Stanislav Chistov	Mighty Ducks of Anaheim	79	12
=	Branko Radivojevic	Phoenix Coyotes	79	12
10 =	Ramzi Abid	Phoenix Coyotes/Pittsburgh Penguins	33	10
=	Dan Snyder	Atlanta Thrashers	36	10

Source: *National Hockey League*

Henrik Zetterberg (born October 9, 1980, Sweden) played for Timra, Sweden, and for his national team, in the 2000–01 season achieving 15 goals and 46 points in 47 games and being named Sweden's Rookie of the Year. He played for Sweden in the Winter Olympics before signing a three-year $2.5-million contract with Detroit in May 2002.

TOP 10 ASSISTS IN AN NHL CAREER

	PLAYER	SEASONS	ASSISTS*
1	Wayne Gretzky	20	1,963
2	Ron Francis#	22	1,222
3	Ray Bourque	22	1,169
4	Mark Messier#	24	1,168
5	Paul Coffey	21	1,135
6	Adam Oates#	20	1,063
7	Gordie Howe	26	1,049
8	Marcel Dionne	18	1,040
9	Mario Lemieux#	15	1,011
10	Steve Yzerman#	20	1,010

* Regular season only

Still active at end of 2002–03 season

Source: *National Hockey League/Hockey Database*

When Gretzky retired after a 20-year career, he held 10 NHL scoring titles and more goals, assists, and points than anyone in League history.

TOP 10 POINT-SCORERS IN AN NHL CAREER

	PLAYER	SEASONS	GOALS	ASSISTS	TOTAL POINTS*
1	Wayne Gretzky	20	894	1,963	2,857
2	Gordie Howe	26	801	1,049	1,850
3	Mark Messier#	24	676	1,168	1,844
4	Marcel Dionne	18	731	1,040	1,771
5	Ron Francis#	22	536	1,222	1,758
6	Mario Lemieux#	15	682	1,011	1,692
7	Steve Yzerman#	20	660	1,010	1,670
8	Phil Esposito	18	717	873	1,590
9	Ray Bourque	22	410	1,169	1,579
10	Paul Coffey	21	396	1,135	1,531

* Regular season only

Still active at start of 2002–03 season

Wayne Gretzky holds, or jointly holds, 61 official NHL records: 40 for the regular season, 15 for Stanley Cup playoffs, and six in the All-Star Game. His point-scoring records include most in a career (2,857), most in a regular season (215 in 1985–86), and most in a season, including playoffs (255 in 1984–85). His final NHL point was an assist scored by Mathieu Schneider for the Rangers against Pittsburgh Penguins on April 18, 1999.

TOP 10 GOAL-SCORERS IN AN NHL CAREER

	PLAYER	SEASONS	GOALS*
1	Wayne Gretzky	20	894
2	Gordie Howe	26	801
3	Marcel Dionne	18	731
4	Phil Esposito	18	717
5	Brett Hull#	18	716
6	Mike Gartner	19	708
7	Mario Lemieux#	15	682
8	Mark Messier#	24	676
9	Steve Yzerman#	20	660
10	Luc Robitaille#	17	631

* Regular season only

Still active at end of 2002–03 season

Source: *National Hockey League*

The first of Wayne Gretzky's 894 goals was against Vancouver on October 14, 1979, while his last was against the New York Islanders on March 29, 1999.

TOP 10 BEST-PAID PLAYERS IN THE NHL, 2002–03

	PLAYER	TEAM	SALARY ($)
1	Jaromír Jágr	Washington Capitals	11,483,333
2	Keith Tkachuk	St. Louis Blues	11,000,000
3	Nicklas Lidstrom	Detroit Red Wings	10,500,000
4 =	Pavel Bure	New York Rangers	10,000,000
=	Paul Kariya	Mighty Ducks of Anaheim	10,000,000
6	Joe Sakic	Colorado Avalanche	9,856,018
7	Brian Leetch	New York Rangers	9,680,000
8	Robert Holik	New York Rangers	9,600,000
9 =	Peter Forsberg	Colorado Avalanche	9,500,000
=	Chris Pronger	St. Louis Blues	9,500,000

Source: *National Hockey League Players Association*

The Washington Capitals' second-highest earner in 2002–03 was goaltender Olaf Kolzig on $6 million. Robert Lang topped $5 million, while the Capitals had four more players on $2 million or more. Top-earner Jágr was drafted fifth overall in the 1990 draft by the Pittsburgh Penguins. He made his NHL debut on October 5 against the Capitals and scored his first goal two nights later against the Devils.

TOP 10 GOALIES WITH THE BEST SAVE PERCENTAGES IN THE NHL, 2002–03

	PLAYER*	TEAM	GAMES PLAYED	SAVES TOTAL	(%)
1	Marty Turco	Dallas Stars	55	1,267	0.932
2	Sean Burke	Phoenix Coyotes	22	588	0.930
3	Martin Gerber	Mighty Ducks of Anaheim	22	509	0.929
4	Dwayne Roloson	Minnesota Wild	50	1,236	0.927
5 =	Roman Cechmanek	Philadelphia Fliers	58	1,266	0.925
=	Manny Legace	Detroit Red Wings	25	630	0.925
7	Emmanuel Fernandez	Minnesota Wild	50	898	0.924
8	Ed Belfour	Toronto Maple Leafs	62	1,675	0.922
9 =	J. Giguere	Mighty Ducks of Anaheim	65	1,675	0.920
=	Patrick Roy	Columbus Blue Jackets	63	1,586	0.920

* *Minimum qualification 20 games; regular season only*

Source: *National Hockey League*

Born in Sault Ste. Marie, Ontario, on August 13, 1975, Marty Turco enjoyed a highly successful amateur career before turning pro. He holds the record for posting the most wins in NCAA history with a 127–28–7 record (.806 winning percentage) for the Michigan Wolverines.

TOP 10 GOAL-SCORERS IN THE NHL, 2002–03

	PLAYER/TEAM	GOALS*
1	Milan Hejduk, Columbus Blue Jackets	50
2	Markus Naslund, Vancouver Canucks	48
3	Todd Bertuzzi, Vancouver Canucks	46
4	Marian Hossa, Ottawa Senators	45
5	Glen Murray, Boston Bruins	44
6	Dany Heatley, Atlanta Thrashers	41
7	Ilya Kovalchuk, Atlanta Thrashers	38
8 =	Brett Hull, Detroit Red Wings	37
=	Alex Kovalev, New York Rangers	37
=	Zigmund Palffy, Los Angeles Kings	37
=	Mats Sundin, Toronto Maple Leafs	37

* *Regular season only*

Source: *National Hockey League*

TOP 10 LATEST STANLEY CUP WINNERS

YEAR	WINNER
2002	Detroit Red Wings
2001	Colorado Avalanche
2000	New Jersey Devils
1999	Dallas Stars
1998	Detroit Red Wings
1997	Detroit Red Wings
1996	Colorado Avalanche
1995	New Jersey Devils
1994	New York Rangers
1993	Montreal Canadiens

Source: *National Hockey League*

TOP 10 TEAM SALARIES IN THE NHL, 2002–03

	TEAM	SALARY ($)
1	Dallas Stars	71,685,169
2	New York Rangers	68,527,085
3	Detroit Red Wings	67,510,506
4	St. Louis Blues	63,217,000
5	Colorado Avalanche	60,470,926
6	Toronto Maple Leafs	54,861,600
7	Philadelphia Flyers	54,645,833
8	New Jersey Devils	52,372,626
9	Washington Capitals	51,402,458
10	Montreal Canadiens	48,647,360

Source: *National Hockey League Players Association*

The average NHL payroll for the 2002–03 season was $42.6 million and the average player's salary was $1.76 million. The Dallas Stars had 12 players above this figure, with an average salary of $2.68 million.

Racket Sports

TABLE TENNIS WORLD CHAMPIONSHIP GOLD MEDAL WINNERS

	COUNTRY	MEN'S	WOMEN'S	TOTAL*
1	China	41.5	48	89.5
2	Hungary	42	26	68
3	Japan	23.5	23.5	47
4	Czech Republic	17.5	10.5	28
5	Romania	–	17	17
6 =	England	8	6	14
=	Sweden	14	–	14
8	US	5	5	10
9	Austria	3	3	6
10	Germany	1	4	5
	All countries	161	154	315

* Includes team events, singles, doubles, and mixed; 0.5 golds were possible when doubles pairs could be of different nationalities—today, only players of the same nationality can play in pairs

Source: *International Table Tennis Federation (ITTF)*

MALE SQUASH PLAYERS

	PLAYER/COUNTRY	AVERAGE POINTS*
1	Peter Nicol, England	1,312.500
2	Jonathon Power, Canada	1,213.844
3	David Palmer, Australia	1,034.375
4	John White, Scotland	634.444
5	Stewart Boswell, Australia	624.219
6	Thierry Lincou, France	474.219
7	Anthony Ricketts, Australia	371.094
8	Ong Beng Hee, Malaysia	354.688
9	Lee Beachill, England	350.781
10	Martin Heath, Scotland	294.444

* As of January 2003

Source: *Dunlop PSA World Rankings*

The players' rankings have been decided by taking the total points they have scored and dividing this figure by the number of tournaments in which they have competed. Peter Nicol confirmed his preeminent position by winning the England National Squash Championship in February 2003.

FEMALE SQUASH PLAYERS

	PLAYER/COUNTRY	AVERAGE POINTS*
1	Sarah Fitz-Gerald, Australia	1,956.471
2	Carol Owens, New Zealand	1,745.278
3	Natalie Pohrer, England	1,322.905
4	Linda Charman-Smith, England	915.471
5	Vanessa Atkinson, Netherlands	876.750
6	Tania Bailey, England	860.342
7	Cassie Campion, England	848,750
8	Rachael Grinham, Australia	833,368
9	Rebecca Macree, England	565.095
10	Fiona Geaves, England	542.158

* As at January 2003

Source: *WISPA World Rankings*

Women's squash has been played at an international level since the 1920s. British players dominated the sport until Australian player Heather McKay played undefeated from 1962 to 1980. Fellow Australian Sarah Fitz-Gerald has been World Open Champion on five occasions (1996–98 and 2001–02).

TABLE TENNIS FIRSTS

FIRST FACT

"INDOOR TENNIS" WAS FIRST PLAYED in the early 1880s by British army officers in India and South Africa, using lids from cigar boxes as paddles and the rounded part of champagne corks as balls. English athlete James Gibb introduced the use of celluloid balls after 1900, developing the game he called "Ping Pong," echoing the sound of the ball in play. This was registered in 1901 as a trade name by croquet pioneers John Jacques and by Parker Brothers in the US. The studded rubber paddle surface was invented by E. C. Goode in 1902. The Fédération Internationale de Tennis de Table (International Table Tennis Federation) was founded in 1926, and table tennis became an Olympic sport in 1988.

COUNTRIES WITH THE MOST WIMBLEDON SINGLES TITLES

	COUNTRY	WOMEN'S	MEN'S	TOTAL
1	US	46	33	79
2	UK	36	35	71
3	Australia	5	20	25
4	France	6	7	13
5	Germany	8	4	12
6	Sweden	–	7	7
7	Czechoslovakia/ Czech Republic	3	2	5
8	New Zealand	–	4	4
9	Brazil	3	–	3
10	Spain	1	1	2

Men's singles championships have been held—with breaks during both world wars—since 1877 and women's since 1884.

FEMALE TENNIS PLAYERS*

	PLAYER/COUNTRY	WEEKS AT NO. 1
1	Steffi Graf, Germany	377
2	Martina Navratilova, Czechoslovakia/US	331
3	Chris Evert, US	262
4	Martina Hingis, Switzerland	209
5	Monica Seles, Yugoslavia/US	178
6	Lindsay Davenport, US	38
7	Serena Williams, US	32
8	Tracy Austin, US	22
9	Jennifer Capriati, US	17
10	Arantxa Sanchez-Vicario, Spain	12

* Based on weeks at No. 1 in WTA rankings (1973 to January 13, 2003)

As well as the most weeks, Steffi Graf achieved the longest unbroken run at No. 1, with 186 weeks (August 17, 1987–March 10, 1991).

TOP 10 | MALE TENNIS PLAYERS*

PLAYER/COUNTRY	WEEKS AT NO. 1
1 **Pete Sampras,** US	286
2 **Ivan Lendl,** Czechoslovakia/US	270
3 **Jimmy Connors,** US	268
4 **John McEnroe,** US	170
5 **Björn Borg,** Sweden	109
6 **Andre Agassi,** US	87
7 **Stefan Edberg,** Sweden	72
8 **Lleyton Hewitt,** US	65
9 **Jim Courier,** US	58
10 **Gustavo Kuerton,** Brazil	43

* Based on weeks at No. 1 in ATP rankings (1973 to January 13, 2003)

Jimmy Connors had the longest unbroken run at No. 1, a total of 160 weeks, from July 29, 1974 to August 22, 1977. Pete Sampras's longest run was 102 weeks, from April 14, 1996 to March 29, 1998.

◄ **For Pete's sake**
Pete Sampras holds more Grand Slam singles titles than any other man in the history of the sport.

Golfing Greats

King of swing
Foremost money-winner and youngest-ever winner of the US Masters, Tiger Woods has taken the world of golf by storm since turning pro in 1996.

TOP 10 PLAYERS TO WIN THE MOST MAJORS IN A CAREER

	PLAYER*	MAJORS#
1	Jack Nicklaus	18
2	Walter Hagen	11
3 =	Ben Hogan	9
=	Gary Player, South Africa	9
5 =	Tom Watson	8
=	Tiger Woods	8
7 =	Bobby Jones	7
=	Arnold Palmer	7
=	Gene Sarazen	7
=	Sam Snead	7
	Harry Vardon, UK	7

* All from US unless otherwise specified

\# To the end of the 2002 season

The four Majors are the British Open, US Open, US Masters, and US PGA. Of these, the oldest is the British Open, first played in Prestwick in 1860 and won by Willie Park. The first US Open was at the Newport Club, Rhode Island, held in 1895 and won by Horace Rawlins, playing on his home course.

TOP 10 MONEY-WINNING GOLFERS, 2002

	GOLFER*	PGA TOUR WINNINGS (2002) ($)
1	Tiger Woods	7,392,188
2	Phil Mickelson	4,311,971
3	Vijay Singh, Fiji	3,756,563
4	David Toms	3,459,739
5	Ernie Els, South Africa	3,291,895
6	Jerry Kelly	2,946,889
7	Rich Beem	2,938,365
8	Justin Leonard	2,738,235
9	Charles Howell III	2,702,747
10	Retief Goosen	2,617,004

* All from US unless otherwise specified

TOP 10 WINNERS OF WOMEN'S MAJORS

	PLAYER*	MAJORS#
1	Patty Berg	16
2 =	Louise Suggs	13
=	Mickey Wright	13
4	Babe Zaharias	12
5	Julie Inkster	10
6	Betsy Rawls	8
7	JoAnne Carner	7
8 =	Pat Bradley	6
=	Glenna Collett Vare	6
=	Betsy King	6
=	Patty Sheehan	6
=	Karrie Webb	6
=	Kathy Whitworth	6

All from US

To the end of the 2002 season

The present-day Majors are the US Open, LPGA Championship, Nabisco Championship, British Open, and the amateur championships of both the US and UK. Also taken into account in this Top 10 are wins in the former Majors: the Western Open (1937–67), Titleholders Championship (1930–72), and the du Maurier Classic (1977–2000).

TOP 10 AMERICAN PLAYERS WITH THE MOST WINS IN THE RYDER CUP

	PLAYER	WINS
1	Arnold Palmer	22
2 =	Billy Casper	20
=	Lanny Wadkins	20
4 =	Jack Nicklaus	17
=	Lee Trevino	17
6	Tom Kite	15
7	Gene Littler	14
8	Hale Irwin	13
9	Raymond Floyd	12
10 =	Sam Snead	10
=	Tom Watson	10

The Ryder Cup was launched in 1927 by British golf enthusiast Samuel Ryder (1858–1936). Held every two years, the venues alternate between the US and Great Britain, the US originally competing against Great Britain and Ireland, but, since 1979, against Europe.

◀ **Iron lady**
Julie Inkster is only the second woman to win all four women's golf Grand Slam tournaments.

TOP 10 CAREER BEST-PAID GOLFERS

	GOLFER*	CAREER WINNINGS# ($)
1	Tiger Woods	35,944,852
2	Phil Mickelson	22,709,944
3	Davis Love III	21,663,495
4	Vijay Singh, Fiji	19,353,024
5	Ernie Els, South Africa	17,168,329
6	Scott Hoch	17,137,297
7	Nick Price, Zimbabwe	17,086,904
8	David Duval	16,195,473
9	Jim Furyk	15,068,084
10	Justin Leonard	14,853,334

All from US unless otherwise specified

As of March 16, 2003

TOP 10 PLAYERS WITH THE MOST WINS ON THE US TOUR IN A CAREER

	PLAYER*	WINS
1	Sam Snead	81
2	Jack Nicklaus	70
3	Ben Hogan	63
4	Arnold Palmer	60
5	Byron Nelson	52
6	Billy Casper	51
7 =	Walter Hagen	40
=	Cary Midlecoff	40
9	Gene Sarazen	38
10	Lloyd Mangrum	36

All from US

FIRST GRAND SLAM

In 1930 Bobby (Robert Tyre) Jones (1902–71) won the Open and Amateur tournaments in both his native US and the UK, thereby completing the first ever golfing "Grand Slam." Jones—who never relinquished his amateur status—remains the only golfer ever to achieve this feat. Considered the greatest player in the history of the game, he was the co-founder of the Augusta National Golf Club and the originator of the US Masters tournament. That event, along with the US Open, US PGA, and British Open, comprise today's golfing Grand Slam.

FIRST FACT

Water Sports

TOP 10 OLYMPIC ROWING COUNTRIES

	COUNTRY	GOLD	MEDALS SILVER	BRONZE	TOTAL
1	US	29	29	21	79
2 =	East Germany	33	7	8	48
=	Germany*	21	13	14	48
4	UK	21	16	7	44
5	Soviet Union#	12	20	11	43
6	Italy	14	13	10	37
7 =	Canada	8	12	13	33
=	France	6	14	13	33
9	Romania	15	10	7	32
10	Australia	7	8	10	25

Not including West/East Germany 1968–88

Includes Unified Team of 1992; excludes Russia since then

Olympic rowing dates from 1900 for men, but as recently as 1976 for women. The total includes several discontinued events. Britain's Steve Redgrave has won five Gold medals at five consecutive Olympic Games, 1984–2000, a unique feat in an endurance sport for which he received a knighthood.

TOP 10 COLLEGES IN THE INTERCOLLEGIATE ROWING ASSOCIATION

	COLLEGE	WINNING YEARS (FIRST/LAST)	WINS
1	Cornell	1896–1982	24
2	California	1928–2002	14
3	Navy	1921–84	13
4	Washington	1923–97	11
5	Pennsylvania	1898–1989	9
6 =	Wisconsin	1951–90	7
=	Brown	1979–95	7
8	Syracuse	1904–78	6
9	Columbia	1895–1929	4
10	Princeton	1985–98	3

Men's varsity eight-oared shells event

Source: *Intercollegiate Rowing Association Regatta*

The Intercollegiate Rowing Association Regatta has been held since 1895, after Harvard and Yale left the Rowing Association to establish their own annual race. The regatta highlight, the varsity eights event, first took place in Poughkeepsie, New York, but since 1995 has been contested in Camden, New Jersey.

TOP 10 OLYMPIC CANOEING COUNTRIES

	COUNTRY	GOLD	MEDALS SILVER	BRONZE	TOTAL
1	Hungary	14	25	21	60
2 =	Germany*	22	16	15	53
=	Soviet Union#	30	14	9	53
4	Romania	10	10	14	34
5	East Germany	14	7	9	30
6	Sweden	14	11	4	29
7	France	3	7	16	26
8	Bulgaria	4	5	8	17
9	Canada	3	8	5	16
10 =	Poland	0	5	10	15
=	US	5	4	6	15

Not including West/East Germany 1968–88

Includes Unified Team of 1992; excludes Russia since then

Canoeing has been an official Olympic sport since 1936, although it was first seen as a demonstration sport at the 1924 Paris Olympics.

ACROSS THE CHANNEL

FIRST FACT

ALTHOUGH CHANNEL CROSSINGS had previously been made using flotation aids, the first swimmer to do so unaided was a British sailor, Captain Matthew Webb (1848–83), on August 24–25, 1875. Sustained by beef-tea, beer, coffee, and an omelette, and despite being stung by a starfish, he landed at Calais after 21 hours, 44 minutes, and 55 seconds in the water. It was not until September 6, 1911, that Thomas William Burgess (UK) became the second man to swim the Channel. The first woman to make the crossing was Gertrude Ederle (US), on August 6, 1926, and in 1934 Edward Temme (UK) became the first person to swim the Channel in both directions.

TOP 10 FASTEST CROSS-CHANNEL SWIMMERS

	SWIMMER/COUNTRY	YEAR	TIME (HR:MIN)
1	Chad Hundeby, US	1994	7:17
2	Penny Lee Dean, US	1978	7:40
3	Tamara Bruce, Australia	1994	7:53
4	Philip Rush, New Zealand	1987	7:55
5	Hans Van Goor, Netherlands	1995	8:02
6	Richard Davey, UK	1988	8:05
7	Irene van der Laan, Netherlands	1982	8:06
8 =	Paul Asmuth, US	1985	8:12
=	Gail Rice, US	1999	8:12
10	Anita Sood, India	1987	8:15

Source: *Channel Swimming Association*

An earlier record, of 9 hours 36 minutes, was set in 1973 by Lynne Cox (US), aged 16—the minimum permitted age for solo swimmers—while the current female record has been held since 1978 by another American, Penny Dean, who was aged 23 at the time.

TOP 10 MEN'S OLYMPIC 100M FREESTYLE TIMES

	SWIMMER/COUNTRY	YEAR	TIME (SECS)
1	Pieter van den Hoogenband, Netherlands	2000	47.84
2	Pieter van den Hoogenband	2000	48.30
3	Matt Biondi, US	1988	48.63
4	Pieter van den Hoogenband	2000	48.64
5	Alexander Popov, Russia	2000	48.69
6	Gary Hall Jr., US	2000	48.73
7 =	Alexander Popov	1996	48.74
=	Michael Klim, US	2000	48.74
9	Michael Klim	2000	48.80
10	Gary Hall Jr., US	1996	48.81

Gary Hall Jr. is a member of a family of swimmers: his grandfather, Charles Keating, was an All-America swimmer at the University of Cincinnati; his uncle a member of the 1976 US Olympics team; while his father, Gary Hall Sr., won silver medals at the 1968 and 1972 Olympics and a bronze in 1976.

TOP 10 WATERSKIERS WITH THE MOST WORLD CUP WINS

	WATERSKIER/COUNTRY	M/F*	SLALOM	JUMP	TOTAL
1	**Andy Mapple**, UK	M	29	–	29
2	**Emma Sheers**, Australia	F	2	15	17
3	**Jaret Llewellyn**, Canada	M	–	16	16
4	**Toni Neville**, Australia	F	4	7	11
5	**Wade Cox**, US	M	10	–	10
6 =	**Bruce Neville**, Australia	M	–	9	9
=	**Kristi Overton-Johnson** (née Overton), US	F	9		9
8	**Freddy Krueger**, US	M	–	8	8
9	**Scot Ellis**, US	M	–	7	7
10 =	**Susi Graham**, Canada	F	6	–	6
=	**Carl Roberge**, US	M	1	5	6

* Male/female

Waterskiing was invented in 1922 by 18-year-old Ralph W. Samuelson of Lake City, Minnesota, using two 8-ft (2.4-m) planks and 100 ft (30 m) of sash cord. The first international governing body, the World Water Ski Union, was established in 1946 in Geneva, Switzerland.

THE 10 LATEST WINNERS OF THE AMERICA'S CUP

	WINNING BOAT/SKIPPER/COUNTRY	CHALLENGER/COUNTRY	SCORE
2003	**Alinghi,** Russell Coutts, Switzerland	**Team New Zealand,** New Zealand	5–0
2000	**Team New Zealand,** Russell Coutts, New Zealand	**Prada Luna Rossa,** Italy	5–0
1995	**Black Magic,** Russell Coutts, New Zealand	**Young America,** US	5–0
1992	**America³,** Bill Koch, US	**Il Moro di Venezia,** Italy	4–1
1988	**Stars and Stripes,** Dennis Conner, US	**KZ1,** New Zealand	2–0
1987	**Stars and Stripes,** Dennis Conner, US	**Kookaburra III,** Australia	4–0
1983	**Australia II,** John Bertrand, Australia	**Liberty,** US	4–3
1980	**Freedom,** Dennis Conner, US	**Australia,** Australia	4–1
1977	**Courageous,** Ted Turner, US	**Australia,** Australia	4–0
1974	**Courageous,** Ted Hood, US	**Southern Cross,** Australia	4–0

One of the costliest and most prestigious of all sporting events, the America's Cup has also been among the most one-sided, with the New York Yacht Club competitor winning every event from 1851 to 1980.

▼ **America's Cup winners**
Team New Zealand crosses the finishing line off its home country to take the 2000 America's Cup.

Tough Guys

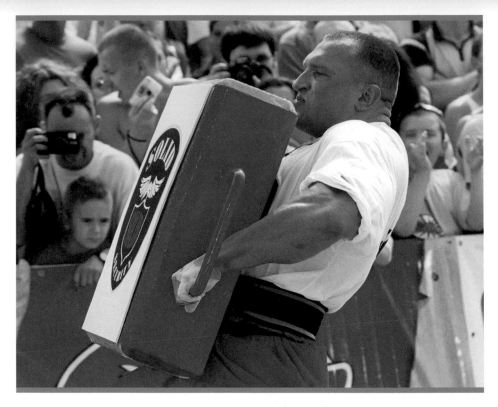

YEAR	STRONGMAN	COUNTRY
2002	Mariusz Pudzianowski	Poland
2001	Svend Karlsen	Norway
2000	Janne Virtanen	Finland
1999	Jouko Ahola	Finland
1998	Magnus Samuelsson	Sweden
1997	Jouko Ahola	Finland
1996	Magnus Ver Magnusson	Iceland
1995	Magnus Ver Magnusson	Iceland
1994	Magnus Ver Magnusson	Iceland
1993	Gary Taylor	UK

Source: *StrongestMan.com*

◀ **Polish performance**
Poland's Mariusz Pudzianowski is the latest winner of a grueling contest that involves such feats as lifting cars and pulling trucks.

TOP 10 | OLYMPIC FREESTYLE WRESTLING COUNTRIES

	COUNTRY	GOLD	MEDALS SILVER	BRONZE	TOTAL
1	US	44	35	24	103
2	Soviet Union*	31	17	15	63
3 =	Bulgaria	7	17	9	33
=	Japan	16	9	8	33
=	Turkey	16	11	6	33
6	Iran	5	9	12	26
=	Sweden	8	10	8	26
8	Finland	8	7	10	25
9	Korea	4	7	8	19
10	GB#	3	4	10	17

* *Includes Unified Team of 1992; excludes Russia since then*

\# *Great Britain's three gold medals in the freestyle event all date from the 1908 Games.*

THE 10 | LATEST UNDISPUTED WORLD HEAVYWEIGHT BOXING CHAMPIONS

	FIGHTER*	YEAR
1	Lennox Lewis, UK	1999
2	Riddick Bowe	1992
3	Evander Holyfield	1990
4	James Buster Douglas	1990
5	Mike Tyson	1987
6	Leon Spinks	1978
7	Muhammad Ali	1974
8	George Foreman	1973
9	Joe Frazier	1970
10	Muhammad Ali	1967

* *All from the US unless otherwise stated*

"Undisputed" champions are those recognized by the main governing bodies (World Boxing Council, World Boxing Association, International Boxing Federation, and World Boxing Organization) at the time of winning their world title. Champions not recognized by all major bodies may coexist with these, so there may be more than one "world champion" in each weight division.

TOP 10 | MEDAL-WINNING WEIGHTLIFTERS (WOMEN)

	WEIGHTLIFTER/COUNTRY	SENIOR WORLD CHAMPIONSHIP MEDALS (1987–2000)
1	Maria Takacs, Hungary	12
2 =	Shu-Chih Chen, Taipei	8
=	Milena Tredafilova, Bulgaria	8
=	Maria Isabel Urrutia, Colombia	8*
5 =	Robin Goad-Byrd, US	7
=	Nameirakpam Kunjarani, Indonesia	7
7 =	Maria Christoforidou, Greece	6
=	Izabela Dragneva-Rifatova, Bulgaria	6
9 =	Jui-Lien Chen, Taipei	5
=	Nan-Mei Chu, Taipei	5
=	Hongyun Li, China	5
=	Erika Takacs, Hungary	5

* *Also won a gold medal in the Olympic Games*

Source: *International Weightlifting Federation*

TOP 10 | MEDAL-WINNING WEIGHTLIFTERS (MEN)

WEIGHTLIFTER/COUNTRY	MEDALS WON (1891–2001)		
	OLYMPICS	SWC	TOTAL
1 Imre Földi, Hungary	3	10	13
2 = Waldemar Baszanowski, Poland	2	10	12
= Seresht Mohammad Nasiri, Iran	3	9	12
4 = Tamio Kono, US	3	8	11
= Norbert Schemansky, US	4	7	11
= Naim Süleymanoglu, Turkey	3	8	11
= Arkadi Vorobiev, USSR	3	8	11
= Marian Zielinski, Poland	3	8	11
9 = Vasili Alexeev, USSR	2	8	10
= Yoshinobu Miyake, Japan	3	7	10
= Nicu Vlad, Romania	3	7	10

SWC = Senior World Championships

Source: International Weightlifting Federation

TOP 10 | OLYMPIC JUDO COUNTRIES

COUNTRY	MEDALS			
	GOLD	SILVER	BRONZE	TOTAL
1 Japan	23	12	13	48
2 France	10	5	17	32
3 Korea	7	10	13	30
4 Soviet Union*	7	5	15	27
5 Cuba	5	7	8	20
6 GB	–	7	9	16
7 Netherlands	4	–	7	11
8 = Brazil	2	3	5	10
= China	4	1	5	10
= Germany#	1	1	8	10
= Italy	2	3	5	10

* Includes Unified Team of 1992; excludes Russia since then

Not including West/East Germany 1968–88

▼ **Hawaii Ironman**
The Hawaii Ironman triathlon was first contested in 1978 at Waikiki Beach, but since 1981 has been held at Kailua-Kona.

TOP 10 | FASTEST WINNING TIMES FOR THE HAWAII IRONMAN

WINNER/NATIONALITY	YEAR	TIME (HR:MIN:SEC)
1 Luc Van Lierde, Belgium	1996	8:04:08
2 Mark Allen, US	1993	8:07:45
3 Mark Allen	1992	8:09:08
4 Mark Allen	1989	8:09:16
5 Luc Van Lierde	1999	8:17:17
6 Mark Allen	1991	8:18:32
7 Greg Welch, Australia	1994	8:20:27
8 Mark Allen	1995	8:20:34
9 Peter Reid, Canada	2000	8:21:01
10 Peter Reid	1998	8:24:20

This is perhaps one of the most grueling of all contests, in which competitors engage in a 2.4-mile (3.86-km) swim, followed by a 112-mile (180-km) cycle race, and end with a full marathon (26 miles 385 yards/42.195 km).

Horsing Around

HORSE RACING BETTING COUNTRIES

	COUNTRY	VALUE ($)*
1	Japan	35,400,000,000
2	US	17,300,000,000
3	China (Hong Kong)	10,610,000,000
4	UK	8,000,000,000
5	Australia	5,800,000,000
6	France	5,700,000,000
7	South Korea	3,400,000,000
8	Italy	2,200,000,000
9	Malaysia	1,400,000,000
10	Canada	1,200,000,000

* *Value of indigenous betting*

◄ **Horse power**
With 725,000 racehorses in the US, the horse industry is estimated to contribute over $112 billion a year to the US economy.

TOP 10 **MONEY-WINNING DRIVERS**

	DRIVER	WINNINGS ($)
1	John Campbell	213,776,639
2	Michel Lachance	147,936,357
3	Bill O'Donnell	94,861,168
4	Jack Moiseyev	88,886,711
5	Cat Manzi	88,643,353
6	Herve Filion	85,574,660
7	Doug Brown	80,452,423
8	Luc Ouellette	79,316,296
9	Steve Condren	74,709,560
10	David Magee	72,421,402

Source: *US Trotting Association*

Harness-racing horses pull a driver on a two-wheeled "sulky" (introduced in 1829) around an oval track. A trotter does not gallop, but is trained so that its diagonally opposite legs move forward together, unlike a pacer's legs, which are extended laterally and with a swinging motion.

TOP 10 US JOCKEYS WITH THE MOST CAREER WINS

	JOCKEY	YEARS RIDING	WINS*
1	Laffit Pincay Jr.	39	9,471
2	Willie Shoemaker	42	8,833
3	Pat Day	30	8,389
4	Russell Baze	29	8,075
5	David Gall	43	7,396
6	Chris McCarron	28	7,339
7	Angel Cordero Jr.	35	7,057
8	Jorge Velasquez	33	6,795
9	Sandy Hawley	31	6,449
10	Larry Snyder	35	6,388

* As of the end of the 2002 season

Source: NTRA Communications

Having broken Bill Shoemaker's record tally on Irish Nip at Hollywood Park on December 10, 1999, Panama-born Laffit Pincay Jr. went on to become the only jockey ever to hit a career wins total of 9,000, which he achieved riding Chicim at Santa Anita on October 28, 2000.

TOP 10 FASTEST WINNING TIMES OF THE KENTUCKY DERBY

	HORSE	YEARS	TIME (MIN:SEC)
1	Secretariat	1973	1:59.2
2	Monarchos	2001	1:59.4
3	Northern Dancer	1964	2:00.0
4	Spend A Buck	1985	2:00.2
5	Decidedly	1962	2:00.4
6	Proud Clarion	1967	2:00.6
7	Grindstone	1996	2:01.0
8 =	Affirmed	1978	2:01.2
=	Fusaichi Pegasus	2000	2:01.2
=	Lucky Debonair	1965	2:01.2
=	Thunder Gulch	1995	2:01.2

Source: The Jockey Club

The Kentucky Derby is held on the first Saturday in May at Churchill Downs, Louisville, Kentucky. The first leg of the Triple Crown, it was first raced in 1875 over a distance of 1 mile 4 furlongs, but after 1896 was reduced to 1 mile 2 furlongs.

THE 10 LATEST TRIPLE CROWN WINNING HORSES*

	HORSE	YEAR
1	Affirmed	1978
2	Seattle Slew	1977
3	Secretariat	1973
4	Citation	1948
5	Assault	1946
6	Count Fleet	1943
7	Whirlaway	1941
8	War Admiral	1937
9	Omaha	1935
10	Gallant Fox	1930

* Horses that have won the Kentucky Derby, the Preakness, and Belmont Stakes in the same season

Since 1875, only 11 horses have won all three races in one season. Since 1978, three horses—Sunday Silence (1989), Silver Charm (1997), and Real Quiet (1998)—came close to winning all three races, but missed out by finishing second in one of them.

TOP 10 MONEY-WINNING HORSES IN A HARNESS-RACING CAREER

	TROTTERS HORSE	WINNINGS ($)	PACERS HORSE	WINNINGS ($)
1	Moni Maker	5,589,256	Gallo Blue Chip	3,944,512
2	Peace Corps	4,137,737	Nihilator	3,225,653
3	Mack Lobell	3,917,594	Artsplace	3,085,083
4	Sea Cove	3,138,986	Presidential Ball	3,021,363
5	Magician	3,133,025	Real Desire	3,159,814
6	Wesgate Crown	2,574,045	Matt's Scooter	2,944,591
7	Embassy Lobell	2,566,370	On The Road Again	2,819,102
8	Grades Singing	2,536,301	Riyadh	2,763,527
9	Plesac	2,370,258	Red Bow Tie	2,673,920
10	Jef's Spice	2,311,271	Bettor's Delight	2,581,461

Source: US Trotting Association

Harness-racing is one of the oldest sports in the US, its origins dating back to the Colonial period, when races were held along turnpikes. After growing in popularity in the 19th century, the governing body, the National Association for the Promotion of the Interests of the Trotting Turf (now the US Trotting Association), was founded in 1870.

TOP 10 OLYMPIC EQUESTRIAN COUNTRIES

	COUNTRY	GOLD	SILVER	BRONZE	TOTAL
1	Germany*	22	13	12	47
2	US	9	17	15	41
3	Sweden	17	8	14	39
4	France	11	12	11	34
5	West Germany	11	5	9	25
6	Italy	6	10	7	23
7	Great Britain	5	8	9	22
8	Switzerland	4	10	7	21
9	Netherlands	8	9	2	19
10	Soviet Union#	6	5	4	15

* Not including West Germany or East Germany 1968–88

Includes Unified Team of 1992; excludes Russia since then

These figures include the medal totals for both individual and team disciplines: Show Jumping, Three-Day Event, and Dressage. German rider Reiner Klimke won eight medals—six gold and two bronze—in Olympic events during the period 1964–88.

On Two Wheels

MOTOCROSS COUNTRIES

	COUNTRY	125CC	250CC	500CC	TOTAL
		WORLD CHAMPIONSHIP WINS*			
1	Belgium	9	13	22	44
2	Sweden	0	6	8	14
3	France	3	5	0	8
4 =	Italy	5	1	1	7
=	US	3	3	1	7
=	UK	0	1	6	7
7	Finland	1	1	3	5
8 =	South Africa	2	2	0	4
=	Russia	0	4	0	4
=	Netherlands	3	1	0	4

* To the end of 2002 season

World Motocross Championships have been held since 1947 when the five-man Motocross des Nations team championship was launched.

FASTEST AVERAGE WINNING SPEEDS IN THE TOUR DE FRANCE

	RIDER/COUNTRY	YEAR	AVERAGE SPEED (MPH)	(KM/H)
1	Lance Armstrong, US	1999	25.026	40.276
2	Lance Armstrong	2001	24.898	40.070
3	Marco Pantani, Italy	1998	24.844	39.983
4	Lance Armstrong	2002	24.804	39.919
5	Lance Armstrong	2000	24.587	39.570
6	Miguel Indurain, Spain	1992	24.546	39.504
7	Jan Ullrich, Germany	1997	24.380	39.237
8	Bjarne Rijs, Denmark	1996	24.374	39.227
9	Miguel Indurain	1995	24.353	39.193
10	Bernard Hinault, France	1981	24.208	38.960

The Tour de France has been staged since 1903. The winning speed did not exceed 18.6 mph (30 km/h) until 1935.

DOWNHILL RIDERS IN THE UCI MOUNTAIN BIKE WORLD CUP, 2002 (WOMEN)

	RIDER/COUNTRY	POINTS*
1	Anne Caroline Chausson, France	1,143
2	Fionn Griffiths, UK	1,043
3	Sabrina Jonnier, France	1,010
4	Tracy Moseley, UK	1,000
5	Marielle Saner, Switzerland	960
6	Celine Gros, France	801
7	Vanessa Quin, New Zealand	779
8	Kathy Pruitt, US	696
9	Nolvenn Le Caer, France	685
10	Helen Gaskell, UK	637

* Total points scored over a series of eight competitions

Source: *Union Cycliste Internationale (International Cycling Union)*

DOWNHILL RIDERS IN THE UCI MOUNTAIN BIKE WORLD CUP, 2002 (MEN)

	RIDER/COUNTRY	POINTS*
1	Steve Peat, UK	1,134
2	Christopher Kovarik, Australia	1,015
3	Cedric Gracia, France	903
4	Mickael Pascal, France	799
5 =	Oscar Saiz, Spain	775
=	Nicolas Vouilloz, France	775
7	Fabien Barel, France	770
8	Mick Hannah, Australia	705
9	David Vazquez Lopez, Spain	687
10	Nathan Rennie, Australia	635

* Total points scored over a series of eight competitions

Source: *Union Cycliste Internationale (International Cycling Union)*

▶ **Riding high**
Lance Armstrong's 1999 Tour de France win, the first by an American since Greg LeMond in 1990, also set an unbeaten record speed.

TOP 10 MOTORCYCLISTS WITH THE MOST GRAND PRIX RACE WINS

	RIDER/COUNTRY	YEARS	RACE WINS*
1	Giacomo Agostini, Italy	1965–76	122
2	Angel Nieto, Spain	1969–85	90
3	Mike Hailwood, UK	1959–67	76
4	Rolf Biland, Switzerland	1975–90	56
5	Mick Doohan, Australia	1990–98	54
6	Phil Read, UK	1961–75	52
7	Valentino Rossi, Italy	1996–2002	50
8	Jim Redman, Southern Rhodesia	1961–66	45
9	Anton Mang, West Germany	1976–88	42
10	Carlo Ubbiali, Italy	1950–60	39

* To the end of 2002 season

All except Biland were solo machine riders. Britain's Barry Sheene won 23 races during his career and is the only man to win Grands Prix at 50 and 500cc.

THE FIRST DAYTONA 200

FIRST FACT

The beach in Daytona, Florida, has long been the venue for speed record attempts and races, and it was there on January 24, 1937, that the first ever Daytona 200 event—known in its early years as the "Handlebar Derby"—took place, with 120 entries. It was won by Californian Ed Kretz on an Indian motorcycle at an average speed of 73.34 mph (118 km/h). The original race combined 1.5 miles (2.4 km) of public roads and 1.5 miles of beach and was carefully timed so that riders did not have to contend with the incoming tide.

▶ Wheels of fortune
Italian motorcycle maestro, Giacomo Agostini, won both the first and last of his record 122 Grand Prix races at the Nürburgring, Germany.

TOP 10 FASTEST WINNING SPEEDS OF THE DAYTONA 200

	RIDER*/BIKE	YEAR	AVERAGE SPEED (MPH)	(KM/H)
1	Miguel Duhamel, Canada, Honda	2003	113.83	183.20
2	Mat Mladin, Australia, Suzuki	2000	113.63	182.87
3	Miguel Duhamel, Canada, Honda	1999	113.47	182.61
4	Kenny Roberts, Yamaha	1984	113.14	182.08
5	Scott Russell, Yamaha	1998	111.78	179.89
6	Kenny Roberts, Yamaha	1983	110.93	178.52
7	Scott Russell, Kawasaki	1992	110.67	178.11
8	Graeme Crosby, New Zealand, Yamaha	1982	109.10	175.58
9	Steve Baker, Yamaha	1977	108.85	175.18
10	Miguel Duhamel, Canada, Honda	1996	108.82	175.13

* From the US unless otherwise stated

Source: American Motorcyclist Association

TOP 10 MANUFACTURERS WITH THE MOST MOTORCYCLE GRAND PRIX WINS

	MANUFACTURER	FIRST WIN	WINS*
1	Honda	1961	536
2	Yamaha	1963	401
3	MV Agusta	1952	275
4	Suzuki	1962	153
5	Aprilia	1987	140
6	Kawasaki	1969	85
7	Derbi	1970	81
8	Kreidler	1962	65
9	Garelli	1982	51
10	Gilera	1949	47

* To the end of 2002 season

Japanese manufacturer Yamaha was originally a musical instrument maker (hence the crossed tuning fork trademark), and did not make its first motorcycle—a single-cylinder 125cc two-stroke—until 1954. Yamaha made its first racing bike in 1961 and had its first Grand Prix win at the 1963 Belgian GP in Spa, when Fumio Ito of Japan won in the 250cc class.

Auto Racing

TOP 10 CART MONEY WINNERS

	DRIVER/COUNTRY	TOTAL PRIZES* ($)
1	Al Unser Jr., US	18,828,406
2	Michael Andretti#, US	17,928,118
3	Bobby Rahal, US	16,344,008
4	Emerson Fittipaldi, Brazil	14,293,625
5	Mario Andretti, US	11,552,154
6	Rick Mears, US	11,050,807
7	Jimmy Vasser#, US	10,627,244
8	Danny Sullivan, US	8,884,126
9	Paul Tracy#, Canada	8,825,270
10	Arie Luyendyk, Netherlands	7,732,188

* As of January 1, 2003

Still active at end 2002 season

Source: Championship Auto Racing Teams

◀ **CART success**
Michael Andretti, one of the most successful CART riders of all time, races toward the finish at the Milwaukee Mile in 1999.

TOP 10 DRIVERS WITH THE MOST WINSTON CUP WINS

	DRIVER	YEARS	VICTORIES
1	Richard Petty	1958–92	200
2	David Pearson	1960–86	105
3 =	Bobby Allison	1975–88	84
=	Darrell Waltrip	1975–92	84
5	Cale Yarborough	1957–88	83
6	Dale Earnhardt	1979–2000	76
7	Jeff Gordon*	1994–2002	61
8 =	Lee Petty	1949–64	54
=	Rusty Wallace*	1986–2001	54
10 =	Ned Jarrett	1953–66	50
=	Junior Johnson	1953–66	50

* Still driving at end of 2002 season

Source: NASCAR

The Winston Cup is a season-long series of races which take place over enclosed circuits such as Daytona speedway, organized by the National Association of Stock Car Auto Racing, Inc. (NASCAR). The series started in 1949 as the Grand National series, but changed its style to the Winston Cup in 1972 when sponsored by the R.J. Reynolds tobacco company, manufacturers of Winston cigarettes.

TOP 10 FASTEST GRAND PRIX RACES, 2002

GRAND PRIX	CIRCUIT	WINNER'S SPEED (MPH)	(KM/H)
1 Italy	Monza	149.807	241.090
2 Belgium	Spa-Francorchamps	140.412	225.970
3 Japan	Suzuka	132.123	212.645
4 Germany	Hockenheim	130.031	209.263
5 San Marino	Enzo e Dino Ferrari	127.763	205.613
6 Spain	Catalunya	126.607	203.753
7 Great Britain	Silverstone	125.300	201.649
8 US-Indianapolis	Indianapolis	125.192	201.476
9 Brazil	Interlagos	124.336	200.098
10 France	Magny-Cours	123.738	199.136

Grand Prix racing is European in origin. Since the late 19th century, car races took place on public roads, which is reflected in the construction of today's circuits, which incorporate chicanes and bends that test drivers' skills to the limit. Formula One began after World War II, when a distinction was made between these and less powerful Formula Two cars.

TOP 10 FASTEST WINNING SPEEDS OF THE INDIANAPOLIS 500

	DRIVER/COUNTRY	CAR	YEAR	SPEED (MPH)	(KM/H)
1	**Arie Luyendyk,** Netherlands	Lola-Chevrolet	1990	185.981	299.307
2	**Rick Mears,** US	Chevrolet-Lumina	1991	176.457	283.980
3	**Bobby Rahal,** US	March-Cosworth	1986	170.722	274.750
4	**Juan Pablo Montoya,** Colombia	G Force-Aurora	2000	167.607	269.730
5	**Emerson Fittipaldi,** Brazil	Penske-Chevrolet	1989	167.581	269.695
6	**Helio Castroneves,** Brazil	Dallara-Chevrolet	2002	166.499	267.954
7	**Rick Mears,** US	March-Cosworth	1984	163.612	263.308
8	**Mark Donohue,** US	McLaren-Offenhauser	1972	162.962	262.619
9	**Al Unser,** US	March-Cosworth	1987	162.175	260.995
10	**Tom Sneva,** US	March-Cosworth	1983	162.117	260.902

Because American drivers start on the run and race around oval circuits, consistently higher average lap speeds are achieved than in Formula One. Car racing in the US on specially built circuits dates back to 1909, when Indianapolis Speedway opened. CART (Championship Auto Racing Teams, Inc.) was formed in 1978, and in 1996 the Indy Racing League was established in response to disputes over regulations governing the Indy 500. Indy 500 races have counted for CART points in 1979, 1980, and 1983–95.

TOP 10 FORMULA ONE DRIVERS WITH THE MOST GRAND PRIX WINS

	DRIVER/COUNTRY	CAREER	WINS*
1	**Michael Schumacher,** Germany	1991–	64
2	**Alain Prost,** France	1980–93	51
3	**Ayrton Senna,** Brazil	1984–94	41
4	**Nigel Mansell,** UK	1980–95	31
5	**Jackie Stewart,** UK	1965–73	27
6 =	**Jim Clark,** UK	1960–68	25
=	**Niki Lauda,** Austria	1971–85	25
8	**Juan Manuel Fangio,** Argentina	1950–58	24
9	**Nelson Piquet,** Brazil	1978–91	23
10	**Damon Hill,** UK	1992–99	22

* To the end of 2002 season

Michael Schumacher started his Formula One career with Jordan in 1991, but after just one race moved to Benetton. He took his first Grand Prix win, the Belgian, in 1992, his first full racing season. He overtook Alain Prost's career points record by winning the 2001 Japanese Grand Prix.

▼ **"The Maestro"**
King of the race track during the 1950s, Juan Manuel Fangio (1911–95) won 24 Grand Prix races and secured a record five world titles.

Sports Media

TOP 10 MOST WATCHED SPORTING EVENTS ON US TELEVISION, 2001–02

	EVENT	NETWORK	VIEWERS
1	Super Bowl XXXVI: New England vs. St. Louis	Fox	42,664,000
2	Fox Super Bowl: Kick Off	Fox	30,632,000
3	Winter Olympics (Feb. 21, 2002, 8pm)	NBC	28,233,000
4	Fox Super Bowl: Post Game	Fox	26,066,000
5	Fox World Series Game 7: New York Yanks at Arizona	Fox	24,826,000
6	Fox NFC Championship: Philadelphia at St. Louis	Fox	23,998,000
7	Winter Olympics (Feb. 19, 2002, 8pm)	NBC	23,574,000
8	AFC Championship on CBS: New England at Pittsburgh	CBS	22,348,000
9	Winter Olympics (Feb. 11, 2002, 8pm)	NBC	20,668,000
10	Fox NFC Playoff—Sunday: Green Bay at St. Louis	Fox	20,620,000

Source: *Nielsen Media Research*

Aside from the annual list-topping Super Bowl, the Winter Olympics from Salt Lake City scored three places in the Top 10, with the February 21 finals of the women's figure skating, giant slalom, and curling events achieving a new record audience for the event. The previous holder was the 1960 Games from Squaw Valley, which was the first Olympics featured on network television in the US.

THE 10 LATEST WINNERS OF THE SPORTS ILLUSTRATED "SPORTSMAN/ SPORTSWOMAN OF THE YEAR" AWARD

YEAR	WINNER	SPORT
2002	Lance Armstrong	Cycling
2001	Curt Schilling and Randy Johnson	Baseball
2000	Tiger Woods	Golf
1999	US Women's World Cup Squad	Soccer
1998	Mark McGwire and Sammy Sosa	Baseball
1997	Dean Smith	Basketball (coach)
1996	Tiger Woods	Golf
1995	Cal Ripken Jr.	Baseball
1994	Johan Olav Koss and Bonnie Blair	Ice skating
1993	Don Shula	Football (coach)

First presented in 1954, when it was won by British athlete Roger Bannister, this annual award honors the sportsman or sportswoman who in that year, in the opinion of the editors of *Sports Illustrated*, most "symbolizes in character and performance the ideals of sportsmanship." Tiger Woods made history on more than just the golf course in 2000, when he became the first sportsman ever to be honored with this award twice.

TOP 10 SPORTS FILMS

	FILM	YEAR	SPORT
1	Rocky IV	1985	Boxing
2	Space Jam	1996	Basketball
3	The Waterboy	1998	Football
4	Days of Thunder	1990	Stock car racing
5	Cool Runnings	1993	Bobsledding
6	A League of Their Own	1992	Baseball
7	Remember the Titans	2000	Football
8	Rocky III	1982	Boxing
9	Rocky V	1990	Boxing
10	Rocky	1976	Boxing

Led by Sylvester Stallone's *Rocky* series, the boxing ring dominates Hollywood's most successful sports-based epics (based on worldwide box-office income), with all those in the Top 10 having made at least $120 million. Were *Forrest Gump* (1994) considered in this category on the grounds that football and table tennis are featured in it, it would top the list.

TOP 10 THEMES OF SPORTS FILMS

	SPORT	FILMS
1	Boxing	204
2	Horse racing	139
3	Football	123
4 =	Baseball	85
=	Auto racing	85
6	Basketball	41
7	Track and field	33
8	Golf	24
9	Wrestling	20
10	Motorcycle racing	15

Source: *Patrick Robertson*, Film Facts (*Aurum Press, 2001*)

A survey of feature films produced in Hollywood from 1910 to 2000 with competitive sports as their principal themes identified a total of 891 films, with boxing accounting for 22.9 percent of the total.

TOP 10 | SPORTING EVENTS WITH THE LARGEST US TELEVISION AUDIENCE SHARES

	EVENT	DATE	RATING
1	Super Bowl XVI	Jan. 24, 1982	49.1
2	Super Bowl XVII	Jan. 30, 1983	48.6
3	XVII Winter Olympics	Feb. 23, 1994	48 5
4	Super Bowl XX	Jan. 26, 1986	48.3
5	Super Bowl XII	Jan. 15, 1978	47.2
6	Super Bowl XIII	Jan. 21, 1979	47.1
7 =	Super Bowl XVIII	Jan. 22, 1984	46.4
=	Super Bowl XIX	Jan. 20, 1985	46.4
9	Super Bowl XIV	Jan. 20, 1980	46 3
10	Super Bowl XXX	Jan. 28, 1996	46.0

Source: *Nielsen Media Research*

Those listed here, along with ten further Super Bowls, back to VI in 1972, are among the Top 50 networked programs of all time in the US. In this extended list, the XVII Lillehammer, Norway, Winter Olympics makes two showings, on Feb. 23 and Feb. 25, 1994 (the latter achieving a rating of 44.2). Despite great national enthusiasm (fueled by media interest in figure skater Nancy Kerrigan, who had been physically attacked before the Games), the US finished a disappointing fifth in the overall medals table.

TOP 10 | MOST EXPENSIVE OLYMPIC GAMES TV RIGHTS

	VENUE	YEAR	RIGHTS ($)
1	Athens	2004	394,000,000
2	Sydney	2000	363,000,000
3	Atlanta	1996	240,000,000
4	Turin*	2006	135,000,000
5	Salt Lake City*	2002	120,000,000
6	Barcelona	1994	90,000,000
7	Nagano*	1998	72,000,000
8	Seoul	1988	26,000,000
9	Lillehammer*	1994	24,000,000
10	Los Angeles	1984	19,800,000

* *Winter Games*

▼ A run for their money
As the Olympic Games attract ever-larger international TV audiences, so the costs, levels of sponsorship, and TV rights have escalated to multimillion-dollar levels.

Leisure Pursuits

TOP 10 PARTICIPATION ACTIVITIES IN THE US

	ACTIVITY	NO. PARTICIPATING* (2001)
1	Exercise walking	71,200,000
2	Swimming	54,800,000
3	Camping (vacation/overnight)	45,500,000
4	Fishing	44,400,000
5	Exercising with equipment	43,000,000
6	Bowling	40,300,000
7	Bicycle riding	39,000,000
8	Billiards/pool	32,700,000
9	Basketball	28,100,000
10	Golf	26,600,000

Seven years of age and older, participated more than once during the year

Source: *National Sporting Goods Association*

In the five years from 1996 to 2001, snowboarding was reported as experiencing the greatest increase in participation, a 106 percent rise from 4.7 million to 9.6 million, while 2x2 roller-skating (as contrasted with inline) dropped by 49.4 percent, from 15.1 million to 7.7 million enthusiasts.

TOP 10 FAVORITE SPORTS ON TV (MEN)

	SPORT	% MEN WITH PREFERENCE
1	Soccer	32
2 =	Football	9
=	Baseball	9
4	Basketball	8
5	Car racing	5
6	Boxing	4
7 =	Golf	2
=	Tennis	2
=	Track and field	2
10 =	Figure skating	1
=	Gymnastics	1
=	Volleyball	1

Source: *Ipsos-Reid*/Screen Digest

This international survey averages out any national enthusiasms, revealing to US audiences the massive global popularity of soccer and the total eclipse of hockey. UK and Australasian readers may be equally saddened to see their love of cricket and rugby so diluted as to be discounted.

TOP 10 FAVORITE SPORTS ON TV (WOMEN)

	SPORT	% WOMEN WITH PREFERENCE
1	Soccer	13
2 =	Baseball	8
=	Basketball	8
=	Figure skating	8
5	Football	6
6 =	Gymnastics	5
=	Tennis	5
8	Track and field	4
9 =	Swimming	3
=	Volleyball	3

Source: *Ipsos-Reid*/Screen Digest

Beyond sports with a long-standing female following, soccer has experienced a particular surge of interest among women, as both participants and spectators. The 2002 World Cup and the film *Bend it Like Beckham* (2002) are credited with initiating a wave of enthusiasm for the game among women, the latter even inspiring the creation of the first women's soccer league in India.

TOP 10 MOST POPULAR TYPES OF TOY

	TYPE OF TOY	MARKET SHARE PERCENTAGE (2000)
1	Video games	23.2
2	Infant/pre-school toys	11.6
3 =	Activity toys	10.8
=	Other toys	10.8
5	Games/puzzles	10.6
6	Dolls	9.7
7	Toy vehicles	8.2
8	Plushes	6.5
9	Action figures	4.4
10	Ride-on toys	4.2

Source: *Eurotoys/The NPD Group Worldwide*

This list is based on a survey of toy consumption in the European Union, and can be taken as a reliable guide to the most popular types of toy in the developed world.

TOP 10 TOY-BUYING COUNTRIES

	COUNTRY*	SPENDING ON TOYS PER CAPITA (2000) ($)
1	US	126.1
2	UK	90.1
3	Canada	87.9
4	Belgium	73.7
5	Japan	72.4
6	Denmark	58.8
7	France	57.4
8	Ireland	56.1
9	Sweden	51.3
10	Switzerland	50.5

* Of those covered by survey

Source: *Euromonitor*

FIRST COMPUTER GAMES

THE FIRST ARCADE GAME, the precursor of all modern computer games, was invented by Nolan Bushnell and Ted Dabney and given the name "Computer Space." Described as "a cosmic dogfight between a spaceship and a flying saucer," it went on sale in 1971, but proved too complicated to achieve wide appeal. Its creators, along with Al Alcorn, then designed Pong, a game launched in 1972 that achieved enormous success, selling about 100,000 units. Nolan formed a company called Syzygy, later renamed Atari, and in 1975 sold a version of Pong to be played on a TV set, beginning the era of the home computer games console.

TOP 10 COUNTRIES SPENDING THE MOST ON CONSOLE AND COMPUTER GAMES

	COUNTRY	SALES (2000) ($) TOTAL	PER CAPITA
1	Canada	1,724,000,000	56.1
2	US	14,348,000,000	52.1
3	UK	2,648,000,000	44.6
4	Japan	4,155,000,000	32.7
5	Germany	2,648,000,000	21.1
6	South Korea	1,724,000,000	20.9
7	Italy	990,000,000	16.5
8	Sweden	113,000,000	12.7
9	Australia	219,000,000	11.4
10	France	639,000,000	9.7

Source: *Euromonitor*

◀ **In the swim**
Second only to walking among the most popular participation activities in the US, swimming also provides one of the best routes to all-around fitness.

TOP 10 ITEMS OF RECREATION SPENDING IN THE US

	CATEGORY	TOTAL EXPENDITURE (2001) ($)
1	Video and audio goods, including musical instruments	66,700,000,000
2	Commercial participant amusements*	63,000,000,000
3	Nondurable toys and sports supplies	60,400,000,000
4	Wheel goods, sports and photographic equipment, boats, and pleasure aircraft	50,400,000,000
5	Magazines, newspapers, and sheet music	32,500,000,000
6	Computers, peripherals, and software	31,400,000,000
7	Books and maps	30,800,000,000
8	Spectator amusements#	25,000,000,000
9	Flowers, seeds, and potted plants	16,700,000,000
10	Clubs and fraternal organizations	15,900,000,000

* Category includes amusement parks, billiards, bowling, dancing, casino gambling, golf, riding, shooting, skating, swimming, sightseeing, etc.

 # Category includes motion picture theaters, theaters, opera, nonprofit entertainments, spectator sports

Source: *US Bureau of Economic Analysis, Survey of Current Business (April 2003)*

Further Information

THE UNIVERSE & THE EARTH

Astronauts & Cosmonauts
http://www.worldspaceflight.com/bios
Biographies and other data on space travelers

Encyclopedia Astronautica
http://www.astronautix.com Spaceflight news
and reference

NASA
http://www.nasa.gov The principal website
for the US space program

National Climatic Data Center
http://www.ncdc.noaa.gov Weather data,
with an emphasis on the US

The Nine Planets
http://www.seds.org/nineplanets/nineplanets
A multimedia tour of the Solar System

Peaklist
http://www.highalpex.com/Peaklist/peaklist.html
Lists of the world's tallest mountains

Space.com
http://www.space.com Reports on events
in space exploration

United Nations Atlas of the Oceans
http://www.oceansatlas.org/index.jsp An
information resource on oceanographic issues

Volcano Live
http://www.volcanolive.com World volcano
news and information

WebElements
http://www.webelements.com

LIFE ON EARTH

Convention on International Trade in Endangered Species of Wild Fauna and Flora (CITES)
http://www.cites.org Lists endangered species
of flora and fauna

Dinosauria On-Line
http://www.dinosauria.com Information and
pictures concerned with dinosaurs

The Electronic Zoo
http://netvet.wustl.edu/e-zoo.htm Links to sites
devoted to animals

FishBase
http://www.fishbase.org/home.htm
Global information on fish

Food and Agriculture Organization of the United Nations
http://apps.fao.org FAO statistics on agriculture,
fisheries, and forestry

The International Shark Attack File
http://www.flmnh.ufl.edu/fish/Sharks/ISAF/ISAF.
htm A database of shark attack records

International Union for the Conservation of Nature
http://iucn.org The leading nature conservation
site

PetsForum
http://petsforum.com Information about cats,
dogs, and other pets

United Nations Environment Programme
http://www.unep.ch Includes the UN's System-
Wide Earthwatch and its Global Resource
Information Database

University of Florida Book of Insect Records
http://ufbir.ifas.ufl.edu Insect champions in many
categories

THE HUMAN WORLD

Death Penalty Information Center
http://www.deathpenaltyinfo.org US-specific data
on the death penalty

Eponym
http://www.eponym.org Links to personal
name websites

Federal Bureau of Prisons
http://www.bop.gov Public information on all
aspects of the US prison system

International Agency for Research on Cancer
http://www-dep.iarc.fr Statistics on the incidence
of cancer worldwide

Inter-Parliamentary Union
http://www.ipu.org Includes data on women
in parliaments

Interpol
http://www.interpol.int Worldwide crime
statistics

National Center for Health Statistics
http://www.cdc.gov/nchs Information and links
on health for US citizens

Rulers
http://rulers.org A database of the world's rulers
and political leaders

United Nations
http://www.un.org The launch site for accessing
the UN's many bodies

World Health Organization
http://www.who.int/en World health information
and advice

TOWN & COUNTRY

CIA World Factbook
http://www.odci.gov/cia/publications/factbook
Detailed country-by-country data

International Commission on Large Dams
http://www.icold-cigb.org A searchable guide
to the world's dams

Population Reference Bureau
http://www.prb.org US and international
population issues

Skyscrapers.com
http://www.skyscrapers.com/re/en A detailed,
searchable guide to the world's tallest buildings

United Nations City
http://www.photius.com/wfb1999/rankings/cities.ht
ml City information for capitals and those with
100,000-plus populations

United Nations Population Division
http://www.un.org/esa/population/unpop.htm
Worldwide data on population issues

US Census Bureau
http://www.census.gov US and international
population statistics

World Bank
http://www.worldbank.org Development and
other statistics from around the world

World's Largest Bridges
http://www.struct.kth.se/research/bridges/Bridge
s.htm The world's longest bridges listed by type

The World's Longest Tunnel Page
http://home.no.net/lotsberg A database of the
longest rail, road, and canal tunnels

CULTURE & LEARNING

American Library Association
http://www.ala.org US library information and
book awards

The Art Newspaper
http://www.theartnewspaper.com News and
views on the art world

Dorling Kindersley
http://us.dk.com The website of the publishers
of this book

Global Reach
http://www.glreach.com Facts and figures on
online languages

The Library of Congress
http://www.loc.gov An online gateway to one of
the world's greatest collections of words and
pictures

National Center for Education Statistics
http://nces.ed.gov The home of federal education
data

Nobel Prizes
http://www.nobel.se A searchable database of all
Nobel Prizewinners

Publishers Weekly
http://publishersweekly.reviewsnews.com
The trade journal of American publishers

The Pulitzer Prizes
http://www.pulitzer.org A searchable guide to
the prestigious US literary prize

United Nations Educational, Scientific and Cultural Organization (UNESCO)
http://www.unesco.org Comparative international
statistics on all aspects of education and culture

MUSIC & MUSICIANS

All Music Guide
http://www.allmusic.com A comprehensive guide to all genres of music

American Society of Composers, Authors and Publishers
http://www.ascap.com ASCAP songwriter and other awards

Billboard
http://www.billboard.com US music news and charts data

ClassicalUSA.com
http://classicalusa.com An online guide to classical music in the US

Grammy Awards
http://www.naras.org The official site for the US music awards

Mobile Beat Magazine
http://www.mobilebeat.com DJ song requests

MTV
http://www.mtv.com The online site for the TV music channel

Recording Industry Association of America
http://www.riaa.org

Rock and Roll Hall of Fame
http://www.rockhall.com The museum of the history of rock

Rolling Stone magazine
http://www.rollingstone.com

STAGE & SCREEN

Academy of Motion Picture Arts and Sciences
http://www.oscars.org The official "Oscars" website

BBC
http://www.bbc.co.uk Gateway to BBC TV and radio, with a powerful Internet search engine

Hollywood.com
http://www.hollywood.com A general US movie site with details on all the new releases

Golden Globe Awards
http://hfpa.org/html Hollywood Foreign Press Association

Internet Movie Database
http://www.imdb.com The best of the publicly accessible film websites; the "Pro" version is available to subscribers

Internet Theatre Database
http://www.theatredb.com A Broadway-focused searchable stage site

London Theatre Guide
http://www.londontheatre.co.uk
A comprehensive guide to West End theater productions

Screen Daily
http://www.londontheatre.co.uk Daily news from the film world—the website of UK weekly *Screen International*

Variety
http://www.variety.com Extensive entertainment information—some features are available only with a subscription

Yahoo! Movies
http://movies.yahoo.com Features and links to the latest movie releases

COMMERCIAL WORLD

Bureau of Labor Statistics
http://www.bls.gov US Department of Labor figures

Forbes magazine
http://www.forbes.com "Rich lists" and other business information

Fortune magazine
http://www.fortune.com/fortune Information on US and global companies

International Currency Converter
http://www.oanda.com/convert Daily exchange rates for 164 currencies, 1990–present

International Labor Organization
http://www.ilo.org Facts and figures on the world's workers

International Telecommunications Union
http://www.itu.int Worldwide telecommunications statistics

National Center for Injury Prevention and Control
http://www.cdc.gov Accidental death statistics for the US

Organisation of Economic Co-operation and Development
http://www.oecd.org World economic and social statistics

United Nations Development Programme
http://www.undp.org Country GDPs and other development data

The World Bank
http://www.worldbank.org World development and labour statistics

TRANSPORT & TOURISM

AirDisaster.com
http://www.airdisaster.com Reports on aviation disasters

International Registry of Sunken Ships
http://users.accesscomm.ca/shipwreck A huge database of the world's wrecked and lost ships

International Road Federation
http://www.irfnet.org Facts and figures on the world's roads

Light Rail Transit Association
http://www.lrta.org/world/worldind.html A guide to the world's light railways and tram systems

National Park Service
http://www.nps.gov The official site of the US national park system

Railway Gazette International
http://www.railwaygazette.com The world's railroad business in depth

Roller Coaster DataBase
http://www.rcdb.com A searchable database of some 1,600 world roller coasters

Tourism Offices Worldwide Directory
http://www.towd.com Contact details for tourism offices for US states and countries around the world

Travel Industry Association of America
http://www.tia.org

World Tourism Organization
http://www.world-tourism.org The world's principal travel and tourism organization

SPORT & LEISURE

Golf On Line
http://www.sportsillustrated.cnn.com/golfonline/golfstats *Sports Illustrated*'s guide to world golf

The International Olympic Committee
http://www.olympic.org The official website of the Olympic movement, with a searchable database

International Association of Athletics Federations
http://www.iaaf.org The statistics and rankings of the world's top athletes

The International Paralympic Committee
http://www.paralympic.org The official website of the International Paralympic Committee

Major League Baseball
http://www.mlb.com The official website of MBL

National Basketball Association
http://www.nba.com The official website of the NBA

National Football League
http://www.nhl.com The official website of the NFL

Professional Golfers' Association (PGA) Tour
http://www.pgatour.com

National Hockey league
http://www.nhl.com The official website of the NHL

Yahoo Sports
http://dir.yahoo.com/Recreation/Sports The directory of sports entries at Yahoo covering all minor as well as major sports

Index

D

E

Index

Index

Index

Acknowledgments

Special US research: Dafydd Rees
Sport consultant: Ian Morrison

Alexander Ash; Caroline Ash; Nicholas Ash; Professor David Ball; David B. Barrett; Richard Braddish; Thomas Brinkoff; Tina Cardy; Pete Compton; Joanna Corcoran-Wunsch; Kaylee Coxall; Luke Crampton; Adrian Crookes; Sidney S. Culbert; Alain P. Dornic; Philip Eden; Raymond Fletcher; Christopher Forbes; Cullen Geiselman; Russell E. Gough; Monica Grady; Andrew Grantham; Stan Greenberg; Andrew Hemming; Duncan Hislop; Doug Hopper; Andreas Hörstemeier; Richard Hurley; Alan Jeffreys; Todd M. Johnson; Tessa Kale; Larry Kilman; Rex King; Robert Lamb; Dr. Benjamin Lucas; John Malam; Roberto Mamrud; Dr. Gregg Marland; Chris Mead; Roberto Ortiz de Zarate; Sarah Owen; Tony Pattison; Adrian Room; Bill Rudman; Robert Senior; Karel Stockkermans; Mitchell Symons; Thomas Tranter; Alexis Tregenza; Lucy T. Verma; Tony Waltham; Dickon White; Nigel Wilcockson; Peter Wynne-Thomas

Academy of Motion Picture Arts and Sciences (AMPAS) – Oscar statuette is the registered trademark and copyrighted property of the Academy of Motion Picture Arts and Sciences; ACNielsen MMS; *Ad Age Global*; The Advertising Association; Aintree Racecourse; *Airline Business*; Air Transport Intelligence; American Library Association; America's Cup; Amnesty International; *Amusement Business*; *The Art Newspaper*; Art Sales Index; Association of Tennis Professionals (ATP); Audit Bureau of Circulations Ltd; Bat Conservation International; BBC Radio 1; BBC Radio 4; Booker Prize; *BP Statistical Review of World Energy 2002*; British Academy of Film and Television Arts (BAFTA); British Broadcasting Corporation (BBC); British Cave Research Association; *British Crime Survey*; British Museum; British Phonographic Industry (BPI); British Record Industry Trust (BRIT Trust); British Video Association (BVA); Broadcasters Audience Research Board Ltd (BARB); *Business Week*; Cameron Mackintosh Ltd; Cannes Film Festival; Central Intelligence Agency (CIA); Centre for Environmental Initiatives; Championship Auto Racing Teams (CART); Channel Swimming Association; *Checkout*; Christian Research; Christie's; *Classical Music*; *The Columbia Granger's Index to Poetry in Anthologies*; Columbia University (Pulitzer Prizes); Commission for Distilled Spirits; CricInfo; *Criminal Statistics England & Wales*; CyberAtlas; Deloitte & Touche Sports; Department of Environment, Food and Rural Affairs (DFFRA); Department of Health; *The Economist*; Electoral Reform Society; Elephant Trade Information System (ETIS); Energy Information Administration (EIA); English Tourism Council; Environmental Technology Center; Euromonitor; European Film Academy; Eurotoys; *Evening Standard*; Fédération Equestre Internationale (FEI); Fédération Internationale de Football Association (FIFA); The Financial Times Ltd; Florida Museum of Natural History; Food and Agriculture Organization of the United Nations (FAO); *Forbes*; Forestry Commission; *Fortune*; Fund for the Replacement of Animals in Medical Experiments (FRAME); Gemstone Publishing, Inc; General Register Office for Scotland; Global Reach; Health and Safety Executive (HSE); Higher Education Statistics Agency (HESA); Home Accident Surveillance System (HASS); Home Office; Imperial War Museum; Indianapolis Motor Speedway; InsideHoops.com; Interbrand; International Agency for Research on Cancer; International Association of Athletics Federations (IAAF); International Atomic Energy Agency; International Coffee Organisation; International Intellectual Property Alliance (IIPA); International Labour Organization (ILO); International Olympic Committee (IOC); International Paralympic Committee; International Shark Attack File; International Skating Union (ISU); International Ski Federation (FIS); International Table Tennis Federation (ITTF); International Tea Committee Ltd; International Telecommunication Union (ITU); International Union for the Conservation of Nature (IUCN); International Water Ski Federation (IWSF); International Weightlifting Federation (IWF); Inter-Parliamentary Union; Interpol; Kennel Club; Lloyds Register-Fairplay Ltd; Lycos; McDonald's; *Melody Maker*; MRIB; MTV; Museum of Rugby; Music Control UK; Music Information Database; National Academy of Recording Arts and Sciences, USA (NARAS); National Aeronautics and Space Administration, USA (NASA); National Basketball Association, USA (NBA); National Football League, USA (NFL); National Fraud Information Center, National Consumers League, USA; Natural History Museum; NetRatings; *New Musical Express (NME)*; Nielsen; Nielsen BookScan; Nielsen Media Research; Nobel Foundation; The NPD Group Worldwide; Office for National Statistics (ONS); Official UK Charts Company; *OperaGlass*; Organisation Internationale des Constructeurs d'Automobiles (OICA); *The Overstreet Comic Book Price Guide*; Penguin Books; Performing Right Society; Pet Food Manufacturers' Association (PFMA); Petplan; Phobics Society; The Poetry Poll; Pollstar; Professional Golfers' Association (PGA); Professional Squash Association (PSA); *Racing Post*; Radio Joint Audience Research Ltd (RAJAR); *Railway Gazette International*; Royal Brompton National Heart and Lung Hospital; Royal Opera House, Covent Garden; RSSSF; Russell Reynolds Associates; Ryder Cup; *Screen Digest*; SearchEngineWatch.com; Shakespeare Centre; Society of London Theatre (SOLT) (Olivier Awards); Society of Motor Manufacturers and Traders Ltd; Sony Radio Academy Awards; Sotheby's; S. P. Consultants; Sport England; Star UK; *Stores*; Students for the Exploration and Development of Space (SEDS); *The Sunday Times*; Swiss Re; Tate Britain; Tate Modern; TeleGeography; TNS; Tour de France; Union Cycliste Internationale (UCI); United Nations (UN); United Nations Educational, Scientific and Cultural Organization (UNESCO); United Nations Environment Programme (UNEP); United Nations Population Division (UNPD); United Nations System-wide Earthwatch; Universal Postal Union (UPU); US Census Bureau; *Variety*; Verifone; VH1, USA; Victoria & Albert Museum; WebElements; Whitbread Book Awards; Women's International Squash Players Association (WISPA); Women's Tennis Association (WTA); World Association of Newspapers (WAN); *World Atlas of Coral Reefs*; World Bank; *World Christian Trends*; World Conservation Monitoring Centre (WCMC); World Health Organization (WHO); World Intellectual Property Organization (WIPO); World Motocross Championships; *World of Learning*; World Snowboarding Federation (WSF); World's Strongest Man Contest; World Tourism Organization (WTO); Zurich World Rankings;

Acknowledgments

Publisher's acknowledgments
Dorling Kindersley would like to thank the following for their contributions: Editorial Sharon Lucas; Design Marianne Markham; Picture Research Franziska Marking, Cynthia Frazer, Marie Osborn; Picture Library Hayley Smith, Richard Dabb, Claire Bowers; Design Revolution

Index
Ursula Caffrey

Packager's acknowledgments
The Bridgewater Book Company would like to thank Susie Behar, Alison Bolus, Stephanie Horner, and Tom Kitch for editorial assistance, and Richard Constable, Chris Morris, Warrick Sears, and Barbara Theisen for their design work.

Picture Credits